AMERICANS AGAINST THE CITY

AMERICANS AGAINST THE CITY

Anti-Urbanism in the Twentieth Century

Steven Conn

OXFORD
UNIVERSITY PRESS

OXFORD

UNIVERSITY PRESS

Oxford University Press is a department of the University of
Oxford. It furthers the University's objective of excellence in research,
scholarship, and education by publishing worldwide.

Oxford   New York
Auckland   Cape Town   Dar es Salaam   Hong Kong   Karachi
Kuala Lumpur   Madrid   Melbourne   Mexico City   Nairobi
New Delhi   Shanghai   Taipei   Toronto

With offices in
Argentina   Austria   Brazil   Chile   Czech Republic   France   Greece
Guatemala   Hungary   Italy   Japan   Poland   Portugal   Singapore
South Korea   Switzerland   Thailand   Turkey   Ukraine   Vietnam

Oxford is a registered trademark of Oxford University Press
in the UK and certain other countries.

Published in the United States of America by
Oxford University Press
198 Madison Avenue, New York, NY 10016

© Oxford University Press 2014

First issued as an Oxford University Press paperback, 2016

Library of Congress Cataloging-in-Publication Data
Conn, Steven.
Americans against the city : anti-urbanism in the twentieth century / Steven Conn.
    pages cm
Includes bibliographical references and index.
ISBN 978–0–19–997366–8 (hardback); 978–0–19–063634–0 (paperback)
1. Urban renewal—United States—History.   2. Urbanization—United States—History.
3. Decentralization in government—United States—History.   4. Urbanization
5. Decentralization in government—United States.   I. Title. HT175.C637 2014
307.3'4160973—dc23
2013044642

For Angela, and for Olivia and Zachary, too—because of all the cities we have explored together

CONTENTS

ACKNOWLEDGMENTS

As Crosby, Stills, and Nash once sang: "It's been a long time comin'..."

This book began on an evening walk with my parents, Terry and Peter, nearly a decade ago; and while I have called in many favors, accumulated many debts, and even relied on the kindness of strangers, my first expression of gratitude belongs to them. They remain models for me in so many different ways.

Lots of things have gotten in the way of finishing this book—many that were rewarding, some that were onerous, much that was necessary. But none have been as gratifying as my two children Zach and Olivia, who transformed from toddlers into teens as I wrote this, becoming more and more interesting, complicated and fun along the way. I owe my second thanks to them.

It gives me great pleasure to look back at all the help I have received from friends and colleagues as I worked my way through this project. I have called upon Kevin Boyle, Saul Cornell, Jacob Dorn, Robert Fishman, Alison Isenberg, Michael Kammen, Chris Klemek, Bruce Kuklick, Max Page, Nathaniel Popkin, Wendell Pritchett, Bryant Simon, Tom Sugrue, and Mike Zuckerman for advice, help, and encouragement. I need to thank Dan Amsterdam, Bill Childs, Bob Fogarty, and Dave Steigerwald in particular for their generosity with me. My students Delano Lopez and Patrick Potyondy asked some very hard questions about the book and made it better in so doing. Nancy Toff, my editor at Oxford University Press, came along at just the right moment to give me a final push. And I would not have finished this project were it not for the help from two very able graduate students, Leticia Wiggins and Renya Esquivel-King.

I benefited from a number of archival collections and the staff at each, including the Van Pelt Library at the University of Pennsylvania, the Rockefeller Archive Center, the special collections at the University of Illinois, Chicago, the Houston Metropolitan Research Center at the Houston Public Library, the Greenhills Historical Society, and the special collections at Wright State University.

Long as it has taken, this book would still not be finished were it not for a grant I received from the American Philosophical Society to support a year of research and writing. I did much of that work in the Olive Kettering Library at Antioch College. The resources of that terrific facility are matched by the generosity of the staff, who have given me so much help. Jim and Sandy and Ritch and Duffy have all amiably put up with me, but Scott Sanders deserves a special mention. I have come to rely on his remarkable breadth of knowledge and his dependable good humor.

My wife, Angela Brintlinger, was along for that walk with my parents on that chilly fall evening. If a partnership is a metaphorical journey, then ours can be measured in the walks she and I have taken together over the years. Hundreds of them. Miles and miles of them. I've treasured every step.

AMERICANS AGAINST THE CITY

THE AMERICAN URBAN PARADOX

DATELINE: Roanoke County. Roanoke County, Virginia, sits in the southwestern part of the commonwealth, just as the state begins to taper to a point. It is, without question, a pretty part of the country. Just south of the Shenandoah Valley, just east of the Appalachians, its hills and valleys, farm fields and forests, range from picturesque to gorgeous. No mystery that tourism is an increasingly important part of the local economy.

At first glance, Roanoke County is part of rural America. As of 2010, there were just 100,000 residents spread over the county's 251 square miles. And like much of rural America, Roanoke County is a politically conservative place. Over the last half-century it has voted reliably and overwhelmingly for the Republican presidential candidate. Barry Goldwater won less than 40 percent of the vote nationally in 1964, but he captured 55 percent of the vote here. Virtually all of those 100,000 residents are white.

That first glance, however, belies the real picture. Roanoke County does not count the nearly 100,000 people who live in the city of Roanoke, which sits as an independent municipal entity in the middle of the county. Further, much of the county's population is clustered around the city. Taken together, Roanokers are not rural Americans, really. They are urban and suburban Americans.

In other words, Roanoke County constitutes a much larger metropolitan region, with a population of roughly 200,000—in fact, the fourth largest county in Virginia, and by far the largest in southwestern Virginia. As with many metropolitan areas, the city serves as the center of the region, economically and culturally. And in the summer of 2011, Roanoke County became a small front in a national battle.

After the election of 2008, when Roanokers gave 60 percent of their vote to John McCain, Roanoke County became Tea Party country. The media have certainly reported about the Tea Party anger directed at "Washington" and the big-spending liberals who reside there. Equally important, though perhaps less discussed, have been the attacks by activists against the actions of local governments. In Roanoke County, that means anger was directed at the five-member board of supervisors.

The board had begun to explore a number of initiatives under the broad umbrella of "sustainability": ideas that ranged from bike paths and "smart" electric meters to encouraging development around public transportation nodes. Tea Partiers in Roanoke County saw these initiatives as a naked attempt to make the county more "urban," and they smelled government conspiracy.

They have been encouraged in their conspiracy theorizing by the Republican Party. On January 13, 2012, the Republican National Committee crystallized its own antipathy toward urbanism when it issued a statement denouncing "sustainable development" as nothing less than an assault on "the American way of life of private property ownership, single family homes, private car ownership and individual travel choices, and privately owned farms." The whole thing, according to the Tea Party, smacked of a communist plot or, worse, something cooked up by the United Nations. One can sympathize with the exasperation of Roanoke County Supervisor Charlotte Moore. After being attacked by the Tea Party, she sighed, "The Tea Party people say they want non-polluted air and clean water and everything we promote and support, but they say it's a communist movement. I really don't know what they want."[1]

Roanoke County is not alone among the nation's metropolitan regions looking at ways to reduce energy consumption, or to combat the loss of farmland and open space. There is a wide consensus now that encouraging more "urban" patterns of development—those that rely less on automobiles, that concentrate people in higher densities, and that permit "mixed" uses—can help municipalities save money, bring better economic growth, and even foster more sociability. Nor is Roanoke County alone in experiencing an angry and irrational backlash against these initiatives.

So let Roanoke County stand as representative. It embodies two kinds of landscapes that characterize America in the early decades of the twenty-first century. The first is physical, and the second is political. The former is the essentially suburbanized landscape of much of metropolitan America; the latter is the deeply suspicious fear of government and the role it should play in our lives that shapes much of our political discourse. The purpose of this book is to describe the relationship between these two landscapes as they developed during the twentieth century. The two landscapes are connected in important ways, each shaping the other and tied together by the same impulse in American life. I call it "anti-urbanism."

To define what I mean by anti-urbanism demands that I define what "urbanism" itself means, and that is no small task. People have attempted to characterize what a city is for almost as long as cities have been part of the human experience. To begin, we can define cities by their demographics because, at a basic level, they are concentrations of human life and activity. We might also define them functionally; a century ago the German social thinker Max Weber created a taxonomy of cities that included market settlements, consumer and producer cities, political and administrative cities, and fortress and garrison cities.[2] To which we might add religious centers and intellectual hubs.

Demographics and function are clearly integral to any definition of what we mean by urban, but they fail to capture fully the more transcendent, aspirational quality that seems to me to be at the heart of what we associate with urbanism. Aristotle chided us long ago that "a great city is not to be confounded with a populous one," though the difference between a great city and one that is merely big is hard to put your finger on. As a number of intellectuals began to notice in the late nineteenth and early twentieth centuries, the rise and astonishing growth of industrial cities created new social and cultural possibilities, in addition to new economic relationships. We can count people and tally economic activity to take the measure of a city, but those numbers do not explain what Langston Hughes managed to capture in four short lines: "In the morning the city / Spreads its wings / Making a song / In stone that sings."[3]

It seems to me that great cities, loaded as that phrase is, combine function and culture in mutually reinforcing, intertwined ways. At the risk of simplifying too much, great cities serve as marketplaces and as meeting places. As marketplaces, cities bring people together to participate in exchange and transaction, whether economically, socially, or intellectually. But the very act of gathering together throws people into all sorts of unexpected interactions and juxtapositions that could not happen anywhere else and out of which grow equally unexpected innovations and change. It is this role as grand meeting place that Margaret Mead had in mind when she wrote, "A city must be a place where groups of women and men are seeking and developing the highest things they know."[4] This combination of marketplace and meeting place creates the sense of possibility and challenge that is unique to the urban environment.

Although intellectuals like Weber and Georg Simmel recognized this cultural aspect of city life a century or more ago, it is probably fair to say that Americans tend to focus only on the economic functions of the city. As a consequence, we have not fully appreciated this equally important, if more ineffable, role that cities play in our civilization. Indeed, the role of meeting place is the factor that turns the merely urban into the urbane.

If these are the two ways in which cities ought to function, then those functions require two urban conditions. The first is density; the second is a public realm. The former is a physical condition of the built environment, whereas the latter is a political and social condition of that environment; and like the marketplace/meeting place roles, they grow or shrink in relation to each other.

Density is the more straightforward of the two conditions. We can measure it by simple long division: take the population of any municipality and divide it by the size of the place, and you get its density. But we are so accustomed to thinking in terms of "big" rather than "dense" that the results of that arithmetic can sometimes be surprising. The 2010 Census lists these as the five largest American cities: New York, Los Angeles, Chicago, Houston, Philadelphia. A familiar enough list. Ranked by density, however, the list of major cities looks like this: New York, San Francisco, Boston, Chicago, Philadelphia. It is worth noting that although New York City is far and away the densest of big American cities, Paris is nearly twice as dense. Size does not matter when it comes to urbanity, but density does.

Density enables—often forces—diverse and heterogeneous populations of people to interact with each other. Those interactions, whether economic or social, casual or intimate, create the cosmopolitanism that is the hallmark of great cities that has so excited some and terrified others. In the main, however, cities have been the places where we have first and most fully confronted the task of living alongside people who do not necessarily belong to our own tribe. The word *cosmopolitan*, after all, originally described someone who moved comfortably in the midst of the unfamiliar and diverse. Familiarity may breed contempt, as the old saw has it, but the lesson of city life is that, more often than not, it also breeds a kind of tolerance.

The way in which cities work to bring different people together in close proximity is causally connected to the creation of a public realm or public sphere. Philosophers and historians have parsed different meanings of that concept, but broadly speaking we can think of the public sphere as a space—metaphorical and literal—that enables private individuals to come together to identify, discuss, debate, and act on areas of shared concern. It is a space that bridges elements of people's purely private lives and the realm of governing authority. The creation of a public sphere makes it possible for individuals to conceive of themselves as a public with its own collective set of interests.[5]

Beginning in the seventeenth century, cities provided the first, best locations for this public realm. They fostered networks of communication and facilitated the exchange of ideas. They provided public streets and sidewalks for people to parade and protest, squares and parks for them to gather in. Likewise, cities hosted institutions that promoted knowledge and culture to a wide public: museums and libraries, schools and universities. No wonder, then, that cities were at the forefront of the democratic revolutions that took place in the eighteenth century. In Boston, members of this newly emerging public threw tea into the harbor in an act of protest against the British crown, and in the coffeehouses of Philadelphia, radicals debated the ideas that would propel the drive to independence. Democracy itself, the process whereby a diverse and heterogeneous group of individuals becomes a "public," and identifies and negotiates matters of shared concern, is an urban creation.

Few Americans, then or now, would reject the idea of democracy, but plenty of them have rejected the city and the "urbanness" from which it sprang. In the pages that follow I will examine the ideas and exhortations of a diverse group of writers, critics, architects, planners, and others who have all shared an anti-urban outlook. More specifically, these intellectuals and others looked at the American city as it evolved during the twentieth century, and they rejected, in varying degrees and with differing emphases, both parts of the urban equation. Broadly speaking, they rejected the density of urban spaces and the public nature of urban life.

Some who objected to density did so because they genuinely believed that the crowded, often unsanitary conditions of industrial neighborhoods were inhumane. Others simply could not abide the ethnic and racial diversity that came to define American cities, first as emigrants from southern and Eastern Europe poured into them, and then as African Americans and Hispanic Americans altered the colors of the city yet again.

Their antidote to density—and they often referred to it as "concentration"—was to decentralize the city, and they offered various proposals and plans to achieve that goal. From garden cities, to a revival of the American small town, to the building of new towns and cities, anti-urban Americans imagined and tried to build a variety of alternatives to the city that were less dense—and presumably less diverse, as well. For many of these anti-urbanists, the early twentieth-century technologies of electricity and the automobile would make decentralization possible without losing the economic advantages that come with urban concentration. By plugging in and driving around, Americans could be untethered from the centralized city. More recently that dream has had a revival in the decentralized promises of a digital age where telecommuting will make it possible for people to work in one place while living somewhere else entirely.

At the same time, and just as important, anti-urbanists objected to the public, collective nature of city life. In the Progressive-era city, urban citizens turned increasingly to the mechanisms of government to shape and improve the quality of urban life. For many anti-urbanists, however, that expansion of government constituted, in and of itself, a grave concern. As the importance of cities and the scale of government expanded across the twentieth century, these anti-urbanists began to see the two as almost coterminous. They grew equally suspicious of both.

If the anti-urbanists felt uneasy with or hostile to the urban public sphere, and even more to the role government played in it, then almost all of them offered the fuzzier notion of "community" as its alternative. Americans of many stripes looked at the dizzying growth of industrial cities and saw loss: the loss of intimate social relations replaced by anonymity, and of nurturing communities replaced by alienation. They were convinced that "community" could not be achieved in the modern city. Central to their anti-urban vision of the United States was a restoration—somehow, some way—of this lost community.

Community has almost entirely warm connotations as we use the term in this country. It implies something more than mere association, but something that is emotionally, perhaps even spiritually, fulfilling as well. A place where everyone knows your name and cares about your well-being. Those who offered community as the alternative to the impersonality of the city, however, seldom acknowledged that any community is necessarily defined by those whom it includes, and thus also by those whom it does not. And there are plenty of examples where "communities" react defensively to outsiders, where they throw up barricades, literal and metaphorical, and where they retreat into themselves. It is this dual sense of community—a place welcoming to those inside it and hostile to those outside it—that makes the recent growth of "gated communities" oxymoronic and redundant at the same time.

Nor did the anti-urbanists recognize that community was not a simple substitute for the public sphere created in and by urban spaces. Indeed, the interactions necessary to form a "public" are different from, but no less important than, the more intimate relationships formed in a community. Without them democratic processes do not work as well, which perhaps helps explain why, as we have moved more and more toward the world of the private in this country, our politics has become increasingly shrill and sclerotic.[6]

In this sense, Roanoke County illustrates the irony central to twentieth-century anti-urbanism. On the one hand, many of the sizable majority of Americans who live in the decentralized, suburbanized landscape of metropolitan America find it to be profoundly dissatisfying. They complain about all the time wasted in traffic, and they lament the ugly sameness of it all. Most of all, they report that these places leave them feeling alienated and alone. They mourn the loss of some sense of community that these sterile physical and social environments have failed to give them. On the other hand, many of them reject the idea that any collective, public action can or should be taken to address these problems. They are thus left feeling powerless to do much about them.

That irony may be the most important consequence of the anti-urbanism impulse as it developed during the twentieth century. As people feel less and less connected to each other and to their surroundings, it becomes more and more difficult to make the collective decisions and take the collective actions that are at the very heart of democratic governance. We may be a highly mobile society, but our democracy is still organized geographically. We elect officials—from county supervisors to mayors, to members of state legislatures and the House of Representatives—based on geographic boundaries. The result is a kind of political disconnect: we elect politicians on the basis of a geography many of us know little about and care about even less. In short, atomized individuals have a difficult time imagining a common good rooted in the specificity of locale.

Indeed, our politics of anger, fear, and paranoia has fermented in the place-less places so many Americans now occupy.[7] Taken together, anti-urbanism adds up to an unwillingness to acknowledge the urban—and metropolitan—nature of American society, and a refusal to embrace the essentially collective, rather than individual, nature of urban life.

The reaction against this equating of "city" and "public" has given twentieth-century anti-urbanism its particular flavor. Though racism and racial tension contributed to the urban crisis of the 1950s and '60s, and the economic tsunami called "deindustrialization" left many older cities economically destitute by the 1970s and '80s, the two components of anti-urbanism laid out here have deeper roots. As a consequence, by the turn of the twenty-first century, our anti-urban rejection of cities and the public has left us with an indifference to the problems of the city. More than that, however, it has also meant a refusal to confront any number of national problems that require public solutions, from education and transportation to health care and the environment.

Thus, anti-urbanism has meant that Americans have abandoned the urban form as we have built our physical environment, and we have denied the shared, public nature of urban life as well. Even as more and more Americans live and work in large, urbanized metropolitan regions, we retreat as far as we can into the world of the private. Our sense of purpose, national and personal, has become disconnected from our sense of place. Like many of the residents of Roanoke County, we are a nation reliant on the engines of our cities, populated with people who do not like cities very much.

In the pages that follow I pair the history of the complex idea of anti-urbanism with a history of places where those ideas were given physical form in several locations around the country. Part of what ties the disparate stories in this book together is this relationship between ideas and places, between anti-urbanism as a critique of American life and the creation of physical alternatives to the city.[8]

Sometimes these ideas shaped policymaking, especially after the postwar expansion of the federal government, but this book is not a history of planning or of urban/anti-urban policy.[9] Nor is it a fine-grained sociology of the lived experiences of urbanites/anti-urbanites during the twentieth century. Instead, this book describes the cultural and intellectual architecture of anti-urbanism, and it examines how those ideas gave shape to the physical landscape in which we live and work today. It examines the ideas and cultural soil out of which our present policy and planning decisions have grown.

To chart these reactions against the city, I have created a very rough periodization of American urban history or, better, of American anti-urban history. In the Progressive era, the city and its problems were repositioned in the public debate in a different way than they had been treated in the nineteenth century. Reformers of the Progressive era were certainly no less concerned than their nineteenth-century predecessors with questions of vice—drinking, prostitution, petty crime—and the philosophers of the era, particularly Josiah Royce, worried a great deal about the corrosive effects of industrial society on the fabric of American "community."[10] But a number of those reformers became convinced that the problems of the city, rather than simply being issues of personal morality, had become matters of public concern; the solutions to those problems, therefore, would come from politics and public policy, not merely from individual salvation. They recognized that the cities which boomed during the industrial age were more than simply the sum of the misbehaving people who lived in them; instead, they had become larger, more complicated organisms. Indeed, they recognized that the United States had become an urban nation, and they insisted that, as an urban nation, the problems of the city and the problems of the nation were coterminous. The "city," in other words, became the "public"; and they believed that the future of the nation would be won precisely in the city.

The interwar period, then, saw the rise of a broad and somewhat inchoate movement of "decentralization." Those who argued that the best way to tame urban problems was to "decentralize" both population and industry included the planners of the Regional Planning Association, the back-to-the-land homesteaders led by Ralph Borsodi, those who shaped the New Deal's new town program, and the writers who contributed to the journal *Free America*.

During those same years, Americans who wanted to leave the city and decentralize American life needed examples of an alternative to urban America. They "discovered" one such alternative in the American "folk"—people whose traditional patterns of living had not been corrupted by urban and industrial America, and who could serve as a model for a de-urbanized future. Aspects of this anti-urban vogue for the folk included the regionalist movement, the "invention" of the New England town as the source of true Americanism, and the romantic celebration of life in the Southern Appalachian highlands.

The end of World War II and the 1980s roughly bookend a period of urban crisis in older, industrial cities and the radical transformation of urban space in cities across the country. In the 1950s and '60s, the twin transformations brought about by urban renewal and interstate highway programs sprang from the anti-urban impulse and left the cities reeling from their effects. Simultaneously, the perceived failure of the federal urban renewal program turned the cities into physical manifestations of a failure of government liberalism.

The reaction against the city in the postwar period was undeniably connected to the question of race, as the African American population continued to urbanize, but race simply amplified much of the anti-urban impulse that had already been circulating in America during the first half of the twentieth century. At the same time, the anti-urbanism of the postwar years contributed in important ways to the broader agenda of the New Right.

One response during these years was the phenomenal growth of the postwar suburb. Another was the emergence of the Sunbelt, whose rapidly developing urban centers embodied many of the anti-urban impulses that appeared in the 1920s and '30s: decentralized, rather than dense, in their spatial organization; and private, rather than public, in their political outlook.

That urban crisis spawned a generation of Americans who searched for a physical alternative to the American city. Some, like Antioch College President and Tennessee Valley Authority Director Arthur Morgan, believed that the American small town could be brought back to life, and that only there could true American values be fostered. At the end of the 1960s, America witnessed another back-to-the-land exodus, this time led by disillusioned hippies and activists who retreated to rural communes. Although their politics might have been on the left, their animus against the city was no different from or less virulent than that of their parents, who had earlier moved to the suburbs. Finally, reacting against the urban chaos of the late 1960s, the Nixon administration proposed another program of building new towns that would allow people to escape the old cities and start over again.

American cities reached a low-water mark during the age of Reagan. If in the Progressive era urban problems were seen as national issues, then by the 1980s that view had been almost entirely negated: urban issues were no longer part of the national agenda. At roughly the same moment, many Americans became concerned with the deterioration of "community." The political scientist Robert Putnam has both studied the problem and captured the Zeitgeist in his book *Bowling Alone* (2000). He was part of a small movement among some philosophers, sociologists, and others—called "communitarianism"—which offered solutions to that pervasive late-twentieth-century American anomie. Alongside the communitarians arose a group of architects and planners called the "new urbanists," whose proposed solutions could be inscribed into physical space by bringing back more traditional urban forms—sidewalks, porches, and common spaces as opposed to cul-de-sacs and strip malls. New urbanist principles informed the Department of Housing and Urban Development's (HUD) new approach to public housing, known as the HOPE VI program. Those principles also influenced a number of HUD housing developments in several American cities, and helped contribute to the so-called urban renaissance at the turn of the twenty-first century.

In 1903, W. E. B. Du Bois made the prescient prediction for the twentieth century when he announced that the problem of that century would be the problem of the color line. Five years earlier, however, Rev. Josiah Strong made his own bold prediction: "We must face the inevitable. The new civilization is certain to be urban, and the problem of the twentieth century will be the city."[11] The century or so that followed has proved Strong correct. Ours *did* become an urban civilization, but even as it did, many Americans continued to dream anti-urban dreams and tried to make those dreams real.

1 ANTI-URBANISM

AN AMERICAN TRADITION

In 1630, John Winthrop declared that the Massachusetts Bay Colony he was about to lead would be a "city on a hill," and in the four hundred years since, the image has become among the most clichéd in our political rhetoric. Though politicians may still find it stirring, Winthrop's metaphor has never really suited the American temperament. More apt, I suspect, is the experience of William Penn. In 1683, Penn founded his great city and "holy experiment," Philadelphia, and laid out its revolutionary grid system. He also built a country estate for himself several miles from his city, though the difference between town and country in the 1690s could hardly have been huge. In so doing, Penn became perhaps the only person in history to have founded a city and become its first suburbanite almost simultaneously. It is fair to say that when most Americans imagine what the good life might be, they think more like Penn than like Winthrop. For Americans, utopia has always been a few acres in the country, a home on the range.

Which is to say that the American argument with the city goes back to the very beginning of English settlement in the "new world"—longer, perhaps, than the American distrust of government.[1] In 1784, Thomas Jefferson published *Notes on the State of Virginia,* in which he valorized and mythologized a nation of independent yeoman farmers; and of all the founding figures, Jefferson provides us with the most flamboyant denunciations of the American city. His language was famously florid and his tone was not subtle:

> The mobs of great cities add just so much to the support of pure government, as sores do to the strength of the human body. It is the manners and spirit of a people which preserve a republic in vigour. A degeneracy in these is a canker which soon eats to the heart of its laws and constitution.[2]

Jefferson also championed the decentralization of government power, though as president he certainly embraced centralized power enthusiastically. But Americans took to heart the Jeffersonian view of government and of cities. Nearly two hundred years after Jefferson wrote that anti-urban invective, Gallup began surveying where Americans wanted to live and the results have been remarkably consistent over the years: not quite 20 percent of us—fewer than one in five—expressed a desire to live in a city.[3]

The two halves of the anti-urban impulse—the fear of the city as a physical form and the suspicion of government—came together when the nation's new capital was established. Article 1, section 8, of the Constitution defines the area of a future national capital as no more than ten square miles, and insists that such a space be created by "cessation of particular States." It further gives Congress the power to locate this district and to govern it entirely. Where that ten square miles might be remained unresolved until the summer of 1790. Northerners wanted the capital in New York, Philadelphia, or near Trenton, roughly halfway between the two. Southerners—Virginians, in particular—wanted a site on the Potomac River. Jefferson, so he claimed later, won the Potomac site when he had James Madison and Alexander Hamilton to his home for dinner and they hammered out a trade: southern votes for Hamilton's financial plans in exchange for a southern capital. The two necessary bills passed in July and August. Jefferson was very pleased with himself.

By moving the capital away from the two major urban centers, New York and Philadelphia, Jefferson set about creating a capital city very different from those in Europe. London, Paris, and St. Petersburg all functioned as their nation's political, cultural, and economic centers, and as such they represented a concentration of power that made Jefferson profoundly uneasy. So he engineered the relocation of politics away from culture and commerce. The final site of the capital, chosen by President Washington, was made purely for reasons of symbolic geography, not because there were any inherent advantages to it.

The site Washington chose was swampy in many places, and certainly did not enjoy the natural advantages that usually attract city-builders. Enthusiasts predicted that someday Washington, D.C., would hum with industry and that the port on the Potomac would bustle with activity of the sort that other cities enjoyed. Things did not quite work out that way. Instead, it began as—and in many ways remains—a one-company town, a city that has grown only with the rhythms of government, rather than with the organic patterns of urbanism.[4]

The plan for the new city did not help matters. President Washington hired the French engineer Pierre L'Enfant to lay out the capital, and the ironies began almost immediately. The plan this Frenchman designed for the capital of the new American republic borrowed heavily from the French baroque style. L'Enfant took a grid pattern of secondary streets, pioneered in Philadelphia, and laid the radiating avenues of the Versailles gardens on top of it. Although the plan attempts to embody the three branches of the federal government, its primary purpose is to map and display power.

Finally, of course, the founders built their anti-urbanism into the very structure of the republic. Scholars have fully explored how much the interests of slave-holding southerners and their agricultural economy shaped the Constitution, but it is worth reiterating that they did so in opposition to the urbanizing manufacturing centers of the north. Further, by guaranteeing two senators for every state regardless of population, the founders created the basis upon which the political interests of the metropolitan majority can be held hostage by the rural minority. Call it the tyranny of Wyoming.

And it is worth remembering that our current practice of redistricting every ten years based on census data is a relatively recent phenomenon. Until the Supreme Court decision in *Baker v. Carr* in 1962, states redistricted on an irregular basis, thus preserving legislative districts that did not reflect the rapidly urbanizing populations of many states. By 1950, half of all Illinoisans, for example, lived in Cook County, the greater Chicago area, but Cook County had far fewer than half the seats in the Illinois legislature, or in the Illinois congressional delegation, because Illinois had not redrawn its districts since 1900.[5] Call this the tyranny of the small town; through it, anti-urbanism was woven into the fabric of power.

Anti-Urbanism in the Nineteenth Century

During the nineteenth century, Americans learned to venerate Thomas Jefferson, and they applauded his anti-urban vision of the nation, but in fact they didn't really listen to him. As a city, Washington, D.C., languished to some extent for most of the nineteenth century. But the rest of Jefferson's nation of yeoman farmers urbanized at an astonishing rate across the century. New York City had approximately 60,000 residents in 1800, and ten times that number by 1860. By 1900, Manhattan alone was home to roughly 2.2 million souls. Perhaps even more shocking, in 1840 Chicago counted just over 4,000 residents and barely registered on the map. By 1900, the city bustled with more than 1.5 million people. It would add another half million by 1910.

By 1900, New York, Chicago, and Philadelphia, each with populations of well over 1 million, stood as embodiments of vertiginous urban growth. But they also symbolized the direction in which the national graph pointed. When Jefferson moved into the White House in 1800, a scant 6 percent of Americans were classified as urbanites. A century later, that number stood at 40 percent and the percentage of farm dwellers declined from over 90 to just 50 percent.

Those numbers underlay the urban crisis of the late nineteenth century, and that crisis was cast largely in moral terms. Cities produced vice—lots of it, and in a bewilderingly salacious variety, to judge by the endless accounts of it in the nineteenth-century press. The city became the place to locate and localize the abstract debates over the nation's virtue and its potential corruption. The solution to the problem of the city, therefore, was also moral or religious.

Cities, in this sense, became the front lines for religious crusaders attempting to rescue a fallen nation. It was no mere hyperbole that when William and Catherine Booth founded an evangelical and social service organization in the slums of East London in 1865, they called it the Salvation Army. That Army mustered its first recruits in the United States fifteen years later, in New York City's Battery Park.

Urban growth did not go uncelebrated, of course. Throughout the nineteenth century, the city was the subject of boosters' enthusiasm, especially boosters who hoped to get rich developing real estate. For people like these, city growth was usually taken as salutary evidence of the nation's growth in general. The language of boosterism pervades much of the writing about cities, as in this 1893 essay about the new city of Denver: "Denver is a beautiful city—a parlor city with cabinet finish—and it is so new that it looks as if it had been made to order, and was just ready for delivery."[6]

Architects like Frank Furness and Louis Sullivan found inspiration in the booming industrial city; the great park-builder, Frederick Law Olmsted, believed that cities could combine the urban with the pastoral. The poet Walt Whitman, perhaps more than any other cultural figure, celebrated and reveled in the cosmopolitan life of his New York and Brooklyn:

> This is the city... and I am one of the citizens;
> Whatever interests the rest interests me.... politics, markets, newspapers, schools,
> Benevolent societies, improvements, banks, tariffs, steamships, factories,
> Stocks, stores, real estate, and personal estate.[7]

Still, these figures stand in the minority. In the nineteenth century, the American city produced precious few real champions among the nation's writers, artists, intellectuals, and politicians. Indeed, most of the country's leading thinkers—from Jefferson to Frank Lloyd Wright—shared with their fellow Americans an uneasiness about American cities, even as they watched them grow. The title of a 1962 survey of American thought summarized this situation succinctly: *The Intellectual versus the City.*[8]

The litany of nineteenth-century American intellectuals who expressed hostility to the city is familiar and requires only a quick review: Ralph Waldo Emerson thought Boston a fine enough place to visit, but he never wanted to live there; Henry David Thoreau did not even like to visit and retreated farther from the city. He wrote to Emerson that in Boston, "the pigs in the street are the most respectable part of the population."[9] Henry Adams, looking back on his own nineteenth century, set up a stark but altogether familiar dichotomy by juxtaposing Boston (town) and Quincy (country) as the competing poles of his childhood. It was an "inherited feud," the tension between Quincy and Boston, and Adams grew up believing that Boston represented all that was wrong: "Quincy had always been right, for Quincy represented a moral principle—the principle of resistance to Boston."[10]

Mid-nineteenth-century American painters—Asher B. Durand, Frederick Church, Albert Bierstadt, John Frederick Kensett, and Martin Johnson Heade, to name a few—established themselves by painting glorious landscapes, first on the Hudson River and in New England, later in the American West. Thomas Eakins painted the people of industrial Philadelphia, though rarely the city itself; Winslow Homer headed for the coast of Maine. By the end of the century, realist writers like Stephen Crane and Theodore Dreiser saw the modern American city as a gargantuan maw that simply swallowed those unfortunates who got swallowed by it.

Nineteenth-century moralizing about the city reached a culmination of sorts when the Reverend Josiah Strong published his 1885 blockbuster *Our Country: Its Possible Future and Its Present Crisis.* Strong was as uneasy as anyone else about the growth of an urban society. In *Our Country,* he updated the old Puritan jeremiad to include a variety of new evils and threats, including immigration, Romanism, and socialism. The last in his list of "perils" was "The City," which had become "a serious menace to our civilization" because in it "each of the dangers we have discussed is enhanced and all are focalized." In the tradition of the nineteenth-century moralists, he asked of urban America, "Is our progress in morals and intelligence at all comparable to the growth of population?" The question was purely rhetorical. Reactionary, perhaps hysterical, though he was, Strong could read the writing on the wall. "The city is the nerve center of our civilization," he wrote, "it is also the storm center."[11]

Strong's warning of impending American decline interests us not simply because of its overheated language. Rather, we can see his book as a mile marker of sorts, a culmination of the nineteenth-century anti-urban tradition and a prescient acknowledgment that the United States had decisively entered its urban moment.

THE MODERN CITY

On the one hand, the city stands for all that is evil—a city that is full of devils, foul and corrupting; and, on the other hand, the city stands for all that is noble, full of the glory of God, and shining with a clear and brilliant light. But, if we think a little more carefully, we shall see that the city has in all ages of the world represented both these aspects. It has been the worst, and it has been the best. Every city has been a Babylon, and every city has been a New Jerusalem; and it has always been a question whether the Babylon would extirpate the New Jerusalem or the New Jerusalem would extirpate the Babylon. It has been so in the past. It is so in the present. The greatest corruption, the greatest vice, the greatest crime, are to be found in the great city. The greatest philanthropy, the greatest purity, the most aggressive and noble courage, are to be found in the great city. San Francisco, St. Louis, Chicago, Cincinnati, Philadelphia, New York, Boston, and Brooklyn are full of devils—and also full of the glory of God.—*Lyman Abbott.*

Storm center and nerve center. At the turn of the twentieth century, Reverend Josiah Strong was among the loudest voices warning Americans about the dangers of the new city. This photo of State Street in Chicago, accompanied by this foreboding paragraph, served as the frontispiece of his 1907 book *The Challenge of the City. Library of Congress LC-USZ60-101148*

Strong's nineteenth-century predecessors could still view the nation's growing cities as abhorrent aberrations, and they could still cling to a Jeffersonian vision of the nation's future as being out on the inexhaustible frontier. By the end of the century, though, those dreams had faded into nostalgia in the face of available evidence. America had become, despite all the rhetorical protestations, an urban nation, and what remained to be seen was how Americans would respond to that reality.

The Nineteenth-Century Urban Paradox Comes to a Head: Frederick Jackson Turner and Josiah Royce

As the nineteenth century drew to a close, the demographics of America's cities astonished: Chicago doubled in size between 1880 and 1890, adding half a million people to its neighborhoods; it added an additional 700,000 between 1890 and 1900. New York's growth and consolidation created a colossus of almost 3.5 million people by 1900. By 1910 it had added another 1.3 million people. These numbers tracked even more astonishing economic developments. The Gilded Age, the rise of corporate capitalism, the "incorporation" of America, the age of the Robber Barons—however one wants to label the American economy in the post-Civil War era, that transformation took place largely in American cities (or was driven by urban capital). The census data of 1890 was unequivocal: the frontier had closed, and the value of manufactured goods now exceeded the value of farm products by a considerable amount.

These shifts, from country to city, from farm to factory, lay beneath much of the politics of the 1880s and 1890s, especially the political movement known as populism. Leonidas L. Polk, a North Carolina newspaper editor, summed up the feelings of people who saw the nineteenth-century world slipping away:

> There is something radically wrong in our Industrial system. There is a screw loose.... The railroads have never been so prosperous, and yet agriculture languishes. The banks have never done a better business, and yet agriculture languishes. Manufacturing enterprises never made more money...and yet agriculture languishes. Towns and cities flourish and "boom"...and yet agriculture languishes.[12]

In the face of railroads and banks, towns and cities, Jefferson's rural America did not stand a chance. For his part, Polk threw himself and his newspaper behind the Populist cause.

The election of 1896 could not have been better scripted as a symbolic showdown between rural and urban America. On July 9, during the Democratic convention, William Jennings Bryan, raised on an Illinois farm and home-schooled on McGuffey Readers and the Bible, and now a young congressman from Nebraska, delivered his "Cross of Gold" speech. He ended that speech—and gave it its name—by telling the nation, "You shall not press down upon the brow of labor this crown of thorns, you shall not crucify mankind upon a cross of gold," and then he stretched his arms out, Christ-like. The stunned crowd was silent for five seconds—and then it went wild. The next day, the Democrats nominated Bryan to be their presidential candidate.

Bryan's speech supported the Democratic proposal for the free coinage of silver. But in the middle of it, Bryan turned the sentiments of Leonidas Polk, and so many others in rural America, into part of his thunderous exhortation. "You come to us and tell us that the great cities are in favor of the gold standard," Bryan railed, setting up the urban–rural antagonism central to his view of the world. "I tell you that the great cities rest upon these broad and fertile prairies. Burn down your cities and leave our farms, and your cities will spring up again as if by magic. But destroy our farms and the grass will grow in the streets of every city in the country."[13] After that speech, the Populists decided to endorse Bryan as their candidate, too.

The election of 1896 was populism's Waterloo, and in its stinging defeat to William McKinley, it stood as a passing of sorts for the Jeffersonian vision that America was still a nation of small farmers. So if the nineteenth-century version of anti-urbanism neither addressed the realities of American life by the 1890s nor offered a compelling vision of the future, what remained was to enshrine that Jeffersonian ideal as the history of the nation.[14]

In July 1893, almost exactly three years before William Jennings Bryan mimicked Christ on the cross, Frederick Jackson Turner came to Chicago to deliver perhaps the most famous paper ever written by an American historian: "On the Significance of the Frontier in American Life." The essay was prompted, Turner told the audience assembled at the World's Columbian Exposition, by the announcement made by the U.S. Census Bureau. According to its data for 1890, the frontier—that mythic but no less iconic place in the American imagination—had disappeared. Turner used this news to muse on the importance of the "frontier" in American history.

In Turner's sweeping synthesis, cities appear only once, and then only as a dismissive aside. The frontier process, Turner wrote, "aroused seaboard cities like Boston, New York, and Baltimore to engage in rivalry for what Washington called 'the extensive and valuable trade of a rising empire.' "[15] Without mentioning the city much at all, however, Turner implicitly acknowledged that the process of urbanization had triumphed. Frontier America, after all, was now gone, and though Turner could not bring himself to admit it on that hot Chicago day in 1893, it had been replaced by urban America. For anyone who

In 1893, University of Wisconsin historian Frederick Jackson Turner offered a sweeping interpretation of American history—one in which cities figured almost not at all. *Courtesy of Wisconsin Historical Society, WHS-1910*

doubted that view, teeming, bumptious Chicago lay just outside the gates of the fair.

"The Significance of the Frontier" stands at the juncture between the older nineteenth-century moralizing tradition of writing about the city and the incipient treatment of the city by professional historians. As John Higham put it some years ago, Turner offered both a "scientific hypothesis" and "a declaration of faith, a romantic invocation of a great national experience."[16] The Turner thesis returns almost directly to Jefferson and the rest in its concern about the relationship between agrarian America (in this case, "the frontier") and democratic virtues. Although Turner acknowledged that it would be "a rash prophet who should assert that the expansive character of American life has now entirely ceased," the question hung in the humid air: What would become of American democracy, and of the nation itself, now that the frontier had closed? "The Significance of the Frontier in American History" thus stands as a thoroughly articulated "rural complaint."[17]

Turner, though trained in the seminar room at The Johns Hopkins University, was a midwesterner—Wisconsin born and bred. His essay can be read as a midwesterner's revenge on what he found to be an overbearing East Coast. But there is more to his midwestern-ness than that. The romantic version of American history that crystallized in the nineteenth century is, first and foremost, a midwestern story. The nation might have begun on the coast, but it was on the rolling prairies of the Midwest that it truly manifested its destiny. The midwestern story, brimming with energy and optimism, filled with the boosters' uncritical celebration of progress, became the American story in the second half of the nineteenth century, free as it was from the darkness of southern history or the nostalgic laments that could be heard in New England. The story of the American heartland, as it came to be told at the turn of the twentieth century, was one of happy success: settlement, steady improvements, much-deserved prosperity, and no end to it all in sight.[18]

The stars of this American romance were the midwestern small town and the farm; the city—though those boomed in the Midwest, too—had only a sinister role to play in this national drama. Turner recognized that the American future was urban. He wrote his essay in order to make sure that the American past at least was understood to be an anti-urban romance, played out in the Midwest.

Frederick Jackson Turner and the philosopher Josiah Royce were almost exact contemporaries—Royce had been born in 1855, Turner in 1861—and they overlapped for a few years on the faculty at Harvard University. On the surface, the historian and the philosopher would not seem to share intellectual concerns. But each in his own way wrestled with the nature of American "community." Turner looked to the pre-industrial, pre-urban past as the place where American community was created. Royce imagined how community could be created in the new urban, industrial circumstances of American life at the turn of the twentieth century.

Royce never turned his philosophical attention to the city in any full or considered way, though his own life ran a Turnerian course in reverse: from the rough-and-tumble California frontier of the 1850s and '60s to the urban and urbane world of Boston and Harvard. As America's leading idealist philosopher, Royce was surely intellectually, emotionally, and temperamentally predisposed to notions of community rooted in a shared sense of spiritual unity and purpose. He made reference repeatedly to an idealized early Christianity—what he called the "ideal Pauline church."

Royce stands as chief among the philosophers who explored the meaning of community in an urban, industrial age. In his own search for transcendence, Royce put the phrase "beloved community" into wide circulation. Seventy-five years after Ralph Waldo Emerson celebrated "the infinitude of private man," Royce countered directly:

Ethical individualism has been, in the past, one great foe of the great community. Ethical individualism, whether it takes the form of democracy or of the irresponsible search on the part of individuals for private happiness or for any other merely individual good, will never save mankind.[19]

Looking back on his own career during a celebration of his sixtieth birthday in 1915, at the Wilton Hotel in Philadelphia, Royce told the assembled crowd: "when I review this whole process, I strongly feel that my deepest motives and problems have centered about the Idea of the Community, although this idea has only come gradually to my clear consciousness."[20]

In an essay written as the First World War erupted, but published posthumously, Royce retained his characteristic and congenial optimism about the future. The "Great Community," as Royce called it, was still in view, even through the smoke of the Western front. "The last two centuries," Royce wrote, "have given us a right to hope for the unity of mankind." He observed that "the modern world has become more international," but Royce insisted that this internationalism "has not been true merely as to its technical and material ties but as to its spiritual union." Thus, he concluded in a statement that strikes us now as almost heartbreakingly naïve:

> while the great community of the future will unquestionably be international by virtue of the ties which will bind its various nationalities together, it will find no place for that sort of internationalism which despises the individual variety of nations, and which tries to substitute for the vices of those who at present seek merely to conquer mankind, the equally worthless desire of those who hope to see us in future a "men without a country."[21]

For his sake, better that Royce should not have lived to see what the twentieth century would bring.

Yet from his own experience of moving from west to east, he certainly understood the allure of the city. He set his novel *The Feud of Oakfield Creek* in frontier California, and he described how Margaret, the female protagonist, fretted over raising her son Tom in such isolation: "Tom suggested bringing him oftener into company with some of the neighbor's children but ... there were few of them whom she wanted him to know, and they were hard to get at. It was all the consequence of living in this lonesome place, she declared." Margaret drew the problem even more sharply: "the older the child grew, the more she felt it was cruel to bring him up here all alone in the country, where he would never find playmates, nor be contented." Margaret knew—and for Royce, she surely stood for almost any parent raising children in rural America in the late nineteenth century—that Tom would soon leave her for the city, and she mused in her melancholy, "One who lived in a city had more chance to keep her boy contented nearby her home."[22]

Further, Royce rooted his optimism about the coming "great community" in the economic circumstances of his moment, and he tried to persuade his readers that these developments justified that optimism. For the first time since that Pauline era, humanity had perfection almost within its grasp. "The idea of the community of mankind," he wrote, "has become more concrete, more closely related to the affairs of daily life, has become more practicable than ever before." He went on a bit more specifically, "At this very moment the material aspect of the civilization favors, as never before, the natural conditions upon which the community of mankind . . . would depend for its prosperity."[23] Though he perhaps could not quite bring himself to say it, the "material aspect of civilization" was the creation of urban, industrial society.

It is, almost, an odd kind of Marxism—a social revolution based on a new industrial prosperity, rather than on industrial desperation. Since the dissolution of that early Christian world, a new, more perfect community lacked the material base upon which it could be built. Now, Western industrial society had created that base—the prosperity necessary for the "community of mankind" to emerge and thrive. And it had done so in and because of its great cities.

Friends and intellectual sparring partners. In the early twentieth century, Josiah Royce (right) and William James (left) both taught in the Harvard University philosophy department. *Harvard University Archives, HUP James, William (10)*

Whatever else one thinks about Royce's philosophy, his assertion that, at the beginning of the twentieth century, the time had finally arrived to make good on Paul's vision of the great community attempted to address one of the contradictions at the heart of American thinking about the very notion of the "beloved community." Throughout the American tradition—indeed, throughout the Christian tradition—prosperity and spiritual perfection have had an uneasy co-existence. From the Puritan anxiety over whether earthly success hinted at eternal salvation, to the founders' fear that wealth and luxury would lead to corruption, to Thoreau's paeans to simplicity as the antidote to rampant materialism, Americans have struggled to reconcile the comforts of this world with their prospects in the next. Royce, however, believed that we could have both. More than that, he resolved this contradiction by suggesting that the "great community" could emerge only when the "material aspect" of life has reached a certain level.

When Royce reminisced for his colleagues and admirers in 1915, he accidentally put his finger on another central dilemma facing those who searched for the meaning of community. He began his remarks by returning to the place of his childhood, the wild and still forbidding landscape of pioneer California. "The sunsets were beautiful," he told the crowd, and he confessed that "my earliest recollections include a very frequent wonder as to what my elders meant when they said that this was a new community." The "Idea of Community"—what Royce called the center of his philosophic inquiries—"was what I was intensely feeling, in the days when my sisters and I looked across the Sacramento Valley."[24] At the end of his life, Royce rooted his career in the place where he grew up.

It is altogether too convenient, too teleological and reductive. Rather than argue over just how much influence Grass Valley, California, had on Royce's philosophy, it is worth pausing to consider why Royce chose to reminisce the way he did. Most of Royce's writings about the idea of community consider it precisely as an idea—or ideal—not as a place. It is a spiritual abstraction, not a physical location. In returning to the Sacramento Valley, Royce acknowledged a dilemma: What is the connection between the idea of community and the places where people have to live their lives? Royce was content to inhabit a "beloved community" of the mind and spirit, but most people need a concrete place to wake up each morning. In front of the dinner audience, even Royce linked his abstract ideas with the experience of living in a real place.

As America entered its urban age, this was the largest, most pressing challenge it faced. If this urban nation was to succeed, it certainly had to solve the logistical problems of city life—water, sanitation, public safety. It also had to confront the glaring and growing problems of social justice and equity—housing, the treatment of immigrants, working conditions in factories. But just as crucially, that urban nation had to address the need for community. It had to nurture the civic virtues and political idealism that Jefferson insisted could be found only on the farm. Urban life had to fulfill the promise of 1776: that not only could we find life and liberty in the city, but we could pursue happiness there as well. Progressive-era reformers, planners, and academics believed that the city could meet that challenge.

By the 1890s, the nineteenth-century version of anti-urbanism reached a culmination of sorts and faced a set of contradictions that could not easily be resolved. Those who clung to the nineteenth-century, Jeffersonian variety of anti-urbanism had to do so by ignoring all the ways in which American society was transforming right before their eyes. A new version of anti-urbanism would emerge after World War I, accommodating itself to a twentieth-century context.

In the meantime, however, the waning of the nineteenth-century version of the anti-urban impulse in American life led briefly to an enthusiasm to embrace urban America, at least among some. They saw its future as inextricably bound to the fate of the nation, and they worked to re-imagine the city as a place of civic virtue, shared public responsibilities, and humane community. The way Progressives altered the place of the city in American life might be summarized this way: if the nineteenth-century moralists saw the rise of the city as *the* problem in American life, Progressive reformers saw the city as a place *with* problems, and thus as a place where problems could find solutions. The city was no longer viewed as a moral battleground where sin competed with redemption but, rather, where specific problems could be identified and solutions rationally applied.[1] A constellation of Progressives used the techniques of social science and political organizing to make urban life better. Through their writings and their work they tried to convince a skeptical nation that cities could indeed be the best hope for America's future.

From Necessary Evil to Positive Good: Planning the Progressive City

In 1906, Frank Carlton lamented to readers of *Popular Science Monthly*, "On the very threshold of a new century these questions are forced upon a reluctant people: Can a nation grow strong, vigorous and progressive if a large percentage of its population are dwelling in cities? Is city life natural?"[2] Put this way, the questions sound rhetorical.

The nineteenth-century anti-urban tradition certainly did not disappear entirely across the threshold of the twentieth century. Indeed, it never has, and at the turn of the twentieth century plenty of writers gave voice to it even while acknowledging that the United States was fast becoming an urban nation. Watching the rush of population to the cities, Carlton moaned that "long-established modes of living are quickly changed; old customs and habits, upheld and cherished by the dearest traditions, are suddenly brushed aside." The editor of *World's Work* magazine did not even phrase this sentiment in the form of a question. "In a country like ours," a 1906 editorial proclaimed, "of great area and of rich productive land—life in cities and towns is not the normal life for any large proportion of the people. Nor is it the best or most wholesome life."[3] Natural, normal, wholesome—for many Americans during the Progressive era these remained things that the city was not, nor would ever be.

Urban Progressives wanted to change that, both in perception and in reality. In fact, putting aside some of the resource-conservation projects and the legal fights over trusts, most of the reform efforts we associate with the Progressive era were designed to solve the problems of urban life. Progressives looked at the city and saw its constituent parts; they attempted to take the great, chaotic whole and dissect it into smaller, more rational pieces. Run down the litany of their reform efforts, and after you pause to be profoundly impressed, you recognize the way in which the Progressives identified and categorized urban problems in order to formulate urban solutions. Concern over the living conditions of city dwellers led to housing reform and zoning codes; the self-evident problems of sanitation led to improvements in sewers and municipal water supplies; the danger so many industrial workers faced on the job generated tentative efforts to improve workplace safety and establish a system of workers' compensation; the bewildering variety of immigrants crowding with astonishing speed into Chicago and New York and Cleveland created demand for English classes and citizenship training. These are the things for which the Progressives are best remembered; and notice the way in which Progressives took the *problem* of the city and turned it into a more manageable *set* of problems—labor, children and family life, immigrant assimilation, public health, and the like. In confronting the challenges of urban life, Progressive reformers responded to the various dislocations of the urban industrial age by re-imagining the city as central to the path of American progress.[4]

Anyone who walked the streets of the turn-of-the-century city could see the variety of problems to which Progressive reformers turned their attention. But

The Progressive city on the move. As the big industrial cities grew at astonishing speeds, Progressive reformers recognized that if urban life was to be made livable, government would need to act, sponsoring public works such as this 1907 sewer project in Philadelphia. *Photo courtesy of PhillyHistory.org, a project of the Philadelphia Department of Records*

for many of those reformers, most of the specific problems—whether health or housing, sanitation or transportation—stemmed from the same root: density. Too many city people made their lives in too little space, and thus the challenge for those who embraced the city was to make city life humane and fulfilling at densities the world had never experienced before.

In the past, some historians have interpreted the Progressive concern with crowding as an aversion to the urban life that newly arrived immigrants made for themselves when they settled in American cities. In those "teeming" immigrant districts, middle-class proprieties and bourgeois virtues disappeared amid a welter of customs, languages, and expediencies.

It may well be right that ethnic aversions and class condescension lay beneath some of the responses to crowding. But consider this: by 1910, the island of Manhattan housed people at a density of 166 people per acre. In an era before high-rise apartments, that figure is astonishing. In lower Manhattan, however, the numbers boggle the mind. There were nearly 730 people per acre in the Lower East side; in some sections of that immigrant neighborhood people lived at a density of more than 1,000 people per acre.[5] No place in the Western world squeezed more people into less space.

Admittedly, Manhattan stands at the far end of the spectrum, but all the boom cities of the industrial age faced variations of this problem. None of them had the infrastructure—streets, water, sanitation, schools, lighting, transportation—to cope with the number of people who now made demands on it. Congestion, as it was often called, was a real and genuine problem in the American city, and it begat a number of other problems besides.

For Progressives in every major city, crowding was the scourge that had to be eliminated. "It is the overcrowding that breeds crime and vice," exhorted one writer, who insisted that the residents of these areas were not inherently bad, but were made so by their surroundings. "Are the American people going to allow in their metropolis the germs of revolt and revolution to flourish and grow?" the writer asked.[6]

Almost immediately upon taking office in 1910, reformist New York Mayor William Jay Gaynor appointed a Commission on the Congestion of Population. Gaynor chose Benjamin Marsh to chair the committee. Marsh came to New York by way of the Pennsylvania Society to Protect Children from Cruelty, where he served as secretary. He had been educated at Grinnell College, at the University of Chicago, and at the University of Pennsylvania. Having taken the job in New York, Marsh first went to Europe to study the latest in city planning. It was a return trip of sorts—he had been born in Bulgaria to missionary parents. His own politics were a blend of political economist Henry George's single-tax theories and British Fabian socialism.[7]

Marsh's views on urban crowding were already a matter of public record. In a 1909 book he sardonically made the case for overcrowding: "Congestion Profits: The Undertaker; The Saloonkeeper; The Land Speculator; The Tenement Sweater; The Politician; Some Trust Companies."[8] Joining Marsh on the commission were two veterans of the settlement house movement, Florence Kelley and

Mary Simkhovitch. In some ways, Kelley stands as an archetypical Progressive crusader. Born just before the outbreak of the Civil War, her family had been abolitionists. She, in turn, devoted her life to causes like female suffrage, child labor, and factory safety. In the 1890s she lived in Chicago's Hull House and by 1899 had relocated to the Henry Street Settlement in New York. At almost exactly the same moment Mayor Gaynor appointed her to his commission, she helped to found the National Association for the Advancement of Colored People. Simkhovitch, too, grew up in the shadow of the Civil War and helped found the Greenwich House settlement in 1902. She remained an activist for housing in New York for the rest of her life.

The commission issued its report in 1911, making twelve broad recommendations to solve the "evil" of congestion in what everyone agreed had become the most overcrowded city in the world. That list reveals two things about the way Progressives viewed the city and its problems.

First, the majority of recommendations involved changes to the physical space of the city. The suggestions made by the commission include regulating the height of tenement buildings; limiting lot occupancy and providing space for parks, playgrounds, and recreational centers; regulating maximum occupancy for residential units; and locating factories in a more deliberate and rational way.[9] More often than not, the social problems the Progressives found in the American city had spatial solutions. A better urban society could be created through the better use of urban space.

Second, every one of those recommendations required the intervention of the government in one way or another. Whether through the creation of public parks, the imposition of building regulations, or the establishment of zoning codes, the space of the Progressive city could be remade only through politics and policy. "In the ideal city," one writer asserted, "the multitude of problems that arise from the congestion of population will not be abandoned to the inhumanity of commercialism or to the chance of philanthropy. They will be taken up by the city itself."[10]

Planning and zoning became ways cities took on the problems that resulted from congestion. When the New York commission's report came out, a writer for *Survey* practically begged, "We need an official city plan."[11] In fact, between 1907 and 1916, half of the nation's fifty largest cities did commission or publish comprehensive city plans to deal with overcrowding.[12] It was surely no accident that New York Mayor Gaynor appointed Benjamin Marsh to chair his congestion committee. Marsh had already made his reputation in the emerging world of planning and had made clear his commitment to the Progressive agenda. Writing a year before his appointment to the commission, he trumpeted, "All public improvements should be scrutinized with a view to the benefits they will confer upon those most needing such benefits."

In 1909, Marsh published his *Introduction to City Planning* and dedicated it this way: "To the increasing group of citizens in every American city—who recognize that government is the most important factor in securing good living conditions and preserving the life, health and well-being of all citizens, and who desire their city's best development." Marsh was also centrally involved in the first national conference on city planning, which took place in Washington in May 1909. According to the *Washington Post*'s front-page story, the conference was "attended by a number of widely known sociological workers from all parts of the county, men and women who believe in having this generation plan for the physical and moral welfare of the future generations who are to live in the centers of population." [13] Thus did city planning arrive in the Progressive city.

To a great extent, however, it had arrived from Europe. Progressive reformers who traveled to Europe came back impressed with what they saw. Whether in the development of decent affordable housing or in the public ownership of gas and electric systems, Europeans seemed well ahead of Americans in using the power of government to plan their cities. Indeed, Marsh filled his book with examples of city planning from European cities—especially Frankfurt, Germany—and concluded that in Europe, "every aspect of city development is carefully considered and arranged." [14] As it happened, L'Enfant's plan for Washington, D.C., had languished during the nineteenth century, much as the city itself did. Charles Dickens could memorably describe it as a city of magnificent intentions, but those intentions remained largely unfulfilled. In 1901, however, the federal government was persuaded to dust off L'Enfant's plans and to get serious about shaping the nation's capital and creating a proper city for the capital of a now urban nation. When the federal government appointed an architectural committee to restart the work on the nation's capital, the committee immediately took a trip to Europe to see European cities. In this sense, the nation's capital city was a European import twice over. [15]

Americans do not take kindly to newfangled European ideas, and so it was with European-style city planning. Although city planning did flourish in the early years of the twentieth century, much of what planners intended wound up twisted by private real estate interests. Zoning codes, for example, had been used in Europe to curb real estate speculation; in the United States they were embraced precisely because they were shaped to the advantage of real estate dealers, and in this way American zoning had little connection to improving the condition of working-class housing, as it did in Europe. The failure of translation as zoning moved across the Atlantic resulted from the reluctance of Americans to embrace the public nature of urban problems and urban solutions. City planning might well be a public enterprise, but it was not permitted to trump private real estate interests. [16]

Benjamin Marsh certainly recognized this in 1909. One can feel his anger when he wrote,

> American city planning in the main has been a method of rewarding speculation in land at the expense of the taxpayer.... In any city, the right of the citizen may be emphasized to escape from the ugly demoralizing and devitalizing conditions of his own home life, for a time in the parks or playgrounds; but we have not as yet dared to insist upon the right of the citizen to have these conditions removed. In this respect, as in many others, American cities have capitulated to real estate and other financial interests.[17]

This, then, was the challenge of the Progressive city. Progressives had to persuade people that in an urban nation the problems of the city demanded solutions, and that those solutions must come from the public sphere—from government at all levels; that they would not come from the private market or private philanthropy. Frederic Howe saw this quite clearly and anticipated the predictable reaction by embracing it: "All these functions are, in a sense, socialistic. But...it is the care and protection of the people, that inspire love and affection for the city. For these new activities will enlarge our life, not limit it." Marsh summarized the situation more succinctly: "Charity in congested districts is exploitation's most powerful ally.... Government must prevent what Charity can only Mitigate."[18]

No one ever accused President William Howard Taft of being a socialist, and it was surely only a cold that caused him to lose his voice. But there is a certain symbolism to it: Taft was slated to open the national conference on city planning in 1909, but this attack of hoarseness forced him to send his regrets.[19] His sore throat meant that the conservative president would not have to attend an event where "socialistic" ideas might be swirling.

The City Beautiful vs. the Progressive City

Benjamin Marsh had another fight to pick in his 1909 book: with the City Beautiful movement, which, he complained, "has...concerned itself chiefly with these outer and more interesting aspects of the city's development, such as parks, playgrounds, civic centers or groupings of public buildings. It is true that some American cities have destroyed slums but in the main they have been destroyed to give place to parks and boulevards."[20] Marsh wanted city planning to lead to social justice, not prettier buildings. In the *Washington Post*'s list of those who attended the first national conference on city planning, architects are notably absent.

It is easy enough to see the new city planning, driven by Progressive social values, as the opposite of the City Beautiful movement, which was driven by architects' dreams and boosters' desires. The City Beautiful movement took off after the Columbian Exposition in Chicago had dazzled millions in the summer of 1893 and had demonstrated the possibilities of an entire city planned with architectural rationality and aesthetic uniformity. As Marsh suggested, Progressive city planners were less interested in the "groupings of public buildings" and the laying out of grand boulevards, and more interested in eliminating the conditions that left city dwellers demoralized. City Beautiful projects appealed to the city's wealthy and elite—indeed, they often were started at the behest of those people—though efforts to reform housing and institute zoning served the city's working poor. Different visions of the city, directed toward different city constituencies.

In fact, the two approaches to reshaping the space of the city shared a great deal in common, whatever Benjamin Marsh might have said. First, and most obviously, both responded to the central fact of American life at the turn of the twentieth century: the United States had entered its urban moment, and the problems of the city—however they might be defined and however they might be solved—were the problems of the nation. Second, and more specifically, each group saw "congestion" as a major cause of what ailed the city. Third, both saw that "congestion" as the result of the failure of the private real estate market to create a decent city. Left only to the greed of private interests, the city would invariably grow denser, more chaotic, and more unlivable. Both groups, therefore, recognized the need for cities to become public affairs, regulated by political processes rather than by business interests.

Two maps, one a pure product of Progressivism, and the other an iconic image of the City Beautiful, can take us on a tour of these two, overlapping visions of the city. Each map was heralded when it appeared, each was intended to be instrumental, and each has had an enormous influence. On their face, the maps could not be more different. Look more closely, however, and you can see how much common ground there was in the Progressive city.

In 1895, the residents of Hull House on the Near West Side of Chicago published *Hull House Maps and Papers*. The fruit of their collective labor, the book consists largely of written essays, ranging from an analysis of the "Bohemian People in Chicago" to a meditation on the relationship between "Art and Labor," written by Hull House co-founder Ellen Gates Starr. The volume has become justly famous as a landmark in sociology and social work.

Hull House Maps and Papers covered a relatively small area of immigrant Chicago: from Halsted Street on the west to Jefferson on the east; Polk Street on the north to 12th Street on the south. The area measured one-third of a square mile, lying just to the east of Hull House itself, which sat on the west side of Halsted Street. It was, essentially, Jane Addams's front yard.

Attentive readers noticed how the systematic nature of the information presented the neighborhood in an almost scientific way. As the reviewer for the *Atlantic* pointed out, social problems "have come to what is known as 'the reading public' through the medium of fiction and the treatment of fact which pictures and magazines render easily digestible."[21] *Hull House Maps and Papers* was thorough, factual, and avoided cheap sentiment.

What grabbed the attention of many readers, however, were the maps—two of them, multi-colored, folding out from the book. One displayed the astonishing ethnic variety to be found in this tiny patch of the city: Irish, Russian, Italian, Bohemian, even a few French Canadians. The other mapped the wages that residents of these twelve square blocks earned. For most families, that amounted to between $5 and $15 for a six-day week (approximately $120 to $360 a week in current dollars).

Hull House workers walked these streets, knocking on every door, and collected all this information on a standardized survey schedule (a sample schedule was included in the published book). "Not only was each house, tenement, and room visited and inspected," wrote Hull House worker Agnes Sinclair Holbrook in an introductory essay, "but in many cases the reports obtained from one person were corroborated by many others."[22] It was an exhaustive and doubtless an exhausting project.

The challenge was how to turn all that information into something visual. To do so, the Hull House staff borrowed the techniques of Charles Booth, who had created similar maps of sections of London's East End, though as Holbrook opined, "the eyes of the world do not centre on this third of a square mile in the heart of Chicago as upon East London when looking for the very essence of misery."[23]

The results look almost like an abstract expressionist painting, an early Chicago precursor to Piet Mondrian's *Broadway Boogie Woogie*. An irregular pattern of colored blocks arranged on the very regular grid of city streets. The blocks themselves represent individual buildings or addresses; the colors correspond to nationalities on one map, to wages on the other. Study the maps carefully and you see that there is a remarkable, painstaking degree of detail. Taking the two together, it becomes hard to discern larger trends, patterns, or correlations in these maps. And maybe that was the point. What emerges in visual form is a colorful cacophony that must have echoed the experience of walking on those bustling, chaotic streets in the 1890s. Still, the maps give order to a part of Chicago that would have struck most people at the time as lacking it. An undifferentiated mass of immigrants could be broken up into specific nationalities; a great lump of the *Lumpenproletariat* could be grouped by different occupations and income. In that sense, the maps participated in the larger Progressive project of taking the overwhelmingness of the city and making sense of it.

Holbrook used her introduction to supplement the maps with a more conventional narrative of the area. Though the lines on the maps simply traced property boundaries, the buildings themselves were as heterogeneous as the people:

> The proportion of wooden buildings to brick is approximately two to one throughout [one] section; but on the south side of Polk Street it is about four to one, and on Ewing more than five to one.... Structures of mixed brick and wood are counted in with brick buildings, and a few stone fronts form an exclusive, if inconsiderable, class, by themselves.

In front of these structures, ramshackle and temporary most of them, "stand garbage-receivers,—wooden boxes repulsive to every sense...shocking to both mind and instinct when rotten, overfilled, and broken, as they often are." The spaces in back are "used as a stable and outhouse." In between "the unpaved and uncared for alleys [are] an especially threatening feature in all this unpleasing picture." Worst of all was the condition inside:

> One feels very clear...after long acquaintance with the neighborhood, and after many visits to many of the homes, that the poorest of the tiny wooden houses, damp and unwholesome as they may be, offer nothing to compare with the hideousness shut up in the inside rooms of the larger, higher and to the casual eye the better tenements of more prestigious aspect.... Rear tenements and alleys form the core of the district, and it is there that the densest crowds of the most wretched and destitute congregate.[24]

Holbrook took readers on a walk, giving the two dimensional, parti-colored blocks a grimmer, three-dimensional reality.

Although they capture a sense of the neighborhood's busy heterogeneity, the maps provided only a snapshot, and the Hull House staff knew this quite well. As the process of getting the book into print dragged on, Jane Addams wrote to Richard Ely, the pioneering Progressive and famous economist who served as an editor for the project, begging that the volume come out "as quickly as possible. We have letters every week asking about it." More to the point, the longer the publication took, the more dated the information in it: "Mrs. [Florence] Kelley's office is already making great changes in the condition of the sweater shops in the neighborhood, the Jewish population is rapidly moving Northward, and all the conditions are of course, more or less, unlike what they were July 1st, 1893, when the data for the maps was finished." Holbrook, too, acknowledged this in her introductory essay, telling readers that "Frequent house-movings...alter the face of the district more or less within a year....Families also move about constantly, going from tenement to tenement, finding more comfortable apartments when they are able to pay for them, drifting into poorer quarters in times of illness, enforced idleness, or 'bad luck.'"[25] Having set out to create a visual portrait of the Near West Side by turning data into maps, the Hull House staff discovered that the subject would not sit still.

Holbrook insisted that *Hull House Maps and Papers* aimed "to present conditions rather than to advance theories," but she and her fellow Hull House workers clearly hoped that the study would stimulate "inquiry and action" that might lead to "new thoughts and methods." Only at the end of her introduction did she permit an explicit appeal:

> The painful nature of minute investigation, and the personal impertinence of many of the questions asked, would be unendurable and unpardonable were it not for the conviction that the public conscience when roused must demand better surroundings for the most inert and long-suffering citizens of the commonwealth. Merely to state symptoms and go no farther would be idle; but to state symptoms in order to ascertain the nature of disease, and apply, it may be, its cure, is not only scientific, but in the highest sense humanitarian.[26]

Hull House Maps and Papers resulted from a federal mandate to study slum conditions in several major American cities. It became a model for how to do that, and thus was hugely influential in the nascent discipline of sociology. Just a few years later, W. E. B. Du Bois, who admired Jane Addams a great deal and hosted her visit to Atlanta, would produce his extraordinary study of Philadelphia's largest black neighborhood, *Philadelphia Negro*, using many of the same techniques (a project even more heroic, since Du Bois did virtually all of it by himself). In their 1922 survey review of settlement house work, Robert Woods and Albert Kennedy summarized the way settlement house workers studied the neighborhoods in which they worked: "Physical environment is studied almost foot by foot....The staff comes to have a clear mental picture of all streets, alleys, vacant lots, and public buildings."[27] Foot by foot, and, they might have added, on foot. This was the way settlement house Progressives understood and imagined the city. It was a view of the city from its sidewalks.

On December 4, 1907, the nation's best known social reformer met with the nation's preeminent city planner when Jane Addams joined Daniel Burnham

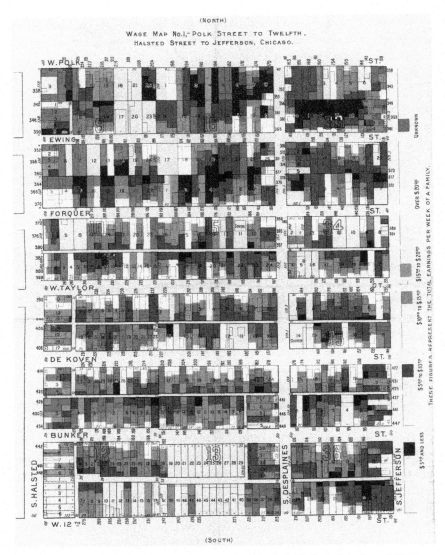

(NORTH)

WAGE MAP No.1.- POLK STREET TO TWELFTH.
HALSTED STREET TO JEFFERSON, CHICAGO.

(SOUTH)

The city from the sidewalks. Hull House workers walked the sidewalks of Chicago, knocking on every door to research several maps of their neighborhood. Originally produced in color, the color-coded blocks in this map charted wages for neighborhood residents. *From* Hull House Maps and Papers

for lunch in his office. They worked within two miles of each other and in two entirely different Chicagos. Not surprisingly, though their work brought them together with some of the same politicians, businessmen, and civic leaders, they imagined the city quite differently. Addams had presented her sidewalk view of the Near West Side a dozen years earlier. Burnham would publish and present to the public his vision of the city two years later.

It makes for an intriguing scene. The diminutive yet indefatigable Addams, who lived and worked among the city's immigrant masses, lunching with Daniel "Big Dan" Burnham, who was undoubtedly clad in a suit hand-tailored in London. Burnham had grown rich in Chicago even while Addams tended to the city's poor. The food was surely good, at any rate. Burnham's gourmand tastes wreaked havoc on the man's waistline to such an extent that by 1905 he had hired his own fitness trainer to keep it under control.

We do not, alas, have Addams's record of this meeting. Indeed, in her meticulously indexed correspondence, Burnham's name is not listed. We do know that Burnham wanted to discuss his Chicago plan with Addams, and specifically to get her endorsement for his proposal to turn the entire lakefront into a set of public parks. She responded enthusiastically, envisioning the lakefront as an escape for the poor, an opportunity to leave the crowded, fetid tenements for a breath of fresh lake air.[28] Burnham may very well have blanched at the prospect of a lakefront full of immigrants, though we can only speculate about his reaction.

Nor do we know what Addams thought of the rest of the plan, or if Burnham even shared it with her. When she saw the final product, as she surely did after it appeared in 1909, some part of her must have been miffed. Burnham's Chicago Plan has become part of the folklore of city planning, the first real "master plan" for an American city. In fact, Burnham imagined nothing less than the transformation of the entire region within a sixty-mile radius of the city's center.[29] "Make no little plans," he is alleged to have said, "they have no magic to stir men's blood," and his Chicago Plan is blood-stirringly big.

It had been percolating probably since the 1893 World's Columbian Exposition, which Burnham oversaw and which made him something of a celebrity. The White City on the city's far south side was only a plaster-and-lath fantasy that lasted some six months. We do not know what Jane Addams thought of the fair either, though Hull House became part of the tourist itinerary for visiting reformers, "a kind of Mecca for philanthropists," she complained. She did have to deal with the aftermath, as the boom city that the Exposition celebrated proved just as illusory as the buildings themselves. By the time the gates of the fair closed, the city was reeling from the full effects of a national economic collapse. Unemployment in Chicago reached 20 percent by December, and Addams wrote that mothers were now bedding down with their children in the Hull House nursery.[30]

In 1897, with the economy beginning to recover, the Merchants Club, a group of striving Chicago businessmen, approached Burnham and asked him to develop a plan for remaking the whole city, the real city—something that would turn Chicago permanently into the White City. He worked on the plan off and on for the next dozen years. By the time he invited Addams to lunch, the project had the sponsorship of Chicago's Commercial Club (which had merged with the Merchants Club), and Burnham was working on it full time. It appeared in the form of a lushly produced book put out by the Commercial Club, and it received acclaim locally, nationally, and internationally. Kaiser Wilhelm thought the plan "the most perfect and satisfactory that he had ever seen" and vowed to remake his own capital in Berlin along Chicago's lines.[31]

Burnham incorporated ideas about planning and aesthetics that swirled on both sides of the Atlantic. He mixed parts of Haussmann's Paris Plan with parts of Washington, D.C.; he drew from his own previous work in Cleveland and San Francisco. Most of all, he used Chicago's lakefront as the place from which the city would radiate. Indeed, he turned the lakefront into a great expanse of public spaces, and he relocated rail yards and factory districts to the outer edges of the city. Most dramatically, Burnham proposed order for the chaotic city both by widening many of the existing streets and even more by creating a web of radiating boulevards on top of the grid. These terminated in a complex of civic buildings with a grand plaza at the center of this new city. It is a hierarchy of space moving away from the lake: a public waterfront with spaces for public and cultural functions like museums and parade grounds; transportation and industry at the far edge; government and civic pride at the center.

It is a magisterial vision, sweeping and grand. That grandeur was made visible through more than 140 illustrations, 50 of them beautifully painted renderings by French artist Jules Guerin. Burnham treated the grid of streets simply as a blank canvas, and he filled it with the order and uniformity of the Beaux Arts aesthetic. In a speech he gave to the Merchants Club in 1897, he told the businessmen who prospered in hog-butchering Chicago, "Beauty has always paid better than any other commodity and always will."[32] With the planner's hubris, the old city could be swept away even more entirely than it had been when it burned down in 1871. In its place would rise truly a city beautiful.

Jane Addams might well have been impressed with this vision, and the lakefront parks surely pleased her. But as she looked more closely at the great civic center, the focus of the entire plan, she undoubtedly noticed that the center was sited on Halsted Street, almost exactly on top of her Hull House.

Perhaps that was simply a coincidence—perhaps the decision to erase Chicago's most famous address and replace it with a government center was driven entirely by the internal logic of Burnham's planning. He certainly was not sentimental even about his own earlier Chicago buildings, which had vanished in the plan as well. Not for nothing did fellow Chicagoan and architect Louis Sullivan call him "elephantine, tactless and blurting."[33]

Still, it seems like more than a coincidence. At some level, Hull House—and the neighborhood surrounding it—represented everything that Burnham wanted to eliminate from the city. As the *Hull House Maps and Papers* fully documented, the neighborhood was crowded and ugly, and perhaps worse, the architecture was as messy and heterogeneous as the people—built to be temporary, just like the stay of so many residents. In response, Burnham planned to put a colossal neo-classical building where Hull House sat and to turn much of the Near West Side neighborhood Addams had documented into a plaza. If Holbrook had hoped the *Maps and Papers* might lead to a "cure" for the ills of the neighborhood, Burnham instead performed an amputation of it on his drafting table.

The poor, or at least their slums, make a brief appearance in the plan. In one paragraph Burnham assured his readers that regulating crowding and sanitation posed "no attack on private property" because "society has the inherent right to protect itself [against] gross evils and known perils."[34] Otherwise, this was a businessman's plan. It had been sponsored by them and had been written for them. In his speech to the Merchants Club back in 1897, Burnham had complained that "thousands of people all over the country are becoming wealthy, and thousands are already so. These people go to New York to live, but many would come here if we should create the conditions which would attract them."[35] Chicago, Burnham believed, could plan its way past New York to become the preeminent city in the nation.

The city seen from the heavens versus the city seen from the sidewalks: it is easy enough to make that distinction between Big Dan and Saint Jane. Hull House residents focused their lens almost microscopically, gathering details about the people who lived in this small corner of Chicago. Burnham pulled his lens back as far as he could and produced a vision devoid of real people. The plan is a visual embodiment of urban forces—transportation, industry, commerce—and above all, it envisions growth. At the time of the plan's publication, Chicagoans routinely and casually predicted that their metropolis would grow to be the largest city in the world within a century, rightful heir to Athens, Rome, and London.

But Addams and Burnham also saw some of the same things as they stared at their city and imagined its future. Foremost, perhaps, they saw the same basic problem with the city, though it went by several names: crowding, congestion, density. More than anything else, at the root of what was wrong with Chicago lay overcrowding, and this would have to be addressed to improve the city. For Progressives in every major city, overcrowding was the scourge that had to be eliminated.

Still, the question of density was particularly urgent in Chicago when Burnham presented his plan. In 1911, Jane Addams and the University of Chicago professor Sophonisba Breckinridge conducted a study that followed up

The city from the heavens. Daniel Burnham illustrated his Plan for Chicago with lush images like this one. This view of Chicago shares more in common with the Hull House map than might first be apparent. Plan of Chicago, architectural drawing, Chicago, IL, c.1908. Daniel H. Burnham, designer. Jules Guerin, renderer. *HALIC, Ryerson and Burnham Archives, The Art Institute of Chicago. Digital File #80380*

on a 1901 study of housing conditions. After ten years, they found conditions barely improved. Although Chicagoans city-wide lived at a density of nearly 20 people per acre, across many of the slum districts the figure was closer to 100 per acre, and in worst areas of the study the figure rose to a staggering 350 per acre.[36]

Burnham's plan solved the problem simply, if radically. Crowded districts would be leveled; crowded people would be relocated, though in fairness he acknowledged in his plan that some of these people might have to be housed by the city itself "in common justice to men and women so degraded by long life in the slums that they have lost all power of caring for themselves."[37] For the city that invented the skyscraper, Burnham imagined a more low-rise, horizontal future.

For Addams, and for all those who saw the city from its sidewalks and back alleys, the solutions revolved around zoning and regulation, of the sort the New York Congestion Commission had recommended for Gotham. Different solutions to the same problem, perhaps, but Burnham and Addams also saw that either would require the intervention of government—on the municipal level surely, but at the state and federal level as well. Benjamin Marsh called for a "civic census" conducted by the federal government to study city planning nationally. Likewise, landscape architect Robert Anderson Pope and settlement house worker Mary Simkhovitch both called for a federal commission devoted to city planning.[38]

Burnham hoped that many of his improvements—the relocation of rail yards, for example—would be undertaken voluntarily. But he recognized that much of his plan would require public authority. He had lawyer Walter Fisher write a chapter in the book analyzing the legal aspects of the plan. Fisher concluded that the city and state already had the power to do most of what Burnham proposed. Upon official receipt of the plan, Chicago Mayor Fred Busse gave it his blessing by appointing a 328-member commission to implement the project.

From the heavens or from the sidewalks, Burnham and Addams both saw overcrowding as the plague of the city. They both viewed government as the way to alleviate the problem, even as they differed on specific solutions. In this sense, Burnham and Addams both acknowledged a fundamental change in the nature of the city itself. The city and its problems would no longer be the subject of moral exhortation, religious revivals, and campaigns against vice. Both saw the problems of the city and the people who worked and lived there in physical rather than spiritual terms. Both saw the solutions to those problems as a matter of reorganizing space rather than of reforming individual shortcomings. Both, therefore, saw the need for politics and government to take a central role in the planning of the city.

However else it may have changed in size, in economics, in ethnic composition, by the early twentieth century the city had become a public rather than a private matter.

From City Wilderness to City Neighborhood

"The stuff of which the city planner is made is that of the old pioneers of liberty and he persists."[39] So wrote American Civic Association president J. Horace McFarland in 1908 as he lauded the work of city planners. It is a wonderfully preposterous image: the city planner as frontiersman, a new heroic figure who has exchanged axes and rifles for maps and drawing pads. A clumsy analogy to be sure, but entirely of its moment.

As Americans confronted their cities at the turn of the twentieth century and tried to comprehend them, they resorted to the language of the frontier, the wilderness, the jungle. Consider this passage from Stephen Crane's novella *George's Mother*:

> She looked out at the chimneys growing thickly on the roofs. A man at work on one seemed like a bee. In the intricate yards below, vine-like lines

had strange leaves of cloth. To her ears came the howl of the man with the red, mottled face. He was engaged in a furious altercation with the youth who had called attention to his poor aim. They were like animals in a jungle.

Crane's better known novel *Maggie: A Girl of the Streets* opens with a scene of feral children hurling rocks at one another. As one of them lies on the ground, blood gushing from his mouth, Crane tells us that "there were notes of joy like songs of triumphant savagery." Jacob Riis, as he showed his readers how the other half lived, sounded fatalistic about the effect of the urban wilderness upon its smallest residents: "Very soon the wild life of the streets holds him fast, and thenceforward by his own effort there is no escape." Descriptions of city life like these, fictional or journalistic, are too numerous to count. Most famously, and most succinctly, Jurgis Rudkus, Upton Sinclair's Lithuanian immigrant protagonist, came to Chicago dreaming dreams of wealth and success only to find himself living in *The Jungle*.[40]

The metaphor of wilderness or jungle worked on two related levels. On the one hand, it served as the quickest shorthand to describe the lawless, savage, and essentially incomprehensible character of the new industrial city—and more specifically, those parts of it crowded with immigrants. "Isolated and congested working-class quarters with all the dangers to moral and material well-being that they present grow along with the growth of all our great cities," pronounced Robert Woods, the founder of the South End Settlement in Boston, stating what was surely obvious to most observers.[41] The city had become a brutal place of man-made nature that reduced the people living in it to animals.

On the other hand, the language of wilderness was familiar to Americans, and Frederick Jackson Turner had put it at the very center of the American experience. For Americans at the turn of the twentieth century, especially those of a Turnerian frame of mind, the dangers of the frontier implied the challenge of their conquest. By extension, those who wrote about the urban frontier drew on this metaphor to insist that the urban wilderness could be tamed as well. Woods titled his 1898 study of Boston's South End *The City Wilderness: A Settlement Study*.

That title is worth pausing over. Ostensibly, it referred to Woods's South End settlement house, and the fact that the information presented in the book had been gathered through his work there. But by juxtaposing *wilderness* and *settlement*, Woods underscored the metaphoric relationship between the frontier, that mythic place with which most Americans were already familiar, and the newer urban frontier. If the former could be settled—and as Frederick Jackson Turner pointed out, that process was now complete—then so too could the latter. Not for nothing did the *Atlantic* magazine title its review of Jane Addams's *Hull House Maps and Papers* "Settlers in the City Wilderness."[42]

All that was missing was an analytic tool with which people could better decipher the undifferentiated chaos of the urban wilderness, a re-imagining of urban space that could help to tame the city frontier. Out on the western prairies it was homestead farms, quarter sections, and railroad towns that served to divide, manage, and tame the vast, empty expanses. Back in Chicago or Boston or New York, the analogue was the neighborhood.

Neighborhood is an old idea—the word itself goes back to the fifteenth century. But the notion that neighborhoods could be found in cities was new. Consider this use of the word by Francis Bacon in 1625: "In a great Towne…there is not that Fellowship…which is in lesse Neighborhoods."[43] Progressive reformers, however, went searching for city neighborhoods, hoping to find along with them all the social order and comity that the word implied. None did so more eagerly than Robert Woods.

He was a big man, over six feet tall and bulky, but he was by all accounts soft-spoken to the point of diffidence. Born in Pittsburgh just as the Civil War ended, he went east to college at Amherst and farther east to London to visit Toynbee Hall, the settlement house that provided inspiration to so many American Progressives. He returned to Boston and in 1895 established the South End settlement, where he worked until his death in 1925.

If Progressives believed that the issues of the city were coterminous with those of the nation writ small, Woods insisted that the neighborhood represented the city in microcosm. "The neighborhood is large enough to include in essence all the problems of the city, the state, and the nation," Woods wrote in a 1914 essay, "and in a constantly increasing number of instances in this country it includes all the fundamental international issues."[44]

That last reference carried significance in two directions. With Europe on the brink of war, Woods reminded readers that Europeans of every variety lived in relative harmony in American city neighborhoods.[45] At the same time, by linking city neighborhoods to "the fundamental international issues," Woods took aim at those like Josiah Strong who fretted that the massive influx of immigrants to American cities had corrupted the nation politically, socially, and racially. Describing what he termed "the neighbor instinct," Woods wrote of immigrants: "Here the neighbor instinct demonstrates its priceless value as the cement of twentieth century democracy.…It would be only too easy for the neighbor sentiment to bring about a kind of assimilation among immigrants which would be only a foreign composite, hardly nearer to American standards than were its original constituents."[46]

More than that, Woods firmly believed that the neighborhood was the stage upon which was played out the civic and public life necessary for democracy. "The neighborhood is the vital public arena to the majority of men, to nearly all women, and all children; in which every one of them is a citizen and many of them, even among the children, are statesmen," Woods argued. He elaborated:

> It is in the gradual public self-revelation of the neighborhood—in its inner public values, and in its harmony of interest with the other neighborhoods—that the reverse detachments of citizenship are to be swung into the battle of good municipal administration.... [I]t is this process which will turn the balance definitely and decisively in the direction of a humanized system of politics, of industrialism, and of morality."

After all, as the former Secretary of the New York City Federation of Churches Walter Laidlaw reminded readers in 1911, "Christianity originated in an urban community."[47]

It must have been a provocative analysis in 1914. Woods linked many of the concerns of the Progressive age—citizenship, family life, harmonies of interest, even "good municipal administration"—and said they were found and fostered in the city neighborhood. By reconceiving those teeming immigrant districts as city neighborhoods, Woods turned the anxieties about those places on their head. They were places of positive good, Woods insisted, and then in a coup de grace he mused, "I am inclined to think that on the whole there is a certain dignity in the sentiment of the neighborhood about itself which is not equaled in fact by any of our other forms of social self-consciousness. The family may be abject; the neighborhood is never so. The city may admit itself disgraced; the neighborhood always considers disgrace foisted upon it."[48] "Dignity" was just about the last thing many Americans thought city neighborhoods and their residents had, but as he stared out at Boston's South End and walked its streets, Woods found just that.

Whether or not Woods was too sanguine or saw the neighborhood through romantic lenses, Progressive reformers needed the concept of neighborhoods. Reformer Clarence Perry, who worked for the Russell Sage Foundation, tried to give analytic rigor to the streets and storefronts by creating the "neighborhood unit."[49] For Progressives like Perry, Woods, and others, the neighborhood was the building block of the humane city.

It stretches things only a little to say that if Progressives had not found neighborhoods in American cities, they would have had to invent them. In truth, they probably did a little of both. When Woods elaborated on the connection between the neighborhood and the city, he wrote:

It is large enough so that the facts and forces of its public life, rightly considered, have significance and dramatic compulsion; so that its totality can arrest and hold a germinating public sense. On the other hand, it is small enough to be comprehensible and manageable; ... The neighborhood is concretely conceivable; the city is not, and will not be except as it is organically integrated through its neighborhoods.[50]

It is not clear, by the end of this passage, whether neighborhoods functioned to make the city "comprehensible and manageable" for those who lived there, or for those who studied them. Perhaps they served both groups, each a little differently. Either way, neighborhoods became the imaginative construct with which to tame the urban wilderness and the key to deciphering the otherwise inchoate nature of the city.

From Urban Wilderness to Urban Ecology

In 1914, as Robert Woods published his thoughts about the South End, Robert Park returned to Chicago from a set of professional and personal wanderings remarkable even by turn-of-the-twentieth-century standards. Born in 1864 in rural Luzerne County, Pennsylvania, he grew up comfortably in Red Wing, Minnesota, where his father played the role of big fish in the proverbial small pond. He left that small town almost as soon as he could, venturing first to the University of Michigan. After that he spent a decade as a journalist, which took him to Detroit, New York, and Chicago; then he decided to go to Harvard for an MA, then on to Germany for a PhD, which he received from Heidelberg in 1903. His formal education now complete, he went back to Harvard to teach. By the time he returned to Cambridge, he had studied with John Dewey, William James, and Georg Simmel, among others.

Harvard did not hold him long. In 1904, none other than Booker T. Washington offered him the chance to serve as publicist for the Tuskegee Institute, which provided him with the opportunity to observe and study American race relations at close hand. He worked at Tuskegee for ten years and then packed his bags again, this time for Chicago's Hyde Park neighborhood and the University of Chicago's department of sociology and anthropology. He was forty-eight years old, his longish hair graying, and he had finally found a place to settle in.

Park arrived to become a founding member of the "Chicago School," a remarkable group of scholars who found themselves with a remarkable opportunity. They worked in a new discipline at a new university, and they situated their work in a virtually brand-new city. They wanted to build on the work of settlement houses to turn the study of the city into a science proper, and they made Chicago their laboratory. Park had said as much, titling one of his essays "The City as a Social Laboratory," and in it he announced that "As a matter of fact civilization and social progress have assumed in our modern cities something of the character of a controlled experiment."[51] Rigorous analysis applied to contemporary processes and problems. The romance of the Chicago School has long since become a touchstone for the discipline of sociology, a golden moment when theory, practice, and purpose seemed to converge. Park served as its leading man.

A year after his arrival in Chicago, Park published a road map for exploring the urban wilderness. His 1915 article "The City: Suggestions for the Investigation of Human Behavior in the Urban Environment" is a classic in the field. In it, Park sketched a research agenda for the sociological study of the city, which proved hugely influential for at least a generation.

What Park and those who followed him found—and perhaps what they went looking to find—when they ventured into the urban jungle was not so much a wilderness as an ecology. Underneath the bustle and the disorder, the change and transformation, lay rules and frameworks. Urban dynamism had a structure that shaped the physical space of the city. After all, despite all the fractures, tensions, and obvious problems with the city, and despite all the invectives directed against it, the city had not fallen apart. Indeed, as an entity it thrived. Observing this, Park surmised that there must be "natural" principles at work making sure that the center did, in fact, hold. The members of the Chicago School set out to find and describe those natural forces, and their "discovery" of stability and order amid what otherwise looked like tremendous upheaval stands as perhaps the most important find the Chicago School sociologists ever made.[52]

As one scholar described it tersely, "One may sum up Park's conception of the city in a sentence: the city represents an externally organized unit in space produced by laws of its own."[53] Park himself reached for a more poetic definition, writing that:

The city is a state of mind, a body of customs and traditions, and of organized attitudes and sentiments that inhere in this tradition. The city is not, in other words, merely a physical mechanism and an artificial construction. It is involved in the vital processes of the people who compose it, it is a product of nature and particularly of human nature.[54]

For Park the city stood as "the natural habitat of civilized man."[55]

Whether the city could usefully be analyzed ecologically, like a forest, hardly mattered. The ecological model was the first, closest thing Americans had come up with to a theory of urbanism. More than that, it was a brilliant metaphor because it turned that most artificial of creations into a "natural" one and in so doing linked the experience of the city with the romantic naturalism of the nineteenth century. No wonder the ecological approach to the city dominated urban sociology for roughly the next half-century, regardless, in fact, of the profound changes cities underwent during those years.[56]

And like those naturalists of the nineteenth century, Park and the others set about to study urban ecology by breaking up the space of the city into smaller constituent parts, almost like a taxonomy. These, in turn, could be analyzed more completely to determine how each played its own vital role in the way the city functioned. As Park put it, "the city is a constellation of natural areas, each with its own characteristic milieu and each performing its specific function in the urban economy as a whole."[57] Surely the most important of these was the neighborhood or "community." What Robert Woods found almost intuitively and by accident in Boston's South End, Chicago's sociologists set out to find and map much more exactly and scientifically.

Park's colleague Ernest Burgess turned out to be the most intrepid of Chicago's neighborhood explorers. In the 1920s, Burgess, along with other Chicago social scientists, undertook to define, label, and map all of Chicago's communities, using Park's notion that any neighborhood constituted a distinct social milieu. The result of Burgess's work verges on the epic. He identified no less than seventy-five different neighborhoods, overlaid their boundaries on a map of the city, and gave them all names. In so doing, he gave Chicagoans a label for the place they called home, and presumably a more intimate identity in an otherwise impersonal urban milieu.

To what extent Burgess's designations reflected or invented the reality of Chicago's neighborhoods remains up for debate. Many who looked at Burgess's map scratched their heads, for example, when they discovered that the part of town known to everyone as "Back of the Yards"—the section filled with immigrant slaughterhouse workers that Upton Sinclair made famous in his novel *The Jungle*—had summarily been renamed "New City." No matter. The map has proved remarkably enduring. In 1947, planners subdivided these seventy-five larger areas into even smaller neighborhood units—513 in all. In 1980, two more "community areas" were added to the original seventy-five; by then, of course, Chicago had long fixed its identity as a city of neighborhoods.[58]

Just as Progressive reformers had broken up the problem of the city into more manageable problems, so too the urban explorers of the Chicago School ventured into the uncharted urban wilderness and came back with a coherent map of neighborhoods.

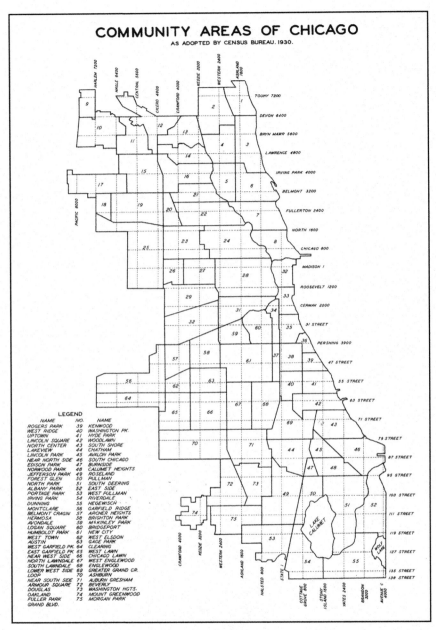

A city of neighborhoods. The Chicago School sociologists hit upon the idea of the neighborhood as a way of bringing conceptual order to the otherwise chaotic city. Ernest Burgess created this map of Chicago communities around 1930. *Ernest Burgess Papers, Special Collections, Regenstein Library, University of Chicago*

The Hope of Democracy

It was all well and good for Progressives to insist that the problems of the city be taken on as public responsibilities, but everyone knew at the turn of the twentieth century that the mechanisms through which to do that—city governments—were hopeless at best, venal and corrupt at worst. Lincoln Steffens traveled from place to place documenting *The Shame of the City* in 1904, and his muckraking exposé simply confirmed what many already suspected. For the Reverend Josiah Strong, this truism could be expressed by a simple, almost mathematical ratio: "As a rule, our largest cities are our worst governed. It is natural, therefore, to infer that, as our cities grow larger and more dangerous, the government will become more corrupt, and control will pass more completely into the hands of those who themselves most need to be controlled." Also writing in the 1880s, James Bryce refrained from using Strong's vicious invective, but acknowledged that cities in the United States stood as our most conspicuous political failures.[59]

If Progressives wanted to expand the notion of public responsibility and obligation, then they had to persuade the rest of the nation that government, especially local government, could be trusted to take on the task. They did this in two ways. First, Progressives initiated a series of political reforms designed to clean up city governments. These are well known: reformers in some places organized political movements that resulted in the election of reform-minded, clean-government advocates like Sam "Golden Rule" Jones in Toledo, Ohio, and Hazen Pingree in Detroit, both of whom brought the "civic idea" to their cities. These efforts worked within existing political frameworks. In other places, reformers pushed through what might be called "extra-democratic" plans to accomplish their goals. A number of cities appointed commissions and city managers so that the control of city affairs could circumvent the messy and frankly corrupt world of electoral politics.[60] Effective management would make effective city government.

At a more abstract, almost philosophical level, however, some Progressive thinkers insisted that the city could be a positive good for democracy, and could be the place where a democratic society realized itself in full. The anonymous writer for *Outlook* magazine, for example, pulled no punches in asserting the relationship between cities and democracy. "Men are made to live together," the writer announced, and went on, "Cities represent living together in its highest estate." Airy enough, but the writer went on to challenge the individualism that lay behind the Jeffersonian strain of anti-urban hostility. If independent yeoman farmers constituted Jefferson's ideal citizens, this writer turned that formulation upside down: "A man becomes a citizen when he recognizes his responsibility and obligation to the community." In this sense, the writer continued, New York City is the most democratic place in the nation because "it has welcomed more races and more men and women to the continent than any other city."[61] This was certainly a nervy way to describe a city whose "democracy" was best known for producing Tammany Hall.

Charles Hatch Sears, the general secretary of the New York Baptist City Mission Society, echoed this anonymous writer. Sounding much like Sinclair Lewis, though well before Lewis created the character Babbitt, Sears believed that "the crux of the difficulty is that the average American citizen is primarily a business man. He has not seen that his own best welfare and that of the city are identical; he has failed to realize that no man can be a citizen worthy of respect...if he sacrifices the public good to his own selfish ends." Sears was more specific about the role of city government in what he called "the redemption of the city." The numbers did not lie, Sears pointed out, saying "the success of the city in improving sanitary conditions is reflected by vital statistics. The death-rate has been lowered steadily." And he reminded readers of the truly astonishing accomplishment of city government in providing the basic infrastructure of human dignity: "The modern New Yorker looks to the municipality to give him pure water, to assure him pure air, to light his streets, and to guarantee him light at fair rates in his home." Plenty of people found plenty of reasons to carp about the state of the American city. But Sears was right. Delivering clean water to the residents of cities that had grown so large so fast was nothing short of miraculous.

But Sears was not finished. In addition to sewer systems and electric lighting, the city taught the modern New Yorker "to have regard for the rights of others when he builds his house; it educates his children; it provides his own culture and recreation; and it cares for his neighbor when helpless in sickness, poverty, or death."[62] Body and soul, city government could indeed redeem the city.

Frederic Howe evangelized for the redemptive potential of city government perhaps more vigorously than anyone else of his era. His was a peripatetic, almost quixotic career which bridged the Gilded Age and the New Deal. Born in a small western Pennsylvania town just after the Civil War, he got a law degree in Ohio and a PhD at Johns Hopkins, and got some additional education in Germany before settling in Cleveland.

There, Howe recognized that the city needed a vocal champion, and he fashioned himself in that role. "Up to the present time," he wrote, "the boss has been the American city's only apologist. He alone is proud of his city, and stands ready to defend it before the world." An urban civilization seemed inevitable in the years before the First World War, and Howe wanted to seize the opportunity rather than bemoan the current state of affairs. "To many people," he acknowledged, "any belief in the city is the idlest of dreams. They see only a loss in the passing of the rural population to the crowded industrial life of the modern city." Many Americans viewed that shift from country to city in almost apocalyptic terms, but Howe was insistent: the city was not merely the future, "the city is the hope of the future."[63]

Ironically, although Howe chided Americans who yearned for an agricultural past, his own vision for American cities drew from the past as well, albeit a very different, more distant one. The real political problem facing American cities, Howe believed, was not corruption but precisely that cities did not have enough independent power. "Our cities are not free to solve their problems as they will," Howe proclaimed, and as a result, "the American city is not a city at all. It is an agent of the State like a county, a township. . . . Many of our city failures should be laid on the principal, not on the agent."[64] It was a swipe at those who did not think urban residents ought to govern themselves.

Expanded home rule—that was the solution Howe came to, over and over. Give cities greater authority and autonomy to deal with their own conditions, including the power to expand municipal ownership over many sectors of urban life. And more than once Howe drew this historical analogy: "Home rule would create a city republic, a new sort of sovereignty, a republic like unto those of Athens, Rome, and the medieval Italian cities."[65] Never mind that for many Americans New York was already as imperious as Rome, and the prospect horrified them, or that they looked at Chicago and saw Sodom and Gomorrah, not Florence and Venice.

The point for Howe was not the recreation of the Italian city-states, but the reinvention of democracy in an urban, industrial society. Like so many other Progressives, Howe looked to Europe for lessons that could be applied in the United States. Urban, industrial society was at least a generation further along in England, and there Howe believed "the city is the most democratic institution in Great Britain. In many ways, it is the only evidence of democracy in that country." Urban democracy, self-government at the local level, was the only mechanism through which the problems of urban life could be ameliorated. As America faced its urban industrial future, Howe insisted that the city would be the place where democracy was reinvented to meet the challenges posed by large corporations, the reorganization of capital, and the unprecedented concentrations of people. The older traditions of American democracy were simply not up to the task. "To the city," Howe wrote triumphantly, "we are to look for a rebirth of democracy, a democracy that will possess the instincts of the past along with a belief in the power of co-operative effort to relieve the costs which city life entails."[66] For this reason he titled his book *The City: The Hope for Democracy*.

In the end, Howe was not interested in recreating the Italian city-state in Chicago and Detroit as a goal in and of itself. The mechanisms of urban democracy that Howe advocated—municipal ownership, home rule, and the like—were means to a larger end. "The city is being inspired by a new morality," Howe wrote.

"It lies latent in every community, and only needs a leader to call it into life. It is the morality of social justice, which is the mission of industrial democracy to the modern world."[67] This was the way that Howe connected the city, democracy, and the larger, more elusive quest for a moral community in an urban nation.

And he was not alone. Whatever their scientific detachment, the Chicago School sociologists also saw the disintegration of community in American life, and that concern lay at the foundation of much of their work. For his part, Robert Park believed that "we are living in such a period of individualization and social disorganization. Everything is in a state of agitation—everything seems to be undergoing a change. Society is, apparently, not much more than a congeries and constellation of social atoms."[68]

Neighborhoods provided some sense of stability for the congeries of social atoms, and ecology gave that unsettling agitation a more comprehensible framework at least metaphorically. These were the constructs with which Progressive sociologists domesticated urban space. Combined with the promise of reinvigorated urban democracy of the sort Howe and others imagined, the city could indeed create and foster genuine communities. Those communities could generate both love and loyalty.

That desire, that hope, lay at the foundation of the settlement house phenomenon in the first place. At their loftiest, settlement houses aspired not simply to deliver social services or conduct social surveys but also to heal the rifts of an increasingly fractious society, to create among disparate people in an urban neighborhood some sense of shared community. Jane Addams wrote that her work had been motivated "by a desire to get back to the people, to be identified with the common lot." When Robert Park died, an obituary quipped that if anyone aroused the suspicion of this otherwise broadly tolerant man, it was a reformer, but in fact his work dovetailed nicely with the work of Addams and others. By describing urban neighborhoods in ecological terms, Park gave a more formal language to the analyses and intuitions many Progressives already had. After all, in writing "The Subjective Necessity of Social Settlements," Jane Addams had said that settlement house workers like herself "are bound to regard the entire life of their city as organic" and that their role is "to make an effort to unify it." Addams wrote that in 1892, calling the city "organic" long before Park became a University of Chicago sociologist.[69]

Developing a sense of civic loyalty was another goal that Progressives like Jane Addams shared with Daniel Burnham and those who wanted to see his plan for Chicago made real. Just as Addams wanted to use Hull House as a place where social rifts could be healed, so too those who promoted Burnham's plan wanted Chicago as a whole, not any particular faction of Chicagoans, to be the beneficiary. As Charles Merriam, one of the plan's major boosters, put it, the purpose of the plan was to make all Chicagoans "a part of a common group, to integrate them in the life of the community, to induce men to think in terms of the common enterprise of which they are a part; to develop personalities, policies, symbols that cut across the lines of other loyalties and raise the flag of the City itself, supreme for local purposes over all others."[70]

To speak of civic loyalty and an identity-defining commitment to place at the turn of the twentieth century takes us back to Josiah Royce. Central to Royce's conception of community was "loyalty." He wrote a great deal about that. As Royce meditated on the idea of loyalty, he spent most of his time in the abstract realm of philosophers. But he did recognize the problem of loyalty as a more specific by-product of a rapidly changing society. When Royce wrote that "the great task that now lies before our American people" was "the task of teaching millions of foreign birth and descent to understand and to bear constantly in mind the value of loyalty," he certainly acknowledged the ways in which new immigrants challenged the existing fabric of American life.

Wherever he looked, Royce saw fractiousness, the inevitable result of a nation of rampant individualism and rootless, grasping individuals. "We have that total indifference to all forms of loyalty," Royce complained, "which our seekers after individual power sometimes exhibit, and which occasionally appears as so serious an evil in the conduct of the business of certain great corporations." Nor did Royce approve of those occasions where people did band together to exhibit certain kinds of loyalty:

> For where the special loyalties are, amongst our people, most developed, they far too often take the form of a loyalty to mutually hostile partisan organizations, or to sects, or to social classes, at the expense of loyalty to the community or to the whole country. The labor-unions demand and cultivate the loyalty of their members; but they do so with a far too frequent emphasis upon the thesis that in order to be loyal to his own social class, or, in particular, to his union, the laborer must disregard certain duties to the community at large, and to the nation.[71]

If large corporations and labor unions stood as part of the problem, then he offered a vision of "provincialism" as the solution.

As he worried about the disappearance of loyalty from American life, Royce equated "loyalty" with "place" and argued that the former had necessarily to be rooted in the latter. Before we could be loyal to something as large and diffuse as the nation, we needed to develop loyalty to some smaller place—what Royce called a province or a region. He worried about "men who have no province, wanderers without a community, sojourners with a dwelling-place but with no home." As he envisioned it, "it is not the sect, it is not the labor-union, it is not the political partisan organization, but it is the widely developed provincial loyalty which is the best mediator between the narrower interests of the individual and the larger patriotism of our nation." Ever optimistic, Royce thought he saw a "new and wiser provincialism" just on the horizon. "I mean by such provincialism," he explained, "no mere renewal of the old sectionalism. I mean the sort of provincialism which makes people want to idealize, to adorn, to ennoble, to educate, their own province; to hold sacred its traditions, to honor its worthy dead, to support and to multiply its public possessions."[72]

Royce did not define the geography of provincialism any more exactly than that, and he was uneasy about the growth of the city. He noted that "our modern great cities swarm" with those rootless cosmopolites. But the Progressive urbanists believed the city could create loyalty and give people that sense of province. When Robert Woods described the "neighbor instinct" that he found in Boston's South End, he was describing just the sort of loyalty Royce yearned for. Royce suggested that the way to adorn and ennoble a local province was through the building of institutions like libraries, museums, historical societies, and improvement associations, which was precisely what City Beautiful advocates were doing in any number of cities at that moment. Royce was no urbanist, and he regarded his frontier childhood in California as the formative experience of his life, but Jane Addams found enough relevance in Royce's ideas to use his writings in several of her Hull House courses.[73]

Nor was Addams alone among Progressive reformers and sociologists in linking community, loyalty, and the city. Ohio State University sociologist Cecil North, writing about "The City as Community," argued that the reason most Americans saw the city as somehow antithetical to community was that they did not really understand how the modern, industrial city functioned. "The chief reason for casting the modern large city outside the community fold," he wrote stiffly,

is that many observers have been more impressed with the evidences of absence of unity in the city than with the signs of its presence.... Such a point of view, however, fails to take account of certain aspects of social unity that are exceedingly significant for modern society. To think of group unity as confined exclusively to situations where simple, face-to-face relations prevail is to neglect some of the most important phases of the present social order.[74]

He went on, acknowledging that the extraordinary heterogeneity of the American city would seem to preclude any kind of unity, much less community: "The reason the city is looked upon as a confused mass of people without essential social unity is because ... the citizens of the city are not bound together by any unique loyalty to a self-sufficient locality. They are highly diverse in their culture and their interests."[75]

Still, writing from Columbus, Ohio, North found the same thing that Woods found in Boston, and Park and Addams found in Chicago: a growing sense of "community" in American cities, and, he was clear, one that grew harmoniously with an expanded government. North pointed out that "the urban population is co-operating in many more things than are the citizens of the state." This was largely because "the functions of city government ... are much more numerous than those of the state." He was certain that "it cannot be doubted that a larger number of co-operative projects is carried on by the urban population than by the state or nation."[76]

From his apartment in Greenwich Village, the essayist and critic Randolph Bourne saw an even more transcendent possibility in the American city. In 1916, the year after Josiah Royce died and two years before his own untimely death from the Spanish flu, Bourne published his essay "Trans-National America" in the pages of *The Atlantic*. In it, Bourne pronounced the goal of assimilating new immigrants to an Anglo-Saxon hegemony not simply a failure in practice, though it surely was, but also a failure of vision. With immigrants arriving from all corners of the globe, Bourne believed, America had the opportunity to create an identity from the grand sum of all its cultural parts. He presented a view of a possible America, an emerging America, and he found it thrilling and exhilarating.

"The failure of the melting-pot," Bourne wrote, "far from closing the great American democratic experiment, means that it has only just begun. Whatever American nationalism turns out to be, we see already that it will have color richer and more exciting than our ideal has hitherto encompassed. In a world which has dreamed of internationalism, we find that we have all unawares been building up the first international nation." It was no accident that Bourne closed the essay by invoking the beloved community:

All our idealisms must be those of future social goals in which all can participate, the good life of personality lived in the environment of the Beloved Community. No mere doubtful triumphs of the past, which redound to the glory of only one of our trans-nationalities, can satisfy us. It must be a future America, on which all can unite, which pulls us irresistibly toward it, as we understand each other more warmly.

As we have discussed, Josiah Royce did not locate his beloved community on a map or in a specific place. Neither did Bourne, but perhaps he felt no need to do so. His vision of transnational America was undeniably an urban vision; Bourne saw transnational America every time he walked out his front door. Far from being the menace the Rev. Josiah Strong inveighed against, those immigrants and the way they interacted in the American city represented the vanguard of a new American identity.[77]

By the first quarter of the twentieth century, many Americans recognized that they no longer lived in anything resembling Thomas Jefferson's nation, nor would they ever again. In place of that vision of the national destiny, Progressive-era philosophers, reformers, academics, and planners had thoroughly reconceived the city. In it, new immigrants could become neighbors, neighborhoods could become communities, communities could band together to reinvigorate democracy itself. The city, finally, could foster the loyalty needed to heal the social divisions that made so many Americans so anxious; and in that healing, in that recognition that America could be more than the sum of its "alien" parts, we would create the first truly international nation. When an anonymous writer for *Outlook* magazine described "The Ideal City" in his 1909 essay, he imagined that in it "love for [the] city will then be as natural for the city dweller as now, in America, it is unnatural and rare."[78]

America's urban moment arrived in the early years of the twentieth century. That moment did not last long, and in the next three chapters we will look at those in the interwar period who thought the only way to restore lost American values was to leave the city, with its heterogeneous density and collectivist spirit.

3 THE CENTER SHOULD NOT HOLD

DECENTRALIZING THE CITY IN THE 1920S AND '30S

If the city in the Progressive era had been repositioned as—in the words of Frederic Howe—the "hope for democracy," then one could make a case that the 1920s was the decade when the American city became central to American life in virtually every way.

As the First World War ended and the doughboys returned from the killing fields of Europe, they came back to a nation driven by an urban economy, filled with a growing number of urbanized people, whose major cultural productions—whether in architecture, painting, literature, music, sports, or mass entertainment—were urban as well. Sinclair Lewis won a Nobel Prize for his acidic attacks on small-town America, though he was hardly more bitter in his scorn than newspaperman H. L. Mencken. At the same time, all that Americans associated with the modern, most of it also urban, generated its own reaction in the period after the war: flappers and jazz clubs on the one hand, fundamentalist religious revival and the Ku Klux Klan on the other. Even those who rejected all that the city stood for could not escape it. As the influential sociologist Louis Wirth wrote in 1938, "The degree to which the contemporary world may be said to be 'urban' is not fully or accurately measured by the proportion of the total population living in cities. The influences which cities exert upon the social life of man are greater than the ratio of the urban population would indicate." Cities, Wirth continued, are "the initiating and controlling center of economic, political and cultural life that has drawn the most remote parts of the world into its orbit."[1]

Even for many who were not members of Mencken's broadly defined "booboisie," however, the city had not been redeemed. Cities grew, yes; their economies boomed in the 1920s; they generated cultural vitality, from spectator sports to jazz. They were also the sites where government intervened to foster the public good, and in all kinds of successful ways. But regardless of whether they could be run efficiently and governed honestly, many American critics still wondered whether they could be made more humane for those who lived in them. Could they satisfy the deeper yearning for social harmony and common purpose? The questions gnawed, and as they did, many Americans between one world war and the next decided the answer was no, and they looked away from the city for answers. The answer they came to, over and over, was to decentralize the city.

The Decentralists Arrive

The announcement the Census Bureau made in 1920 probably did not surprise anyone: a majority of Americans now lived in urban areas. That milestone was perhaps less dramatic than it first appeared, given that at the time the Census defined a "city" as a place larger than 2,500 people. Still, for several generations the demographic arrows had been pointing inevitably in this direction, and the 1920 census bookended the announcement in 1890 that the frontier had closed, underscoring that the United States had truly transformed from a rural nation to an urban one. And although the biggest cities—Chicago, Philadelphia, Detroit, and New York most of all—stood as the great symbols of urban America, other cities were growing all across the nation. By 1920, Boston and Baltimore were both cities of three-quarters of a million people, and Los Angeles had topped 500,000, making it a top-ten city for the first time.

And yet, embracing the realities of urban America was not what most Americans had in mind when, in electing Warren Harding in 1920, they cast their votes for a return to "normalcy." After two decades of an expansive and aggressive federal government, personified by Teddy Roosevelt and Woodrow Wilson pursuing agendas everyone called "progressive," after the traumas and dislocations of war and its aftermath, the 1920s brought a retrenchment and a reduction in the role of the government. Presided over by a small-town Ohioan and then by a Massachusetts Yankee, the laissez-faire of the 1920s was as much ethos as economic theory. At least at the national level.

In fact, it was at this time in American cities that many of the civic projects begun or envisioned before the war finally came to fruition—everything from City Beautiful planning projects to municipal utility consolidations to urban transportation networks. The role of government in creating better, more functional cities decidedly did not shrink after the First World War. It grew. As economist Ralph Woods discovered in the 1930s, "New York City, Chicago, Boston, and Detroit each have larger budgets than the States which contain them."[2]

Consider these numbers: between 1915 and 1929, per capita spending rose 66 percent in Philadelphia and 76 percent in Detroit, figures all the more remarkable because both cities also grew significantly during those years. Detroit's population rose a whopping 179 percent. Taken together, those figures mean that Philadelphia's municipal spending grew 95 percent in that period, Detroit's by 379 percent.[3] That spending represented all sorts of civic projects big and small: public libraries and subway systems, and public school buildings and urban parks and public health initiatives. Government activity buzzed in American cities after the First World War, and it undoubtedly made urban life better.[4]

For the motley assortment of planners, writers, activists, and others who called for decentralization, however, the fact that cities could be made to work better mattered little. Urban problems were symptoms of a much larger disease: the city itself and all that it had come to represent. The only cure was to decentralize American life.

To call it a movement overstates the case. The decentralists of the 1920s and 1930s were a varied bunch, ranging from those associated with the Regional Planning Association, to Catholic and Protestant clergy who worried about the state of rural religion, to the literary crowd at Vanderbilt University who called themselves "The Agrarians" despite their faculty positions in Vanderbilt's English Department.

These decentralists never organized as a political party or issued a manifesto. Nonetheless, they shared a few basic tenets. They certainly saw the increasing concentration of wealth and productive capacity in cities as a danger to the nation. As Woods put it bluntly in his *Plan for Decentralization of Industry*, "The disease is concentration. The nation is the patient." Economic concentration, however, was only part of the larger problem of urban concentration that was discussed in the previous chapter. The city, where most of those factories churned away in the first place, stood as the embodiment of everything the decentralists abhorred. "Naturally, the greatest indictment against the city," Woods went on matter-of-factly, "is its congestion."[5]

No argument about that from the Progressive urbanists. But where they imagined urban solutions to urban problems, the decentralists imagined shrinking the size of big cities, constructing entirely new cities planned in such a way as to avoid the problems of the old ones, or leaving the city altogether for a return to a more rural, more agricultural life.

At the same time, most expressed enthusiasm that new technologies, particularly the car and electrification, would make decentralizing people and the economy feasible. The age of steam demanded centralized industrialized production, just as the age of the railroad had concentrated people. The age of electricity meant production could take place virtually anywhere, and the car would make it possible for people to live where they chose. This is what Stuart Chase had in mind, for example, when he titled his small 1933 book *The Promise of Power*. No nostalgic yearning for the past, or so they insisted, but an attempt to refashion the Jeffersonian yeomanry for the twentieth century.

Even so, many of the anti-urban sentiments of the decentralists simply retreaded old complaints about urban life. Woods sounded less like an economist and more like Rev. Josiah Strong when he asserted that "no matter what your pet abomination may be, you are almost sure to find it manifested in some part or another of the metropolis," and he summoned William Jennings Bryan more than Adam Smith when he warned: "when the city for too long a time forgets its rural base it woos ruin." He went on almost dismissively to say that "the social maladjustments produced by the highly urbanized community are rather obvious," though as he enumerated them he summarized by saying, "Perhaps it would be more reasonable and fair to say that the average city person has little chance for direct participation in activities that reward one with the feeling of being alive and with the glow of accomplishment."[6]

Urban life was unnatural, plain and simple, and Woods hammered the point home by bringing up the hoary contrast between city and country. City children, he wrote, "know nothing of the infinite variety of nature, of landscapes, waterscapes, of natural life, of sky clouds, or the drama of growth and decay.... As children, the city has little to offer them except the opportunity, nay the necessity, to mature along scientific and superefficient lines.... They are robbed of physical adventure and of healthful exploratory experiences of their own." Rhetorically, he pleaded, "Is this tragic condition the price we must pay for our vaunted industrialism, our exaggerated urbanism?"[7]

Beyond these familiar critiques of urban life and exhortations of rural virtues, some of the decentralists also remained committed to the Jeffersonian equating of land ownership with the health of the republic. For these intellectuals, the city deprived people of the opportunity to own their own land. America would survive only as a propertied society, the decentralists felt, and the major threat to a society based on widespread property ownership was the city. The solution, therefore, was to leave the city and return to the country, in one way or another, where every American family could own its own home and a few productive acres.[8]

This was not so much an economic or even a social argument, but something that verged on an ethical appeal. As writer Patrick Quinn put it in 1940, "Subsistence farming simply means farming as 'a way of life' rather than as a business. It means in moral terms, independence, responsibility, security. It means, ultimately, the re-birth of the American property system in land, the second step in the making of a free people."[9] For Woods, decentralizing the economy with a renewed emphasis on farming would preserve the values of American individualism. "Agriculture is primarily an individualistic way of life..." he opined, and contrasted the farm with the city: "Urban life, on the other hand, is an essentially co-operative existence." Cooperation, for Quinn, was not a positive good, and he summarized the key political geography of anti-urbanism: rural life meant individualism; urban life meant something approaching collectivism.

Never mind that real life in rural America during the 1920s and 1930s went from bad to worse. After enjoying a golden moment during the first two decades of the twentieth century, the agricultural economy began to suffer even though other parts of the economy boomed after the war. Then things truly collapsed during the Dust Bowl and Depression years. Urging Americans to abandon the cities for the country in these circumstances might be a tough sell. Northwestern University philosopher Baker Brownell recognized that the key question for decentralists was "how to get people on the land without sending them back to the land in the sense of becoming peasants." Similarly, Woods believed that the hostility between city and country could be left in the nineteenth century and replaced with a synthesis of both: "It is traditional that the city and country are antithetical;...but whereas once individuals had to choose between urban or rural life, today it is possible to have the most desirable features of each."[10]

Still, it was not simply a better economic future that awaited Americans, Reverend Arthur Holt promised them, if they left the cities. It was that larger, more ineffable sense of community. Holt predicted, "If people ever discover what true community life is they are going to desert the city like rats from a sinking ship. It may be the place where they go to work but it will not be the place where they will go to live."[11] For these writers and activists, the only way to replace the alienation of the public life of the city and restore true individualism and genuine community was to leave the city altogether.

Free America

Although they never gathered in a political convention, nor were they ever a movement proper, starting in 1937 the decentralists did share a common place for conversation. In January of that year Herbert Agar brought out the first issue of a new magazine *Free America*, and used it to bring together a motley assortment of writers, critics, and cranks preaching the gospel of anti-urbanism.[12]

Any given issue of the monthly promised a salmagundi of philosophy, polemic, and how-to advice, in no particular order. A 1938 issue, to pull one randomly off the shelf, juxtaposed an essay on the "Crisis of Democracy" with one titled "Our Friend the Earthworm."

Though Agar insisted that *Free America* would be a wide-open forum, in fact its politics drifted decidedly toward the conservative, especially by New

Deal standards. In his introductory editorial, Agar told readers that he had been inspired by the southern agrarians, and several of them, like Donald Davidson and Allen Tate, published in the magazine. When the Depression disappeared as we prepared for war, *Free America* worked hard to position its advocacy of decentralization as the true American alternative to both Marxist collectivism and German fascism. The Nazis, after all, had initiated their own program of back-to-the-land decentralization, but Emerson Hynes took pains to draw distinctions: "We don't want distributionalism the Nazi way. We do not want it as part of a nationalistic or imperialistic program. We do not want it imposed from above or sold by mass propaganda. We don't want it at the cost of our freedom."[13]

Although *Free America* offered its program of decentralization as a way of keeping America from being swept up in the currents of international politics, more central to its agenda was a rejection of urbanized America and all that the decentralists thought it stood for. In fact, for some of the magazine's writers, the two were related. "The fundamental conflict in America today," according to contributor Angeline Bouchard, was not between communism and fascism but, rather, "between metropolis and province." For Bouchard, the former tension was simply a subset of the latter. As she bluntly put it, "The metropolis is the breeder of collectivism and dictatorship." That might seem an extraordinary claim, so Bouchard explained further, "Insofar as [the metropolis] transforms individuals to a swirling, jaded mass, it destroys the spiritual bulwark of democracy. Insofar as it creates economic insecurity on a vast scale, it is the cue for the 'strong man' to rise and offer a way out."[14] Never mind that most of the demagogues who had appeared on the American scene to that point—from Tom Watson and "Pitchfork" Ben Tillman to Huey Long and Catholic priest Charles Coughlin—did not rise from the city.[15]

For those who gathered between the covers of *Free America*, the city was too crowded, too dirty, too heterogeneous, too hectic, and too distant from nature. Bouchard wrote as if it were self-evident that "The truth is that the life of the metropolis is not natural.... The metropolitan is not happy. He has lost the capacity for inner peace and contentment."[16] More than all that, for the decentralists the city represented a collective endeavor, a decidedly public enterprise, one that required a significant expansion of the role of government to achieve. Whatever else decentralists might debate, they all nodded their heads in agreement with those two critiques about the city.

Planning for Decentralization: The RPAA

They called themselves the Regional Planning Association of America (RPAA), though their interests rarely strayed too far beyond the greater New York region. The association lasted only ten years or so, but it still enjoys an almost mythical status, at least in the world of city planners and urban designers. When the group met for the first time, in April 1923, there were eight people in attendance.

Among those eight people, however, was an extraordinary reserve of talents and interests. Alexander Bing, the group's president, was a wealthy real estate mogul and helped finance the group's activities; Charles Harris Whitaker and Clarence Stein both had architectural training; Benton MacKaye was among the first generation of professional foresters; and Lewis Mumford was the organization's intellectual-without-portfolio. They came together because, as Stein put it later, "after the First World War there was a strong surge of enthusiasm for a better world."[17] That better world would be achieved through rational, comprehensive planning.

The world that needed improving, of course, was the urban industrial world. The members of the RPAA shared a hostility to the large-scale modern metropolis, though certainly in varying degrees, and they believed in the need to decentralize industry and population in order to make cities more livable. They also insisted on the interconnections between city and countryside and on the need to think in terms of larger regions; not to do so would be simply to relocate all the old urban mistakes into new places. Regionalism was the only way that the city could be renewed and the countryside with its small towns be reinvigorated.[18]

Part of their solution came from England. Several members had become infatuated with the English "Garden City" idea pioneered by Ebenezer Howard. Hoping to restore a balance between town and country, Howard imagined carefully planned new towns of controlled and manageable size, all surrounded by "greenbelts" of agricultural land and open space. Howard's vision came to an American audience through the publication of his book *Garden Cities of Tomorrow* in 1902, and some Americans were clearly taken. Annie Diggs told readers of *Arena* in her review: "we have located the chiefest evils, and we find them to center almost wholly about 'Environment' and 'Employment.' The Garden City proposition grapples at once with these two problems."

Born in London, Howard spent time in the United States in the 1870s, in Nebraska as a matter of fact, where he decided that the farming life in a remote and isolated place did not suit him. But during his stay he developed a fondness for the writings of Emerson and Thoreau. Back in England, Howard read Edward Bellamy's 1888 utopian novel *Looking Backward* and was deeply moved by it. At the risk of oversimplifying the issue, Howard's garden cities can be seen as a nice combination of transcendentalist ideas about the moral power of nature and the forward-looking, technocratic utopianism of Bellamy. The Garden City idea may have been an English import, but it had important American roots.

When the RPAA drew up its charter on June 8, 1923, it put the Garden City idea front and center among its goals:

> First. The Association will promote the study of housing, industrial decentralization, city planning and regional planning.... Second. The Association will aid the formation of associations and corporations designed to finance, control the land essential to planning, build and operate Garden Cities. Third. The Association will serve as center for information of technical aid to those who seek to erect houses, locate factories and build up communities on garden city lines.[19]

The Regional Planners—Mumford most especially—also adapted the ideas of another Briton, the Scottish biologist Patrick Geddes. Mumford came across Geddes during World War I when he read Geddes's *City Development* and *Cities in Evolution*. They met finally in 1923, the year the RPAA was founded. At the time, Mumford acknowledged Geddes as his intellectual mentor and inspiration; he would do so for the rest of his life.[20]

Geddes applied ideas borrowed from the natural world to develop a wide-ranging critique of modern industrial society and everything that underpinned it. That critique led him to champion small-scale producer economies and people living in small-scale communities. That, in turn, led him from the study of biology to that of city planning.

Mumford took from Geddes his insistence that planning amounted to a great deal more than simply rearranging space to make it more rational and efficient, that the transformations needed could not be achieved merely with cleaner streets and Beaux Arts architecture. The "region" in regional planning was not an arbitrary geographic area but an area that had some degree of natural and cultural coherence—a blend of topography, geology, and climate with historic settlement patterns, transportation routes, and traditions. Applying the ecological model, the notion of the "organic" meant that planning aimed at nothing less than the reconstruction of society.

Mumford, born in 1895, called himself "a child of the city." But as a young man Mumford saw cities where old neighborhoods and institutions had decayed, where the world of intimate associations had been replaced with the colder world of offices and factories, and where maintaining personal connections depended increasingly on technologies of transportation and communication. At the same time, the unstoppable urban tide continued to roll over the countryside, drowning the distinctiveness of small-town life in the process.

In short, the acids of urban modernity had corroded any sense of community. The job of planning, therefore, was nothing less than rehabilitating that sense of civic harmony and balanced social life. "Regional planning is the New Conservation," Mumford announced, "the conservation of human values hand in hand with natural resources."[21]

At virtually the same moment, and using the same metaphor, Robert Park and the other Chicago sociologists thought they had identified an ecology within city neighborhoods that seemed to at least serve some of the purposes Mumford hoped to recreate. But the members of the RPAA advocated decentralization, and their enthusiasm for garden cities revealed that they thought that sort of decentralized life was simply preferable, despite their claim that they would make urban centers themselves better. Architect Charles Whitaker did not hide his growing distaste for cities, and Clarence Stein, though himself a life-long New Yorker, shared some of the same feelings. In 1922, in a speech before the New York Academy of Medicine, Stein complained about the "disease" of concentration—echoing that common refrain of the era—the result of which was that the city had ceased to be "a fit place in which to live." The following year he observed that "as a result of their haphazard and planless growth, the gigantic cities of the old and the new world are becoming more hopelessly unable to carry on their work."[22]

In 1925, *Survey* magazine offered members of the RPAA the chance to write about regional planning, and both Stein and Mumford used the opportunity to position the decentralized region as the antidote to the overly centralized city. Stein tipped his cards with the very title of his contribution: "Dinosaur Cities." Most of the essay was a more or less familiar recitation of urban woes, with Stein insisting that cities were antiquated, increasingly anachronistic, and headed the way of the dinosaurs. "All the breakdowns we have been studying," he concluded, "are the result of a congestion of population."[23]

Nothing new in that, but Stein went on more ominously: "The big city is bankrupt. The little city that has adopted a program of mere expansion…is headed in the same direction." Mumford, as if tag-teaming with Stein, began his essay almost exactly where Stein left off. The opening lines served as a shot across the complacent bow of urban America: "The hope of the city lies outside itself. Focus your attention on the cities—in which more than half of us live—and the future is dismal." Only "drastic public efforts" Stein wrote, in the form of coordinated regional planning, could fix all this.[24]

Some of this was doubtless rhetorical posturing, an attempt to grab readers' attention with a certain level of hyperbole. But the antipathy that Mumford felt toward the cities of the 1920s, and which shaped the attitude of the RPAA, was real and deep. It came roiling to the surface, and helped fracture the RPAA, when Mumford publicly responded to the *Regional Plan of New York*.

The plan was an epic undertaking. Begun at almost the same time as the RPAA formed, the Regional Plan Association (not to be confused with the

RPAA) received funding, to the tune of more than a million dollars, from the Russell Sage Foundation to carry out the work. Frederic A. Delano chaired the committee responsible for the plan, but Thomas Adams oversaw the project and the team of experts assembled to carry it out. The first part of the project consisted of a massive survey of the New York region, an area defined by the working group as a circle with a radius of about fifty miles. Do the math: roughly 7,800 square miles. By the time the survey part of the project was completed, it ran to eight volumes. Only in the final two volumes did the *Regional Plan of New York and its Environs* actually get to planning. The last volume came out in 1931 to much acclaim, and, one suspects, no little exhaustion.

On the face of it, the Regional Plan of New York hit all the right notes. It called for a system of parks and open spaces; it advocated the decentralization of population and industry even though it planned for considerable population growth; it represented the very best available expertise. A year later, Mumford gave his response to it. He hated it.

In two articles that appeared in consecutive issues of the *New Republic,* Mumford tore into the entire plan. He tipped his cap to the public spiritedness of the authors; he acknowledged nothing but the noblest motives. And he found a few things to admire—tasty raisins, as he put it, in an otherwise bland and tasteless pudding. That was about as much generosity as he could muster.

He began by questioning the very definition of the region: "The New York region as described by the Regional Plan is a purely arbitrary concept," he wrote. In fact, the region was defined by commuting time in and out of the city, but Mumford was right that it was not defined by the combination of nature and culture that he believed gave the notion of region its meaning. As he pointed out, "The colossal highway and rapid-transit schemes outlined by the Regional Plan are really an alternative to a community building program; certainly not a means to it." The decentralization envisioned in the plan struck Mumford as equally superficial. "When one speaks of decentralization," Mumford scolded, "one naturally means something more than the decentralization of the over-burdened physical plant.... [O]ne means equally the spread and reintegration of the organs of the common life." The plan, as Mumford saw it, responded to logistical problems rather than human ones, and offered technical solutions instead of cultural ones. Having worked himself into a proper lather by the end of his second installment, Mumford announced bluntly that the plan amounted to "a monumental failure."

Mumford had complaints about the specifics because he condemned what he saw as the governing assumptions of the plan, what he called its "drift":

> One must finally judge the Regional Plan not by its separate details but by its *drift*. Thus, the report talks about garden cities but drifts toward further

metropolitan centralization; it talks about neighborhood planning and better housing but drifts toward our present chaotic methods of supplying both; it talks of objective standards of air and light for building but drifts toward over-intensive uses of even suburban areas.[25]

The "drift" of the plan, in other words, was toward the city as the undeniable center of the region, and Mumford blasted away at the motives of those who

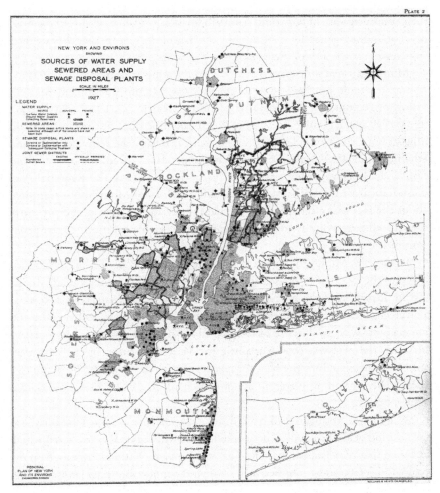

Too much city, not enough region. Though Lewis Mumford complained about the *Regional Plan of New York and its Environs,* it was an epic undertaking. It considered virtually every aspect of regional life illustrated with dozens of charts and maps, including this one of sewers and sewering. Regional Plan of New York and its Environs, *vol. 8, 1929*

produced it. "With the myth of New York's greatness and the desire for metro-politan concentration to spur them," Mumford wrote, "they looked for no other evidence and admitted no other necessities." Believing the new technologies provided the means for a more comprehensive decentralization, Mumford went on: "The influence of the telephone, the radio, the automobile, and the airplane, giant power, skilled industrial planning and rationalization…none of these factors has been completely canvassed and candidly assessed." Having thus indicted, Mumford came to a charge just short of outright corruption: "the Russell Sage Foundation…were so eager to fasten to a viable solution, a solution acceptable to their committee full of illustrious names in financial and civic affairs, to the business community generally, to the public officials of the region, that they deliberately restricted the area of their questions."[26] *J'accuse.*

Mumford's reaction caused real friction among members of the RPAA, though it should not have come as any surprise. Mumford had made his definition of regionalism and regional planning clear in his 1925 contribution to *Survey's* special issue: "In sum, regional planning does not mean the planning of big cities beyond their present areas; it means the reinvigoration and rehabilitation of whole regions so that the products of culture and civilization…shall be available to everyone."[27] By that standard, the Regional Plan did not measure up. Still, it does seem a bit churlish for Mumford to complain about the fact that after spending all that money and nearly a decade of work, the Russell Sage Foundation would want some "viable solution" to the problems of the region.

In the end, Mumford's problem with the *Regional Plan of New York* boiled down to the fact that it focused too much on New York and not enough on the region. It privileged the metropolis at the expense of the hinterland. It took as a given that the city would remain the cultural and economic center, and it did not plan for ways to disperse or develop those kinds of resources more widely. In short, the plan was too city-centric for Mumford's taste. In the same year that Mumford laid into the plan for readers of the *New Republic*, he wrote to a friend. "My notion of heaven is an apple-orchard on a warm mid-afternoon in September."[28]

Whether or not Mumford treated the *Regional Plan of New York* fairly—to say nothing of all the people who worked on it—the regional vision upon which he based that criticism still has an undeniable appeal. With its insistence on the ecological interconnections between town and country, between landscape and culture; and with its desire to turn space into place, to use the techniques of planning to restore meaningful human community, it verges on utopian. Who among us, after all, could resist Mumford's call for a regionalism shaped not by engineers and architects but by "the artist, the poet, the philosopher?"[29]

But vision is not synonymous with policy, and neither Mumford nor his RPAA colleagues ever developed a plan or process to translate ideas into actions. Their ambivalence about the city was matched by a not-coincidental ambivalence about the role government ought to play in planning and in the reconstruction of community that they desired. Ideas can indeed be powerful, but without some mechanism to translate idea into practice, they can languish for years without doing much work in the world.

In the 1920s, in a climate of Babbitry, the RPAA felt that planning might emerge as a counterweight to corrupt politics and avaricious business, as a progressive agent of social change. There is something almost sweet about that, naïve perhaps—a faith that disinterested expertise could persuade without having to dirty its hands with politics or money. Stein certainly recognized that the kind of regional planning the RPAA advocated was not going to happen on its own. Writing in the *New York Times* he said, "Regional planning cannot be carried out by any separate community. It is a function that must be stimulated and assisted by the state."[30] Just how, Stein did not say.

He was more specific when trying to tackle the chronic housing shortage in New York City. The private sector had clearly failed the housing market, and the program of rent control enacted by the state legislature was not ambitious enough. Stein suggested a program of affordable housing, built on a for-profit basis but with subsidies from the state. Small-town Republicans in Albany killed that idea.[31]

Likewise, even Mumford's faith in localism did not lead him to think that local government could take over the functions of larger government structures. In his 1938 book *The Culture of Cities,* Mumford acknowledged that in order to "reapportion the existing balance of power with the nation, to equalize the privileges of different regions and groups, and to distribute the benefits of human culture" would require some sort of state intervention.[32]

They came by their suspicions honestly. Like so many Americans, Mumford in particular looked at the experience of the First World War as a colossal mistake. More than that, Mumford saw it as proof of what evil states could commit in the name of their people. Randolph Bourne was right: war was the "health of the state," and as a consequence the state ought to be viewed skeptically. Instead, Mumford believed, a new politics could only grow in the soil of local regions and come to bloom only after American culture itself had been reborn along those lines. In this sense, Mumford offered culture as a solution to political problems and decentralization as the alternative to socialist centralization for Progressives. Bourne died in 1918, and after his death Mumford assumed his role among those critics known as the Young Americans as the writer most deeply committed to the reconstruction of "culture" as an antidote to the state.[33]

Principled or myopic, the RPAA's failure to connect its agenda to any political process not only meant that its ideas had nowhere to go but, in turn, it also hindered the group's own attempts to make its recommendations more coherent and consistent. Catherine Bauer, who moved on from the RPAA to work on public housing projects, chided Mumford, her colleague and lover, that the RPAA "would rather see 'perfect' housing developments issuing solely from a sort of supertechnical machine than less perfect (possible) ones which represented a real gain in understanding, power and responsibility for the people who live in them." In a rebuke that must have stung, she wrote, "There isn't a society in which the isolated intellectual ... as an *individual* writing and talking to the general public, can expect to provide *direct* leadership, straight-line influence on policy and action."[34] By contrast, the Progressives of the previous generation had used the mechanisms of politics to address land planning and natural resource conservation issues, and with some success. The RPAA, by a combination of choice and circumstance, could not or would not reproduce that model.[35]

The problem of how to turn their decentralized vision into some sort of meaningful reality, of how to use culture as the basis for an anti-statist democratic revival, haunted Stein and Mumford. In 1967, when both were old men, Stein wrote to his friend mulling some of the same questions that had vexed them between the wars: "Cities must set population limits, but how? ... [T]he land must be owned by ... the community: but what community? District? City? County?"[36]

It is unfair to characterize the RPAA as simply "anti-urban." But its agenda of regionalism and decentralization, its ambivalence toward the city, and its suspicion of government meant that the work stands largely as a road not taken in American life. It led neither to the organic regionalism it hoped for, nor to the revitalization of cities during the Depression and after. The group held its last meeting in 1933, the year after Mumford lambasted the Regional Plan of New York. Three years later, Mumford, who called himself a "child of the city," and whose happiest childhood education came from walking with his beloved grandfather through the neighborhoods of New York, had relocated permanently to a small farmhouse in the Hudson River valley.

The RPAA Builds (or Tries to) Radburn, New Jersey

Although Mumford served as the RPAA's in-house intellectual, and though he did some of his most important writing during his years with the group, architect Clarence Stein built two developments he thought would be equally influential: three-dimensional examples of RPAA ideas. In 1924 he teamed up with

RPAA members Alexander Bing and Henry Wright to form the City Housing Corporation (CHC), a limited-dividend development company to build "better homes and communities." There was no question that this would be a money-making, for-profit venture, but with the higher purpose of creating "the Future Garden Cities of America."

Their first venture came on seventy acres of Pennsylvania Railroad yard in Queens, and when it was completed in 1926 the site had been transformed into a mixed residential development for 650 families. Houses faced each other across small courtyard gardens, residents had their own tennis courts, and because of the innovative site planning—handled mostly by Wright—there was space enough for a three-acre park. It all seemed a splendid success. Sunnyside Gardens served as a demonstration project proving that the Garden City model could be moved across the Atlantic. The Mumfords moved into one of the cooperative apartment units in September 1925.

Buoyed by their experience in Queens, Stein, Wright, and Bing set their sights on an even bigger project across the river. Not just a housing development—no matter how creative—within the city, but an entirely new city. A Garden City proper, with its own economic base, cultural life, and properly planned housing. In 1927, the CHC bought 1,000 acres of farmland in northern Jersey, roughly three miles from the industrial city of Paterson and just ten miles from New York. They called the place Radburn.

To visit Radburn, New Jersey, today is to find a pleasant but utterly unassuming place, its colonial and Tudor revival houses surrounded now by Jersey suburbs that have filled virtually all the space between Paterson and the Hudson River. When the first three hundred houses went up for sale in 1929, however, Radburn was greeted as a harbinger of the future. The *Times* suggested that it might be "a pioneer of the 'new city' to which many minds have been turning as a cure for the congestion of the centralized city."[37] Indeed, in terms of its influence on future development, Radburn has punched well above its weight.

People noticed the road design right away. Radburn was not built on a grid—that much was obvious—but it was more than that. Wright and Stein had designed the roads to segregate modes of transportation from one another, just as Progressive-era zoning had begun to separate industrial areas from residential areas. Radburn had a few roads that went in and out of town, but once inside, car traffic was calmed by the extensive use of cul-de-sacs that prevented a great deal of through-traffic. Further, Radburn was crisscrossed with pedestrian paths complete with tunnels underneath the vehicular roads. Cars and walkers never had to intersect. "Homes in the Town for the Motor Age," trumpeted the promotional brochure put out by the CHC, and the name stuck. An editorial in *Survey* magazine, almost breathing a sigh of relief, announced: "A city in which

Perhaps the most influential overpass in American planning history. When Radburn, New Jersey, opened in 1929, critics applauded the way vehicular traffic was separated from pedestrian traffic. They saw this separation as the best accommodation to the age of the automobile. *Library of Congress, LC-USF34-000673-D*

the automobile and the pedestrian may live in peace."[38] Stein and Wright even planned for a gas station.

That Stein and Wright worked so hard to broker peace between drivers and walkers reflects two assumptions of the RPAA and the decentralist vision more broadly. First, the decentralists believed in the promise of new technology to facilitate their goals. In a 1931 report on Radburn written for municipal leaders in his home state of Michigan, Tracy Augur insisted, "The modern facilities for individual transportation have emancipated the modern individual from the forces that made the metropolis. It is no longer necessary to herd humanity en masse, that the larger undertakings of the modern world may find their manpower."[39]

The flip side of that faith, however, was the belief that, more than any other new technology, the automobile underscored just how inadequate and antiquated urban life and urban space had become. The overbuilt urban gridiron could never accommodate the automobile. That much was obvious to anyone in New York in the 1920s (and, truth be told, one could come to the same conclusion today, and not just about New York). The modern world was an automobile world. Such a world demanded entirely new towns with an entirely different conception of roads and traffic patterns. "The modern occupation with the minutia of city life," Augur wrote, tweaking those new urban technocrats who did occupy themselves with fixing the minutia of city life, "is excused by the fallacy that because the cities are already here, we must make the best of them." Radburn stood as the correction of that "fallacy" and as "the first tangible product of a new urban science." [40]

Augur might not have wanted to admit it, but Radburn had exported some urban minutia to the Jersey countryside: Clarence Perry's "neighborhood unit." Perry turned the idea of the neighborhood into a planning tool. He believed neighborhoods ought to be organized around public spaces and institutions—parks, schools, and the like—and that they ought to be big enough to sustain those institutions while being small enough to foster the neighborliness and community that was ultimately the goal of urban planning for the Progressives in the first place. Perry attended several RPAA meetings and was involved in working on the Regional Plan of New York. One of the few things Lewis Mumford found to admire about the plan was its inclusion of Perry's ideas, though he was grudging even about that: "That the growth of the city is something other than a process of extending transit lines and laying down blank subdivisions is obliquely presented in just one part of the Report—that on the neighborhood unit." [41]

Stein and Wright brought the neighborhood unit out of the city and built Radburn around it. More specifically, they took the most basic physical element of city life—the city block—and made it "super." These superblocks, of between 30 and 40 acres each, would be bounded by arterial roads that took the through-traffic in and out without disturbing the quiet and calm within the superblocks themselves. With the traffic shunted off to the edges, the life of each superblock could center on green spaces, schools, and other shared activities.

For Progressives, the urban neighborhood was the key to an expanded and reinvigorated civic and community life. For some of those reformers and sociologists, the 1920s caused a loss of faith. Studying neighborhoods in Columbus, Ohio, sociologist Roderick MacKenzie had to concede that the turnover and mobility of modern urban life meant that the "neighborhood" could not effectively function as a unit of analysis or as the center of social reform. His Chicago colleague Ernest Burgess agreed. In 1924, Burgess wondered if the study of neighborhoods and their work as social catalysts could be put on a scientific footing. He concluded: "It can have a scientific foundation if it will base its activities upon a study of social forces." Fair enough, but Burgess immediately identified a paradox: "the social forces of city life seem, from our studies, to be destroying the city neighborhood." He went on, almost in lament, "Is the neighborhood center to engage in a losing fight against the underlying tendencies of modern urban society?... There are those who are convinced that the function of the neighborhood center is passing, with the decay of the neighborhood in the city."[42]

Jesse Steiner agreed when he assessed the "community movement" in America at the end of the decade. "The community cannot be easily made the unit of social administration," he concluded, "at a time when deep-seated forces are working toward its disintegration. The community movement, it might be said, was ushered in a generation too late."[43] Almost as quickly as Progressives had discovered and described urban neighborhoods, and invested them with so much possibility and potential, those neighborhoods slipped out of their fingers.

But Stein and Wright believed that neighborhood and everything that went with it could be planned and built. Whereas the urban neighborhood seemed to arise and then disappear because of large forces at work in the city, Radburn offered the opportunity to plan with a clean slate, to manage all the variables before they spun out control. In the end, of course, Stein and Wright saw managing the traffic flow and developing in self-contained superblocks not as goals in and of themselves but as means to a greater purpose. They hoped that Radburn would foster that elusive sense of community whose absence remained one of the primary indictments of the city. They wanted to transform space into a meaningful place, to use the techniques of planning to create community.

Survey magazine looked on approvingly. "Radburn has learned a lesson the importance of which many older communities fail to recognize," the editors wrote in 1931, "that is, that good houses alone do not make a community, but that common interests and associations are essential." And the editors added a cautionary, decentralist note, in case readers might forget: "a real community cannot be too large." That was the lesson of Radburn, and looking back on his career, Stein remained committed to the beliefs that motivated the Radburn superblock: "Small neighborhoods are essential for eye-to-eye democracy. This is basic, not only for local contentment, but for national freedom and world-wide security."[44] The goal, finally, was not to build a better place to live, but a place to live better.

Shortly after the first residents moved in, Robert Hudson, a researcher from the American Association for Adult Education, arrived to measure just how well this project in community-building had succeeded. Hudson started his report by noting that Radburn featured two major innovations, "the physical plan and the community idea," and he was persuaded that the two were connected to each other: "in order to approach the problem of community living properly, it is most essential that the physical side of the community be considered." Community life could be planned, just like physical space; indeed, it must be planned "to realize the full possibilities of an ideal community." Hudson found that in Radburn "only 3.27 percent of the adults . . . failed to take part in some phase of the planned community life."[45]

That number, and its faux exactitude, might be impressive, but it deceived a little. In 1934, when Hudson published his study, 336 families called Radburn home, a far cry from the thousands that Stein, Wright, and Bing had envisioned. *Business Weekly* might write in the summer of 1930 that the "business depression has had practically no effect upon sales in Radburn," but in fact it did bring a halt to Radburn's development.[46] Nothing of the original plan got built after 1929, the CHC went bankrupt several years later, and today roughly 600 families occupy a town of just under 150 acres.

For all its influence, the Radburn experiment left many with varying degrees of disappointment. It never attracted—in fact, was never designed to attract—low-income or working-class people, no small irony since the decentralists always claimed they wanted to alleviate the overcrowded housing of working people. "No miracle is promised here," wrote Geddes Smith as Radburn's houses were under construction, "and the wage-earner at the bottom of the economic scale is still unprovided for." Robert Hudson confirmed that prediction six years later when he came to visit: "Radburn residents belong chiefly to the business and professional classes."[47]

Nor did Radburn develop an autonomous economic life or its own, home-grown cultural life. Stein and Wright did not plan for any real industrial activity, at least not in the Radburn that was ultimately completed. "Economically," Hudson concluded, "Radburn is at the opposite end of the scale from a self-contained community."[48] Likewise, although there seem to have been some attempts at a local cultural life, Radburn was sold as being conveniently located just minutes from New York and all the cultural life the city had to offer. In other words, Radburn never developed into a Garden City on the English model—a place where an economically diverse population would find work, culture, and community independent of the big city.

In other words, Radburn became a suburb. Stein recognized as much later in his life when he called his model city "more of a country club without the golf course." And like most suburbs, rather than develop a life of its own, it functioned to reject the city while simultaneously taking advantage of it. As William Elbow, one of the original Radburn residents, put it, "Being out of the city was what appealed to us most when moving to Radburn."[49]

Radburn, like so much else, became a victim of the Great Depression. Although the money for private real estate ventures like Radburn dried up almost entirely in the 1930s, the urgency felt by the decentralists only increased. Whatever had made cities intolerable in the 1920s became worse with mass unemployment and the potential for violence and volatility. The bind in which the decentralists found themselves during the Depression years was whether decentralization, with all that it meant, could be accomplished with the federal government as a partner rather than as an antagonist.

Going Borsodi

Dayton, Ohio, never shows its best aspect in January, unless alternating shades of gray and subtle differences of raw appeal to you. But in January 1933, the city must have looked particularly grim. In the first quarter of the twentieth century, Dayton had prospered as a small but busy manufacturing city whose industrial innovations were utterly disproportionate to its size. In 1913, it had been devastated by an epic flood that left $100 million in property destroyed in its wake and 350 of its citizens dead. It had rebounded, like Chicago had after the fire, without missing a beat; and by the 1920s, Dayton's industries had thoroughly insinuated themselves into the fabric of every day American life—from the electric cash registers made by the National Cash Register Company, to the self-starting automobile engines pioneered by Charles Kettering and his Dayton Engineering Laboratories Company (Delco), to the publications that issued forth in their thousands from the huge McCall's publishing plant, to the Frigidaires which had become synonymous with "ice box" in the American kitchen. Of course, the Wright brothers had carried on some interesting experiments in their bicycle shop. Local lore had it that more patents had been issued per capita to Dayton than any other place in the nation.

By 1933, needless to say, the Depression had taken its toll. Statewide in Ohio, unemployment stood at over 35 percent; in workshops and factories across the state over 40 percent of workers had been idled. In Dayton, whose factories produced all sorts of things that Americans could no longer afford to buy, 17,000 families were on some sort of relief. Roughly 70,000 people; roughly one-third of the residents of Dayton.

This was the city that Ralph Borsodi came to visit in January 1933. What he found inspired him. He was so enthusiastic that he told readers of the *Nation* a few months later: "Dayton promises to make social history."[50] Borsodi was a New York City boy, born in 1886 and raised in Manhattan. By the 1920s, however, he chucked the world of advertising and publishing, which had been his father's business, and set about creating a life of simple self-sufficiency on a small homestead farm in Suffern, just north of New York City. He called himself an economist, though a self-taught one to be sure, and he first put his ideas in front of a national audience in a book called *This Ugly Civilization,* which appeared just on the eve of the Depression in 1929.

The book is an unsparing dissection of the American economy—each chapter begins with an epigraph from Nietzsche's *Thus Spake Zarathustra*—and its politics do not map comfortably onto the spectrum of right and left. On the one hand, for example, Borsodi had no use for contemporary sexual mores, which trapped women between "the Scylla of frigidity and the Charybdis of prostitution";

on the other, he complained that women's colleges had created in women "an abnormal appreciation of careers and an equally abnormal depreciation of marriages." Taken as a whole, however, these idiosyncratic observations amount to a jeremiad, preaching the doctrine of decentralization. Borsodi wrote that the only way to cure our sick society was to replace industrial production and large-scale market agriculture with home-based industry and small-scale production.

Filled with data and examples ranging from the price of canned food in Indiana to an analysis of household electric use, the book is also implicitly a diatribe against the city. "This is an ugly civilization," the book begins, "[i]t is a civilization of noise, smoke, smells, and crowds—of people content to live amidst the throbbing of its machines; the smoke and smells of its factories; the crowds and discomforts of the cities of which it proudly boasts."[51] Like the Reverend Josiah Strong in an earlier generation, Borsodi believed that the city was both cause and symptom of everything wrong with American life, of an ugly, urban civilization.

In the 1920s, Borsodi's decentralizing crusade, his exhortation that Americans turn away from large-scale industrial production and the cities that went along with it, struck most as quixotic. As one reviewer of *This Ugly Civilization* put it somewhat skeptically: "Borsodi's proposals have plausibility as a means of personal escape from the humdrum of urban life of people in comfortable circumstances....But it is difficult to see how their realization of his program of social change would benefit the millions of factory workers who are the real victims of the system which the author indicts."[52]

By 1933, however, the quixotic had become the prophetic. Written during the very end of the 1920s boom, the book gained an audience as the American economic collapse seemed to ratify much of what Borsodi said. Tellingly, Harper and Brothers came out with a second edition of *This Ugly Civilization* in 1933.

In the preface to that second edition, Borsodi wrote that "men and women from all over the country, and even from Europe, keep asking for more and more details about 'how to go Borsodi.'" As his grand economic treatise and manifesto, Borsodi's *Ugly Civilization* did not provide the sort of practical advice that people now wanted. Borsodi responded to that demand with another book that also came out in 1933, and its title made it absolutely clear where the decentralized promised land lay: *Flight from the City*.

"It is not an exaggeration of the situation today to say that millions of urban families are considering the possibility of flight from the city to the country," Borsodi began, thus identifying his audience and speaking directly to them. The rest of the book alternates between memoir and how-to manual. It tells the story of Borsodi's own family and their successful experiment in self-sufficiency. With *Flight from the City*, Borsodi extended an invitation to those millions to join him in creating, as the subtitle put it, "a new way to family security."

Borsodi wanted it understood that those who took flight from the city did not have to retreat to some pre-industrial, technophobic past. Quite the contrary, like other decentralists, Borsodi was particularly enthusiastic about the way new technologies could remove the drudgery of much domestic work. After all, the growing availability of electricity and widespread car ownership made decentralizing production and population perfectly feasible. Nor was Borsodi exhorting Americans to return to the farm and to some warmed-over version of the Jeffersonian yeomanry: "Farming as an exclusive business, a full means of livelihood, has collapsed," he insisted, and went on, "Talk of 'back to the farms,' in this meaning, is in view of the condition of the farmers, the sheerest nonsense, almost a crime." But with unemployment standing at roughly 25 percent nationally when the book came out, Borsodi was just as adamant that the industrial system of production had also failed—"Laboring as an exclusive means of livelihood has also collapsed"—and went on to conclude: "Who, then, is for the moment safe and secure? The nearest to it is this home and acres-owning family in between, which combines the two. It is the only city of economic refuge anywhere in sight."[53]

Flight from the City is an appealing book, filled with an almost folksy common sense. By telling his own story, Borsodi managed to update the Jeffersonian vision of American independence on the land for an industrial, technological age. A review of the book in the *New York Times* was titled "Away From the City, But Not From Machines." If the great story of the nineteenth century had been the movement from country to city, then Borsodi believed the great story of the twentieth century would be the move of people from the city to small-scale farms like his, and he wrote the book to show Americans how to do it without pain or sacrifice. A review in the *Nation* did point out that to "go Borsodi," "you must have a husky wife with a positive taste for domestic production, with no desire to do anything else with her time, and a gift for home education as well...." Still, as the *Times* reviewer put it: "He and his wife hoped and believed that better health, stronger bodies, increased energy would be gained, thus making possible home-grown and home-prepared food, and apparently their convictions have been justified." Borsodi, the *Nation* wrote a bit archly, "documents what is at once the most romantic and the most concrete fulfillment to date of that vague ideal of landed self-sufficiency which has been bothering the American intelligentsia—and raising the value of Connecticut real estate—with such cumulative vigor."[54]

Catherine Bauer wrote that review for the *Nation*, and when she did she was part of the inner circle of the Regional Planning Association of America. She was a champion of affordable and public housing and not nearly as city-phobic as many other decentralists. That she wrote such a sharp review of Borsodi's book only underscores that although the decentralists might agree broadly on the problems facing American society, they did not necessarily agree on the solutions.

After her somewhat cheeky remarks about Connecticut real estate, Bauer took off the gloves: "*Flight from the City* in its wider prescriptions and implications [is] an exceedingly dangerous and even a dishonest piece of propaganda."[55]

By the early 1930s, according to the Census Bureau, just about as many people were leaving the cities and moving back to the country as were moving in other direction—a first perhaps in American history. By 1940, Philadelphia and Cleveland had actually experienced small population losses while other top-ten cities had grown almost not at all. No wonder, then, that by 1933 Borsodi's ideas had found an audience and Borsodi believed himself to be at the center of what seemed like a movement waiting for its leader. Riding that Zeitgeist took him from New York to Dayton.

He came at the invitation of Elizabeth Nutting, who held the wonderful if inscrutable job title of Director of the Division of Character Building for the Dayton's Council of Social Agencies. She and other social service leaders in Dayton had been trying to deal with the city's relief needs by patching together private and public sources of money. As the Depression deepened, they hit upon the idea of organizing "production units" as a way of assisting the unemployed and struggling families to achieve some measure of economic independence and security. They organized roughly a dozen such units and enrolled between 350 and 500 families.

Apparently, by late 1932 or early 1933, Nutting and the others had concluded that these "production units" within the city were not effective, or not fully adequate, and they began to think about moving some number of Dayton's unemployed families into the surrounding countryside and onto homestead farms. Nutting already admired Borsodi's writings, and now her work seemed to intersect his perfectly. He came to visit Dayton not once but three times. By May, he was the homesteading project's "official" adviser. The City of Dayton, it appeared, stood poised to "go Borsodi." The project had its public debut on May 14, 1933. The map of his homesteading scheme that appeared in the *Dayton Daily News* looked remarkably like Ebenezer Howard's map of Garden City.

Bear Creek ran through Walter Shaw's 160-acre farm, and in addition to making the place pretty, it provided an easy source of water. There was also an impressive brick house, of the sort that prosperous farmers built in the nineteenth century, and a few outbuildings as well. These were surely what attracted the Unit Committee to the property. But it must have provided a satisfying symbolism to Borsodi and the others that the Shaw place sat on Dayton-Liberty Road in the country, west of the city but just four miles from it. In the spring of 1933, Borsodi preached that decentralizing the nation's cities would indeed bring economic liberty to millions, and it would begin on Dayton-Liberty Road.

Whatever technical assistance Borsodi provided to those families who moved to the Shaw farm, he certainly used the Dayton experiment as a platform to broadcast his ideas and to demonstrate that they could be translated on a large scale. A month before the public dedication, Borsodi explained to readers of the *Nation* with barely restrained enthusiasm why Dayton was now the center of the decentralizing movement. "In one respect," he wrote,

> the Dayton movement is quite different from the hundreds of self-help, barter and scrip movements which have sprung up all over the country. It is an experiment in production for use as against production for sale or exchange. From the very beginning the leaders of the Dayton group have had in mind not only a temporary solution for the problem of the unemployed but a permanently better way of living for every man, woman, and child now struggling for happiness in our industrial civilization.[56]

The homesteaders on Dayton-Liberty Road, though Borsodi did not mention them specifically in this article, promised to make real Borsodi's vision of domestic rather than factory production and of an economy centered on the home rather than on the market. "Dayton is not waiting for economic planning in order to find some way of taming the machine," he trumpeted, "[i]t is decentralizing production, instead of integrating it...it is making the home, rather than the factory, the economic center of life." This was how Dayton would make "social history."[57]

June found Borsodi in New York, speaking before the Coordinating Council of that city's Welfare Council. He assured the gathering that the success of Dayton's homesteading project could be repeated to "rehabilitate" the unemployed of Gotham. [58] Later that year, when *Flight from the City* appeared in bookstores, readers found it dedicated "to the Homesteaders of Dayton, Ohio and to All who have Embarked on the Great Adventure."[59] At the end of 1933, Borsodi helped to organize a national homesteading conference in Dayton chaired by the president of Ohio State University.

Whatever else that great adventure might entail, it meant leaving the city. Catherine Bauer recognized that even if one could find a "husky wife," pursuing the Borsodi solution meant that "finally you must be actively convinced that schools, colleges, theaters, lectures, libraries, museums, art galleries, concerts, automobiles, doctors, dentists, hospitals, travel, leisure, and most forms of social intercourse or communal recreation belong to a world well lost."[60] Speaking at that national homesteading conference in December 1933, Reverend Charles Wesley Brashares, who was pastor of Dayton's Grace Methodist Church, made explicit the anti-urban alternative represented by the homesteading project with a blunt set of contrasts: "The city suffers extreme wealth and extreme poverty; the village is democratic. The city renders multitudes unemployed; on the land about the village there is always work to be done."[61]

And although Borsodi insisted that the Dayton experiment "will be modern and efficient," even his descriptions of it dripped with nostalgia for the simpler world of pre-urban America and of small-scale production:

> The outstanding fact about these homesteads is that they are designed not only for family gardening but for family weaving and sewing and family activities in all the crafts which have been neglected for so many years.... They are being brought back to the home in Dayton to fulfill the same functions that they fulfilled in the early American home—to furnish economic independence, security, and self-sufficiency.[62]

In Dayton, Borsodi had found a new frontier, and he found pioneers willing to settle it.

As Borsodi worked to draw the eyes of the nation to Dayton, the actual work on the Dayton-Liberty Road sputtered. The families who moved in with great fanfare in May 1933 planted some small gardens and broke ground on new housing, but by the end of that summer the residents were still living in huts, sheds, and even tents. In September, a fire destroyed one building on the site and with it a fair bit of equipment. The project's promoters also had to revise the cost per household figure up from $750 to over $1,000.

Borsodi remained undaunted, at least publicly and in front of national audiences. Though the dozen or so homesteading families on the Shaw farm struggled to build shelter, publicity for *Flight from the City* claimed that "hundreds" of families had already been successfully relocated to homestead farms near Dayton. Before the first vegetables had been planted along the Dayton-Liberty Road, Borsodi began talking about creating fifty more homestead sites in concentric rings around the city and settling upwards of 1,700 families on them.

By March 1934, this empire of homesteads had been scaled back to four, all located in townships in Dayton's hinterland. Three of them were planned much like the original homestead project; the fourth, a place called Valley View to be built west of Dayton on Carrollton Road, made the experiment in self-sufficiency available to black residents of Dayton. Although much of the New Deal excluded African Americans, either by design or by practice, the Unit Committee in Dayton at least imagined that their vision of decentralized independence would be available to all, if only on a segregated basis.

None of these homesteads, as it happens, ever took root. Residents in those outlying townships saw the homesteaders as invaders from the city who would raise property taxes and overcrowd the schools. Some of the settlers, so people had heard, were nudists. In Jefferson Township, home to the future Valley View, residents had a straightforward objection: they resented the "arbitrary implanting of a colony of thirty-five or more families of colored people with their lower standards of living" near white people who enjoyed by "inheritance and culture the higher standards of living."[63] It was a small foreshadowing of the racial conflicts that would erupt in post-WW II suburbia.

Borsodi and the homestead project faced an even more basic problem: capital. It is not clear that Borsodi saw the irony of that. Removing people from the economic grid, it turned out, required a fair bit of up-front money, and in this sense his essentially nineteenth-century vision of capitalism based on local production crashed up against the realities of twentieth-century capitalism based on finance. Borsodi and the others thought they could raise the money for the first Shaw project by selling their own "independence bonds." It did not work. So the project's leaders turned to the federal government to finance their dreams of independence. Surely Borsodi saw the irony there: the great decentralizer had to turn to an increasingly centralized federal government to fund his plans.

Borsodi's anti-urban vision for a decentralized America was of a piece with other anti-urbanists. On one hand—and he spent most of his time proselytizing about this—his vision was economic and focused on small-scale, home-based production and the destruction of large-scale industrial production. This was as much a moral imperative as it was an economic one. As he put it in *Flight from the City*:

> Domestic production, if enough people turned to it, would not only annihilate the undesirable and non-essential factory by depriving it of a market for its products.... It would release men and women from their present thralldom to the factory and make them masters of machines instead of servants to them; it would end the power of exploiting them which ruthless, acquisitive, and predatory men now possess; it would free them for the conquest of comfort, beauty and understanding.[64]

The city, for Borsodi, stood as a metaphor for the factory, for exploited wage labor, and for social alienation.

At the same time, Borsodi and others assumed that the flight from the city would be a flight from the state, from the control of an impersonal government, and from the wider sphere of public obligation that the Progressive urbanists had imagined. As Reverend Brasheres told participants at the Dayton homesteading conference, "The city presents the unsolved problems of self-government; the village governs itself."[65] For his part, Borsodi had made his views of government quite explicit in his book *This Ugly Civilization*: "For government is, at best, a necessary evil. It does not become less evil because it seems necessary."[66] Evil or not, Borsodi found government money necessary if the Dayton project was to succeed.

Immediately after Borsodi tried to rally enthusiasm in New York for homesteading, he jumped on a train and headed to Washington, D.C., where he had been authorized by the Dayton committee to request $2.5 million from Franklin Roosevelt's Reconstruction Finance Corporation. With that money, Borsodi told officials, he could build his network of self-sufficient homesteads and relocate upwards of 2,000 families. He did not get it.

But at virtually the same moment, Congress passed the National Industrial Recovery Act, and buried in that massive piece of legislation lay $25 million to fund homesteading projects, administered through the newly created Division of Subsistence Homesteads. Between 1933 and 1935, the division funded the creation of thirty-four homesteading projects.[67] By the fall of 1933, Borsodi had assurances from the division director, Milburn Wilson, that the project would receive a loan of $50,000. Not quite $2.5 million, but a start. Early in 1934, Borsodi submitted another loan application for just over $300,000 to fund the four new homestead projects and called publicly for the Roosevelt administration to commit $1 billion to the Division of Subsistence Homesteads.

A billion here, and a billion there, as Everett Dirksen famously said, and pretty soon we're talking about real money, but as far as Secretary of the Interior Harold Ickes was concerned, a loan of $309,400 was already real money and he had no intention of simply writing a check to Borsodi without some serious federal oversight. The first $50,000 loan had been issued before Ickes put new regulations into effect giving the federal government more authority over how these loans would be spent. It was not going to happen like that again.

Still, evil or not, the federal government seemed supportive of Borsodi's work in the spring of 1934. On April 1, the press reported an announcement by Harold Ickes that the Dayton, Ohio, homestead project would be enlarged with more loan money, and director Wilson continued to see Dayton as a vanguard in a national movement: "The Dayton project with its five units presents a demonstration in self-help which has many possibilities for repeatability in other areas."[68]

In the end, Borsodi and a majority of those on the Unit Committee governing board could not abide the federal strings attached to federal money. By a four-to-one vote, they decided to withdraw their loan application. Borsodi saw federal ownership of the land and the loss of local control over the money as turning his homesteads into something akin to Indian reservations. Gasping his last for the Dayton project, Borsodi thought he might find the money in a different, less regulated federal pot, but here too he failed. On July 10, he fled the city of Dayton, returning to his home in Suffern. Dayton had not made social history.

Looking back on it, Borsodi believed that asking for federal money in the first place had contributed to the demise of the Dayton project, dooming it to a fate of "red-tape, absentee bureaucratic dictation and politics."[69] Borsodi bristled at what he felt was an intrusion by the federal government, but some homesteaders found Borsodi to be just as overbearing, forcing them to adopt his particular brand of homesteading. As one told a Dayton journalist:

> The powers and functions of the unit as a self-governing group exist in name only, and are in reality being replaced by an increasingly rigorous paternalism. The spirit of this paternalism is *not* benevolent. It is stubborn, somewhat ill-tempered, and dictatorial. The spirit being engendered among the homesteaders as a result is one of resentment. Nothing could be further from the ideal of a cooperative community.[70]

Borsodi also seems to have misunderstood the relationship between his homestead units and the city from which homesteaders had fled. Borsodi might have imagined a return to canning and sewing, but it isn't clear that residents on the Shaw farm did. Some reported being forced by Borsodi and Nutting to purchase looms, for example, though no one had any intention of weaving on them. And as the *New York Times* inadvertently noted in a report on the proposed expansion of the Dayton project, the homesteads would all be "located within a ten-mile radius of the center of Dayton, thus enabling homesteaders to commute to their work in the city."[71] Hardly a flight from the city, except daily at 5 o'clock.

Borsodi's ill-fated adventure in Dayton underscored that, in the mid-1930s, many decentralists found themselves on the horns of a dilemma. On the one hand, the New Deal held out the promise of federal support—financial and otherwise—for their broad programs to decentralize the nation's population and its economy. The Division of Subsistence Homesteads wanted to help, and other New Deal agencies did as well. One Father Ligutti, for example, used money from the Farm Security Administration to create the Granger Homesteads, northwest of Des Moines. And given their enthusiasm for the promise of electric power, the decentralists also applauded the creation of the Rural Electrification Administration and the Tennessee Valley Authority. Clarence Stein, writing to FDR as head of the Regional Planning Association, enthused that the group "publicly endorsed your plan for the development of the [TVA]." No small irony there, since the TVA was accused by right-wing critics of being Exhibit A when they charged the New Deal with being a socialist plot. Economist Ralph Woods expressed a certain level of optimism with the New Deal because "for the first time centralization was officially recognized as a national problem, if not a national curse."[72]

On the other hand, the decentralists shared degrees of suspicion about the federal government. The National Housing Act of 1937, for example, provoked a particular outrage for two reasons. First, the act's goal of clearing urban slums and replacing them with better quality housing seemed designed to keep people living in the cities, not to encourage them to leave altogether. That simply reinforced everything already wrong with American society. Second, the act called for the construction of *public* housing that would be owned by the government and rented to these city dwellers. Nothing in the act made it possible for residents of these units to own their own property. The 1937 act only confirmed for Borsodi the reasons he walked away from the Dayton project. He railed that the New Deal made it "virtually impossible for anyone to own property, to engage in business large or small, without paying constant and obsequious tribute to bureaucracy."[73] As it happens, Catherine Bauer, who had written that harsh review of *Flight from the City* four years earlier, played a major role in writing the National Housing Act.

A genuine dilemma, then: Could decentralization be achieved in any other way except through the sponsorship of the federal government? Could the decentralizers use the federal government temporarily, as it were, without having to pay tribute to the bureaucracy? Borsodi recognized the problem. He remained convinced that governments "are the worst instruments for experimenting with

Catherine Bauer was an indefatigable advocate for public housing. Here, however, in a photo taken by her colleague and one-time lover Lewis Mumford, she has taken a break from that work. *Lewis Mumford Papers, Rare Book & Manuscript Library, University of Pennsylvania*

fundamental social reform to which a society might turn."[74] But where else could he and the others turn to undertake a large-scale flight from the city?

By the second half of the 1930s, the political cast of these questions had altered. With war looming, the stakes for the decentralists became more urgent, and they portrayed their efforts as a way for America to avoid the ideologies of Europe. Decentralism, and the nostalgia that went with it, became a middle path between fascism and communism. That was certainly the theme of two conferences held at Northwestern University in 1937 and 1938, organized by Baker Brownell.

Brownell grew up in St. Charles, Illinois, now at the far reaches of the ever-expanding suburban frontier of Chicago, but in the late nineteenth century an outpost of the rural Midwest. After an education both formal and experiential, Brownell wound up on the faculty at Northwestern University, where he began teaching courses in modern thought. Like so many others he fretted that the bonds of the human community were dissolving, though from his office in the philosophy department he interpreted this as being the result of the fragmentation of knowledge and understanding. His courses tried to help students integrate knowledge, and thus their understanding of the world, into something more unified and coherent. In the spring of 1937, Brownell invited a number of people to Evanston to talk about how to revive "the early American spirit of personal and community enterprise." He asked Ralph Borsodi to deliver the keynote address. The topic, naturally: decentralization.

Brownell specifically linked a revival of what he termed that American pioneer spirit of personal and community self-sufficiency with an opposition to communism and fascism. As the *Chicago Tribune* quoted Brownell: "Discouragement of collectivism, communist or Fascist, will be the chief objective of the conference." Number 3 among the conference themes underscored that point of view: "In view of the distrust of political, financial and social centralization and opposition to collectivism of any kind, how may the American pioneer spirit find its way through the present situation."[75] In the face of economic dislocation and global crisis, Brownell, Borsodi, and any number of other Americans thought the answer could be found not in some newfangled ideology but in an old-fashioned, refashioned American tradition.[76]

Dreaming of Broadacres

It is surely more than coincidental that the most celebrated architect of the American twentieth century was also the most aggressively anti-urban. Frank Lloyd Wright enjoyed making provocative, outrageous statements of the sort that would get him quoted in the press. But he reserved some of his best invective for the American city. "To look at the plan of a great City," he wrote, "is to look at something like the cross-section of a fibrous tumor." In a speech in St. Louis, he told the American Municipal Association that "The modern city is a place for banking and prostitution and very little else."[77] Good stuff.

Nor is it coincidental that Wright arrived at the apex of his profession in the 1930s. Not only did he do some of his most stunning work in those years, but the ideas he had been developing since the turn of the century found a more receptive audience. Wright did not join the Regional Planning Association, nor did he have anything to do with the New Deal. He was an architect, first and last, but he also believed in decentralization and gave it the imprimatur of high architectural theory and his own indomitable celebrity.

Born and raised on a farm near Madison, Wisconsin, after the Civil War, Wright migrated to Chicago, where he worked in Louis Sullivan's studio. By the turn of the twentieth century, he had established his own office and was quite successful building large single-family homes for well-to-do clients, especially in the near-west Chicago suburb of Oak Park. These were the "prairie style" houses that first brought him fame. But Wright's tumultuous personal life ran afoul of suburban respectability. He had an affair with the wife of a client, abandoned his own wife and six children, and then there was that sordid business at Taliesin, his compound near Spring Green, Wisconsin, that involved an arson fire and a murder. Wright's career went into something of a decline. Between the wars, Wright regained his professional stature. He wrote to Fiske Kimball, director of the Philadelphia Museum of Art, in 1928 and quoted Mark Twain: "I have been reading my obituaries to a considerable extent the past year or two…the reports of my death are greatly exaggerated."[78] These were the years when Wright promoted what he called "organic" architecture, of which his 1936 house Fallingwater south of Pittsburgh is the most spectacular exemplar.

Wright shared two positions with the other decentralists. Like them, Wright wanted to denounce the city and enjoy its benefits at the same time. His own commissions depended on clients firmly rooted in urban money. Fallingwater, after all, was the vacation home for the Kaufmann family, department store barons from Pittsburgh, and is within an easy day trip from the Steel City; his last commission, of course, came from the Guggenheim Museum and sits on New York's Fifth Avenue. Wright established his studios in rural Wisconsin and at Taliesin West in Arizona, but late in his life he kept a permanent suite at the Plaza Hotel.

Likewise, Wright believed in modern technology, and he shared the decentralist faith that technological advances made it possible to dream of a decentralized future. Wright pioneered the use of concrete and steel and glass in bold new ways in his buildings. But he also loved the automobile, and when he imagined his brave new world, it was filled with cars speeding unimpeded along very big roads.

The buildings speak eloquently for Wright's inventive genius. Less well remembered, perhaps, is that Wright also saw himself from the very beginning as a planner. Over the course of his career, he drew plans for at least two different new developments. Before the First World War, Wright began work on a summer retreat complex in the Bitter Root Valley in Montana. The plan was financed by Chicago railroad money and it went bankrupt during the war. In 1932, he unveiled a much more comprehensive, more elaborate project called Broadacre City.[79]

Wright launched the idea in a book fittingly titled *The Disappearing City*. In that book, Wright described the city with typical hyperventilation: "Like some tumor grown malignant, the city, like some cancerous growth, is become a menace to the future of humanity."[80] The title was not descriptive but, rather, wishful—the city was not, in fact, disappearing. As if by force of his own will, Wright thought he could simply make the city go away.

His alternative to it, as represented by Broadacre City, relied on the new technologies of decentralization, the car first and foremost. "No hard road in the new city would have less than three lanes," Wright described, and added that the "Communal Center" of his new city "would be an automobile objective situated near some major highway."[81] The magazine *Free America* put the book on its must-read list.

Car technology to one side, Wright's vision of the future leaned heavily on his romance with the past. Early in the book, Wright paralleled his "organic modern architecture" with the "spirit that built the majestic cathedrals of the middle-ages." Later, he conjured the ghost of William Jennings Bryan by writing "Without the farmer the cities would starve and go naked." In fact, Broadacre City can be seen as Wright's attempt, right down to the geometry of squares, to recreate and update the nineteenth-century homestead. "In the City of Tomorrow," Wright announced, "ground space will be reckoned by the acre: an acre to the family." "Pioneering," he went on, "now lies along this new frontier: decentralization." Elsewhere he echoed this sentiment with more insidious language: "The White man must pioneer again along the New Frontier. The true course for Democracy is now Decentralization."[82]

The goal for Wright, and for the other decentralists, was not simply to rearrange people and space. Rather, in so doing, they all believed they could restore the social cohesion, unity, and democratic community that the city had destroyed. In looking back to medieval Europe for his analogy, Wright believed that the "medieval spirit was nearest the communal, democratic spirit of anything we know. The common-spirit of a people disciplined by means and methods and materials, in common, will have—and with no recognized formula—great unity." In this sense, Broadacre "demands a return to democratically endowed village life in modern geometric functional form." More bluntly, Wright made the equation between physical space and the nature of politics: "Let us repeat: as Monarchy was the ideal of Centralization…so Democracy is the ideal of reintegrated decentralization."[83] When Wright elaborated his Broadacre City ideas in a new book, he titled it *When Democracy Builds.*

In 1934–35, interns at Taliesin built a 12-square-foot model of the "city." It went on tour, stopping at a number of places including the Industrial Arts Exposition held at New York's Rockefeller Center. Daniel had come to the lion's den. That is where Lewis Mumford saw it, and he told readers of *The New Yorker* that it was the only reason to go to the expo. He called it a "new type of decongested city that the motorcar… [has] made technically possible." Broadacre City, Mumford wrote, "is both a generous dream and a rational plan." The model represented a new city four miles square, with woods and park spaces, arterial roads to carry the car traffic in and out, separated from schools and other public amenities. But the central idea of the plan is residential. The houses are standardized and made for people with lower incomes—here, Wright responded to the charge that his was an architecture for the rich—each sitting on a plot of five acres complete with a workshop and a garden. "Wright is a man of the open country," Mumford told his readers, "and the basis of his city is private cultivated land.…" Mumford concluded his review by saying that with Broadacre City, "Wright's philosophy of life and his mode of planning have never been shown to better advantage."[84]

Mumford and Wright carried on a thirty-year correspondence, though as one might expect from two prickly, egotistical men, even amid their expressions of admiration and friendship there was a great deal of prickliness and ego. Mumford was the younger of the two—when Wright wanted to condescend, he referred to Mumford as "my young friend"—and he admired Wright a great deal. He wanted to admire him more, one senses, but Wright's personality and his politics got in the way. They broke for nearly a decade after Wright joined the isolationists opposing American involvement in World War II.

One senses, too, that Mumford wished Wright would have been a more rigorous thinker, more analytic and less bombastic. They both shared a disdain for the modern city, but as Mumford described the difference between Wright's anti-urban vision and his own in a 1936 letter, Wright "dismisses megalopolis with a wave of his hand," whereas Mumford "[took] it apart stone by stone, from foundation to pinnacle."[85]

It was never intended, of course, to be a real place. It was a model, a vision, and a polemic. It was a three-dimensional diatribe against the modern city and a clarion call for decentralizing the nation. But through his admiration,

Mumford saw the essential flaw with Broadacre City. In a letter to Wright he complained: "Economically speaking—apart from the fact that you guarantee a minimum amount of land—the pattern of Broadacre City too closely resembles that of a contemporary suburb with a few manufacturing industries."[86]

Exactly right. Since Broadacre City was only a model, it did not need to be located in a specific locale. Wright produced a geography of nowhere, which foreshadowed in many ways the coming geography of everywhere.

Dateline: Central Florida

It was not another Florida swampland promotion to be sure, but it did have a "too good to be true" ring to it:

"NOT in the hurricane belt"
"Located 'where there's magic in the good earth'"
"Established on a site of unusual natural beauty"
"A variety of cash income opportunities"[87]

The place is called Melbourne Village, about halfway down Florida's east coast, and in 1946 Elizabeth Nutting, Margaret Hutchinson, and several others left Dayton to move there. The group purchased roughly 1,000 acres of what was then largely empty scrubland and built the homesteading paradise they dreamt of in Dayton but had been unable to create. As the umbrella for the project, they founded the American Homesteading Foundation.

Their ambitions had clearly been tempered by experience. They made no claims to be a national model, or to point the way to the future for the rest of the nation. A refuge, to judge by some comments, rather than a harbinger; a place for personal rather than political agendas. In an appeal published in the first issue of the *Melbourne Village News,* the writer stated simply: "Here is an opportunity not to be cast aside. Those who lived on the land in the last depression of the thirties, lived exceedingly well, and knew no scarcity. Already the storm clouds are gathering for us, and no one knows when the deluge will start, how long it will last, or how hard it will be. But it's coming." Looking back on her experience, Margaret Hutchinson summed up Melbourne Village by saying, "All that anybody claims for Melbourne Village is that it is a good way of life in a troubled world."[88]

Settlers bought a membership in the foundation and got in return a deed to a small plot—half an acre, one acre, perhaps as big as two. Although settlers built their own houses and grew what they wanted to grow, they also contributed to building a shared community life. Among the first things they did was to lay out and grade dirt roads. They named one of them Dayton Boulevard. By early 1948, according to the *Miami Herald,* this "planned community for creative living" had nine houses completed or under construction.[89]

It is still there, incorporated as its own municipality in 1957 with a mayor and council. It feels the pressure from the real estate development that has swallowed up so much of the rest of the state, and several years ago they drew up a plan to preserve the character of this 6-square-mile oasis. The American Homesteading Foundation still exists too, and it maintains the village's shared spaces. In Melbourne Village now live roughly 700 people, in modest houses in a place they are proud to call home.

Nutting and Hutchinson came to Florida inspired by Ralph Borsodi, and he remained an inspiration for the original settlers, though he was an irregular and perhaps not altogether constructive presence. After he left Dayton, Borsodi returned to Suffern, New York, and founded the School for Living, an educational operation promoting everything from organic farming to alternative banking. Things did not turn out much better there. In 1940, Borsodi had been forced to resign as the president of the Independence Foundation, Inc., the financial entity he had created to finance his experiment in Suffern.[90]

During his stay in Melbourne Village, Borsodi dreamed that he could turn the School for Living into the University of Melbourne. It never really got off the launch pad, in part because Borsodi's own racial politics proved increasingly embarrassing during the 1960s. The planned Valley View in Dayton notwithstanding, Borsodi had worked in the 1950s with several school districts to help them circumvent desegregation orders—and he did not want to admit any black students to the University of Melbourne's programs. It disbanded finally in 1969, and Borsodi returned north, this time to Exeter, New Hampshire.

Borsodi died in the fall of 1977. Six months earlier, the *New York Times* ran a story that proved to be an inadvertent obituary of sorts. Reporter William Tucker went out to Rockland County, New York, where Borsodi had established four homesteading communities right after the war. The homesteaders, almost all from New York City, came with nothing and, in true pioneer fashion, cut down trees to build their own houses. Thirty years later, the remaining original settlers, many now quite elderly, shared their memories with Tucker. Mostly they looked back with fondness—nostalgia—on their experiment: on their time spent raising chickens and goats, cooking over wood fires, and drawing their own water. "When my parents came up to visit," Greta Mason recalled, "they were hysterical. They thought we had gone out of our minds. But we loved it. It was a great adventure. Our kids said if we ever moved back to the apartment they'd murder us."[91]

By the late 1970s, however, these communities of self-sufficient homesteaders faced the pressures of affluence. Rockland County was not nearly as far from New York City as it had been in the 1940s, and real estate prices were booming. As Tucker reported, "Many of their custom-built homes are now in the $70,000–$90,000 bracket [mid-$300,000s, in current dollars] and are among the most-sought after dwellings in Rockland County." Borsodi's pioneer frontier had become desirable suburbia in the space of a generation.

The old residents were more equivocal about Borsodi himself. Whatever he may have learned in Dayton, the capacity to let people deviate from his plans or pursue their own dreams was not one of them. "Borsodi had all sorts of plans on how we were going to make our own clothes and grow our own food," cackled eighty-three-year-old Evelyn McGregor, "but as soon as we got our house built, we kicked him out." A fitting remembrance in its own way.

Still, there remained something attractive about Borsodi's vision and something powerful in the forces he tried to tap: the desire for some level of independence within the context of a supportive community. Retired now to sunnier climes, Louis Sabini looked back on his time in the Skyview settlement and mused: "It's been a lifetime experience. We proved to ourselves that you don't have to be completely alone in this world."[92]

The homesteads in both Rockland County, New York, and Melbourne, Florida, grew in the immediate postwar moment, but they represented a last gasp rather than a new beginning. Whatever large audience decentralists had for their ideas in the 1930s had trickled away during the Second World War. Some decentralists, notably Lewis Mumford, hoped that war, rather than economic depression, might offer the necessary impetus to move people out of the cities. After all, they pointed out, large concentrations of people and centralized industrial production were both vulnerable to enemy attack. If the war forced a decentralization of manufacturing and drove people out of the city, then a positive good might come out of it.

Things didn't happen that way, of course. The war certainly did move Americans around, most dramatically to the West Coast, where the Pacific War demanded boats and planes and troops. But this was hardly the decentralization that Mumford imagined, nor a return to small-scale self-sufficiency of the sort Borsodi had preached. The war made decentralism and its emphasis on smallness seem small and trivial indeed, and in the buoyant, forward-looking America that emerged after the war, the decentralists' message of foreboding and their call to return to a simpler, smaller America no longer resonated. *Free America,* which once the war started had ceased to be a venue for the debate of decentralist ideas but became, rather, a bulletin of various projects around the country, stopped publication altogether in 1947. In that same year, Harper and Brothers came out with a new edition of Borsodi's *Flight from the City*.

In a new preface to the book, Borsodi vented even more angrily at the federal government and at the rest of us who had been seduced by the goodies provided by big government: "The masses of people are frantically calling upon Washington for old age pensions, unemployment compensation, and other forms of security from the cradle to the grave," he complained. "Most self-respecting Americans used to" provide these necessities for themselves, he went on, until "the gospel of depending upon the government began to be substituted for the gospel of independence."[93]

The *Washington Post* gave the new edition a small dismissive squib: "Prophet of Doom Repeats Solution."[94]

4 NEW DEAL, NEW TOWNS

THE ANTI-URBAN NEW DEAL

It is hardly worth saying that the New Deal had a tremendous impact on American cities. How could it not, given that the industrial sector of the economy was in near collapse and the vast bulk of that sector had been urbanized for nearly two generations? The mass unemployment. The bread lines. The evictions. The marches in the streets. These were all urban phenomena, and Franklin Roosevelt had to address them.

Yet it is probably fair to say that although the effects of many New Deal policies—beginning with the National Industrial Recovery Act passed in FDR's first 100 days—were felt in cities, the New Deal did not have an urban policy as such, certainly not the way it had an agricultural and rural focus. Indeed, it is also probably fair to say that significant parts of the New Deal were shaped by the decentralizing ideas that swirled in the 1920s. Certainly, many New Dealers were not afraid to use the power of the federal government to advance their agendas—though Roosevelt himself was perhaps more reluctant about this than some of his advisers—but to a remarkable degree those agendas were shaped by some of the same anti-urban assumptions circulating more widely, especially the idea that industry and people ought to be decentralized.

In fact, it is not clear that Roosevelt had much use for cities at all. Rexford Tugwell called his boss a "child of the country," who, like so many whose attitudes were shaped in the late nineteenth century, saw the city as "a perhaps necessary nuisance," and he found Roosevelt's progressivism to be "rooted in country soil." He seems to have been altogether uneasy to get the federal government involved in urban affairs because "if the Federal Government started to finance cities, it would give us some kind of obligation to see that they were run right." Indeed, the thirteen-volume collection of Roosevelt's *Public Papers and Addresses* does not include "cities" or "urban" in its exhaustive Cumulative Topical Table. The listings under "Agriculture," on the other hand, run to nearly a full page. No wonder that a 1940 biography of the president called him the "Country Squire in the White House."[1]

Roosevelt's view of cities shaped a paradox about his presidency that has not received as much attention as so many other aspects of his transformative New Deal. Though critics, journalists, and historians have debated the extent to which FDR restructured the American economy, centralized the power of the federal government, or reoriented the relationship Americans have with their president, they have not commented much on how when Roosevelt looked at American cities, he wanted to decentralize them. The dilemma for him was not unlike the one Ralph Borsodi faced in Dayton. Could a newly centralized and powerful central government achieve a decentralized nation?

We can see this dilemma in FDR's enthusiasm particularly for the Civilian Conservation Corps, which offered urban men that chance not just for a job but also for the restorative effects of being in the country, close to the earth. Perhaps the most ambitious manifestation of the paradox could be seen in the form of the

The country squire with some of his CCC boys: President Franklin Roosevelt shares lunch with Civilian Conservation Corps workers at Shenandoah National Park. The CCC was just one of FDR's New Deal programs to deal with the crisis of urban, industrial America by decentralizing the city. *National Park Service Historic Photograph Collection*

dams, flood control, and electrification projects created by the Tennessee Valley Authority. The TVA came as close as the New Deal ever did to large-scale, centralized planning, but its purpose was in line with what other decentralists advocated. For those who wanted to decentralize the population and the economy, electricity promised all the benefits of modern life with the need for urban concentration. Much of the TVA's work involved environmental repair in a region suffering from deforestation and erosion. But the electricity generated by those hydroelectric dams had the potential to transform the economy of the entire watershed, making it possible for people to earn a living there. They would no longer have to flee to the cities.

New Deal approaches to housing aimed for similar decentralizing goals, proposing to use the federal government to move people out of the city. After all, Roosevelt himself, according to Tugwell, never "had a vision of the city as a high expression of human aspiration. He always did, and always would, think people better off in the country."[2]

Decentralizing the Housing Market

For Catherine Bauer, a member of the Regional Planning Association of America in the 1920s, the New Deal seemed to be her moment. Unlike many of her colleagues in that group, she was not afraid to enter the world of politics to achieve her policy goals. In 1934, impressed with what she had seen of public housing on a European trip, she wrote *Modern Housing,* in which she argued that some of those European experiments ought to be carried out here. On the strength of her experience and expertise, she influenced some of the early housing projects undertaken under the auspices of the Public Works Administration's (PWA) Housing Division. Among the most influential of these was the Carl Mackley Houses, built in 1935 in Philadelphia by the American Federation of Hosiery Workers with a limited-dividend subsidized loan from the PWA. The push for public housing, clearly a high priority for American cities, reached a climax of sorts in 1937, with the passage of the Wagner Public Housing Act, the second major housing act of the New Deal. Bauer, along with the veteran Progressive reformer Mary Simkhovitch, helped draft that legislation.

The act proved an incomplete triumph at best. As it emerged in its final form, it provided money for slum clearance, but it limited the availability of public housing to the poor, cementing the equation between public housing and poverty that haunts it to this day. The act gave a great deal of discretion to local authorities over where such housing could be built, and it created strict construction cost limits for projects. Thus did public housing become synonymous with bad neighborhoods and shoddy building. Bauer and Simkhovitch might have helped draft the bill, but the final version of it had the footprints of the real estate lobby all over it.[3]

Roosevelt's embrace of public housing might have been flaccid, but his commitment to homeownership was unequivocal. During his first term, the federal government entered the private housing market in a big way. Bauer and the others offered their models of subsidized housing as an alternative to a private sector that had failed to provide adequate housing for the urban working class in the 1920s and that had ground to a halt altogether in the 1930s. The Housing Act of 1934 put the power of the federal government to work in order to stimulate the housing industry.

In certain ways, the Housing Act expanded the Home Owners' Loan Corporation (HOLC), which had been created in 1933 to staunch the flood of foreclosures by offering homeowners refinancing with long-term loans at low interest rates. In urban areas, HOLC assumed roughly 15 percent of mortgages and thus halved the number of foreclosures between 1933 and 1937. The Housing Act's most significant creation, though, was surely the Federal Housing Administration (FHA). The FHA, in turn, created loan programs to bolster the private housing market. It insured private mortgages, making it less risky for banks to lend, it lengthened the duration of mortgages, and it reduced the monthly payments for home buyers, as well as the down payment to qualify for mortgages, thereby opening up the mortgage market to those with less cash on hand. And for those who did not want to buy a new house, the FHA made loans available for home renovation and repair.

James Moffett served as FDR's first head of the FHA. Shortly after the Housing Act that created his new job was passed, Moffett published an explanation of its goals in the pages of the *New York Times*. He began by insisting that the FHA enjoyed wide support across many sectors of the economy: "men prominent in many lines of business, finance and industry, including labor leaders...building trades, employers' associations, publishers of business, architectural and general magazines, real estate boards and manufacturers of almost every type." With their blessing, Moffett went on, the FHA was poised to make "effective use of private rather than government capital."

More than any other sector of the economy, the construction industry stood poised to benefit from these FHA programs. As Moffett reminded readers, there was a wide consensus that "there cannot be complete recovery with so important an industry as construction paralyzed as it has been for five years or more." And he was certainly right about that. Since 1928, new housing construction had dropped off by about 95 percent, and the amount spent by homeowners to repair and renovate their properties had dropped during the early 1930s from

$55 million to a scant $500,000 a year. Moffett was confident that the FHA "will have the effect of immediately putting the construction industry back to work with the transfer of its wages into merchandise purchasing power and the subsequent stimulation of economic recovery and restoration of normal conditions."[4]

It certainly seemed to work. In November 1935, roughly a year after the FHA launched its lending programs, the Federal Home Loan Board reported that October had been "the nation's biggest home-building month in four years," rising 109 percent over the previous October. For its part, the FHA was quick to take the credit, and it also reported that its lending activity had already topped $1 billion.[5] Two years into the FHA's work, economist Arthur Weimer tallied the results and concluded that "the Federal Housing Administration provides an example of federal underwriting of private enterprise." He did not want to comment on "whether or not this is a 'proper' function of government," but no doubt the housing and mortgage industries thought it was.[6]

Weimer's research also hinted at how the FHA's programs would affect the overall drift of the housing market. One of the FHA's initial programs provided loan money to repair and renovate buildings. Though Moffett had insisted that the loans would be made "for work on all types of buildings," Weimer charted that, after two years, 54 percent of that loan money went to single-family residences and less than 18 percent went to buildings listed as "multiple residential." Nor, as Weimer saw it, was FHA money supporting housing construction for those most in need. "The effects of the FHA program will probably only reach those in the low-income groups indirectly by a process of 'filtering up.'" By this he meant that as new construction attracted residents currently living in "older residences, rents of the latter will tend to decline, and those in the lower-income groups can then command more desirable housing facilities." James Moffett had hinted as much from the outset. He promised that "loans for modernizations will be 'character loans.' They will be based solely on the character of the home owner, and his ability to re-pay out of his income."[7]

In other words, from the outset the FHA worked to subsidize lower density, single-family housing for largely middle-class (or at least securely employed) people. Moffett's reassurance that loans would be based on "character" also foreshadowed the FHA's practice of redlining—discriminatory lending that often involved drawing red lines, quite literally, around certain city neighborhoods to define areas that would not receive FHA loans. These neighborhoods tended to have the oldest housing stock, the poorest city residents, and were more often than not black sections of town.[8] Thus, FHA (and HOLC) loan criteria effectively excluded African Americans (and to a lesser extent Jews) and the poor. But it bears mentioning that, by subsidizing new construction and by steering loans to rehabilitate single-family houses rather than denser multi-family buildings, the

FHA's policies also encouraged the neglect of the older, more densely built urban cores; promoted building on the urban edges; and after the war, helped fuel the boom of suburban construction. Racial and ethnic prejudices doubtless played a role in the way the FHA loaned its money, but so, too, did the anti-urban enthusiasm of decentralization and its emphasis on reducing housing density.

When compared to the failure of a broad public housing program to gain traction during the New Deal, the FHA's success in "underwriting private enterprise" provides a wonderful example of how Americans prefer their government interventions to be indirect, hidden from plain sight, and funneled through the private sector. But it also underscores that from Roosevelt on down, many New Dealers wanted to use the power of an expanded central government to decentralize the nation's cities. Public housing was decidedly a city phenomenon and so was given short shrift; the private, single-family home was the American dream, and the government would make it come true.

New Deal, New Towns

Just before Franklin Roosevelt took the presidential oath of office, Clarence Stein wrote him a letter. In it, he outlined what he thought would be necessary for the "location and design of new communities with industrial decentralization with the object of building a usable environment." In order to create new towns successfully, Stein wrote, they had to be planned: "All of our experience of the past indicates that this cannot be attained by speculative land development, individual house building, and chaotic town and village growth. It can only be secured by planning and building complete integrated communities."[9] Case in point: Radburn, New Jersey.

On the face of it, it might seem a bit presumptuous for an architect and real estate developer to be offering advice to the new president. But Stein and FDR were already acquainted. The two had had lunch in Albany in 1931 to discuss regional planning, and Roosevelt had attended an RPAA conference at the University of Virginia in 1931. His wife Eleanor served on the RPAA board. Roosevelt expressed a keen interest in regional planning, or so Stein reported, and in particular in figuring out ways to revive small-scale farming and industry and to move people from the cities back to the country. In fact, as Tugwell described him, Roosevelt sounded positively Borsodian. "He saw no reason," Tugwell wrote a decade or so after Roosevelt's death, "why millions of [urban] families might not have subsistence farms. He persisted, even in contending that urban workers could succeed in part-time farming, thus relieving city congestion." According to Tugwell, Roosevelt "recoiled instinctively" from that "city congestion."[10] With FDR's election as president, Stein and others felt that decentralization had arrived in Washington.

Just how the federal government would promote decentralization proved to be complicated. Those involved in the back-to-land, subsistence homesteading movement could not, or would not, abide any partnership with the New Deal. Mumford, too, had a phobia of the federal government, believing that decentralization needed to bubble up, somehow, from the grassroots. Stein, among the RPAA members, wanted to work with Washington.

In the wake of the Dayton experiment—though perhaps not precisely because of it—the New Dealers created a new umbrella agency to run a variety of programs designed to move Americans to better locations. Fittingly, they called it the Resettlement Administration (RSA), and it was created by Executive Order 7027 in April 1935. Roosevelt put Rexford Tugwell in charge. It had been his idea in the first place.

When Roosevelt summoned him to Washington to join the "brain trust," Tugwell was an economics professor at Columbia University; after he left Washington, he served—briefly—as the head of New York City's Planning Commission. But despite these New York connections, Tugwell shared FDR's general attitude about the contrast between city and country. The overarching goal of the RSA was to "rehabilitate" rural America. By this, Tugwell meant both a transformation and a return. A transformation—of farming practices, of agricultural economics (this had been Tugwell's academic specialty), of the perceptions of rural life in the first place—in order to create the conditions for Americans to leave the cities and return to the country, where they belonged. The problems of the urban unemployed, in Tugwell's view, were the problems of temporary relief; rural America required a more ambitious, more fundamental program if life there was to be sustained. "Resettlement's goal," Tugwell told the nation, "is to lay the basis of a sound and permanent reconstruction of rural life." That life, Tugwell added, was "the parent and protector of American individualism."[11]

The RSA had the same grab-bag quality of so much of the New Deal. It took responsibility for resettling farmers driven off their land and for trying to rehabilitate rural areas to keep farmers on their land, and it tried to coordinate a program of more rational land use. It also recorded its work photographically and even sponsored the Pare Lorentz film *The Plow that Broke the Plains*. And like so much of the New Deal, the RSA did not last long. After about a year and half, it disappeared, its programs absorbed by the new Farm Security Administration.

The project that generated the most excitement, at least for those who wanted urban decentralization, fell under the RSA's Division of Suburban Resettlement. This division would undertake to build satellite cities—twenty of them in all: ten around the ten largest cities and another ten around mid-sized cities, all shaped by the most "advanced town-planning theories." Some people called them "Tugwelltowns."

Observers saw a grand decentralizing strategy where there might or might not have been any. "After the present PWA [Public Works Administration] slum-clearance projects are finished," the *New Republic*'s Jonathan Mitchell wrote enthusiastically, "it is very doubtful whether the government will undertake further low-cost-housing construction in congested city areas."[12] Here, then, was how the New Deal would undertake urban decentralization on a massive scale—one hand of the New Deal clearing urban ghettos and another moving displaced people out of the city altogether.[13]

By the end of 1935, those hypothetical twenty new towns had been scaled back to four. In the final event, only three were built: Greenbelt, Maryland; Greendale, Wisconsin; and Greenhills, Ohio. Even thus reduced in number, they were watched as important experiments. According to Henry Churchill, "The four [sic] new towns being built by the Suburban Resettlement Division of the Resettlement Administration constitute the most far-reaching and significant effort in housing today. They are the first large-scale attempt in this country to integrate all the factors that go to make a community." And to put these new towns into some large perspective, Churchill continued that "next to the TVA [they were] the most significant of the New Deal's attempts to be a new deal."[14]

For some, the Suburban Resettlement's greenbelt towns represented, finally, a serious attempt to bring the Garden City idea to the United States. But in so doing, the RSA thoroughly Americanized the idea. Looking back on it, Lewis Mumford insisted, "had it not been for the ideas that the Regional Planning Association...put into circulation during the twenties, the Greenbelt Towns undertaken by the Re-Settlement Administration in 1935 would have been inconceivable."[15] That might be a tad self-serving on Mumford's part, but it is certainly fair to say that the greenbelt towns owe at least as much to Clarence Stein and Radburn, New Jersey, as they do to Ebenezer Howard.

Each town plan grew from the specifics of its location—topography, existing transportation infrastructure, even the peculiar preferences of the local residents who might move into them. But they shared some broad similarities as well. Straight from Radburn, each town took the idea of segregating pedestrian and vehicular traffic to make the streets safe in an automobile age. In a short article about the new towns, written in 1940, the *New York Times* crowed almost exclusively about the traffic—the lack of accidents or even arrests for moving violations. Along with this, the towns shared the superblock concept, also borrowed from Radburn. Finally—and this, too, is more Radburn than Garden City—the new towns would decidedly not have their own industrial base. The expectation was that residents would commute back into the city for their jobs. This represented a disappointment for the decentralists and a departure from earlier New Deal impulses. As the *New Republic* stiffly pointed out, "It will be noted that, to some degree, this runs counter to President Roosevelt's frequently expressed wish to bring about the decentralization of industry."[16] Perhaps, but this was the model developed at Radburn, after all, and that seemed to have been a success.

Besides, however much the New Dealers wanted decentralization, they had also learned some lessons from their experience with subsistence homesteads and with Ralph Borsodi. The greenbelt towns grew in response to those. As Jonathan Mitchell reminded his readers, "For many months, the New Deal objective was a community in which the inhabitants would support themselves partly by work in a privately owned factory, partly by the cultivation of truck gardens and fruit orchards." That hadn't worked, or at least Tugwell was no longer interested in that kind of arrangement, and the *New Republic's* Henry Churchill for one was pleased that the new towns would not go down this road: "It is important to note that there is nothing of the subsistence-homestead idea in these towns. The inhabitants will depend on nearby industry for support, not on not-quite farms."[17] Borsodi must have bristled at that.

Though the greenbelt towns could solve the technical problems of relocating urbanites into attractive new settlements, complete with safe streets and cul-de-sacs, the RSA had larger ambitions. They wanted these towns to foster a rich civic life and a larger sense of community. That might be done in two ways.

First, the new towns could provide a set of amenities designed to nurture community activity and feeling. That posed a potential problem, according to Mitchell:

> Perhaps the chief unsolved question is how elaborate these communal facilities should be. A minority of Resettlement Administration experts are opposed to such things as, for example, community theatres, studios for groups interested in painting, music and handicrafts, tennis courts and golf links. With every evidence of moral indignation, they assert that it would be intolerable and un-American for the government to foist the more abundant life upon people seeking only cheap living quarters.[18]

Ironically, although some inside the RSA worried that providing theaters and art studios in the new towns would simply inflame the political opposition, the other experiment set up in the towns to create a shared community was in some ways more radical: a cooperative economy. Though the primary source of jobs for new town residents would remain in the city and in the private sector, the local retail enterprises inside the towns were set up as co-ops.

Tugwell was, after all, an economist, interested in developing a more collective economy because he believed it was a better way to achieve a more organic society than, say, cultural activities.[19] In a sense, his notion of retail co-ops rec-ognized the consumer nature of the American economy and tried to make it more democratic. It was an implicit critique of Borsodi and the other subsistence homesteaders who clung to a nostalgic belief that Americans could be turned into producers again. The *New York Herald Tribune* expressed some sarcasm about this aspect of the new towns: "Those who lament that America's last frontier is gone should visit Greenbelt, Md., the little resettlement town founded by the New Deal…[where residents] have voluntarily decided to try something never tried before in a modern American community. They are about to buy, and oper-ate for themselves, all the stores which serve their town." Still, *Business Week* sent a reporter out to Greenbelt to investigate just how those stores were doing.[20]

When a University of Maryland political scientist, Hugh Bone, came to visit Greenbelt a year after its first residents had moved in, he found much that encouraged him. In particular, he commented on the "intense community life and civic activity" in the town, and he spent some time detailing it. Observers who were rooting for the new towns saw what they wanted to find: an answer to the housing problem, to the urban problem, to the problem of meaningful com-munity. Bone declared the first year of Greenbelt's existence a victory and in that victory a hope for the future:

> The Greenbelt experiment during the past year has been a particular suc-cess in the humanitarian and psychological sense. Whether it will be able to repay the federal government financially and become self-supporting is still conjecture. If it is able to fulfill the latter test, there will be a great impetus in the direction of "garden cities," which bid fair to revolutionize urban life.[21]

The *New Republic's* Churchill and Mitchell were similarly hopeful. Each acknowledged that Greenhills, Greenbelt, and Greendale represented small, ten-tative beginnings, but crucial ones nonetheless. "These towns are not a panacea, they will not solve the problem of housing for the masses," Churchill concluded, "but they will be a demonstration of what new civic patterns can do towards making a better and more pleasant way of living. We have inherited smoke and stones and dirt, chaos and confusion: these experiments may help lead us back to air and grass and sunlight, order and harmony." Mitchell was even more airy about it: "The new communities do not represent the more abundant life; they are merely models of what the more abundant life will be like, when and if the government provides it."[22]

Grass and sunlight. Order and harmony. An abundant life. These remained the things that defined the American vision of the good life. The industrial city had destroyed them. Industrial capitalism could neither restore them nor replace them with something better. For a brief moment during the Great Depression, some thought the New Deal could provide them.

In the Greenhills

Traveling just ten miles north from downtown Cincinnati put a person well out into the country in 1935. A landscape of gently rolling hills, crisscrossed by a number of streams and creeks all making their way southward to the Ohio River. The land had been cleared in the nineteenth century and was still farmed by some of the descendants of those settlers. By the mid-1930s, farmers were mostly raising dairy and livestock, but some grew crops and tended orchards. And in 1935 the Resettlement Administration began buying 6,000 acres of this land to locate one of the RSA's new towns.

Officially, the RSA used "objective" criteria when it selected new town sites, making data-driven decisions, though it did not use that phrase at the time. The factors the RSA considered included "reasonable prospects of continued growth in population and employment opportunities," "regular, steady growth without booms and without cyclical slumps greater than average," "the present physical

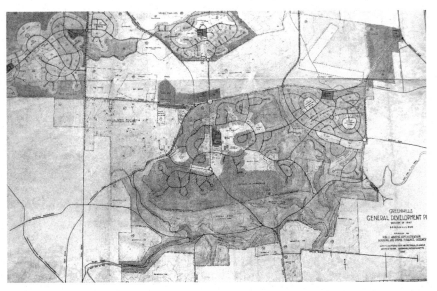

The plan of Greenhills. With its curvilinear streets and encircling greenbelt, Greenhills, Ohio, and the other New Deal new towns were designed to be the antidote to urban living. *Greenhills Historical Society, photo by author*

condition of the housing," and "availability of land on the outskirts."[23] All very rational, and after looking at this data for 100 cities, the RSA chose Cincinnati because it fit the bill snugly.

There was a certain political irony here. In choosing Cincinnati, the RSA put one of its "socialist utopias" in one of the most conservative regions of the county. More than that, Greenhills would sit almost literally in the back yard of Senator Robert Taft—"Mr. Republican," Cincinnati's own, and FDR's chief congressional antagonist. Someone in Washington must have chuckled.

The first purpose of Greenhills, as for the other new town projects, was to put unemployed men to work, even if that meant forgoing certain kinds of construction efficiencies. As a press release informed the public, "In the construction of Greenhills the first emphasis was on supplying the maximum employment to relief labor. In carrying out this objective, hand methods were largely preferred to labor-displacing machine operations." During construction, Greenhills provided jobs to more than two thousand laborers, "many of them unemployed since 1929."[24] The photographs are quite wonderful: men building the future with nineteenth-century, horse-drawn technology.

The future those men built combined Bauhaus-inspired architecture and design with Garden City planning, "an American adaption of the garden city plan first adopted in England nearly 40 years ago," as one publication put it.[25] Some commentators were put off by the modernist architecture, but most were impressed with the layout of the streets, the generous spacing each housing unit enjoyed, and all the green surrounding the residential sections. "Roads are laid out to route through-traffic around the town proper, achieving quiet and safety in the residential districts," an enthusiastic out-of-town newspaper reported. "In sharp contrast to the overcrowded conditions borne in the cities," it went on, "by families of the income groups for whom Greenhills is being built, there will be wide spacing between buildings."[26] One plan even showed a Radburn-style pedestrian underpass, though in the end it was never built.

Around the village, the planners preserved a considerable amount of farmland, which was rented back to tenant farmers who, in turn, sold their produce, milk, and meat to the residents. Central to the Garden City idea was a "greenbelt," and Greenhills is ringed by forest. In fact, when builders arrived at the site there were very few trees left after generations of intensive farming. The greenbelt was not preserved so much as created. Planners estimated that they would plant 1.5 million trees.

Greenhills opened in January 1938. By design, nothing was for sale—all the units were rentals ranging from $18 to $42 a month, and the federal government served as landlord. This certainly struck some at the time as a sensible arrangement. "By maintaining the property under one ownership," the *Decatur Herald and Review* wrote, "the objective of low rents and maintenance of the principles of sound planning embracing durable building and wide spacing can be adhered to. Sale of the land would open the community to the inroads of speculative profit that eventually would frustrate the original objectives."[27]

Potential tenants had to submit applications and have their incomes and housing situation evaluated before they could be approved as renters. In fact, they had to have their incomes evaluated every year by the National Housing Agency to determine if they still met the income eligibility guidelines set up by the RSA. And they had to adhere to a fairly rigid set of guidelines. All residents received a *Greenhills Manual* that provided all kinds of useful information and set out expectations for their behavior. As one original resident remembered, "Rents were cheap...but residents had to accept the government's rules—no one could drive nails into the walls, shake mops or rugs out the doors, or plant flowers in the front yard. Only a government work crew could paint the house, and then only with certain standard colors. It was always kind of a standard joke that you could only have a blue door."[28] Blue doors notwithstanding, 2,000 people had moved into Greenhills by the end of 1938.

In those early days, Greenhills was not only a new town but also a young one—more than 80 percent of its residents were between the ages of twenty and forty. Given that demographic, most of the remaining 20 percent were probably children, and Greenhills in the late 1930s buzzed with youthful energy. Just what kind of people they were, however, caused some controversy. When he came to sell the idea of Greenhills to conservative Cincinnati, Rexford Tugwell promised that it would help clear out the slums of the city, which no doubt appealed to Cincinnati's civic and business leaders.[29] In fact, the first residents came from the ranks of the postal service and from the nearby Pratt & Whitney engine plant that still operated. They included school teachers and downtown office workers—not, in the end, former slum-dwellers. Although Greenhills might have put some of the unemployed to work, it began as a solidly middle-class town. By 1930, the African American population of the Cincinnati area had risen to 8 percent, and yet of all the faces that stare out from the pages of the 1940 second anniversary booklet, only two are black. Nathan Yates and John White are pictured as part of the public works crew, but they did not live in Greenhills. At the center of Greenhills still sits the Greenhills Community Building, an imposing testament to the larger social ambitions of the New Deal new towns. The building itself served as a school, library, recreational space, and movie theater. But it was the focal point and hub of the community life of the town more broadly. "Greenhills offers opportunities in civic and social activities that often are denied individuals in larger communities," new residents were told in their manual. "Its success as a community and its benefits beyond the contribution of good housing, depend upon the extent the residents avail themselves of the advantages offered them. For Greenhills to be what it was planned to be, the residents will have to work together to make it and each of its institutions useful to all." Through this active community life, embodied in the community building, "a complete community life of the city will be possible." All the benefits of urban life, and alongside "these urban advantages are the benefits of rural life."[30]

It worked to a remarkable degree. The town quickly established a co-op grocery store and a pharmacy. Residents could deposit money in their own credit union and read their own newspaper. By one estimate, more than 60 percent of the people who moved to Greenhills participated in some community or civic organization.[31]

Inherent in this best-of-both-worlds was a belief that Greenhills would eliminate all the ills of urban life that reformers had been worried about since the Progressive era. Unlike life in the city, "living in Greenhills will be as healthful, safe and pleasant as modern knowledge can make it." It would be a "wholesome" community, free of urban congestion, and would include within it everything that "has been considered prerequisite to a healthful, convenient and attractive arrangement of homes and community facilities."[32]

And when people moved into this extraordinary experiment, they reached back to the iconic nineteenth-century American image to describe what they were doing: the pioneers. "In calling the first twelve families pioneers," the Greenhills association wrote in 1940, "our newspaper friends anticipated the spirit and tempo of life in our community."[33]

The library room of the Community Building is lined at the top with a splendid mural in the New Deal style. A viewer can follow it around the four walls and read the story of exploration, settlement, and progress in the region. The story culminates in Greenhills, and here the visual imagery is supplemented with text:

> The pioneers climbed the mountains and swept down the river, conquered the wilderness, cleared the forests, mined the earth and tilled the soil; creating from the rich resources of the Ohio Valley a civilization dedicated to providing equal opportunity for all men. Greenhills is dedicated to preservation of the human resources of that civilization and that opportunity. In its means for better community living it seeks to make enduring the social, economic, and free political institutions thus created.

Greenhills might have been planned and designed for the future, but its identity was firmly rooted in the past. It was simply the latest frontier that had to be settled and tamed, even if now the trees were being planted rather than cut down.

Looking back on it all in 1988, Stella Mannix Zieverink, one of the pioneers, said, "It was like a new country."[34]

A new country perhaps, but a dream that didn't last. In 1937, Rexford Tugwell wrote, "There ought to be three thousand such projects rather than three," but even as he made that declaration he probably knew that his greenbelt town project had already run its course.[35] The towns had come under withering attack from several quarters and for all the usual reasons: too expensive, too socialist, too utopian. Some people called him "Rex the Red." The *New York Herald Tribune* scoffed at the whole thing: "Greenbelt critics ask whether it was worth so much of the taxpayers' money to try to prove the worth of resettlement. The people of Greenbelt answer that 'a couple of Greenbelts could be built for the cost of one battleship,' and besides, the government expects to get its money back in rents over 60 years."[36] In fact, Tugwell wrote his essay in the *New Republic* to defend the towns from precisely such criticism. There is a certain weariness in his tone. By the time the *New York Herald* piece ran, the RSA was gone, the greenbelt town program had been declared unconstitutional (*Franklin Township v. Tugwell*, 1936), and Rex the Red had resigned and left Washington altogether.

Shopping in the cooperative market in Greenhills, Ohio. The New Deal new towns came with some economic ideas, too, such as cooperative businesses. After the Second World War it all smacked too much of socialism. *Library of Congress, LC-USF33- 001182-M4 [P&P]*

A decade or so later, with the Depression and WW II now behind the nation, the House Committee on Banking and Currency held hearings on the greenbelt towns. More specifically, in the spring of 1949, Congress considered a bill to sell the three federally owned towns to private groups. The American Legion in Milwaukee had formed its own development corporation and proposed buying Greendale, and on March 18, its representatives came to plead their case. Wisconsin's junior senator, Joseph McCarthy, was the first to testify on behalf of the American Legion proposal.

"These houses were originally built as emergency relief projects," Maxwell Elliott of the National Special Housing Committee of the American Legion reminded the committee, "but they had another purpose, and that was to provide home ownership with a country surrounding at a reasonable price for people who needed housing. At the present time, the people who need decent housing at reasonable prices—more than anybody else in the country—are the veterans." Tough to argue with that, though Elliott conveniently forgot that in Greenhills, at least, residents were never to own their own homes. And he also forgot about the larger decentralizing aspirations of the new town projects.

Some did raise concerns. Representative Lansdale Sasscer of Maryland worried that the 7,500 residents of Greenbelt, which was part of his district, might wind up displaced. "Most of them went in there under the old Greenbelt, where you had an income limitation....As far as Greenbelt is concerned, I have a very definite feeling that it should not be sold at this time." The *Milwaukee Journal* agreed, pointing out that to sell the towns amounted to a public subsidy for private businesses. Public money had been spent to build Greendale, the editorial noted, and now a private group would reap the benefit: "One wonders whether there are adequate safeguards in the Legion proposal against possible profits ending up in the Legion treasury."[37]

Opponents of the sale insisted that there was more than a real estate transaction at stake. They entered this notice from the *Greendale Review* into the record: "Greendale is not merely one of three Federal villages which were created by a couple of men. Greendale means families, people, mothers, fathers and children. It means social institutions that form whenever people live together." The goals of the New Deal greenbelt town program had always been larger than those of mere housing development. Just before the United States entered the Second World War, Philip Brown visited Greenbelt and reported: "The least the town has done is to give natural leaders a chance to use their ability. The most it has done is to plant for the first time in the minds of many men and women a knowledge of the strength of democratic action."[38]

The bill passed, and the three greenbelt towns were sold. By 1952, more than half of Greenhills's original acreage had been purchased by a developer to create the conventional suburb of Forest Park.[39]

The City circa 1939

The decentralists could be forgiven if they thought their moment had truly arrived in 1939. Out in Flushing, Queens, near the Trylon and Perisphere, at the 1939 World's Fair they called "The World of Tomorrow," the decentralists made one last play to grab national attention before the war. Almost a half century earlier, the 1893 World's Columbian Exposition in Chicago had offered a vision for what a planned city could be, and in so doing, provided a generation of architects and planners with inspiration. No doubt, the decentralists hoped they could use the 1939 fair to seize the imaginations of their own generation.

In fact, it was hard for the 44 million visitors who made the trek to Queens in 1939 and 1940 to escape the decentralist agenda of the fair. The diorama "Democracity" was located inside the Perisphere itself, the place where most visitors entered the grounds. It was billed as the "City of Tomorrow," echoing the overall theme of the fair. Up the world's longest escalator they went, into the world's largest sphere, where they perched on two balconies, one above the other,

Visitors to the 1939 World's Fair could hardly avoid the exhibit "Democracity," since it was attached to the iconic Trylon and Perisphere at the main entrance. Millions saw a vision of what a decentralized city could look like—only twenty years into the future. *New York World's Fair 1939-1940 records, Manuscripts and Archives Division, The New York Public Library, Astor, Lenox and Tilden Foundations.*

rotating in opposite directions and looking down on the future. Twenty years into the future to be precise, at an American city circa 1959.

What all those visitors saw must have made the decentralists proud. A city of clean streets, nestled against a river of clear blue water, radiating out from a central tower. Beyond the city itself, a set of five satellite towns each connected to the center by "a web of immaculate highways with turn-off ramps and free of dangerous intersections." Visitors stared down as if from the heavens and a voice intoned: "Here are grass and trees as well as stone and steel. Not a dream city but a symbol of life as lived by the Man of Tomorrow. No longer a plan-less jumble of slum and grime and smoke, but town and country joined for work and play in sunlight and good air." Lewis Mumford could not have put it any better.

In fact, Democracity, the "city of the future," owed a great deal to the planners of the previous generation. Come to think of it, except for the highways filled with cars, Democracity looked a good deal like Daniel Burnham's 1909 plan for Chicago. The full name of the exhibit was "Democracity, the Garden City of Tomorrow." An older man, among the preview visitors to Democracity, reached even further back when he said to his companion: "It's Bellamy's 'Looking Backward.' We've been looking into the future at something we read about sixty years ago."[40] As visitors circled the display they heard the voice of beloved broadcaster H. V. Kaltenborn tell them, "Here it is…and we like it. It's attractive and sensible at the same time. It's pleasant because we've spent a lot of money to make it so." A full 180,000 people came to Democracity in the first week of the fair, as many as 6,500 an hour on the first day. According to a Gallup survey, Democracity was the second most popular attraction during the first month of the fair.

Those who left "Democracity" wanting more of the decentralists' vision could head over to the Science and Education Building and watch it on the big screen. Titled simply *The City*, the film ran for under an hour, all day. Clarence Stein, under the auspices of the American Institute of Planners, brought together some extraordinary talent: Pare Lorenz shaped the outline; Aaron Copland wrote the score; Lewis Mumford wrote the script; Morris Carnovsky narrated; and the Carnegie Foundation paid the bills. *Free America* called it "America's First Decentralist Film."[41]

The result was less than the sum of those talented parts, not so much a documentary as a morality play in roughly four acts. The words on the screen that open the film even before the narration begins set the tone: "Year by year our cities grow more complex and less fit for living. The age of rebuilding is here. We must remold our old cities and build new communities better suited to our needs." There was the juxtaposition at the heart of the anti-urban impulse—old cities vs. new communities.

First, we see scenes of bucolic, small-town life. In fact, one suspects that even for audiences in 1939, most of whom drove cars or took trains to get to the fair, there was something absurdly, anachronistically pre-industrial about these scenes. After all, in 1939 how much commerce was still being conducted with horse-drawn carriages? How many wheel-wrights still operated fixing those wooden wheels? But Mumford uses these scenes to argue his central point about the relationship between geography and culture, about the relationship between space and place: "Art is not something we look at in a showcase," Carnovsky intones. "It's in the blankets we've spun and woven at home," he assures us as we watch a woman weave on a hand loom just like Ralph Borsodi had hoped women would do on the homesteads of Dayton. And he concludes the lesson: "There was lasting harmony between the soil and what we built and planted there."[42]

Then the film cuts. Copland's music moves from sonorous to agitated, and the camera takes us from the idyll of small-town America to Pittsburgh. Infernal Pittsburgh. The humble blacksmith shop morphs into an enormous steel mill, puffy white clouds are replaced with stacks belching black smoke, and children running through meadows give way to children playing pathetically in the streets. There is nothing subtle in these visuals, but Carnovsky narrates them for us just in case we miss the point.

On to New York and its environs. No smokestacks here, but scene after scene of urban chaos. Masses of people, alienated, faceless people, moving in herds through the streets, in and out of the subways, up and down the enormous sky-scrapers that loom ominously. To my eye, some of these scenes look intentionally speeded up, just slightly, to exaggerate the effect of an urban society that has tumbled profoundly out of balance. Faster and faster, until the action comes to a halt entirely with scenes of crushing traffic jams, cut in with shots of a policeman frantically trying to direct it all.

Finally, relief. In the film's fourth act we see the future. Garden cities, well planned and harmonious again. "Safe streets and quiet neighborhoods are not just matters of good luck. They're built into the design and built to stay there." Some of the scenes are from Radburn; not surprisingly, others are from Greenbelt, Maryland, and Greenhills, Ohio. "This is no suburb," Mumford insists, "where the lucky people play at living in the country. This kind of city spells coopera-tion whenever doing things together means cheapness or efficiency or better living." As we watch children riding bicycles safely removed from traffic, and women tending small vegetable gardens, and men playing softball, the message is clear: with the right planning we can restore the social harmony and sense of community that we have lost in urban America.

It would have been hard for audiences not to get the message. As George Weller summarized it in *Free America*: "*The City* declares that the American metropolis is an ugly, inconvenient and unhealthy place to live and work, that cities must be decentralized because they are politically undemocratic as well as unfit for human habitation...." Weller fairly cackled at the ironic "heresy" that such a film would be shown "in the Trylon's shadow" at a world's fair held in the nation's "super-metropolis." "An awkward case of heresy has broken out at the World's Fair," he announced. "The trouble has been caused by a short talkie called *The City*. *The City* denies flatly all the standards of collectivist living, urban expansion, industrial glut and mob entertainment of which the Fair itself is ... the steamroller of exhibits."[43]

Like the film, Weller's review nicely encapsulates the thrust of decentralist thinking: the modern city not only ruined the lives of those who lived in it but it also ruined the nation as a body politic. Decentralizing the city was the only way to save both. Those who came to the 1939 World's Fair were promised a glimpse into the World of Tomorrow, a world filled with exciting new industrial technologies designed to make life for the metropolitans easier and brought to you by some of America's largest corporations. *The City* argued that the decentralist anti-urban vision, rooted in the small towns of the nineteenth century, could be a part of that World of Tomorrow, too. The film closes with a challenge: "The choice is yours."

The war, looming as it already was for Americans in 1939, might have put the decentralizing agenda on hold, but just after it was over, former New Dealer Thomas Hewes expressed the hope that the moment had finally come. In his book *Decentralize for Liberty,* Hewes reminded readers that the city was the worst consequence of overcentralization. They "are the culture for mass unemployment," the place where big business and big labor colluded "abetted by big government."[44]

5 LOOKING FOR ALTERNATIVES TO THE CITY

THE PAST AND THE FOLK

Like so many American reformers, decentralists like Ralph Borsodi and those who wrote for *Free America* walked a fine line. They rejected much about the urban industrialized world and yet they insisted that they did not yearn for a simple-minded return to the past. They embraced the possibilities of new technology to achieve their goals, but they had little interest in the modernist fantasies of creating an entirely new world built on those technologies (and more that had not yet been invented). They wanted a large-scale transformation of American society of the sort that only the federal government could finance, but they wanted it to bubble up on a small scale, somehow, from "the people."

More to the point, they insisted that their ideas—about decentralization and domestic production, about regionalism and the integrity of local cultures, about social coherence and harmony—should command attention precisely because they were deeply rooted in the most fundamental American traditions. Rather than sitting at the summit of American development and progress, the American city represented for them an increasingly gruesome aberration. Their proposals aimed at restoring American traditions while updating them for a technological world. In short, they faced the future with at least one eye firmly set on the past.

Decentralists between the wars offered two sides of the same coin. On one side, planners like Lewis Mumford and Clarence Stein, back-to-the-landers like Ralph Borsodi, and New Deal new town builders presented Americans with visions of what the future might look like, physically and socially. On the other side, a number of Americans looked to the American past not only for models but for legitimacy and inspiration as well. They wanted their ideas to be anchored in something more than planning practice and economic theory. If Americans really were going to flee from the city, they had to have places to go, imaginatively as much as physically; and in addition to building new settlements that would provide attractive alternatives to the city, decentralizers and others needed to persuade Americans that such places already existed, or at any rate once had. They found that anchor, their alternatives to the city, in a particular version of the American past and in the American "folk."

Finding the Folk

Looking back on his career, Louis Jones, former director of the New York State Historical Association, observed, "The decade from 1931 to 1940 was, of course, the period during which America suddenly became aware of the fact that it had a folk tradition." He ascribed this discovery to the New Deal, whose projects "brought to the attention of a confused and struggling people an awareness of their native culture."[1] Those folklore projects sponsored by the New Deal ought to be seen alongside the new town and other RSA programs, and as part and parcel of the New Deal's focus on rural life and the countryside as the location for American redemption.

Jones's recollection is right, but incomplete. Certainly since at least the late nineteenth century, Americans had found a model of a different kind of community in the Pueblo tribes of the American Southwest. Charles Fletcher Lummis, an adventuring journalist, came to New Mexico in 1888 to recover from an illness and he become fascinated by Pueblo culture. He reported to a friend that the converted Indians he met "are all as good Christians as you are—perhaps a great deal better." He went on to say that no "Christian American community in the world…can approach in morality one of these little adobe towns," and in a wonderful irony concluded, "I wish they [Pueblos] would send out missionaries to their American brothers." Lummis was certainly not alone. The Southwest and its Pueblo people attracted the attention of other writers, artists, and spiritual seekers. When Georgia O'Keeffe came to Taos in 1929, she stayed with Mabel Dodge Luhan, who had established an artist colony on her ranch shortly after the First World War.[2] The people of the Southwest had preserved their way of life against the onslaught of American civilization, living in harmony with a harsh landscape and, in turn, with each other, their relationships nurtured by their timeless traditions. That is what Euro-Americans found, at any rate, when they came to the region.

Anthropologists came, too, giving scientific legitimacy to those perceptions. Frank Hamilton Cushing went there first and most flamboyantly. He arrived at the Zuni Pueblo in 1879, and lived with the tribe until 1884—not just with the

Zuni, but as a Zuni. Cushing went native; he was essentially adopted into the tribe and made a member of one the Zuni's priesthoods. In this way Cushing helped pioneer the anthropological technique of participant observation. In 1895, when Cushing posed for a full-length portrait by Thomas Eakins, he had himself depicted as a Zuni. Two generations later, the anthropologist Ruth Benedict presented the Zuni to American readers in her best-selling *Patterns of Culture* as "an unspoiled community," and she found that "their culture has not disintegrated like that of all the Indian communities outside Arizona and New Mexico. Month by month and year by year, the old dances of the gods are danced in their stone villages.... [L]ife follows essentially the old routines."[3]

Louis Jones was certainly right, though, that in the 1930s the enthusiasm for the folk and the "primitive" grew tremendously. Americans broadened their "discovery" of folk traditions to include those that were closer to mainstream American life—traditions that were far enough away to have been protected from the corrosions of urban progress, but near enough that they might still be grasped by Americans looking for an alternative to urban America.

The New Deal fostered much of this activity, sponsoring any number of projects to collect, preserve, and otherwise disseminate the pure products of America's folk: the collection of slave narratives, the Historic American Building Survey, and the publication of State Guides, to name just three instances. None was more important, however, than the way the New Deal reconceived of Native America as an alternative to industrial America.

John Collier was one of those who came to the Southwest and fell under its spell. Looking back on his 1919 visit to the Pueblo country, he marveled at how those tribes fostered "earth loyalties and human loyalties, amid a context of beauty that suffused the life of the whole group."[4] As head of the Bureau of Indian Affairs under Franklin Roosevelt, Collier engineered what became known as the "Indian New Deal." At an administrative level, the Indian Reorganization Act of 1934 attempted to undo the damage done to Native communities by fifty years of the Dawes Severality Act. Among other things, it slowed the allotment and privatization of land and restored a measure of tribal self-governance. As director, Collier also oversaw the decentralization of the Bureau of Indian Affairs (BIA), moving administrative power out into local areas in an analogue to what the decentralizers had hoped to do with urban populations and economic power.

Collier had spent much of the 1920s working as the executive secretary of the Indian Defense Association, and as director of the BIA he was clearly driven by a sense that Native people deserved political justice. Just as important, he believed that preserving and restoring Native life—those human loyalties and earth loyalties—could serve as a model for rebuilding a sense of community in the rest of America as well. Before he came to the Southwest, Collier had worked in New York City at the People's Institute, a school founded in 1897 to teach courses in social philosophy and government to new immigrants. In 1913, he described what he found there: "The economic changes of the late generation have destroyed most of the old social bonds, have substituted economic for human forces, and have in a sense pulverized social life. The need of the age is the creation of new vital social bonds." Some Progressives thought that those social bonds could be forged in the city. Collier found them in Indian country instead.[5]

But this activity was not restricted to government programs. The interwar period stands as a golden age of folklore studies. In fact, in some ways folklore was the domestic version of the anthropology of far away and exotic places: *ethnology* was how American academics studied other peoples; *folklore* was how they studied Americans, though the goals and methods were remarkably similar. And like anthropologists, many folklorists described their work as being out "in the field." The American Folklore Society was founded in 1888, and in 1942 Indiana University began teaching the first academic courses in the subject, bookending the arrival of the field and its formalization in the academy.[6]

American Ballads and Folk Songs remains a magisterial product of this vogue for the folk. Produced by John Lomax and his son Alan, the volume reaches for an encyclopedic completeness. In it they divided America's folk music tradition into twenty-five categories, starting with railroad songs and ending with Negro spirituals. It is a vast and wonderful collection, running to over 600 pages, complete with words and musical notation so people could sing the songs for themselves, which was undoubtedly the point in the first place. If, as Lewis Mumford and others advocated, cultural life could percolate on a small scale and on the local level, then people needed to know the words to the old songs.

In their introduction, the Lomaxes discussed the particularities of folk music, but in so doing they also defined what Americans in the 1930s meant by their discussion of the "folk." "Since America has no peasant class," the Lomaxes quote an Oxford don as saying, "there are, of course, no American folk songs." They argued instead that there are American peasants, if one means by that people living lives "of isolation, without books or newspapers or telephone or radio." The implication is that although much of this musical material originated in the nineteenth or even eighteenth century in isolated pockets of the United States, the songs were real and alive: "Although the spread of machine civilization is rapidly making it hard to find folk singers," the father and son team wrote, "ballads are yet sung in this country."

This was particularly true of African Americans, whose songs are disproportionately represented in the anthology. The Lomaxes recorded black singing on "big cotton plantations and lumber camps in Texas, in farm prison camps in Texas, Louisiana and Mississippi, and in two state prison camps in Tennessee." Though

Between the wars a number of folklorists and others set about to find American folk traditions in the forgotten corners of the nation. None was more energetic than Alan Lomax, demonstrating here that he could play music as well as record it. *Library of Congress, LOT 7414-B, no. N64-1a [P&P]*

the archive of music they collected remains a precious resource, their purpose, as they described it, verges on the insensitive: "Our purpose was to find the Negro who had had the least contact with jazz, the radio, and with the white man.... In the prison farm camps, the conditions were practically ideal." They surely did not mean to sound as callous as that. What the Lomaxes really wanted was authenticity, at least as they defined it. Since "he is apt to sing as he thinks the whites wish him to sing," the Lomaxes did their research where they were convinced the songs "had been entirely in the keeping of the black man."[7]

But African Americans represented only one example of what the folk tradition meant for Americans in the 1930s. Isolated and removed from the influences of urban, industrial culture (for the Lomaxes, "machine civilization" was almost synonymous with jazz and the radio) and still connected to an older economy (agriculture, mining, lumber), the American "folk" could be found in those pre-industrial, pre-urban corners of America just waiting to be explored. Notice, too, that in searching for music on these terms, the Lomaxes made these remote people sound remarkably like the primitives anthropologists sought in even more remote areas of the world. *American Ballads and Folk Songs*, after all, came out in 1934, the same year as Ruth Benedict's *Patterns of Culture*.

Doubtless many reasons contributed to the enthusiasm for the "folk" in the 1920s and 1930s. Chief among them was that as America entered its urban moment, these pre-industrial people—living lives in harmony with their surroundings, creating their own culture rooted in their own traditions, warmed by a sense of community and social cohesion, or so it appeared—appealed to Americans who wanted to imagine an alternative to the city.

A Nation of Regions

If Americans during the interwar years discovered that they had "a folk," then they also discovered that those folks lived in specific places out of which grew distinctive cultures. Frederick Jackson Turner had argued that in the eighteenth and nineteenth centuries, the frontier was the place that created the American identity. By the turn of the twentieth century, many felt that the city could function as the new frontier. Others disagreed. Instead, they searched for a different way to imagine American identity, and they found their answer in the notion of regionalism.[8]

The real America, so the thinking went, was not to be found in the urban centers but in regions that had resisted the onslaught of American progress and thus had retained an authenticity rooted in the land and in the past. Lewis Mumford, who served as the leading voice for regional planning, rooted his entire conception of regionalism in the idea that geographic regions, properly nurtured, produced distinctive societies as well. Those societies grew organically from the particularities of regional landscapes and from the peculiarities of the people who settled them. Regional culture had an integrity and a unity that metropolitan culture did not, and in this sense it stood as its opposite: harmonious rather than promiscuous; authentic rather than commercial; truly American rather than mongrel. Regionalism was not merely a way of solving a set of technical urban problems, like housing or congestion or transportation; it was also a powerful anti-urban vision of an America built on a notion of culture rooted in specific places.

We think about "regionalism" between the wars, if we think about it at all, as a literary and artistic phenomenon. During those years, regionalist writers and painters reacted in opposition to the fad of European modernism and against Europe altogether by asserting and insisting on a culture rooted in home-grown, American traditions.[9] During the 1920s and 1930s, the South and the Midwest announced their defiance of the metropolitan mainstream with the greatest vehemence. Philosopher Josiah Royce believed that loyalty was a fading virtue in American life early in the twentieth century, and that it could be restored only if Americans committed themselves to their local "province" or region. A generation later, "regionalism" was still in the air, and it stood as the easiest antonym to "metropolitanism."

Iowa's own Grant Wood stands as the central figure of the midwestern regionalist painters. Though he grew up in Iowa and made his career there, he also traveled, studying for a while in Minneapolis and at the Art Institute of Chicago. During the 1920s, he made four trips to Europe. But Iowa was home, and he persuaded fellow painters and midwesterners John Steuart Curry and Thomas Hart Benton to come home and hitch the wagon of their careers to the region.

In 1935, Wood published a regionalist manifesto of sorts, fittingly with a publisher based in Iowa City. Talking about the work he knew best, Wood wrote, "In painting there has been a definite swing to... regionalism; and this has been aided by such factors as the rejection of French domination, a growing consciousness of the art materials in the distinctively rural districts of America." Wood cast his diatribe—indeed, titled it as—*The Revolt Against the City*.

Rather than simply extolling the virtues of regionalism, Wood took the opportunity to attack the city and thus offered regionalism as the tonic to urbanism. "This urban growth," he thundered,

> whose tremendous power was so effective upon the whole of American society, served, so far as art was concerned, to tighten the grip of traditional imitativeness, for the cities were far less typically American than the frontier area whose power they usurped. Not only were they the seats of

the colonial spirit, but they were inimical to whatever was new, original and alive in the truly American spirit.[10]

Cities were retrograde, relics of a colonial past and fundamentally un-American. Quite an indictment packed into two sentences. But Wood went on to evoke the liberation from the city that came from regionalism: "Because of this new emphasis on native materials, the artist no longer finds it necessary to migrate even to New York, or to seek any great metropolis. No longer is it necessary for him to suffer the confusing cosmopolitanism, the noise, the too intimate gregariousness of the large city."[11]

In Wood's case, this was a bit disingenuous, more posture than practice. He might announce that artists no longer needed to go to New York, but his work was still being marketed by Associated American Artists, based in that city, and being bought by urban collectors and institutions. Wood is responsible for the best-known painting to come out of the regionalist movement—indeed, perhaps the most recognized American painting altogether: *American Gothic*. It hangs today in the Art Institute of Chicago, smack dab in the middle of the Loop.

Five years before Wood announced his revolt against the city, the South had announced that it would rise again. Or at least some of its leading literary figures did. The southern "Agrarians" who coalesced briefly in the English department at Vanderbilt University began to develop their searing critique of urban industrial America during the 1920s, when all still seemed well with that world. By the time they issued their collective manifesto *I'll Take My Stand* in 1930, of course, the wheels had come off and their essays took on an "I told you so" air. The Agrarians had been prepared to defend southern backwardness on its own merits, but as the Depression settled in, they could offer it as an alternative to the rest of America. They seemed untroubled that the university where several of them had offices had been founded by one of the great industrial pioneers.

I'll Take My Stand—in fact, much of what the southern regionalists wrote—is tough to stomach today. Although striking a defiant pose in defense of southern traditions, the authors willfully ignored southern poverty, penury, and most of all, the system of American apartheid upon which all aspects of southern life rested. Like Royce, the Agrarians insisted that they did not want to renew the old sectionalism, which had caused the nation so much trouble before. But given southern circumstances past and present, it was not entirely clear what the difference was between that old sectionalism and their new regionalism. Donald Davidson, one of the Agrarians, used his 1938 book *The Attack on Leviathan: Regionalism and Nationalism in the United States* to put forward a distinctly southern—that is, Confederate—version of history. "The Union that Lincoln is said to have wanted to establish," Davidson grudgingly asserted, "was never really set up. If Lincoln was a supporter, as in a dim way he may have been, of the Jeffersonian notion of a body of free and self-reliant farmers then why did he fight the South?" Four mil-lion enslaved Africans might have had an answer to that question, but Davidson was not finished with Lincoln. "Lincoln made war upon his own idea, and the fruit of his victory, represented in sprawling, confused, industrial America, is a more pitiful site than the desolate Lee plantations, for it is hardly even a noble ruin."[12] The allusion to seventeenth-century philosopher Thomas Hobbes in the book's title is a nice touch. Even Lewis Mumford, regionalism's chief intellectual, called the Agrarians "a bit reactionary," and he was no crusading progressive.

Still, some people, at least for a while, took the Agrarians seriously as part of the Jeffersonian, anti-urban tradition, and part and parcel of the decentralist movement. Writer Patrick Quinn, asked rhetorically in 1940 "Is the Agrarian claim to a Jeffersonian tradition a valid claim?", went on to answer "That answer is, almost unqualifiedly, yes." And sounding much like those decentralists who denied that they were motivated by nostalgia, Quinn insisted, "Let it be said at once that the Agrarian program of decen-tralization represents no backward step." Quinn also understood that the Agrarians were not simply offering agrarianism as a solution to economic problems. Those prob-lems were mere symptoms caused by a larger sickness in American life. The goal of the Agrarians was to make sure that the South did not succumb to the illness.[13] Neither Quinn nor the Agrarians he admired seemed to acknowledge that large numbers of African Americans still lived in the South, and that many of them were still trapped in an agricultural economy that left them decidedly not free.

During the 1920s and 1930s, neither the Midwest nor the South fully cap-tured the American imagination as a regionalist alternative to the industrial city, however. That was the case for the Midwest probably because it was simply too far away from the urban concentration of the East Coast for many people to care; it was the case for the South surely because of the political history and mal-odorous social situation associated with it. As it turned out, whatever claims the Midwest or the South might stake as America's regional alternative to the city, the most compelling anti-urban, "folk" geography in the 1920s and '30s extended from New England to the Smoky Mountains, along the spine of the Appalachian Mountains. On the map, New England is several hundred miles from the south-ern Appalachians of western Virginia, North Carolina, and eastern Tennessee and Kentucky. Imaginatively, however, the two regions were much closer during those years, and their creation as distinctive folk cultures grew from the same impulses.

Yankees vs. the City: The New England Town

New England, almost by definition, constituted the oldest, most enduring region in the American imagination. Indeed, New Englanders had been singing songs of themselves and their distinctiveness since John Winthrop promised in 1630 to build a city on a hill for the rest of us to admire. For many Americans, New England remained powerfully linked with some of the central themes of the American experience: haven for the religiously persecuted; cradle of the American Revolution; source of the nation's first cultural flowering. Nowhere did Protestants pursue the work ethic as vigorously, nowhere was common sense more common than in New England. New England, more so than any other region, could claim to be both a region apart and central to the very meaning of the nation.

Yet by the early twentieth century, New England had taken it on the chin. Economically, the region languished. Its once nation-leading industries, like shoes and textiles, had shrunk or had vanished altogether; its ports and fisheries had slowed; and it had never been a particularly good place to farm. There was a reason, after all, that all those New England farmers left for the flat and fertile fields of the Midwest. This decline contributed to a reassessment of the place New England ought to hold in the American consciousness. New England had given us Puritanism, and in the pop-Freudian world of the Jazz Age, no one had anything good to say about Puritans. H. L. Mencken defined Puritanism as "the haunting fear that someone, somewhere might be happy"; and insofar as Americans were still stifled by Puritanical restraints, we had only New England to blame.

So for those who wanted to reassert New England's claim as a region filled with its own customs, traditions, and folk types, though simultaneously being central to the very meaning of "American," New England had to be rehabilitated. During the years between the wars, writers and others—often themselves transplants to the region—found a New England that had resisted all the allures and false idols that had seduced the rest of the nation. So, for example, when writer Edward Chapman looked back on his Connecticut village, he took on Sinclair Lewis and his Nobel Prize directly: "on the whole I seem to recall little resemblance to that 'Main Street' upon which Mr. Sinclair Lewis has poured the vials of his eloquent scorn."[14] This generation of New England partisans did not venerate the past of great men and heroic deeds, but did admire a continuity between past and present in the lives of ordinary people.

Case in point, Bernard DeVoto. Born in Ogden, Utah, at the end of the nineteenth century, as a young man DeVoto made his way east, into the world of American letters. He went to Harvard University, headed to the Midwest where he taught for a while in the English department at Northwestern University, and then in 1927, at thirty years old, he quit the academic life to return to New England. And being a man of letters, he wrote about his decision for the readers of *Harper's Monthly*, where he would become a regular contributor for years.

He went to New England, he told those readers, not despite all the nasty things people like H. L. Mencken said about the place but precisely because of them. "What has been important in the development of the almost-perfect state is that New England is not America," DeVoto wrote, drawing a clear line between his adopted home and the places many of his readers resided. "The road it chose to follow, from the beginning, diverged from the highway of American progress." Progress, agreed Chapman, was, if not overrated, then ill-defined. "We have inclined to define it far too much in terms of mere physical convenience, comfort, and well-being... but the standard leaves so much to be desired," Chapman wrote in the very year that Franklin Roosevelt saw one-third of the nation as ill-housed, ill-clad, and ill-nourished. For his part, Chapman preferred "to go back to the old days."[15]

The heart of this newly imagined New England moved from the seaport towns, whaling ports, and the Boston area inland and northward to Vermont, New Hampshire, and Maine.[16] Here, in the northern states, many of the refugees who fled the city—Helen and Scott Nearing, and E. B. White—found the escape they imagined. And, in keeping with a New England tradition that stretches back to the seventeenth century, many of these transplants wrote essays and books about their experiments and experiences to let the rest of the world know what they were up to. Louise Dickinson Rich, a schoolteacher from Boston, came to remote Maine, where she met and fell in love with a transplant from Chicago and married him. In 1942, she published *We Took to the Woods*, a chatty, charming book largely about her domestic life in Maine that became a remarkable best-seller.

Needless to say, this New England of small towns and village greens ignored or erased the New England of cities and industry. DeVoto, for one, was strident about his anti-urbanism. The only hopeful sign he found in New England's cities was exactly their decline. Someday, he believed, they would disappear altogether:

> I cannot praise some aspects of the Yankee city. Such ulcerous growths of industrial New England as Lowell, Lawrence, Lynn, Pawtucket, Woonsocket, and Chelsea seem the products of nightmare.... It is only when one remembers Newark, Syracuse, Pittsburgh, West Philadelphia, Gary, Hammond, Akron, and South Bend that this leprosy seems tolerable. The refuse of industrialism knows no sectional boundaries and is common to all America.... [I]ndustrial leadership has passed from New England, and its disease will wane.[17]

Just as obviously, a New England re-imagined without cities and located in the three northern states was a New England without much in the way of immigrants or ethnic diversity. A Yankee kingdom. Writing in *Yankee* magazine, Claude Moore Fuess made it clear, if there were any doubt, just who constituted a Yankee: "No Latin or Slav, even in the second generation, can properly be called a Yankee. The true Yankee comes down from Anglo-Saxon stock and from branch to branch of the family tree."[18] Just as the Agrarians could project an image of the South absent of any black people, these neo-Yankees saw New England without any Irish or Italians.

So where did that road lead, if not to progress? In the 1920s and '30s, New England increasingly became synonymous with the small town—the New England village. That is where real Yankees lived. Real New England, the New England that captured the attention of Americans between the wars, therefore, was small-town New England. According to writer Clarence Webster, writing in 1945, in every region there "is a central force that has molded the thought and behavior of the people of the region.... [A]lways some dominant power creates man's folkways." Without question, he continued, "In New England it is the town."[19]

Lewis Mumford rhapsodized about the New England town as almost utopian, a "complete and intelligent partnership between earth and man," and he believed it ought to serve as the model for all new planned towns. After all, according to Mumford, "the fact of the matter is that the New England village up to the middle of the eighteenth century was a garden-city in every sense that we now apply to that term."[20] The New England town was the connection between America's Garden City future and its pre-urban past.

Never mind that at this moment in the history of the region most of the indicators that measure social health pointed in the wrong direction. As early as 1900, the census reported that those New England towns were shriveling up. At the very end of the roaring twenties, the *New Republic* asked "Whither New England?" and found that it was largely stagnating: "within twenty-five years the whole face of America has changed.... But the ruling caste in New England has remained substantially the same." When Louis Adamic visited the area to report for *Harper's,* he found the towns "tragic" in their economic despair. Doing a study of the "hill country" of New England—that rural northern part of New England that remained unspoiled by urbanism or industry—Harold Fisher Wilson found that during the first three decades of the twentieth century, the amount of agricultural acreage had decreased by 30 percent in Maine, 34 percent in Vermont, and an astonishing 51 percent in New Hampshire. Farms throughout the hill country stood abandoned as the rural population declined, its young people having been lured away by "urban attractions."[21] Perhaps this explains how writers and artists could afford the real estate and could transplant themselves there.

Jonathan Daniels came to New England in the 1930s. As a southerner, he came, "secretly respectful" of New England and its traditions and history. He expected to find the Yankees who had haunted the imagination of southerners since at least 1861, and to experience the civilization they had created. When he left New England, he was still "frankly full of admiration" but also sobered by the distance between the image of New England and the hard reality he saw:

> The fish and the forests, which were what they had to begin with, were depleted long ago. The water power, which now runs by so many less productive mills, is a resource no longer unique. The region has to spend a billion dollars or more every year to feed itself. A million of the eight million eaters within the land were, when I rode it, people who wanted work and could not get it. There were more old people and fewer young ones in the old land than in most other American regions. Twice as many freight cars—and probably twice as many trucks—brought food and fuel and materials in as took products out. And the more valuable products which went out had, in an America which New Englanders had helped spread to the Pacific, a longer way to go.[22]

Welcome to the New England of the Great Depression.

No matter. For some, like Mumford, who wanted to decentralize urban America into smaller units, the New England village was the model for all he hoped to achieve. It had a physical compactness and logic to it, complete with common spaces and agricultural land in close proximity. When Mumford talked about returning to the settlement patterns of the American past, he had New England primarily in mind. In addition, those towns fostered a distinct regional culture, a culture that Mumford had celebrated in his book *The Golden Day*. For Mumford, New England was a *real* place—and plenty of others agreed.

No wonder, then, that when Clarence Stein began advertising Radburn, his new town in suburban New Jersey, he promised that the "[h]omes will have all the peace and quiet which existed in the old New England towns."[23] Stein not only had New England in his sights as he planned the town but he also recognized the pull that the image of a New England village would have on his potential buyers from the New York City area. At the end of the film *The City*, when we are shown scenes of greenbelt towns, the narrator tells us: "This works as well for modern living as once it did in old New England towns." The push for the decentralized Garden City idea in the 1920s was thus directly connected to, and perhaps inspired by, this valorization of the New England town.

Those villages had an undeniable aesthetic appeal, especially as they were romanticized in words and pictures, like those Norman Rockwell, another transplant to New England, produced for the *Saturday Evening Post*. He helped spread an idealized version of New England to a national audience. But the physical environment was not the final significance of the New England town. Those spaces had fostered the New England town meeting, and thus served as the very cradle of American democratic practice. They had given the nation the model of citizen democracy in the heroic eighteenth century, and if Americans used New England towns as their guide, they could save American democracy in the uncertain twentieth century. "When town meeting comes around," audiences watching the film *The City* were told, "we know our rights.... In all that matters we neighbors hold together."

When introducing his own survey of "town meeting country," Clarence Webster made this clear. The New England town was more than the sum of its buildings and spaces, more than a dot on the map: "It is a concept of political philosophy and, also, a deeply satisfying spiritual reality." For Webster, that philosophy and that "spiritual reality" put the New England town at the center of the American experience. "This, then, is the story of the New England town," he wrote triumphantly, "To know it is to understand in part why the United States can be a democracy."[24]

Webster's tone alternated among self-satisfaction, defensiveness, and caution. He nodded toward some of New England's obvious problems. "True, of course, there have been some defeats and many more compromises," he acknowledged, "but the small cities and the hill towns are once more showing the world what a sound unit of living can be." Here he sounded more like a midwestern booster than a hill country Yankee. "The greatest danger that faces the small town of Town Meeting Country," he wrote, echoing Ralph Borsodi,

> is that too many of its places will cease to produce. Then the end is near; for we are supported by an economy of production with the community itself, and I doubt if we could survive as a summer playground or the home of workers who commute to an industrial civilization. You have to work a place, and work for it, before you can make it live and be *worth* keeping alive for a few hundred years. [25]

In a region where production both agricultural and industrial had been on the decline for years, Webster could still find hope for producer-based communities.

In the same breath, Webster dismissed the notion that these small towns existed now only in the gravitational orbit of larger cities. "Some 'experts' will tell you blithely, 'Oh yes, the small town is now part of the city that is only ten miles away, and the rural amusements have been discarded in favor of the movies.' That is another of those one-eighth truths printed by the man who spent three weeks visiting... ordinarily the trip to the city is made only when there is nothing going on in town."[26] New England villagers can amuse, entertain, and enlighten themselves, thank you very much. *Yankee* magazine ran a regular column on New England folk dancing for those subscribers who wanted to learn.

It is not hard to see, therefore, why the New England village appealed so strongly to writers, planners, and other anti-urban dreamers in the 1920s and '30s. For those decentralists who believed that economic production had to return to smaller scale, domestically based work, New England towns had never lost that production; for those regionalists who wanted culture to percolate naturally from local traditions, people, and landscapes, New England stood as the first genuine American culture and its most lasting. And for those who simply thought American cities stood in the vanguard of American ugliness—well, no one would argue with the beauty of New England villages.

Finally, for those who believed that the American city corrupted American democracy, New England offered the town meeting. At those meetings, New England towns achieved a near-perfect civic balance between individual freedom and community obligation. Webster was certainly not alone when he wrote that the New England town "gives the New Englander exactly what he demands—a sensible and efficient form of government with the freedom to be himself." As another writer put it, the New England town meeting "is as really a Mother of Parliaments as her great Elder Sister at Westminster. The experience in self-government and willingness to hear many men of many minds thresh out things of public moment in free conference was, I believe, of inestimable worth to New England, and to the Nation." It defined the region to the point almost of being synonymous with it: "There is final proof that our 1940 New England towns are still strong and are worthy of the people who built them: we still hold town meetings."[27]

The irony here was apparently lost entirely on these writers. Part of what made New England towns attractive to disgruntled urbanites was precisely its demographic sameness—they were inhabited by those real Yankees of naught but Anglo-Saxon stock. Indeed, that same writer worried that the New England town "has been hard pressed by the incoming of foreign elements in great force and numbers." And yet Chapman could still write in 1937 that the town meeting represented the meeting of "many men of many minds."[28] New England towns offered all the unspoken and retrograde comforts of ethnic and racial homogeneity to those who found cities nothing but a welter of people decidedly not Yankees. Chapman, and others like him, did not acknowledge that this version of "community" was predicated on a tightly defined ethno-racial exclusivity.

It hardly requires saying that these celebrations of New England in the interwar years had an anti-urban subtext that was never far below the surface. Clarence

Webster was familiar enough with city folks coming as tourists or as summer residents to New England, and he dismissed them this way: "On the whole, the city folks we get are not too hard to understand, if you want merely a rough working estimate. They are just children playing in an extra-large back yard, and they have all the cussedness, charm, and general unpredictability of brats." The brats could cause trouble in town meetings, however. Webster claimed that town meetings got as "heated" as they ever got when, "city folks present a petition and force the calling of a special meeting to vote on appropriating two hundred dollars for beautification of the village street."[29] Of course, by this time, tourist dollars increasingly supported those New England towns across much of the region.

If New England towns were portrayed to the American public as the ethnic and economic antithesis of the American city, then by the Depression years they were presented as the political antidote to an overweening government as well. Plenty of New England partisans found government regulation and relief programs offensive to their traditions of individual freedom and self-reliance. "Yes, the town meeting is unmistakably from and of us," Webster argued, implicitly setting New England against what he saw as the drift of the rest of the nation; "It is not put over us by a beneficent father or social order apart from ourselves; we do not elect it; it could not exist without us—it *is* us."[30]

When DeVoto wrote about his retreat to New England, he told his readers about his new neighbor Jason. Jason and his wife exemplified all those Yankee traditions. They ate food they grew and canned themselves; they cooked and stayed warm with wood they split; and DeVoto assured his readers that, although "Jason lives far below 'the American standard,' yet he lives in comfort and security.... [M]ore than anyone else I know, he lives...the good life."[31]

Who knows if Jason really existed? He may have been some composite DeVoto put together, or indeed invented from whole (homespun) cloth. For DeVoto, Jason served a larger purpose and came into the essay bearing the indictment DeVoto had really written: "There are thousands like Jason on the hillside farms of Vermont, New Hampshire, and northwestern Massachusetts, and there have been for three centuries. They have never thrown themselves upon the charity of the nation. They have never assaulted Congress, demanding a place at the national trough."[32]

It is worth noting that DeVoto's essay appeared in *Harper's* in 1932, well before the New Deal came to the nation. And yet DeVoto was already offering Yankee-ism as an alternative to government relief and intervention programs. New Englanders were tough, DeVoto insisted; they took care of themselves and their own. The Depression would not change that. Indeed, the rest of the nation had grown fat and flabby with material prosperity, and thus had to belly-up to "the national trough." By contrast, New Englanders had never succumbed to

Between the wars, New England was portrayed as the one region in the country that had retained the true American virtues of independence and self-reliance. But despite the contempt some of its residents felt for outsiders, even in the 1930s tourism accounted for a major part of many local economies, as on the Mohawk Trail in Massachusetts. *Library of Congress, LC-USF34-080818-D*

that easy prosperity and thus went on unchanged and unmoved: "How, indeed, should hard times terrify New England? It has had hard times for sixty years—in one way or another for three hundred years. It has had to find a way to endure a perpetual depression, and had found it. It began to look as though the bankrupt nation might learn something from New England."[33]

Louise Rich sounded the same notes, though with a little less drama, when she described an annual town meeting during the depths of the Depression. The local relief fund had not been spent down, and as a consequence the citizens voted to reduce the coming year's contribution to it. "This was the year when Relief money was running out all over the country, and when food riots were common in the big cities," she reminded readers. She did not draw her conclusion as dogmatically as some writers, and she was more honest about New England realities than others, but she drew it just the same: "And that doesn't prove that New England didn't feel the depression. What it proves is that rural New England, with its starved farms and hand-to-mouth living, is chronically so near depression that a big slump doesn't matter much." She went on to define deprivation as a form of Yankee virtue: "It simply means pulling in the belt another notch, wearing the same clothes one or two or three more years, and going without butter. We don't get guns for our butter, either. We get something even more necessary to the self-guarding of Democracy. We get self-respect and the right to spit in anyone's eye and tell them to go climb a tree."[34]

Politics in the town of Grover's Corner, New Hampshire, during these years had changed little since the Civil War: 86 percent of its citizens voted Republican, just as their fathers and grandfathers had. Thornton Wilder invented the town in his 1938 play *Our Town*, but he exaggerated the politics of the region only slightly. New England away from the coasts and the immigrants and the cities clung to a Republicanism where any intrusion by government was regarded as an assault on personal freedom; it was one in which all government beyond the town meeting was viewed contemptuously, just as the world outside the self-sufficient village was viewed with suspicion. "A society is here founded on granite," DeVoto thundered:

No one supposes it is perfect. It is not an experiment; it was not planned by enthusiasts or engineers or prophets of any kind. But out of the Yankee nature and the procession of blind force somehow dignity and community decency were here evolved. The New England town, that is, has adjusted itself to the conditions of its life. It is a finished place.[35]

Clarence Webster was no less emphatic. His 1945 description of New England's town meeting and the freedom it guaranteed must have sounded irresistible to a nation just catching its breath from the twin traumas of depression and war:

First, these men and women are individuals. . . . Second, they are folks who can come together in town meeting and act for the good of the community. Those are the common denominators of this country. We are free men and women, doing as we please. We can also act as the town demands, for we are bound by its old and wise customs. That is why we can vote in the main wisely in town meeting. You have to be free before you can endure being bound by society; and you must be bound before you can build a society in which you can be free.[36]

Robb Sagendorph, who began publishing *Yankee* magazine in 1935 as a way to celebrate the region with attractive illustrations and local-color stories, in addition to folk-dancing instruction, was another who believed freedom preceded society. By 1937, he was actively campaigning against the New Deal and contemplating starting his own regional political party: the Yankee Party.[37] The New Hampshire license plate reads "Live Free or Die," doesn't it?

The image of New England created between the wars, and all the meaning attached to it, has proved remarkably potent and enduring. In 1931, for example, when Stuart Chase published his book *Mexico: A Study of Two Americas,* he extolled the virtues of the Tepoxtlan region. There he found that "community spirit is strong—as in old New England barn raisings."[38] After the war, the founders of Melbourne Village, the Borsodi-inspired community on the east coast of Florida, promised that the new town would be "a democratic community where each member has one vote, and where the New England Town Meeting can come alive again."[39] An odd reference at first glance, because Melbourne's founders hailed from the Midwest. In 1969, Michael Kittridge began manufacturing scented candles in South Hadley, Massachusetts, and his business—Yankee Candle—is now the largest of its kind in the country, with franchise stores in malls around the country.

For those who saw decentralization, the creation of small-scale communities, and a retreat from the cities as the only way to revitalize American democracy, New England towns, their town meetings, and that ineffable but intoxicating sense of community they fostered assumed an almost mythological place in their imaginations. The New England town, past and present, became the touchstone for those who wanted to build the new communities of the future on their own and without an interfering government

Anti-Urbanism, Mountain Style: The Invention of Appalachia

Before he came to New York to study at Columbia University and then work with the city's poor, John Collier hiked in the southern Appalachians. He went first in the summer of 1901 with his brother, both seeking to recover from the death of their parents. Collier found solace in the mountains and among its people, and he returned to the area periodically when he felt the need of spiritual restoration.[40] Perhaps he crossed paths with John Campbell.

John Campbell came to New England from a home in Indiana. He studied theology, married a New England girl, and then went to the southern Appalachians in the early years of the twentieth century as an educator and missionary.

Remote as his posting seemed at one level, Campbell was certainly not alone. The southern Appalachians were dotted with educational and economic uplift projects started by northerners, which dated back at least as far as Berea College in Kentucky, whose connections to Oberlin College and Yale University were crucial to shaping its work. By the time Campbell arrived, Vassar graduate Susan Chester had already opened the Log Cabin Settlement in Asheville, North Carolina; Frances Goodrich had started her Allanstand cottage industries project nearby; and the Hindman Settlement School in eastern Kentucky was several years old. These would be joined by the Biltmore Industries, founded by Edith Vanderbilt; the Berry schools in northern Georgia; and the Crossnore and Penland craft schools in North Carolina.[41] Many of those who came to the mountains, like their predecessors a generation earlier who went there to work for the Freedmen's Bureau, were from New England.[42]

They came ostensibly to help indigenous Appalachians better their lives. In so doing, they participated in the creation of the very notion of Appalachia. "Appalachia" as a region with a distinct cultural identity began to emerge in the national consciousness late in the nineteenth century. It appeared first in local-color stories and in fiction. The term "hillbilly" made its debut in the *New York Journal* in a story printed in 1900—defined then as "a free and untrammeled white."[43]

Initially, these northern reformers discovered the region as a place full of social problems that needed to be solved. They came to bridge the gap between primitive mountain life and contemporary America. Once they arrived and began their work, however, many altered their view and began to see Appalachians not simply as benighted but as having preserved all sorts of pre-industrial, pioneer virtues that were now sorely lacking in modern America: self-reliance, independence, and in their isolation, all sorts of "cultural" traits, from music to language to furniture making. Those who live in the Southern Highlands had avoided many of the woes of urban, industrial society, especially economic specialization and the alienation that went with it, as well as ethnic and racial mixing. In other words, these reformers found a true "American folk."[44]

For his part, Campbell's work convinced him that he had as much to learn as to teach and that the region was not quite as backward as he thought when he had arrived. He persuaded the Russell Sage Foundation that, in order to solve the region's problems, there needed to be the same kind of systematic study that others had brought to bear on the city. In 1912, the New York-based foundation created its Southern Highlands Division, with an office in Asheville and with Campbell as its director.

The division did not survive Campbell's early death in 1919. But the foundation maintained a connection to the region through John's widow, Olive. Born and raised in West Medford, Massachusetts, she carried on her husband's work and persuaded the foundation to posthumously publish her husband's magnum opus, *The Southern Highlander and His Homeland*, in 1921.

It is not clear when Olive Campbell decided that opening a school would be the best way to honor her husband's memory, but it seems to have occurred to her quite quickly. In 1923, she left the country for a tour of Scandinavia and the folk schools that had been established there. She was particularly taken with Danish folk schools, and she published a small book about them in 1928. She came back from that trip convinced that some version of the folk school was just what the southern Appalachians needed.

She persuaded the Russell Sage Foundation to advance her some money so she could travel the Southern Highlands, scouting the right location for the school she intended to start. As she explained her goal to the foundation's director, John Glenn, "We want a region characteristically enough mountain as to difficulties, but if we are doing this in the spirit of an experiment or demonstration, we should be somewhat accessible—even preferably central."[45]

Difficulties, to be sure. By the interwar period, perhaps the only other region more economically desperate than New England was Appalachia. Without engaging in technical economic arguments, it does not exaggerate too much to say that Appalachia had been colonized by northern capital and corporations, and that the region suffered all of the predictable consequences of that colonial exploitation.

Timber camps and coal mines and rail yards attracted workers from countless isolated and rural settlements, who hoped to trade that isolation for better wages and larger economic opportunities. Rarely did they get them. More often, those mountain workers were left no better off than the region as a whole, which never saw much return on the wealth of its natural resources. Ironically, this most remote and rural of American regions was thus deeply dependent on the forces of the urban industrial economy—and was whipsaw-sensitive to its fluctuations. For instance, Appalachia was hit hard when that economy collapsed in the 1930s; by 1936, nearly 50 percent of all mountain families were on relief; and according to the federal government, the region had a lower per capita income than any other part of the country.[46]

Campbell and others in her circle understood the problems of the mountains, yet they did not want simply to create economic opportunities for mountain people by bringing them into the mainstream of American economic life. "We measure success by urban standards," she wrote in 1925, before the Depression made life worse, insisting that the "rural problem" required a different set of standards and a different kind of educational strategy.[47] She did not come to the region to convert mountain folk with the gospel of middle-class prosperity; she wanted to make their lives better without changing them too much. After all, she wrote to a friend, "if we insist upon our way being the right way, then there is no logical halfway point to stop in preparing them to compete with the outside.... [T]here is no reason why we should try to make country people conform to city standards."[48]

Instead, she wanted to promote the traditional craft traditions of the southern mountains while making them profitable. She wanted to preserve Appalachian folk culture and sell it in a larger marketplace. She wanted to make it economically viable to remain "folk." In short, Campbell and her collaborators wanted an anti-urban solution to the problems of the rural Southern Highlands.

More specifically, she wanted mountain folk to stay in the mountains. Earlier educational efforts in the region, she believed, had helped create a sort of brain drain—the most talented and the most ambitious wound up leaving. She thought her school could train students to make their lives where they were. As she was laying the groundwork for the school, she wrote excitedly to John Glenn at the Russell Sage Foundation about a meeting with a possible funder, a "Cincinnati millionaire" who had made his fortune cutting Appalachian timber. Campbell reported that he was looking for a project just like she was proposing, "something which will help make country life fuller and yet not drain the mountains of their best." In a story covering the folk school, the *Sentinel* in Winston Salem, North Carolina, told its readers that its goal was to make "the rural life so interesting and so attractive that the most promising boys and girls will find happiness and contentment right on the farm instead of flocking to the great cities which often so completely absorb them that they are scarcely heard from again."[49] Olive Campbell wanted a school that would answer the age-old question: How are you going to keep them down on the farm?

Back in New York, the Russell Sage Foundation debated whether this kind of work fell within its scope, whether "education"—even as broadly conceived as Campbell had in mind—truly constituted "social work." Glenn's reservations extended beyond those of the foundation's core mission. He wondered whether the Danish model, with which Campbell was so smitten, really fit the American landscape. "As I read your letters and reports," he wrote to Campbell, "I get the impression that the folk schools in the mountains will be a very different proposition from the folk schools in Denmark. The latter is a small, compact, open country.... They can influence the national life with comparative ease. In the southern mountains, on the other hand, any folk school is chiefly a neighborhood or county affair."

He was also dubious about Campbell's larger goal of stemming the flight of youth, talent, and ambition from the mountains to the cities, asking, "You lay stress on the importance of keeping pupils in the mountains. I question whether the influence of your folk schools will do this. Is it likely that an energetic, thoughtful young man or woman who has been taught to care for himself or herself intelligently and given wider aspirations will wish to stay in an isolated mountain country?"[50] Undaunted by these questions, Campbell found her spot later in 1925–Brasstown, North Carolina. Not so much a town as a cluster of families. Average annual income was less than $100 a year—before the Depression arrived.

Having found her location, she set to work establishing the school, converting buildings into a campus and recruiting some of her first students. By the end of

Olive Campbell came to Appalachia ostensibly to help its residents, but she stayed because she fell in love with the region. She is shown in 1926 or 1927, third from right, with several others who helped start the John C. Campbell Folk School in Brasstown, North Carolina. *Printed with permission of the John C. Campbell Folk School*

1925, Campbell was using letterhead that proclaimed "The John C. Campbell Folk School." Among the first staff members, fittingly enough, was a Danish farmer who came to teach Danish farming techniques to the locals.[51]

The school offered no formal academic curriculum, no grades, no credits; rather, there was educational programming designed to provide "practical training for life in a rural mountain environment." The goal, according to a fundraising appeal, was "to awaken, enliven, enlighten. Through its varied program—cultural and practical—young people come to sense the hope for the mountains."[52]

The reference to "young people" elided some of Campbell's own anxieties about just who would benefit from the school's offerings. Initially she saw the school as part of a larger movement in American life for adult education, and she advertised that it was designed for eighteen- to thirty-year-olds. Her first class of seven students, however, were sixteen- to twenty-two-year-olds and their academic background was sorely lacking: "In our history lesson this morning not one knew what other nation spoke English beside ours and could not point out England on the map....I assure you there is plenty of work to be done in the coming months."[53]

In fact, when she looked into the faces of those who attended to the school, she saw the decline she had come to reverse, and that sense of generational declension bothered her a great deal. The region itself had "declined far from the once pioneer plenty," but so had the people. In a report she sent to the Russell Sage Foundation, she acknowledged that although "we have a large group of older people of the splendid old pioneer type," the younger generation left something to be desired: "When, however, one gets down into the late twenties or early thirties, one finds that on the whole the more energetic have gone, especially if they have had an education." Writing to Mrs. John Glenn, she crowed that "It would be hard to find a stronger group of young married couples—thirty to forty years old. They have the best of the mountain traits." But then she worried, "One cannot help wondering what their children will turn out to be, and how many will stay here in the country."[54]

There is something both nostalgic and romanticized in those references to "pioneer plenty" and "pioneer types." The school's motto proclaimed "I Sing Behind the Plow," capturing succinctly a happy view of those pre-industrial farmers who whistled while they worked. It is the same nostalgia exhibited by those who imagined a return to the country's pioneer past as an antidote to the overurbanized present. The difference is that in the Southern Highlands, just as in New England, Americans believed that the past remained close enough to touch. Or, as it turned out, close enough to buy.

Campbell was a central figure in the development of the handicraft economy of the southern Appalachians. She recognized that selling handicrafts might be a way of turning mountain traditions into something profitable enough that it would give mountain people the ability to stay at home and out of the mainstream economy. It was a tricky proposition, to be sure, because it meant tying mountain producers even closer to the vagaries of the consumer and tourist economies, which were threatening the very isolation that had preserved those craft traditions in the first place.

Campbell recognized the dilemma and wrote to Russell Sage's John Glenn about it in 1928. "Some of the schools," she noted, "get out extremely fine work, others poor work—not what I feel ought to represent mountain handwork as it might be and not that which calls forth the best in the people." The problem is that "good and bad work compete as mountain output on the market with each other." She wondered about a solution to this problem, something that would give "a clearer insight of what types of handwork should be begun. Is it time, for example, to stop the setting up of looms because the market is overstocked with handmade cloth as I heard one woman say?"[55] In other words, should schools like hers foster only the traditions a middle-class market could bear?

The following year, Campbell spearheaded the creation of the Southern Highland Craft Guild. The guild served as an arbiter of "quality" and facilitated the marketing of southern Appalachian products in larger, urban markets. In the 1930s, the guild began marketing and selling crafts in New York City and participated in several exhibitions, including the Rural Arts exhibition held in the Department of Agriculture building in Washington, D.C., in 1937. That same year, the Russell Sage Foundation published *Handicrafts of the Southern Highlands*, a lushly illustrated "art book" of the sort the foundation had never published before.

As a result of this explosion of Appalachian handicrafts into the urban marketplace, however, the federal government now recognized the essential conundrum between tradition and modernity, between artifacts and commodities. A Department of Labor study of the southern Appalachians argued that these craftspeople should really be classed as "industrial houseworkers," rather than "tradition-bound descendants of Anglo-American pioneers."[56] Nor was Campbell oblivious to the paradox. When she proposed a new craft-education project in 1943 she parsed it this way: "Handicrafts have always played an important part in the mountain economy, first in meeting home needs, and increasingly today by furnishing a cash income through satisfying tourist demands." This seemed to be the way to the future because the Southern Highlands were an "almost limitless tourist resource, in which handicrafts have a prominent place."[57]

This, in the end, was the compromise—or the irony—of "discovering" the Appalachian folk. Their value to the rest of the nation lay in their unspoiled isolation and in their preservation (real or imagined) of a pre-industrial, pioneer way of life. The only way to keep them down on their farms, it turned out, was to invite greater and greater numbers of middle-class urbanites to visit as tourists and, conversely, to export their handicrafts to urban markets. Campbell, perhaps more than some of the other anti-urban fantasists of the time, recognized the connections between the city and its opposite. She understood that although Appalachia might stand apart from the rest of urban America, it could not survive as a culturally (and economically) autonomous region without the city.

Above all else, however, Olive Campbell devoted her life to the southern Appalachians not because of the handicrafts but because she believed, like so many others, in the therapeutic possibilities of community. "We get more and more interested in the community," she wrote to Mrs. John Glenn during a driving January snowstorm in Brasstown, and she insisted that a "people's college" of the sort she established "might be a real part of the community in which it is situated." She believed, as so many others did, too, that real community must be rooted in the particularities of place; but she also believed that the idea of community transcended those particularities and could help tie the nation together.

Campbell was not alone in her concern with Appalachian community. Although the mountain folk had preserved much of their pre-modern life style, they suffered from a lack of any larger sense of community. Campbell wrote of her own frustrations trying to establish agricultural cooperatives in the region: "Certain definite obstacles stand in the way of cooperative movements in the Highlands. Prominent among these [is] the pronounced individualism of the people." Promoting Appalachian culture—handcrafts, songs, music, and the rest—became the mechanism to achieve that larger sense of community, the glue which would hold together an isolated population that was dispersed across a difficult geography. It would define what Appalachians shared and simultaneously distinguish them from the rest of the nation. Culture would constitute who they were and who they were not.[58]

Olive Campbell had followed her husband to the Southern Highlands. She stayed after his death because, despite the human deprivation and environmental degradation, this child of New England found that the southern Appalachians fulfilled her own yearnings for an alternative to urban America. In a 1929 speech she explained, "When I have been away in the cities and return to our mountain country, I am struck anew with its beauty. I find myself wondering why anyone lives anywhere else. Why the noise, the confusion, the dirt, the scramble, when one may have the fresh stillness, the independence of life among these blue and green hills."[59]

Not everyone agreed. In the second half of the twentieth century, 4 million Appalachians left the region, mostly headed to the industrial cities of the Midwest.

Linking New England Towns and Appalachia: Anti-Urbanism and the Appalachian Trail

It is just over 1,000 miles from Springer Mountain, Georgia, at the southern end of the Appalachians, to the small town of Shirley Center, Massachusetts. Shirley Center sits in the middle of Thoreau country, northwest of Boston, beyond Concord and Walden Pond, but not quite as far out as the end of the train line in Fitchburg. Nearly 300 years after the place was first settled, Shirley Center has grown to a town of just over 6,000 residents.

It remains a small town in the classic New England mold. It was settled and incorporated in the mid-eighteenth century and it retains much of its eighteenth- and nineteenth-century charm. The First Parish Church opened its doors in 1773, and it remains picture-postcard worthy today. The 1939 film *The City* opens with bucolic scenes of horse-drawn carts, kids splashing in a swimming hole, and men harvesting grain with scythes in a quaint New England village. According to the road sign that flashes briefly on the screen, the name of this idyll is "Shirley."

The most famous son of this quintessential New England village struck all who knew him as a quintessential Yankee, though he wasn't precisely. Benton MacKaye was born in Stamford, Connecticut, in 1879, his father an actor and a failed businessman. He grew tall and impossibly lean, with spectacles, smoked an ever-present pipe, and displayed a stoic tolerance for personal discomfort and deprivation. Lewis Mumford once mused of his friend that MacKaye must subsist on pipe smoke. A Yankee sent straight from central casting.

Shirley Center was not his ancestral home. Benton's older brother William had bought "The Cottage" in Shirley when Benton was a kid, and he fell in love with it—with the freedom and the access to nature it allowed and the escape it afforded from the bustle of the urban world. Nor did he root himself in Shirley Center and make it his life's work. In fact, he led a peripatetic existence, teaching for a while at his alma mater, Harvard; working in New York and in Washington, D.C.; and going down to Knoxville, Tennessee, to work for the Tennessee Valley Authority in its first heady days. He did not make a career—or a living—out of any of them. But he returned to Shirley every time one of these jobs ended, or when he needed respite from a world he found far too noisy. As an old man he described the appeal that the town exerted on him: "Shirley Center, always somewhat insulated from the dust storms of the Sahara of general life…constitutes the essence of community culture vs. metropolitan cacophony."[60]

The year 1921 proved the pivot point in MacKaye's life. In April, his wife Betty, a crusader for women's rights, killed herself after struggling for several years with mental breakdowns. MacKaye never remarried. And in October he published "An Appalachian Trail: A Project in Regional Planning," in *The Journal of the American Institute of Architects*. The unintended symbolism of those six months is almost too obvious: he lost his wife and found his calling.

With that article, MacKaye embarked on the project of his life, the work for which he would earn the name "Father of the Appalachian Trail." At an abstract level, MacKaye's conception of the trail was shaped by two sets of ideas. One came from the Progressive-era ethos of resource conservation advocated most vigorously by President Theodore Roosevelt and his director of the Forest Service, Gifford Pinchot. MacKaye had studied forestry at Harvard, and had worked for the Forest Service, which sent him to Madison, Wisconsin, to study the forest conditions in the Great Lakes region just before the First World War. MacKaye looked at Pinchot as a hero and Pinchot, in turn, wrote an admiring note to MacKaye about the Appalachian Trail project.

The landmark Meeting House in Shirley Center, Massachusetts, where New England met Appalachia. Appalachian Trail founder Benton MacKaye lived here throughout his peripatetic career. He envisioned the Appalachian Trail as a route by which the virtues of the New England town could be brought to everywhere else along its 2,000-mile route. *Library of Congress, HABS MASS 9-SHIR, 1-1*

At the same time, the idea for the Appalachian Trail grew out of the decentralist, anti-urban impulses that gained currency after the First World War. On his way to Madison, MacKaye passed through Chicago, and what he saw appalled him and confirmed what he felt in his guts about American cities. He was revolted by Chicago's "sardined humanity," squeezed in among the smokestacks, "each issuing a grim black cloud that streamed indefinitely across the prairie." Watching bathers on Lake Michigan, MacKaye found a juxtaposition that summed up his feelings about metropolitan civilization: "Here on the beach was the feeble attempt at obtaining Heaven; back in the phalanx of smokestacks was our titanic triumph in attaining hell."[61]

MacKaye met Clarence Stein in 1921, and he joined the Regional Planning Association of America. Stein spoke to the Appalachian Trail Conference in 1925, applauding the trail as a way to counter the pernicious effects of the "possible giant city" he saw swallowing up the eastern seaboard. In the same year, in an article for *Survey* magazine, MacKaye put it more bluntly, "The metropolis is a harbinger of death...the end of the present western mechanical regime." Two years later, MacKaye described the trail in even more colorful terms when speaking before the Appalachian Trail Conference: "And now I come straight to the point of the philosophy of through trails. *It is to organize a Barbarian invasion.* It is a counter movement to the Metropolitan invasion.... The Appalachian Range should be placed in public hands and become the site for a Barbarian Utopia."[62]

For MacKaye, the recreational trail was a means to a much larger end. He hoped to use the trail as a way to promote decentralized development of the entire region. As he described it in his 1921 article, his vision for the Appalachian Trail was of "a project to develop the opportunities—for recreation, recuperation, and employment—in the region of the Appalachian skyline.... It is a project in housing and community architecture."

As he stood on the ridgeline of the Appalachians and looked out, MacKaye saw a nation in distress and a region full of possibilities. "The rural population of the United States, and of the Eastern States adjacent to the Appalachians, has now dipped below the urban," he noted, making reference to data from the 1920 Census, "There are in the Appalachian belt probably 25 million acres of grazing and agricultural land awaiting development. Here is room for a whole new rural population. Here is an opportunity—if only the way can be found—for that counter migration from the city to the country that has so long been prayed for."

As he sketched it, the "project in regional planning" included four components: first the trail; then a series of shelter camps for hikers on the trail; then a set of "community camps" that MacKaye imagined "would grow naturally out of the shelter camps and inns." As he put it, "Each would consist of a little community on or near the trail where people could live in private domiciles." Finally,

MacKaye believed that "food and farm camps" would grow naturally out of the community camps where "in the same spirit of cooperation and well-ordered action the food and crops consumed in the outdoor living would as far as practicable be sown and harvested." This fourth phase of development would "provide one definite avenue of experiment in getting 'back to the land.'"[63] The hiking trail itself was simply a way to link the new communities MacKaye envisioned.

In other words, MacKaye wanted to use a 2,000-mile hiking trail running from Maine to Georgia as a way of exporting the New England village ideal to the underdeveloped, in some cases abandoned, areas of Appalachia, on the one hand, and of providing an escape route for those trapped in the conurbation between Boston and Washington, on the other. Along the spine of the trail, a series of new communities, rooted to the land and built around the spirit of local democracy, would grow. The Appalachian Trail would create a region, like New England, where "cooperation replaces antagonism, trust replaces suspicion, emulation replaces competition."[64] The Appalachian Trail does not run through Shirley Center, Massachusetts, but on it MacKaye believed he could bring Shirley Center all the way down to north Georgia.

It did not work out that way, of course. MacKaye, who had helped convene the Appalachian Trail Conference in 1925 to promote the project, clashed with Myron Avery, the conference chairman, over whether the project should support road-building projects along the Appalachian ridge and the commercial development that would inevitably come with it. Avery, who oversaw much of the nitty-gritty work of putting the trail together, wanted to focus on just that. As he quarreled with Avery, MacKaye became increasingly committed to wilderness preservation for its own sake. "The Appalachian Trail," he told the Conference in 1930, "is a footway and not a motorway because it is a primeval way and not a metropolitan way, because its purpose is to extend primeval environment and to set the bounds to the metropolitan environment.... To preserve the primeval environment: this is the point, the whole point, and nothing but the point of the Appalachian Trail."[65] MacKaye recognized the extent to which public roads would be the way the "metropolitan invasion" would arrive. MacKaye lost these arguments and he walked away from the Appalachian Trail Conference in the mid-1930s.

The trail itself has proved a stunning success. It was pieced together with remarkable speed, all things considered. "Thru" hikers—those who walk the entire trail in one season—began making the journey in the 1930s. But it never came to include the levels of community settlement that MacKaye first proposed. Nor did it stand as the bulwark against metropolitanism—not quite the "retreat from profit" that MacKaye had hoped it would be. In fact, the Appalachian Trail, and the amenities that have grown up alongside it, have contributed to the tourist economy that has developed in the region.

Still, looking back on it once it had been completed, Benton MacKaye believed that the Appalachian Trail stood as "a folk product, pure and simple."[66] MacKaye had worked for the federal government in several capacities, but he needed to believe that his great life's work was really a grassroots "folk product." So did all of those American writers, intellectuals, and policymakers who looked to the American folk for their urban escape.

A New Deal New Town in Appalachia

If you visit the little town of Cades Cove, Tennessee, today, you will find one of the most picturesque settlements in the region and one of the most beautiful places in the country. Tucked into an isolated valley surrounded by the Smoky Mountains, Cades Cove is as perfect an example of Appalachia as one could hope to find. Like Shirley Center in New England, Cades Cove is what Appalachia ought to look like.

Do not expect too much by way of solitude, however. If you take the trip you will join literally millions of other visitors who come every year. Cades Cove is part of the Great Smoky Mountains National Park. Though this is not the largest national park, it is the most visited by a factor of two—more than 9 million people come every year. Cades Cove is the most popular destination within the park. And as you tour the buildings and wander the meadows, you are visiting an elaborate fiction.

Congress officially authorized the creation of the park in 1926, though building the park proceeded in a desultory fashion until the New Deal. The park was established in 1934, and six years later Franklin Roosevelt came down to give it an official dedication. At over 800 square miles, straddling the Tennessee–North Carolina border, Great Smoky Mountains National Park is among the largest protected areas east of the Rocky Mountains and includes some of the highest peaks in the Appalachians, as well as some of its last stands of old-growth forest.

That the park was ready to welcome visitors by 1940 is a testament to the energy of the New Deal and to the hard work of the thousands of Civilian Conservation Corps workers who were sent there to blaze hiking trails, pave roads, and replant trees. They came from big cities, many of them, and the ones from New York renamed their anonymous barracks after grand Manhattan hotels: The New Yorker, the Savoy, and the like.

The workers stare out at you, lean and sinewy and all white, in a short 1936 movie about the building of the park. We see them wielding picks and shovels and little else, leaving the impression that the park's extraordinary infrastructure was built largely by hand. They do not speak to us, but a narrator describes them in a way that makes the connection between urban distress and Appalachian relief: "Here are boys who were struggling in the congested areas of large cities.... The Corps transported them physically and transformed them mentally. They are happy, healed, and saved for better days." The promise here, by extension, is that once the park is open, urbanites of all kinds can come to be healed.

The narrator also describes the cultural value being preserved along with the natural beauty of the area. "The southern mountain folk," he intones, "retain the pure Anglo-Saxon influence in their songs, legends, and characteristics of speech."[67] In just a few years, deracinated Americans could come to the park to find these cultural restoratives, too.

This vision of the region, around which the Great Smoky Mountains National Park was built, was itself created by the folklorists and reformers who came to the southern Appalachians in the first several decades of the twentieth century. And those responsible for the park made sure that what visitors experienced would conform to expectations. When some locals asked the Park Service for permission to run campgrounds and gas stations within the park, they were told in uncertain terms: no. The Park Service vowed to use "every ounce of energy to prevent the hot-dog stand, the soft drink stand, the gaudy filling station ... and the billboards from marring the natural beauty of our gates." Likewise, when local gift-shop owners hoped to sell their wares inside the park, the Park Service decided to deal only with the Southern Highland Handicraft Guild, thus avoiding "an influx of peddling of wares by irresponsible mountain people."[68] Nowhere in the park, however, was a popular image of Appalachia more thoroughly recreated than at Cades Cove.

Recreated, most importantly, by the federal government itself. Just as the centralizing forces of the New Deal attempted to create decentralized new towns, so too the federal government played the main role in turning Cades Cove into a stage set of pre-industrial Appalachia for millions of tourists.

People still lived in the Cove when the Park Service arrived, some of them descendants of the white settlers who arrived early in the nineteenth century. They still made their living farming and lumbering. In fact, the Cove had never been quite as isolated as it now appears. Cove residents had been selling lumber to the outside market throughout the nineteenth century, and the post office had arrived as far back as 1833.

But when Cades Cove was incorporated into the park boundaries in 1930, the Park Service had no intention of letting its current residents stay. Lawsuits ensued and the park ultimately won. The Cades Cove visitors to the park would see a town evacuated of its inhabitants. With the people gone, the Park Service then removed any evidence of twentieth-century life, destroying modern buildings and preserving only those that resonated with the pre-industrial, "pioneer"

Appalachia as it ought to be. When the federal government created Great Smoky Mountains National Park, it also recreated the settlement of Cades Cove to make it more congenial to the tourists who now flocked to see it. *Library of Congress HAER TENN,78-GAT.V,6-20*

life the southern mountains had come to represent. The Park Service returned Cades Cove to a past its own people had left behind, creating a ghost town where it is not clear who, exactly, is haunting the place.[69]

In fact, the federal government did a great deal more to promote tourism in the region as a way of saving it. In 1935, Congress chartered Shenandoah National Park, just a few hours drive from Washington, D.C., and built the Skyline Drive through the middle of it. Benton MacKaye thought of that road as the antithesis of his Appalachian Trail; but in 1942, Olive Campbell and the Southern Highland Craft Guild negotiated a partnership with the National Park Service to sell crafts in a store on the newly built road.

A tourist economy is exactly the opposite of an economy anchored in the geographic and cultural particularities of place. But by the mid-twentieth century it is what linked New England, the Southern Highlands, and the Appalachian Trail. Rather than serving as models for an alternative to centralized, urban life, those places have become weekend excursions from it. The tourist economy is the ultimate expression, therefore, of the metropolitanism that MacKaye, Mumford, and others despised—an economy driven by people in motion, by outsiders in search of something they cannot find otherwise.

Neither the past of New England nor the folk of the Appalachians prompted Americans to decentralize their cities in the ways that many had hoped; instead, they came to feel evacuated and abandoned. The American city would finally be decentralized in the decades after World War II.

6 THE CENTER DID NOT HOLD

THE CITY IN THE AGE OF URBAN RENEWAL

Looked at from one perspective, the decentralizers of the 1920s and '30s got much of what they wished for in the decades after the Second World War. Cities did indeed decentralize, with people and jobs leaving—fleeing—the older, urban cores; Garden City ideas finally found a receptive audience among politicians and policymakers; and the car, the new technology that figured most centrally in the plans of decentralizers, did indeed become both an indispensable feature of American life and the one around which all space was planned.[1]

Looked at head on, what Americans witnessed was the almost complete transformation of the American landscape, urban and rural, in ways that made some incredulous and others heartsick. And that transformative decentralization was funded and facilitated by the federal government. Thus, although the Progressive-era goal had been to use the powers of government to foster urban life, in the postwar period the federal government was instrumental in recreating American metropolitan areas along lines that can only be described as anti-urban.

The story is familiar, but here is a quick review of some numbers nonetheless: Between 1950 and 1960, the nation's population grew by roughly 28 million people. Two-thirds of them resided in the new and burgeoning suburbs.[2] During the decade of the 1950s, eleven of the twelve largest cities in the country saw their populations decline. Some, like New York, Chicago, and Baltimore, saw small drops of between 1 and 2 percent; for Boston, Pittsburgh, and St. Louis, however, the percentages registered in the double digits.

And the 1960 figures were only the beginning. For the next quarter-century or so, the older American cities would continue to bleed population. Chicago began the postwar era as home to 3.6 million souls; it began the age of Reagan with just over 3 million; Philadelphia lost slightly more than 300,000 residents during the same thirty years, roughly 25 percent; Cleveland just over 325,000, a loss of about one-third its population; Detroit lost almost 650,000, going from 1.8 million to 1.2 million people. At the same time, the areas around those cities grew, in some cases spectacularly. As the war broke out, for example, roughly 85 percent of the people in Cook County, Illinois, lived inside Chicago's city limits; by 1990, only 55 percent did.[3] The urban evacuation of the postwar period led to urban crisis, rather than to the kind of urban regeneration the decentralizers had envisioned. The flight from the cities into the new postwar suburbs happened with even less planning than the great urban concentration had half a century earlier. Be careful what you wish for.

Pause over the two ruptures those numbers represent. First, and most obvious, the 1950s stood as the first time since the nation began counting its people that the venerable American cities had not grown. Certainly, the new cities of the South and West grew during this era—Los Angeles exemplary among them—but the nation's population as a whole and its economic life remained centered in the Northeast and around the Great Lakes. Growth had shifted to those regions even as their core cities shrank.

Perhaps more important, the 1950s stand as the decade when the health of the great American cities was divorced from the health of the American economy in general. For a century and a half, the growth in the American economy had been inextricably bound to the growth of American cities. By 1960, that was no longer true. Now, an increasing percentage of the nation's economic activity followed the city residents out to the suburbs, leaving cities not only smaller in numbers but also with disproportionately shrunken revenues and withering job bases as well. As older American cities contracted during the 1950s, the nation's GDP grew by an astonishing 80 percent, from $294 billion to $526 billion.

The flight from the cities was racial as well as economic. White people primarily left the cities; cities thus became increasingly black. Economic activity also left town, and cities became increasingly poor and black. Anti-urban Americans have disliked cities for a long time, but after the war that suspicion was amplified by ongoing racial animosity.

I can cast the story in personal terms. My mother was born in Brooklyn while my grandfather was off fighting in the Second World War. When her sister was born, the family had moved to Queens, to a newly developing area of the borough. By the time the third child came along a few years later, my grandparents had relocated to a brand-new house in the wilds of Long Island. Theirs was the first house in the new subdivision, but it would not stand alone for long.[4]

As they abandoned the older industrial cities, big and small, growing numbers of Americans abandoned liberalism as well. By the mid-1970s those cities—from the deteriorated streets of the South Bronx to the racially volatile section of Watts—represented for the Americans who left them everything that had gone wrong with the liberal agenda. The government's apparent inability to fix the cities—even to keep order in the streets, much less solve the problems of poverty, unemployment, and race relations—represented the folly of big government and was perceived as such from both ends of the political spectrum.

The efforts to renew the cities in the thirty years after the Second World War instead turned them into battlegrounds—sometimes literally—that pitted neighborhoods against city hall, neighbors against each other, planners against citizens, white against black. Perhaps most significantly, in the American consciousness the cities became the places where the public good was set against the sanctity of private interests. At the end of the era of urban renewal, private interests had won, and growing numbers of Americans no longer wanted even to discuss a common good. As Americans abandoned the city, the nation moved from Kennedy's 1961 exhortation, "Ask not what your country can do for you, but what you can do for your country," to Ronald Reagan's 1980 accusatory question, "Are you better off now than you were four years ago?" The sense of collective obligation was being replaced with a demand for individual entitlement. After all, when he was inaugurated the following year, Ronald Reagan told the nation that government was not the solution to our problems, it *was* the problem.

My grandparents' story was recapitulated tens of thousands of times in the postwar era. But as they and those thousands of others transformed the countryside into suburbs, the cities they left behind were changed no less dramatically. This was most true for the "inner cities," as they were called in a code that neatly swirled together race, poverty, and destitution. As America entered its suburban age, cities experienced the age of urban renewal.

We might also call it the "age of planning," an era when cities were torn apart and rearranged by powerful and often unaccountable figures like Robert Moses, Edmund Bacon, and Chicago mayor Richard Daley. The bills that those big-city planners ran up were paid, in turn, by the federal government through the urban renewal and interstate highway programs. Those two programs lasted for roughly a quarter-century, from the late 1940s through the mid-1970s. In 1965, *Look* magazine ran a special issue on "Our Sick Cities," and editorialized "Our cities are seriously sick.... Many of us are worried, and some of us are ready to give up cities for dead." By 1975, few would argue that cities had in any way been renewed. Indeed, the older industrial powerhouses were just entering their worst years of crisis.[5]

How, Exactly, to "Renew" the American City?

In one of his least politic quips, Frank Lloyd Wright once suggested that perhaps the bombing of London by the Nazis was not so bad after all, since it destroyed an overcrowded urban area and thus would force Londoners to plan for decentralization.[6] It was a revealing, if utterly callous, remark.

Wright's provocation to one side, he had inadvertently pointed to a central irony of American cities after World War II. Many European (and Asian) cities did indeed need to be rebuilt in the wake of wartime destruction. From East London to Stalingrad, planners and architects had an extraordinary opportunity to remake these urban spaces, though the results have proved more often than not disappointing. American cities, by contrast, had escaped the bombing. Although people in European cities had to be evacuated or risk death, American cities grew, with factories converting to wartime production and hiring tens of thousands of workers. In 1950, the populations of eight of the ten largest American cities reached their peak.

Expansive with the flush of victory, Americans finally took up the call to rebuild their cities after the war, with the seriousness and on a scale that some had been advocating for nearly fifty years. Europeans had to rebuild out of necessity; Americans did so by choice. As a result, the older cores of American cities came to resemble, on a small scale, the ruined cities of Europe, razed by bulldozers rather than blitzed by bombers. After the war, American cities had to be destroyed in order to be saved. They called it "urban renewal."[7]

After years of agitation by writers, critics, architects, planners, and politicians for a large-scale urban program, Congress passed the Housing Act of 1949. Title One of the Act created the mechanism and formula for urban renewal. Cities could acquire buildings, blocks, or whole neighborhoods deemed "blighted" through eminent domain; the federal government would pay two-thirds of the cost of the acquisition, and the land would then be turned over to private developers for building.[8] The 1954 Housing Act expanded the program so that hospitals, universities, and other institutions could use it for their own expansion, and the program was made even more attractive to private developers by the provision of Federal Housing Administration (FHA)–backed mortgages for urban renewal projects.

In that same year, the Supreme Court removed any legal ambiguities surrounding the use of eminent domain for redevelopment projects in its ruling in *Berman v. Parker.* The case in question originated from a redevelopment project in Washington, D.C. As part of it, a small department store, itself not blighted, was seized by the city through eminent domain. The owner of the store objected, arguing that his store was being taken as part of a larger effort to make the area more attractive, and that the redevelopment plan amounted to stealing land from one businessman in order to give it to another. The Court disagreed and in so doing expanded the interpretation of the "taking" clause of the 5th Amendment to include public "purpose" in addition to public "use." Urban renewal constituted, in the Court's view, public purpose.

Just like the Court's other epochal ruling that year, *Brown v. Board of Education*, this one was unanimous; and just as in *Brown*, the Court saw its decision as fostering a public good and improving life for minorities and the poor. In his opinion, Justice William O. Douglas sounded like a member of the old Regional Planning Association: "If owner after owner were permitted to resist these redevelopment programs on the ground that his particular property was not being used against the public interest, integrated plans for redevelopment would suffer greatly." With the *Berman* decision, the principles of professional planning had been invoked to uphold the larger principle that the public good superseded the rights of private property. And as in the *Brown* decision, the Court believed that *Berman* would lead to a more equitable society.

As it happens, 1954 was also the year that the phrase "urban renewal" came into popular use. No longer would cities merely be "redeveloped"; they would be "renewed" instead. "Redevelopment" smacked of real estate guys doing deals. "Renewal" conjured images of springtime and spirituality, and something almost moral.

In 1954, the *Berman* case opened the door for urban renewal if it served a "public purpose." The case originated in Washington, D.C., where this 1935 photo was taken. Though urban renewal projects would become quite controversial, the image reminds us that the conditions that prompted those projects were not good, either. *Library of Congress, LC-USF33-T01-000138-M2*

But urban renewal meant different things in different cities. It even meant different things in different parts of the same city. Public housing projects. Luxury apartment towers. Small-scale commercial developments. Large downtown office blocks. Whatever and wherever the project, it almost inevitably began with demolition. After a half-century of complaint and concern about overcrowded, dilapidated, unsanitary, and dangerous urban neighborhoods, cities finally had the tools necessary to clear out their slums. And replace them with—what? That was in some ways urban renewal's foundational problem.

Most of the ideas circulating in the 1920s and '30s to solve the urban crisis involved leaving the city, one way or another. Ebenezer Howard and his devotees in the United States, such as Clarence Stein and Lewis Mumford, argued for creating self-contained satellite cities; Frank Lloyd Wright imagined his Broadacre City as essentially rural and certainly disconnected from actual urban places. Much less thought had been given to how to refashion the cities themselves, or to what might become of them if and when people left them in large numbers, as they were clearly now doing.

Urban planners and reformers during the Progressive era found much of their inspiration and many of their ideas in Europe, especially in England and Germany. By the 1940s it was no longer necessary to travel to Europe for that inspiration—and indeed, war made that impossible. Instead, as a result of Europe's turmoil, European refugees came to the United States, and leading European modernists ensconced themselves in American universities. Most significantly, Walter Gropius fled Germany just after the Nazi take-over and became a presiding figure at Harvard's School of Design. But Harvard was not the only place where new ideas about architecture and about the city percolated. MIT launched a PhD program in city planning in 1958, and even more influentially, the University of Pennsylvania combined sophisticated social science research with architecture and planning. Together, these three institutions created a new professional expert: the "urbanist."[9] These urbanists shaped policy in Washington, and they shaped individual projects in dozens of cities.

Perhaps the most influential of the European imports came not from England or Germany but from Paris. It was called "La Ville Radieuse"—the Radiant City—and its creator called himself Le Corbusier. *The Radiant City* was the title of a book Le Corbusier published in 1935, the same year he visited the United States, the year the Museum of Modern Art brought him over for a one-man show of his work.

The Radiant City is at once an architectural program and a statement of urban philosophy. Though it represents the extension and development of some of Le Corbusier's earlier ideas, the Radiant City also reflected the circumstances of the 1930s. Architectural space, along with just about all else in society, needed to be planned and organized centrally by elites and experts in order to eliminate the inefficiencies and chaos that characterized cities, especially in the wake of economic collapse. His was, in some ways, a profoundly anti-democratic vision; the Depression had caused Le Corbusier to lose faith in the power of private markets to build a better society and in the ability of the populace to make wise choices. Le Corbusier came to the United States, but unlike Gropius and the others, he went back to Europe. He did not, as they say, have a good war. When the Nazis invaded France, he cozied up to the Vichy government.

The central feature of the Radiant City, or at least the feature with which it became most associated, was the tall apartment tower set in a large swath of open space that was traversed by high-speed roads. For Le Corbusier, the solution to low-rise density and overcrowding was to tip everything 90 degrees and make it vertical rather than horizontal. The solution to the dirt and disorder of city streets was to eliminate them and replace them with parks and plazas and highways. Born and raised in Switzerland before he moved to Paris, Le Corbusier looked at the city with the fastidiousness and controlling instincts of a watchmaker.

During his American visit, which lasted into 1936, Le Corbusier did the lecture circuit, including talks at some of the nation's most important architecture schools. The specific lines of his American influence are difficult to trace, particularly because his voice joined those of other European modernists who immigrated to the United States in the 1930s and helped to shape the American version of High Modernism. Nonetheless, he clearly had an impact on those who heard him speak and the students who got to know his work during the 1930s. In some of their early work, Marcel Breuer, William Lescaze, and I. M. Pei, among others, owed a debt to Le Corbusier.[10]

Which takes us back for a moment to Queens in 1939. For its display at the World's Fair, General Motors hired a theatrical and industrial designer named Norman Bel Geddes. The result was certainly the most spectacular of the decentralist contributions to the fair. In keeping with the fair's theme, "The World of Tomorrow," the exhibit was called simply "Futurama." Democracity ranked as the second most popular fair exhibit, according to a Gallup poll. Futurama came in first.

Bel Geddes was among those American designers influenced profoundly by Le Corbusier's version of urbanism. Bringing industry and theater together seamlessly, Bel Geddes built a 35,000-square-foot vision of the American metropolis linked to the hinterland by a system of interstate highways. As the Futurama guidebook explained, "Here is an American city replanned around a highly developed modern traffic system.... Whenever possible the rights of way of these express city thoroughfares have been so routed as to displace outmoded business sections and undesirable slum areas."[11] As visitors rode around the exhibit in cars, just like an amusement park ride, the audio script tried to convince them, according to the eminent journalist Walter Lippmann, that if the American people wanted "to enjoy the full benefit of private enterprise in motor manufacturing, it will have to rebuild its cities and its highways with public enterprise."[12]

The intellectual architecture that undergirded American urban renewal after the war was a mixture of all these elements: equal parts Garden City, Radiant City, and what we might call social-scientific modernism coming out of the most important planning and architecture schools in the country.[13] Whatever the merits of any of these on their own, thrown together as they were in the American context they created a set of governing assumptions that in turned shaped specific projects that were, in the end, fundamentally anti-urban.

This assessment isn't mine, though I agree with it. It was offered by journalist and city-lover William Whyte in 1958. As an editor at *Fortune* magazine, Whyte responded in horror to the phenomenon of urban renewal by assembling a collection of essays into a book he titled *The Exploding Metropolis*. In his introduction, he reminded his readers that "each year more people are living in metropolitan areas than ever before, and urban redevelopment has become a fashionable if not always well-understood cause." He went on to present the thrust of the essays he collected: "It is the contention of this book that most of the rebuilding under way and in prospect is being designed by people who don't like cities. They do not merely dislike the noise and the dirt and the congestion. They dislike the city's variety and concentration, its tension, its hustle and bustle."[14]

The litany here is as good a summary of urban virtues as any other. What made the city different from the suburbs, Whyte insisted, were precisely all those things planners wanted to eliminate: variety, concentration, tension, action. Planners and others in the 1920s and '30s saw these urban attributes, in varying proportions, as what was wrong with the American city. And if, in Whyte's assessment, urban activity in all its variety had created specific kinds of urban spaces and forms, then the planners of the urban-renewal age agreed. The solution to urban problems, therefore, was to demolish and rebuild those older urban spaces into something exactly the opposite. That desire coincided nicely with the emphasis of the modernist aesthetic on order and uniformity and its rejection of the past. In fact, desire and aesthetic were mutually reinforcing.

Whyte made an angry accusation, and it was probably a little unfair. Surely many of those city politicians, policymakers, and planners believed that urban renewal was necessary to update the cities for a modern age and to bring a measure of justice to those who lived their lives in urban slums. For better or worse, the road to urban renewal was paved with good intentions, along with naked profit motive. Besides, Whyte did not seem to recognize just how many compromises were necessary between the moment an urban renewal project began and the time it was finally completed—compromises that always put cost ahead of design and expediency often before common sense.

Catherine Bauer, planner and housing advocate, was a thorough insider in the world of public housing and policy by the 1950s, and even she recognized the disappointing results of urban renewal. In 1955, six years into the federal experiment in renewing cities, Bauer firmly believed that progress had been made since the 1930s in housing and planning. But she also acknowledged that the physical environments being created left a great deal to be desired: "This is true whether you look at the results of the FHA formula, with its monstrous and monotonous expanse of suburban chicken-coops, or those of the public housing-insurance company formula, which seems to produce either railroad cars on a siding, or vast institutional buildings that look like veterans' hospitals."

She blamed this in part on the inexperience of planners and designers, who had been given new tools with which to work but had not yet figured out how to do so effectively. After all, they had no tradition of positive, proactive urbanism upon which to draw. She also complained about the "dogma" of architects and planners who

> too frequently assume that there must be a *single* rational, logical solution...which results in vast housing projects that are apparently viewed by their designers mainly as huge pieces of technocratic sculpture, abstract forms that have little to do with satisfying, pleasing or delighting the occupants, as places to *live* in.[15]

More than that, however, she criticized the disconnect between those who did the planning and those who would have to live with it. Plans are presented to the public, she chided, *fait accompli*—no debate, no discussion, no attempt to involve the public in the process before the final results have been unveiled. "This is one of the most backward countries in the world," she offered, "from the viewpoint of public debate about the big issues in architectural design and city planning. Isn't it partly our own fault?"[16]

Whyte was far less charitable. He directed his anger at the results of urban renewal projects without caring much how those results came to be. "The projects are cut off from the life of the city as much as possible," he complained. More specifically, he railed against the physical transformation of urban space, from "variety and concentration" to sameness and sterility. In other words, he objected to the architectural monoculture of modernism that defined so many urban renewal projects, which he summed up as "the standard design for every kind of big housing project, for rich or poor—the wrong design in the wrong place at the wrong time." Whyte quipped about the irony that "the 'garden city' movement may turn out to have had its greatest impact on the central city." [17] That was not quite right. In fact, American urban renewal resulted from a confluence of Ebenezer Howard, Le Corbusier, and the new technocratic urbanists.[18]

Through the 1950s and '60s, the physical and social fabric of American cities would be ripped apart, often savagely, by the housing projects and commercial developments built in the name of urban renewal. The ultimate result was that the American city looked less like Le Corbusier's Radiant City and more like Bel Geddes's Futurama. It might have been the case, as General Motors CEO Charles Wilson told Congress during his 1953 confirmation hearings to be Secretary of Defense, that "what was good for the country was good for General Motors and vice versa." But what was good for General Motors turned out to be not very good for the American city.

Further, public spending on renewing cities through the urban renewal program, though it certainly did benefit private interests, came to be seen more and more as part of a social justice and civil rights agenda, about which a growing number of Americans were becoming disenchanted by the 1970s. The attack on urban renewal—and on the mid-century liberalism with which it became virtually synonymous—arose from both sides of the political spectrum.

The Attack on Urban Renewal, Part I: Enter Stage Left

James Baldwin usually gets credit for coining the phrase, though one suspects it might have had many authors. In a 1963 interview with the pioneering social psychologist Kenneth Clark, a tense and visibly agitated Baldwin accused "urban renewal" of really meaning "Negro removal." The phrase proved irresistibly clever and painfully germane, and whether or not Baldwin came up with it himself, once he used it on television it immediately entered the discussion about urban renewal.

Baldwin was not wrong. By anyone's best estimate, two-thirds of those who were being displaced by urban renewal projects were nonwhite. According to economist Martin Anderson, by 1963 slightly more than 600,000 people had been forced out of their homes by urban renewal projects, meaning that roughly 400,000 of them were black or Hispanic. The enabling legislation provided for relocation assistance, but many people at the time found that assistance inadequate. When it did help people find new housing, the housing was often significantly more expensive. Relocation frequently came to mean moving people from one slum to another.[19] By the late 1950s, the mechanics of urban renewal had come to be seen as part of a racist pattern.

The demographics of displacement, which Baldwin so archly encapsulated, reflected the tectonic shifts in urban demographics that had taken place over several decades. Although it might have come as something of a shock for Americans to see cities like New York and Chicago shrinking between 1950 and 1960, those numbers really reflect a tremendous influx of new urbanites. Between 1940 and 1960, approximately 3 million African Americans continued the great migration from the rural and small-town South to northern cities. During a decade in which it lost 1.4 percent of its total population, New York City saw its nonwhite population jump by nearly 50 percent; Chicago's African American population grew nearly 65 percent. Without those new arrivals, the population loss in America's older cities during the 1950s would have been dramatically larger. New York alone saw 1.3 million of its white residents leave during the decade; 270,000 white Chicagoans left the city between 1950 and 1956. On some afternoon in approximately 1955, a Slovak family from Cleveland or an Italian family from Brooklyn loaded up a moving van, headed to the suburbs, and in so doing reached the tipping point at which more whites began to reside outside of major cities than inside them. Standing on the outbound lanes of any American urban highway in the 1950s, you could watch the white flight pass by.[20]

Given this demographic shift, it was inevitable that large-scale urban renewal projects would have an overly large impact on African Americans. Last to arrive in the city, they occupied the cheapest, often the oldest, and thus shabbiest urban neighborhoods—the ones vacated by earlier immigrants who had pursued their own American dreams up and out of those places. They occupied buildings that did not qualify for FHA loans, owned by landlords who might or might not maintain them. The codes of de facto racial segregation then worked to keep blacks in those neighborhoods. Whether urban renewal represented a conspiracy of white political and business leaders to warehouse African Americans in segregated neighborhoods, or whether it followed its own internal logic by targeting the worst physical conditions, which also happened to be black areas, the result was largely the same: in American cities in the 1950s and '60s, the color of blight was black.[21]

People at the time recognized the potentials and the hazards in this coincidence. Housing analyst B. T. McGraw cautioned that in this confluence of urban renewal and black neighborhoods there was "at once vast potential for improving, as well as great dangers for worsening, the housing opportunities of colored minorities."[22] Just a few years later, however, growing numbers of Americans, black and white, saw conspiracy instead of coincidence, and they reacted to urban renewal with anger rather than optimism.

This criticism irritated supporters of urban renewal, black and white, perhaps more than any other group. The notion that urban renewal destroyed functional, if poor, urban neighborhoods was simply a "romantic illusion," or so Robert Weaver, the administrator of the Housing and Home Finance Administration and the highest ranking black member of the Johnson administration, told an audience at Harvard University. It was an illusion about the ghetto perpetrated by those who did not actually have to live in those neighborhoods. It is a "misconception that they are all stable neighborhoods to which the residents have strong ties," Weaver told the gathering, and he went on in his own measured, understated way: "The typical American slum is not necessarily a neighborhood which has great attractions for its occupants."[23]

So here was another way in which urban renewal foreshadowed a major fault line in American politics of the 1960s. Beyond their undeniable physical squalor, the slums of America's older cities, especially for older liberals like Robert Weaver, represented all the betrayed promises and false hopes of American life for African Americans. Tearing them down must have provided many people with almost visceral satisfaction. For this generation of liberals, urban renewal was another example of positive action from the federal government, the Civil Rights Act in bricks and mortar.

For a younger generation—younger than James Baldwin, though he already sensed the changing mood—urban renewal was a pure product of American cynicism, a way for wealthy and powerful white Americans to make even more money at the expense of impoverished black city dwellers, aided fully by a federal government paying lip service to the concerns of black America. Housing became in the northern cities what lunch counters and bus seats had been in the South.

The Attack on Urban Renewal Part II: Enter Stage Right

Martin Anderson had no interest in urban renewal. Or so he claimed in 1964. He was a young, unknown economist and systems engineer, working as a research fellow at the Center for Urban Studies, run jointly by Harvard University and MIT, and he had a much narrower research focus. He wanted to know "how private enterprise would be affected by the program"—that is, where private investment money for the program would come from, how private construction companies would participate, and whether there was money to be made by the private sector from this federal program.

Imagine Anderson's surprise, then, at his discoveries: "there was not much known about the federal urban renewal program, that government statistics did not support the optimistic reports of some journalists, and that the estimated $20 billion of private investment began to melt away as I began to examine the data."[24] Faced with that discovery, Anderson decided to undertake a much broader examination of urban renewal, drawing on published materials, unpublished government reports, and interviews with people involved in various aspects of the program. What he found shocked him still further, and he summarized his findings in the very title of his 1964 book: *The Federal Bulldozer*. When it came out, it caused an immediate sensation. *Reader's Digest* even excerpted the book in its April 1965 issue.

Anderson insisted that he supported the goals of the original 1949 legislation which promised to provide "a decent home and a suitable living environment for every American." But in the book, Anderson made it devastatingly clear that urban renewal projects failed to deliver on that promise. Anderson built his case with page after page of data, salted liberally with charts, tables and graphs, all documenting failure. By the end, Anderson offered four policy choices for the future of urban renewal: stay the proverbial course and continue the program unchanged; tweak it around the edges to address some of the problems that clearly plagued the program; close the urban renewal program but continue its work through agencies already established; or stop urban renewal altogether. After two hundred pages of analysis, that last one was the course Anderson advocated.

The dispassionate tone of the book, with its social-scientific reliance on statistics and regression analysis, verged on the disingenuous and failed to mask Anderson's agenda. He made it clear in the book that the rights of private property trumped all notions of the "public interest" and that the private market was the only force that could—more to the point, should—solve the problems of urban housing. In fact, Anderson was among the early influential devotees of the novelist Ayn Rand.[25]

To achieve Congress's original goals, Anderson saw two options: "One of these is private enterprise, guided by the complex interplay of the market place." The other "is the federal urban renewal program, guided by over-all plans prepared by housing and city planning experts and approved by politicians." The latter, and Anderson made it sound almost insidious, "relies primarily on the use of public authority and public subsidy and reflects the desires of planners and public officials." Private enterprise, on the other hand, "relies on the voluntary trades in the market place, and thus can reflect the diverse desires of millions of individuals." [26] Faced with those options, who would not choose free enterprise?

That description of the miraculous marketplace—"the diverse desires of millions of individuals"—as somehow more democratic than the actions of politicians and public officials elected through democratic processes was as facile and jejune then as it is today. Anderson resorted to quoting the eighteenth-century British politician William Pitt to make his ideological case in defense of property rights: "The poorest man may in his cottage bid defiance to all the forces of the Crown. It may be frail; its roof may shake; the wind may blow through it; the storms may enter, the rain may enter, but the King of England cannot enter; all his forces dare not cross the threshold of the ruined tenement."[27] Anderson was apparently oblivious to the historical irony: between 1760 and 1832, the English enclosure laws, passed largely at the behest of wealthy landowners, dispossessed tens of thousands of English peasant farmers and drove them into the industrializing cities.

Anderson was just as oblivious to the contemporary American situation. After all, the African American family in Chicago or Cleveland, redlined into their own "ruined tenement," rented to them by an unresponsive absentee landlord, probably did not take much solace in Pitt's exhortation. Indeed, Anderson was either being deliberately obtuse or was simply not paying any attention when he insisted on the impartiality of the free market to make us all happy. As B. T. McGraw succinctly put it in 1958, "only in the markets for housing and home finance will a dollar buy less value in a colored hand than in a non-colored hand."[28] Anderson, like all free-market fundamentalists, simply could not acknowledge that the "market" does not function the same way for all Americans. "Location, location, location" goes the mantra of real estate agents, but in the residential dynamics of the mid-twentieth century, "location" was racially coded. Likewise, when Anderson insisted that "the right of property is probably the most important of all human rights," he betrayed that his concerns lay with the owners of condemned property, not the very sizable percentage of ghetto residents who did not own their own homes.

Nor did Anderson seem aware of the irony that sat at the very heart of his argument. Anderson began his book by challenging the assumption upon which urban renewal was built: that the nation suffered from a housing crisis, most acutely in American cities. He countered:

> This is not true. By any objective, consistent measure the decade from 1950 to 1960 witnessed what was probably the greatest improvement in over-all housing quality ever shown in the United States, especially in cities.... This has been accomplished primarily by private market forces operating independently of the federal urban renewal program.[29]

Presumably—Anderson was not entirely clear about this—he was referring to the enormous boom of suburban construction that took place during that decade. He neglected to mention the ways all of that development was also being subsidized by the federal government, from FHA mortgages to interstate highway construction.[30]

The book quickly generated a firestorm of debate across the pages of several major journals, attracting some of the nation's leading social scientists. Some simply dismissed the book out of hand because of the politics of its author. Sociologist Herbert Gans, for example, called Anderson "an ultra-conservative economist and often irresponsible polemicist."[31] Others took Anderson to task because he relied on data that was already out of date (the data cited ran up to 1962; the book appeared in 1964). Robert Weaver was among those impatient with Anderson's findings for this reason.[32] Those complaints seem both easy and evasive. They allowed critics of the book to chastise Anderson for what was not in it rather than deal head-on with what was, and it offered them the chance to say that more recent data would prove Anderson wrong. Still others argued that Anderson's data, out of date or not, were simply incorrect—or perhaps that he had misread, misunderstood, and/or misused his numbers. Anderson, for example, pointed out that urban renewal projects took an absurdly long time to finish, and on the face of it he was right. But as George Raymond, who chaired the planning department at Pratt Institute, pointed out, many of these projects had in fact been completed but were still carried on city ledgers in an accounting mechanism.[33]

Yet despite his dismissal of Anderson for his politics, Gans largely agreed with the conclusions in *The Federal Bulldozer*: urban renewal had destroyed far more housing units than it had created; it paid scant attention to the question of relocating residents whose housing was demolished; those who did find new, better housing paid a great deal more for it; and the primary beneficiaries of these projects were affluent urbanites, city politicians, and real estate developers. In short, Gans too believed that urban renewal had proved a failure.

Although Gans accepted on its face all of the constituent criticisms that Anderson leveled at urban renewal, from his own ideological point of view, Gans could not accept Anderson's big, final conclusion. Laissez-faire economics, itself an intellectual sham alive only "in reactionary minds and dated economics textbooks," gave us the slums in the first place, he reminded readers. Government intervention was necessary precisely because the market had failed so miserably. Rather than abandoning urban renewal altogether to the wishful thinking of the free marketeers, Gans sketched an even more ambitious program of federal intervention to solve urban problems. It included a regional, rather than strictly city-wide, program of rehousing. He also called for the elimination of poverty through "the deliberate creation of new jobs by government action." [34]

The fight that Gans picked with Anderson in 1965 staked out the battle lines that would define politics for the next generation. Agreeing, at least to a certain extent, on the facts of the situation and insisting that they each had the same goals, Gans and Anderson disagreed fundamentally on how to achieve those goals. Gans, in the spirit of Lyndon Johnson's liberalism, saw federal urban renewal efforts as too timid, too constrained, and he called for more federal action to achieve a greater social justice. Anderson, in his libertarian way, distrusted government altogether and insisted on the empowering forces of the marketplace to house people and improve their lives. Bigger government versus no government, and, crudely put, we have been fighting that fight ever since.

This debate between Gans and Anderson reminds us, however, that the battle lines concerning the nature of American liberalism were first drawn in the postwar era, on the pavement of the American city. Even before the long, hot summers of urban riots, urban renewal became a great symbol of the failure of liberalism to solve social problems. The city, and urban renewal public housing projects perhaps most acutely, became the place where, to borrow Anderson's dichotomy, "private property" was pitted against the "public interest," and where the very notion of the "public interest" began to turn sour for Americans. Take, for example, this 1955 complaint from the local newspaper of the Chicago neighborhood of South Deering and the way it contrasts private homeownership with public housing: "a working man purchases a home...secures a mortgage, improves the property and enjoys the fruits of his labor...city planners and do-gooders decide that they are going to dump a project in his back yard and resettle the entire community."[35] The city provided the first, biggest referendum on the future of liberalism in the mid-century, the most visible, physical manifestation of its promises and its shortcomings. By the mid-1960s, the results of that referendum were not good.

Anderson's book not only propelled his academic career but it launched his political career as well. It made him a force in conservative circles, and as a consequence he became Richard Nixon's director of policy research during the 1968 presidential campaign. He then served in the White House during Nixon's first term. (He is credited with bringing Alan Greenspan, another Ayn Rand acolyte, to Richard Nixon's attention.) From there he went on to advise Ronald Reagan during his presidential campaigns in 1976 and again in 1980. He served Reagan for both terms, including as chief domestic policy adviser. The line that connects the perceived failure of urban renewal in the early 1960s to the New Right's attempt to dismantle the Great Society in the 1980s runs straight through Martin Anderson.

Failure Any Way You Look at It: Urban Renewal as Anti-Urban

Born in controversy and maturing in controversy. That is how Robert Weaver described urban renewal in 1965, but by then there was little controversy about its results. Either from the left or the right, urban renewal was being judged by more and more Americans as a grand and bitter failure. No less a luminary than Martin Meyerson, one of the academic urbanists who created the nexus of policy and university, concluded in 1970 that "it is not debatable that much of urban renewal has caused inconvenience and suffering to the low-income families who lived in the slums, particularly low-income black families."[36] At least it provided some rare common ground for the left and the right by the mid-1960s.

This growing bipartisan rejection of urban policy ignored some notable successes. After the war, cities undertook a number of projects that made urban life unarguably better. New sewer and water lines, for example, in a number of cities. And in those centers of industry, government took the lead in cleaning up the environment by reducing the smoke in the air and the chemicals in the rivers. Most notably, Pittsburgh came out of the smog during those years.[37] As the 1960s wore on, however, urban policymakers got very little credit for these kinds of triumphs.

Likewise, as some people pointed out at the time, cities battled against a number of forces beyond their control: deindustrialization, racial animosity, the flight of people and capital. Political progressives demanded that cities eliminate their slums and with them all of the other social problems afflicting urban America. Conservatives insisted that liberal urban policy caused the slums in the first place. The expectations of the former were as unreasonable as the analysis of the latter was intellectually dishonest.

Even with hindsight, however, one would be hard pressed today to find many willing to defend the urban renewal projects of the 1950s and '60s, so thoroughly has the whole enterprise been discredited in the public's imagination, and in most policy circles as well. Still, its supporters at the time had a point: the criticisms leveled at it with increasing anger were not entirely fair. To those who complained that the relocation assistance promised to people being forced from their homes was insufficient, one might point out that people evicted by the forces of the private real estate market got no help at all. If poor people now paid more rent each month for their new apartments, that was because they had often moved from something squalid to something better. Fifty years on, it is also clear that some of the urban renewal projects did succeed in their objectives, though at the time the obvious failures dominated the debate.[38]

Indeed, some of those "failures" might now be tallied as successes, however unintended. Take, for example, one of Gans's sharpest accusations: that urban renewal, thanks to the broadened parameters of the 1954 legislation, facilitated land grabs by big institutions like universities and hospitals. He was surely right, whether by the University of Chicago in Hyde Park, by Columbia University in Harlem, by the University of Pennsylvania in West Philadelphia, by Ohio State University on its north side, or by any number of other urban institutions. In fact, provisions in the 1959 Housing Act made it easier for institutions to use urban renewal programs for their own growth. Regarding Hyde Park, in 1960 the University of Chicago's plans to buffer itself from the surrounding neighborhood generated one of the earliest organized protests against urban renewal, and as student activism increased during the 1960s, institutional expansion plans often became the focus of local battles because they symbolized larger battles between "the establishment" and "the people."[39]

At the University of Pennsylvania, one such land grab involved the acquisition of a "blighted" six-square block area between 38th and 40th Streets to the east and west, Walnut Street and Spruce Street on the north and south. The late-nineteenth-century houses were leveled and their residents evicted in order to make room for a classic modernist, Corbusian "superblock" of high- and low-rise dormitories, park space, and pedestrian walks created by closing city streets to traffic. Students joined with local community activists to protest the project (and another one that created the University City Science Center several blocks away), and together they applied pressure on the university's trustees to modify or scrap the expansion plans. Today the three high-rise towers loom over a

Urban renewal comes to campus. The expansion of the federal urban renewal program enabled institutions such as hospitals and universities to expand into older urban neighborhoods now deemed "blighted." At the University of Pennsylvania, a modernist "superblock" of dormitories replaced roughly six square blocks of late-nineteenth-century Victorian homes. *University of Pennsylvania, University Archives and Records Center: [ID 20020806001]*

surrounding area where residents of a certain age still feel resentment toward the university for what it did to the neighborhood back in the day.

Fair enough. And yet, a generation after those events, in many of the older industrial cities, hospitals and universities now stand as the largest private employers in places that have seen their industries wither. In turn, they are the major purchasers of local goods and services, making their role in urban economies even more vital. Indeed, in the postindustrial "knowledge" economy, the competitive advantage that older cities have resides precisely in those "meds and eds" institutions, many of which expanded through urban renewal in the 1950s and 1960s.[40] Without those land grabs, several had contemplated leaving their host cities and moving to the suburbs. The University of Chicago might have been bluffing when it made that threat; Temple University, another of Philadelphia's major employers, had the real estate all picked out. So, half a century after Gans criticized urban renewal for enriching hospitals and universities, one could argue that cities made a wise investment.

The point here is not to redeem the reputation of urban renewal, though its legacy may be more complicated than many have allowed. Rather, urban renewal was a conceptual failure, a failure of ideas and imagination. Urban renewal began with demolition, and even after two decades there was still no good answer to the question of how to rebuild after the debris had been cleared.

In the end, urban renewal failed because it was anti-urban. William Whyte's angry complaints about urban renewal weren't merely about aesthetics. They pointed to a flawed set of assumptions about what should be destroyed and what should be built in its place, a misconception that the urban should be made more suburban, a fatal mistake that the city of today could be replaced with Futurama. And in this sense, urban renewal was probably doomed from the start.

Urban renewal began its life as a housing program, though it was later expanded. That urban renewal should focus primarily on housing reflected real conditions in American cities. During the Great Depression and the Second World War, very little new housing had been built anywhere in the country, including in American cities. That changed after the war, but the pent-up demand for new housing and the aging and deterioration of older housing stock meant that housing was a pressing issue for many city residents and urban policymakers. At roughly the same moment that President John F. Kennedy announced his intention to put a man on the moon, more than one-third of the housing units in Manhattan were "old-law" tenements built before 1901.[41] Likewise, when the area of Washington, D.C., at the center of the *Berman* case had been surveyed as part of the redevelopment plan, the results were not pretty: nearly two-thirds of the dwellings were deemed to be beyond repair. The survey also found that residents in almost 58 percent of the dwellings were still using outhouses; 84 percent of the houses had no central heat.

So although the equation of housing and urban redevelopment reflected a genuine desire to improve living conditions, it also resulted from the politics of the legislation itself. As the nation emerged from Depression and war, the notion that the federal government ought to undertake a housing program enjoyed broad, bipartisan support. Even the Senate's leading Republican, Ohio's Robert Taft, stood behind the idea. Having been taken on tours of the slums of Cleveland and his own Cincinnati, Taft "found no alternative to public housing as a method of providing low income rentals to those at the bottom of the income scale."[42] In 1943, as member of a Senate subcommittee, Taft issued a report calling for the government to finance 500,000 units of public housing.

Taft's support of public housing doubtless stemmed from a certain patrician *noblesse oblige*, but it also grew from his almost nineteenth-century sense of domesticity, and his convictions about the relationship between home and morality. His report put it bluntly: "Every family must have a decent home in which to live. The character of that home determines more than anything else the character of family life, the conditions in which children grow up and the attitude of people toward the community and government."[43] The Senate's leading conservative sounded like a Progressive-era reformer.

Housing, however, was as far as it went for Taft, and for many others. As Robert Weaver recalled, "In 1945 [Robert Taft] was joined by other members of the Subcommittee on Housing and Urban Redevelopment of the Senate Special Committee on Post-war Economic Policy and Planning in believing that all redevelopment projects should stress housing... and that the federal government should not 'embark upon a general program of aid to cities looking to their rebuilding in more attractive and economical patterns.'"[44]

It was fitting, really, that Robert Taft should have been behind the narrow focus on housing. As the most prominent conservative ideologue throughout the 1930s and 1940s, this wealthy child of Cincinnati helped position the Republican Party as the anti-urban party in the postwar period. Though he supported the creation of public housing for the poor, he had no interest in a broader program of urban revitalization. And thus, neither did the Senate during the years when he held sway.

By the mid-1960s, therefore, the urban renewal program was being judged primarily on its record as a housing program—and being judged a failure, both because it did not replace nearly as many housing units as it destroyed and because it did an inadequate job of relocating displaced people, as well as on its record as a civil rights program whose purpose was to improve the lives of urban blacks. That dynamic was what James Baldwin condensed into the pithy phrase, "urban renewal means Negro removal."

Furthermore, urban renewal was a mechanism used to create a variety of urban transformations, from commercial centers to office towers to new hospital wings. But for many Americans the most potent symbol of urban renewal and all its ills was public housing. Here, the equating of race and squalor, of urban chaos and federal spending, of taxpayer money and social dysfunction could be seen most starkly. More than any other part of the urban renewal agenda, the "projects" stood for everything that had gone wrong.

But Baldwin's phrase was not entirely right, either. Fully one-third of those forced out of their homes by urban renewal were white, and often these people constituted what remained of ethnic enclaves formed at the turn of the twentieth century. Herbert Gans had come to national attention as a critic of urban renewal because of his 1962 book *Urban Villagers*, a study of Boston's white, working-class (mostly Italian) West End as it became the site of urban renewal. Urban renewal could also mean Italian (or Polish or Irish) removal.

The racial dynamics of urban renewal were more complicated than Baldwin allowed, even in cities without those old ethnic villages. Between 1959 and 1964, for example, the city of Columbus, Ohio, initiated four major urban renewal projects, three of which were located in the center of the city. Columbus was decidedly not like Boston or Chicago in a number of ways. Never home to large-scale industry, it never attracted great waves of southern or Eastern European immigrants. The city had a small workshop economy, but by the 1950s it was already on its way to establishing a postindustrial economy based on state government, the state's land-grant university, insurance and banking, and overland shipping.

Overall, roughly 2,300 households were forced out of their homes in Columbus. Just north of the state capitol, the Goodale Project Area's displacement mirrored the national statistics exactly: 66 percent of those who had to move were black; in the Children's Hospital Clearance Area, the figure was 86 percent; but in the Market-Mohawk Project, only 11 percent of those displaced were black. Just as interestingly, though the average annual incomes of black and white residents of these three areas were similar (and low), in two of those areas black income was higher than white income. And although Columbus's projects were small compared to Chicago's, the end result seems to have been little change in the patterns of racial segregation: black Columbus-ites moved into slightly more integrated neighborhoods whereas whites moved into more segregated areas.[45]

Gans spent almost a year living in the West End in order to write *Urban Villagers*. He wondered whether the way of life among these Italian Americans could be attributed to their Italian heritage or to their class. Gans concluded that it was mostly the latter. And though he insisted that he did not present a romanticized view of his subjects, it is a story of loss. The area, after all, was about to be leveled and the social webs that held it together were about to unravel. Many readers found in Gans's description of the West End a coherent urban community, a functional neighborhood, a genuine village. Gans himself had fled the Nazis as a teenager and wound up studying sociology at the University of Chicago. Robert Park was gone by that point, and so were some of the other founders of the Chicago School, but Gans found in the West End the kind of neighborhood that they had found in Chicago a generation earlier. Already in eclipse, what remained of those neighborhoods died when urban renewal came to town. Even the progressive community organizer Saul Alinsky insisted that people recognize "the legitimate self-interest of white communities."[46]

Commentary captured the tension between urban renewal as a program to save American cities and as a program of social justice when it published a forum on urban renewal in 1965. On one side stood Herbert Gans, who had long believed urban planners ought to focus on social problems rather than on physical space. He argued in almost moralistic terms that urban renewal must lead to social justice for the urban poor. On the other side, George Raymond argued that if urban renewal focused entirely on the poor it would miss the urban forest for only some of its trees, and would leave the urban ecology fundamentally out of balance. "Cities deprived of their upper and middle classes, and thus composed chiefly of the poor," Raymond insisted,

> would inevitably entail a serious deterioration in the quality of our entire civilization, since it is the *cities*, not the suburbs, that have always carried and nurtured this precious, complex heritage.... In [Gans's] legitimate concern with the problem of the poor, he is much too ready to sacrifice the city.[47]

In the context of 1965, it was a provocative suggestion: cities needed their wealthy and middle class; the city's primary role was to create a civilization; cities could not survive if they simply became large social service projects. To focus exclusively on civil rights and on questions of poverty and social justice risked sacrificing the larger health of urban civilization.

It was also a suggestion easily dismissed.

The exchange between Gans and Raymond appeared in July, a month before the Los Angeles section of Watts exploded in violence and destruction, eleven months after Harlem and North Philadelphia had done the same. The problems of African America were the problems of urban America, and to plead on behalf of the urban upper class verged on the reactionary. Besides, Gans quipped in reply, to judge by the proliferation of movie theaters and the like, American "civilization" seemed to do just fine in the suburbs.

This was how urban renewal, which had been conceived of as primarily a housing program, became the battleground pitting various urban constituencies against each other: poor against wealthy; black against white; business interests against "community" interests. Had James Baldwin given his interview to Kenneth Clark a year later, in 1964, he might have used the term "gentrification" to describe all this. The British sociologist Ruth Glass coined the term that year to describe neighborhood transformations in English cities, as middle-class people moved into working-class areas. The term quickly crossed the Atlantic and became both a description and an epithet.

The irony is that, although gentrification was denounced and resisted in dozens of urban neighborhoods, the larger problem that American cities faced was systematic disinvestment, which left neighborhood after neighborhood, from Roxbury to Watts, without jobs, banking services, or even grocery stores.

Lyndon Johnson Doubles Down

In the spring of 1965, Walter Reuther, president of the United Auto Workers, called on President Johnson to create a "Marshall Plan" for American cities. The Marshall Plan had helped rebuild European cities destroyed by war. American cities had been scarred in the short term by urban renewal projects and in the longer term by the plate tectonics of the American economy as it shifted away from the industrial cities.

American cities did not get their Marshall Plan. In 1965, Johnson assembled a Task Force on Metropolitan and Urban Problems, chaired by MIT professor Robert Wood. The committee was something of a hodge-podge and ultimately found little consensus to offer the president about urban problems or solutions. Indeed, not everyone on the task force even cared about the American city. As chairman Wood complained, one task force member, psychologist Karl Menninger, "didn't believe in cities. He kept coming in saying we ought to all go back and live on the farm."[48]

On September 9, 1965, Johnson signed the Housing and Urban Development Act, which created a new cabinet-level agency: Housing and Urban Development. In so doing, he gave federal bureaucratic permanence to the equation of housing issues with urban issues. The conflation between the two could now be summarized by the less-than-mellifluous acronym: HUD.

Having created HUD in 1965, Johnson dithered before appointing its first secretary. He finally chose Robert Weaver, who thus became the first African American cabinet secretary in the nation's history. Though he was eminently qualified for the post, by the mid-1960s Weaver was seen, at least by some younger activists, as out of touch with African Americans and out of step with the march of the civil rights movement. That this was unfair misses the point: these were the terms by which the founding secretary of the new HUD would be judged. Though Weaver's appointment made sense in all sorts of ways, it confirmed the growing sense that "housing and urban development" was merely an extension of a larger civil rights agenda, not necessarily an urban agenda.

It was certainly true that housing emerged as a pressing civil rights issue in the metropolitan regions of the North. If state legislatures had created the tangled web of Jim Crow laws in southern states, then northern segregation had been created by a less formal, though no less effective, collaboration of block-busting realtors, discriminatory mortgage lenders, and local politicians anxious to placate angry white homeowners.[49] Martin Luther King Jr. felt the full force of that anger when he tried to march into the Chicago suburbs to demand open housing.

The connection between urban issues and civil rights issues was made even stronger in the public mind in 1966, when Johnson created the Model Cities program. Ostensibly, this was Johnson's response to the urban riots of the previous year, but Model Cities also offered an opportunity to address some of the critiques of the urban renewal program. It demanded more comprehensive planning, and it also attempted to join physical projects with the coordination and delivery of social services. Run by the new HUD, Model Cities joined Johnson's urban agenda tied even more tightly to his War on Poverty.

By 1966, therefore, before the worst of the urban riots, the equation was complete: the urban crisis was synonymous with the racial crisis.[50] The prophecies made by Josiah Strong and W. E. B. Du Bois—Strong predicting that the problem of the twentieth century would be the urban problem and Du Bois claiming that it would be the color line—had converged in the mid-century city.

Further, cities provided the best (or worst, if you prefer) example of the folly of large-scale federal programs and the failure of postwar liberalism; the city was the place where the "common good" was made the enemy of "private interest." As the 1960s wore on, this was how a growing number of Americans came to view their cities. These were also the terms through which the backlash against the city became a larger backlash against liberalism altogether. When Atlanta mayor Sam Massell said of urban renewal early in the 1970s, "Federal encroachment is Federal salvation," he summarized how by the end of the decade the city and the federal government had become entirely linked.[51] He also inadvertently captured how Americans who rejected the city were rejecting the expansive federal government as well.

At Weaver's swearing-in ceremony, President Johnson made a few remarks reaffirming his commitment to the American city. Critics, he noted, claimed that "the city has become unmanageable, unworkable, and unbelievable." But he did "not believe for a moment that the cause of the American city is yet lost.... We are setting out to make our cities places where the good life is possible."[52]

That was the problem exactly, was it not? Johnson's fine words only underscored that the nation had not developed a vision of positive urbanism and did not really know what it meant to live the good life in the city. There was little in the American tradition to suggest that such a life was even possible. The "good life" was what people left the city in order to find. Urban renewal may not have achieved its intended goals, but the larger failure was at the level of urban vision. As one policy expert put it in 1966, "there was no clear conception of a way of urban life that could be achieved through a good urban renewal program."[53]

Five years later, Chase Manhattan Bank CEO David Rockefeller began promoting his own plan to save the city (or at least New York City). When asked about the billions the federal government had already spent trying to fix urban America, Rockefeller responded by saying,

> I think as we look back now at the federal program... [a criticism] that perhaps could be made of it: It concentrated almost exclusively on housing and not on other related community activities, and I think this has proved to be a mistake. The funds were not used to build a rounded community; they merely built houses.... Often, in fact, the vital element of community life was less than it was before.

Rockefeller believed that a proper program of urban revitalization would "develop whole new communities rather than units of housing, or commercial establishments, or industrial areas separately."[54] In other words, Rockefeller reached for a holistic conception of an urban ecology. Urban renewal had for twenty years proceeded without one.

It remains an irony that the era of urban renewal coincided with a low-water mark in American architecture, and that architecture made an easy target for critics like William Whyte. But the failure of urban renewal was not, in the end, a failure of architecture, awful though so much of it was. Architecture alone could not address the myriad problems cities faced, nor could it provide the answer to the question of what the "good life" meant in the city.

That lack of an urban vision, that failure of imagination might well explain the appeal of Le Corbusier for the architects and planners who imported the Radiant City into the American city. Say what you will about Le Corbusier, but he was indeed an urbanist, someone who did not shy away from the scale of modern life or from urban concentration. Big cities, he believed, were inevitable. The challenge was to make them work.[55] In this sense, Le Corbusier stood as the antithesis of Mumford—who hated him from the moment his writings made it to American shores—and the other decentralists who saw the salvation of the cities in shrinking and dispersing them. He was the antithesis, too, of Frank Lloyd Wright, America's home-grown utopian planner of the era. Wright denied the city altogether and fantasized that it could simply disappear. William Whyte had a point in saying that Le Corbusier's ideas were wrong for the city, but America's anti-urban tradition meant that few had an alternatively compelling vision of what the new city could be, even as the old city was torn down.

Meanwhile, across town…

Urban Roads as Urban Renewal

On February 10, 1952, the *Washington Post* ran a Herblock cartoon that featured a set of city buildings—more New York, frankly, than Washington, D.C.—each festooned with banners and billboards advertising new cars. In the middle, two passengers sit in a convertible on top of a mammoth heap of other cars, some with passengers who are reading the newspaper, others covered in cobwebs. It is a stylized rendering of a traffic jam. And on the top of the heap, one passenger in that convertible delivers the punch line to the other: "What I Want Is A New Model City."

Not bad. The juxtaposition of the old city streets with the ads for new model cars that results in a literal traffic pile-up is worth a chuckle. But it also captures nicely two elements of the postwar urban discussion. First, Herblock summed up the desire to rebuild American cities in that neat phrase "model city." In fact, Herblock anticipated the use of that phrase for a Great Society program by more than a decade. Second, the cartoonist put his inky finger exactly on what would drive the reshaping of the American urban landscape: the car.

In the years after the war, the full flowering of Automobile America was stunted by the condition of the nation's roads, and even more by the urban traffic jams that had become so common that Herblock could joke about them. Urban "congestion" had been a major concern for the Progressive urbanists, but they meant the crowding of people into small spaces. In 1939, when all those Americans went to Queens to see the World of Tomorrow, the Public Roads Administration issued a report calling "for the construction of broad express highways, extending into and through the hearts of great cities."[56]

By the 1950s, the urban congestion problem meant cars even more than people. A panel of Yale professors said so in a 1950 report: "city streets [have] become totally inadequate. As a result, all larger cities today are plagued by a near paralysis of traffic."[57] Rushing into this gridlock, the federal government promised to solve the crisis.

Walter Lippmann could not have known just how right he would prove to be when he quipped in 1939 about Futurama that, if America was "to enjoy the full benefit of private enterprise in motor manufacturing, it will have to rebuild its cities and its highways with public enterprise." After the war was over, public spending on highways did indeed stimulate—subsidize, really—not just the auto

"What I Want Is A New Model City"

This 1952 Herblock cartoon captured the mood of many Americans who were eager finally to rebuild their cities, particularly to make them friendlier to automobiles. *A 1952 Herblock Cartoon, © The Herb Block Foundation*

industry but the real estate and construction industries as well. That spending enjoyed wide public support and still does.

In fact, the federal government had been in the highway-building business since the passage of the Federal Aid Act of 1916; $400 million for highways had been allocated as part of the National Industrial Recovery Act of 1933. Plans for an integrated national system of highways had been percolating ever since, when the Federal Highway Act called for the design of 40,000 miles of interstate highway. By that time, a powerful highway lobby had formed that included interests ranging from civil engineers to auto makers to concrete producers. Their diligent lobbying reached an apotheosis with the 1956 Interstate Highway Act, whose broad outlines were shaped by the 1944 blueprint.[58] They called it the biggest public works project in the nation's history and the greatest engineering feat of all time.

The bill called for $26 billion to be spent on the highways, with a goal of completing the now 41,000 miles of road by the end of the 1960s. Road-graders fired up their engines almost immediately after President Eisenhower signed the legislation. By the end of 1956, Bureau of Public Roads general counsel Clifford W. Enfield crowed: "Perhaps the greatest advancement to be enjoyed by Americans during the 20th century may not come about because of nuclear energy, startling medical advances, or interplanetary communications, but by enactment of the Federal Aid Highway Act of 1956." Enfield added, "This legislation calls for environmental changes for the United States on a scale so staggering as to dwarf any prior peacetime endeavors of mankind." [59]

He was right. Searching for comparisons, the bureau issued a report asserting that the total dirt and rock removed to grade the roads would cover an area the size of Connecticut "knee-deep"; the total concrete used "would build six sidewalks to the moon"; and the amount of drainage pipe required "equals the quantity used in the combined water and sewer-main systems in six cities the size of Chicago."[60]

Within approximately twenty-four months, therefore, the federal government created two programs that would profoundly alter the physical and social landscape of the American city. And with an area the size of Connecticut covered in two feet of construction fill, the Interstate Highway Act made urban renewal look trivial.[61]

The road engineers headed to the city, where the traffic problems made the promise of cars zipping effortlessly along high-speed, multi-lane roads most seductive. City officials saw urban interstates as part and parcel of urban renewal plans, and many city mayors lobbied on behalf of the Interstate Highway Act. They believed that highways would revitalize downtown commercial districts by making it easier for suburban shoppers to get into the city; they would clear out crowded nineteenth-century neighborhoods whose density made them unworkable in the twentieth century. They thought real estate values would rise in neighborhoods where choked streets were transformed by on-ramps; they saw decrepit buildings replaced by that most American symbol of progress, fast-moving cars.

Highways would facilitate finally the reorganization and decentralization of urban space in the rational ways planners had been dreaming up for years.

City officials did not express any doubts about all this, at least not publicly, and there is something naïve, almost poignant about the enthusiasm with which they embraced the new urban expressways. None of them seemed to realize that a high-speed expressway designed to bring shoppers effortlessly downtown would make it that much easier for people to leave the city as well. And people did just that—in the millions, taking their jobs with them, along with their disposable income and their school-aged children.

The Philadelphia Planning Commission report of 1950 called for an expressway to "relieve Philadelphia's traffic congestion," and to "provide the necessary links in the internal circulation system of the city... thereby adding to the convenience and efficiency of the city structure."[62] The result was Interstate 76, running north and south through the heart of Philadelphia, completed in 1960. Three years later a modest shopping mall opened at the western end of the highway in an inconsequential place near Valley Forge called King of Prussia. Today, that mall is the largest retail mecca on the East Coast and its very name has become synonymous with "going to the mall." Meanwhile, the eastern stretch of Market Street that was once the center of the city's downtown retail has seen the number of its big department stores dwindle from five to one. And so it has gone in any number of American cities.[63]

How many? That is an interesting question. Although people at the time attempted to do a full and honest accounting of the urban renewal program and its consequences, the highways plowed through the American city without quite the same level of scrutiny. In his 1958 assessment of urban renewal, B. T. McGraw casually mentioned that the highway projects "will involve similar urban population displacements with the first year's estimates under current plans already at ninety thousand families." And though people had begun to complain already that the relocation assistance provided by urban renewal was not adequate, McGraw noted that there was no such requirement for highway projects. By his estimate this left 90,000 families to fend for themselves.[64] According to a 1969 estimate by the National Commission on Urban Problems, highway construction had destroyed at least 330,000 buildings in the previous ten years, roughly 33,000 each year. But in 1971, Ben Kelley wrote that highway construction displaced more than 50,000 people each year. This astounding figure seems too big to be correct, but Kelley was in a position to know. From 1967 to 1969 he served in the Department of Transportation as the public affairs director for the federal road program.[65] Since rural roads went through largely uninhabited areas, one can assume that those 50,000+ lived primarily in cities and surrounding areas.

If those figures are too large and abstract, then perhaps looking at specific places can help us understand the scale of urban destruction that took place. As Interstate 40 rolls through Nashville, Tennessee, it swings away from the downtown core and travels through an area where 626 homes and 27 apartment buildings used to stand. In Baltimore, Maryland, by 1964 highway projects had leveled one out of every five houses occupied by poor blacks. In St. Paul, Minnesota, construction of the St. Anthony-Rondo expressway began by tearing down 433 houses. The tangled mess of urban interstates that came to eviscerate Cleveland forced 19,000 people from their homes by the early 1970s in a city where people were already leaving. [66]

Every city that built a highway during the 1950s and '60s—that is, every city in the country—tore out older neighborhoods, displaced poorer residents, and created concrete scars across its surface, house by house, building by building. And there is some evidence that the road engineers were even more indiscriminate in their destruction than the urban renewal planners. In Topeka, for example, 30 percent of the housing destroyed for urban renewal projects had been graded "good"; for highway projects the figure was almost 50 percent.[67]

Highway projects could destroy city neighborhoods even if they were never built. The simple announcement of a new highway usually created upheaval in the real estate market in the affected area. Early in the 1960s, engineers announced plans to build a piece of I-79 through a section of Pittsburgh. By 1970, the project was still on the drawing board. However, as *Business Week* reported,

> The knowledge that an expressway would be built changed—and is still changing the neighborhood.... People long ago stopped painting their houses or making repairs. Buildings have been abandoned and boarded-up doorways are common.... The pattern of squalor duplicates the right-of-way of plans on Highway Department maps, stretching three miles and ranging in width from little more than a block to seven blocks at a point where a major interchange is planned.[68]

Likewise, when plans to build a crosstown expressway in Philadelphia along South Street were announced, the real estate market took a dive. Neighborhood activists killed the project, though only after years of fighting and uncertainty. By the time of their victory, however, significant sections of the South Street area had deteriorated just as they had in Pittsburgh. It took more than a generation for the neighborhoods along the two-mile corridor to recover. If a neighborhood was not quite a slum when a project was announced, it might well become one after the announcement.

To say that construction projects involving wholesale demolition, countless numbers of bulldozers, dump trucks, and concrete mixers, and thousands upon thousands of workers flew under the radar screen in the 1950s and '60s is to exaggerate more than a little. Certainly, a handful of proposed road projects in high-profile places generated high-profile protests: even before Philadelphians fended off the South Street Expressway, neighborhood activists had stalled work on San Francisco's Embarcadero freeway and their counterparts in Greenwich Village had killed a crosstown expressway slated to go straight through Washington Square. That fight would bring the writer and activist Jane Jacobs to national attention.[69]

Still, there is something remarkable in the fact that highway projects did not seem to attract nearly the same level of critical attention that urban renewal projects had at virtually the very same moment. In one survey of the displacement problem, researchers looked at ten cities, but in only two of them did they include data about highway displacements along with data about urban renewal. By 1970, only three major court cases had been filed opposing the construction of highway projects. [70]

Even on the question of displacement and relocation, highway projects seem to have escaped the same kind of attention as came to urban renewal projects. In 1962, Congress demanded that states provide relocation assistance for people displaced by highways. States simply ignored this mandate, even while they kept spending federal money on the projects. Ignored it and then lied about it. According to one report, "there appears to be a nation-wide trend by state highway departments to falsify certifications to the federal highway officials of the existence of adequate housing for those displaced by highway construction.... State highway officials are giving totally inaccurate certifications of relocation housing to the federal government in order to gain approval of their projects."[71] Only in 1968, with one year left in the original program authorized in 1956, did Congress begin providing federal money to assist those whose homes had been paved over.

By that time, an anti-highway movement had developed, and it was large enough for *Newsweek* to cover it. The story focused on fights in five cities—San Francisco, Chicago, New Orleans, Washington, D.C., and Cambridge, Massachusetts. *Newsweek* quoted an anonymous highway planner who despaired: "The people are not as foolish as we used to think. They won't let you shove a plan down their throats anymore." In response to the growing protest movement, Secretary of Transportation Alan Boyd threatened that he might enforce an existing law and withhold federal funds for highway projects that "fail to allow for sociological, economic and esthetic considerations." That heresy drew a hysterical blast from a spokesman for the Firestone Tire and Rubber Company, who accused the Department of Transportation of being "dedicated to the damnation of anything automotive."[72]

It was also clear to some highway opponents that the same racial dynamic at work in urban renewal projects was at work on the interstates, as those figures from Baltimore demonstrate. In St. Paul, 72 percent of the housing destroyed had been occupied by black residents. Never big on subtlety, the white establishment in Alabama proposed in 1961 to run a new highway directly over the house of Martin Luther King's adviser, Ralph Abernathy.[73] Activists tried to capture this intention in the same kind of pithy slogan as Baldwin had used to critique urban renewal, and they came up with "No more white highways through black bedrooms." In truth, the phrase did not have the same ring, and it never caught on to the same extent. Although housing and its relationship to urban renewal became a central part of the civil rights agenda, highway construction did not, despite all the evidence that highways destroyed black neighborhoods at least as effectively. A 1968 collection of academic essays considering the relationship between urban planning and social policy devoted an entire section to "housing and urban renewal"; it mentioned "highway construction" just five times in 450 pages and then only in passing.[74]

Simply put, urban issues caused political fracture while interstate highways enjoyed widespread public and political support. There was certainly broad political support to solve the housing "crisis" after the war, and the 1954 Housing Act passed in the Senate comfortably by a vote of 59 to 21. Two years later, the Interstate Highway Act passed with only a single no vote. Initially, the highway builders raced against a thirteen-year clock. The original 1956 act was designed to expire in 1969. Projects got under way quickly and pushed forward relentlessly; by 1959, there was already $8 billion worth of work being done.[75]

Yet even with opposition to highways mounting in American cities and the program set to expire, in 1970 Congress tacked on another seven years. Roughly 26,000 miles of the planned 41,000 had opened to traffic by that time, but more to the point, highways had thoroughly insinuated themselves into every aspect of American life, altering the social and physical landscape more profoundly and more quickly than anything else in American history. By that time, highways had become a central fact of the American economy as well. By one estimate, one out of every five workers in 1970 worked directly or indirectly building roads; similarly, 20 percent of the gross national product was associated with road construction.[76]

As the first phase of the program was expiring, and as Congress crafted its extension, Federal Highway Administrator Francis Turner could claim that opposition to the highway program involved fights over about 150 miles of road, out of a sum total of over 40,000, and took place in just sixteen of the 200 cities where highways were being built. "A small percentage in anybody's figure book," he said, and who could argue?[77] Even as *Newsweek* reported on highway protests across the country, it reiterated, as if it needed saying, that "the need for more superhighways is not questioned," even by those who protested them. As late as 1970, as community groups in Chicago mobilized in response to the proposed Crosstown Expressway, which would displace an estimated 4,000 black residents from Englewood to Woodlawn, they did so not to kill the road but to mitigate its effects. As Charles Wise, the president of the Organization of Southwest Communities, put it, "We're not opposed to the highway. We just hope the city can plan its route so 4000 people won't lose their homes."[78]

Indeed, the destruction and displacement caused by highway projects represented such an unalloyed public good at the time that the *Chicago Tribune* used them as a way of justifying the urban renewal project in the Hyde Park/Kenwood neighborhood. "Objections have also been made that the plan will cause the displacement of 4,500 families, of whom about 2,100 are Negro," the *Tribune* editorialized, but it went on to reassure readers: "Displacement of people is a regrettable but unavoidable result of nearly all large civic improvements." The proof of that? "The expressways, for example."[79]

One explanation, perhaps, for the different way the public reacted to these federal initiatives may lie in the mechanisms through which they were carried out. Broadly speaking, urban renewal projects created partnerships between the federal government and city officials—elected and appointed—in order to plan and execute urban renewal. The money came from Washington, but the actors in each city were local. Therefore, anyone who wanted to complain about urban renewal had a relatively easy time figuring out where the buck stopped. Even if these city officials could not be held accountable, in many cases they were handy targets for people's anger and frustration.

Highway projects worked quite differently. The money still came from Washington, and even more generously. The federal government paid 90 percent of the cost of a new expressway. But the money was channeled through state departments of transportation. Working from a national blueprint conceived in 1944 and cast in concrete in 1956, state road engineers worked out the details of projects from their offices in Harrisburg, or Springfield, or Albany—far away, in other words, from the people whose lives they proceeded to disrupt. Accountable to no one.

Although there were doubtless racial implications in the way highway projects were built, it is not clear just how deliberate this was. Without question, these roads took the path of least resistance, which meant through poor neighborhoods, declining industrial districts, and often along waterfronts or through parks. But whether these roads had racial segregation as a primary goal seems murky at best. Whatever else might be said about the state highway engineers, they had certainly mastered their basic geometry. For them, the shortest distance between two points was usually a six-lane straight line, and they had little interest in what might be in the way. A 1944 report that became the basis for what would become Interstate 25 through Colorado put this quite wonderfully, if inadvertently. As the highway approached Denver, the report concluded, "the city interposes a traffic obstacle measured by a time loss of fully one-half hour. It is the function of the proposed new thorough-fare to remove this obstacle."[80]

Likewise, though urban renewal projects had come to be seen by the mid-1960s as symbols of the failure of federal policy by both right and left, the highways did not produce the same anti-government feeling, though they surely represented an enormous expenditure of public money and a huge imposition by the federal government on states and localities.

Although a 90–10 percent funding formula seems on its face to be a great deal for individual states, the aggregate costs to states in the first year of the program came to nearly $1 billion, 30 percent higher than state spending on roads the year before. Some states had their budgets affected even more dramatically. Take the state of Vermont, for example. Still a rock-ribbed Republican bastion in the 1950s and early '60s, Vermont embraced the federal highway money. But to meet the federal match, Vermont had to double its own highway budget. Reluctant to raise user fees of any sort to cover these costs, Vermont borrowed money by issuing bonds. Between 1955 and 1973, a staggering 84 percent of state highway spending came from bonds, leaving Vermont with an equally staggering debt to service. Cheap roads turned out to be quite expensive in state after state. So much for "states' rights."[81]

Early on, the *Wall Street Journal* called the interstate highway project "a vast program thrown together, imperfectly conceived and grossly mismanaged, [that] is in due course becoming a veritable playground for extravagance, waste and corruption."[82] The *Journal* was right, but few agreed or even bothered to look too closely. Critics who railed against the follies of urban renewal remained largely silent about highway projects. Martin Anderson had no counterpart denouncing the public funding of highways and insisting that the private sector should build them instead.

And in the final irony, the interstate highway program often subverted the major goal of the urban renewal program. Though city mayors saw the two programs as part and parcel of their goals to reshape their cities, and those whose lives were being upended probably made little distinction about why they were losing their homes, by the end of the 1960s it was clear that the highway program was exacerbating rather than solving the housing problem that had been the purpose of urban renewal in the first place.

The editors of the *Yale Law Review* came to this conclusion in 1972, and they minced no words. "The housing acts have failed to achieve their goals," they wrote, and went on to point the finger squarely at the interstate: "The construction of urban highways continues to frustrate the national goal of providing every American with a decent home." They elaborated:

> In no small part, this failure has been due to the federal highway program. During the first decade of the Interstate Program, right-of-way clearance for federal highways destroyed more units of low-and moderate-income housing than were built by the federal government's public housing program. City planners have used highways to get rid of the oldest and least desirable housing in the existing inventory, housing usually inhabited by low- and moderate-income families.

The result, according to the editors, was not simply that highways were destroying more homes than were being built, but even more important, "The failure of the federal highway program to account for all the economic and social costs of highway construction has contributed significantly to the problems of urban decay and urban–suburban economic polarization in America."[83]

The sins committed against the city in the name of urban renewal were many and great. Urban renewal projects cleared out "slums," displaced the people who lived in them, and replaced them with office buildings, institutions, and commercial developments in addition to public housing projects. Without question, urban renewal needs to be held accountable for the damage done to individual lives and the vitality of neighborhoods and communities. Highway projects, however, did all that and more besides.

Once completed, the urban interstates left a legacy of inhospitable, unusable spaces; neighborhoods bifurcated or isolated entirely from the rest of their cities; park space destroyed, waterfronts made inaccessible to city residents; to say nothing of the increasingly foul air that settled over cities issuing forth from an ever-increasing number of tailpipes. Most of all, they eased the exodus to the suburbs, making it possible, in turn, to abandon the city. Without them, suburban sprawl simply could not have happened in the way that it did or on the scale that it did. The interstate highways represent the greatest free gift ever given to real estate developers since the federal government gave away large sections of the American west to railroad companies after the Civil War.

By the early 1960s, federal officials like Robert Weaver had begun to acknowledge some of the criticism leveled at urban renewal, and they tried to some extent to address it. Not so those responsible for building the highways. In a 1962 interview, Federal Highway Administrator Rex Whitten parried the accusation that highways might damage cities by saying, "I don't agree that freeways tear up a city. I think the great majority of people stand to benefit.... You don't hear from the vast majority that really wants traffic congestion eliminated."[84] It would take several more years for Washington to acknowledge the damage these urban expressways had done to cities.

Indeed, until the late 1960s the effects of highway projects on the physical and social fabric of American cities were not only recognized but celebrated. When the Clay Commission—established by President Eisenhower to study the effects of the highways—issued its report, it cheered: "We have been able to disperse our factories, our stores, our people; in short, to create a revolution in living habits. Our cities have spread into suburbs, dependent on the automobile for their existence." And if that notion of auto dependency strikes us as a bad thing, the commission's report went on to reassure readers: "The automobile has restored a way of life in which the individual may live in a friendly neighborhood, it has brought city and country closer together, it has made us one country and a united people."[85]

It was everything that the decentralists of the 1920s and '30s had dreamed of, only more so.

The End of Liberalism and the End of the City

By the early 1970s, the interstate highway program was seen as a triumph of American can-do, whereas urban renewal stood as the failed program, emblematic of an entire liberal agenda centered on the city. On March 16, 1972, the same year that the *Yale Law Review* published its scathing critique of the highway program, officials in St. Louis began demolishing the first of the thirty-three buildings called Pruitt-Igoe, as if to acknowledge that failure in a stunning fusillade of dynamite.

By 1972, Pruitt-Igoe had been transformed from a mere public housing project in St. Louis into a national morality play. The complex was an almost archetypal piece of urban renewal in the Corbusian vein. Planning for it had begun in the late 1940s, but the Housing Act of 1949 made it possible. A fifty-seven-acre section of the city's largely African American neighborhood near north side came down, replaced with thirty-three eleven-story blocks of nearly three thousand apartments. The first apartments opened in 1955 to applause, optimism, and some good reviews.

Things went bad fairly quickly. Bad design decisions, forced in many cases by cost cutting, took their toll on residents of the buildings themselves. Most risibly, the elevators operated on a "skip-stop" basis. They did not serve every floor, which quickly became an unworkable nightmare for elderly people who had to get off on one floor and walk up or down to another, or for parents with small children desperately in need of the bathroom. Intended to be racially segregated—some

Before the fall. Though the Pruitt-Igoe housing project in St. Louis became a national symbol of the failure of urban renewal and public housing, when it opened it was greeted with broad enthusiasm. Even as late as 1967, people could still put together a baseball game there. *Missouri History Museum, St. Louis, PHO 40818*

buildings for whites, others for blacks—the apartments and the occupants become overwhelmingly black after the Missouri Supreme Court banned racial discrimination in public housing in 1956. More significantly, the residents were disproportionately poor or unemployed, and with that demographic came crime. According to local lore, St. Louis police referred routinely to "Pruitt-Igoe crimes." The planned density—fifty housing units per acre—turned out to be higher than the neighborhood it replaced, and the complex never filled to capacity.

When the drawings for Pruitt-Igoe first began to circulate in 1951, *Forum* announced that it had "already begun to change the public housing pattern in other cities." It was everything that a High Modernist project ought to be: "vertical neighborhoods" achieving economies of scale, surrounded by plaza and park space. By 1965, James Bailey, writing in *Architectural Forum,* said that Pruitt-Igoe was "a case history of failure."[86] But it got worse; by 1971, roughly 600 people lived in seventeen buildings. The remaining sixteen stood boarded up, haunting a sinister and dangerous Corbusian ghost town.

When the dynamite was detonated in March 1972, it blew up more than abandoned buildings. Charles Jencks announced that March 16 marked the day modern architecture died.[87] That's a terrific piece of hyperbole, but it hardly seems adequate. Urban renewal, as it had been envisioned for more than two decades, died on that day, too—the dynamite punctuating for many Americans the growing sense that public housing, the War on Poverty, and everything associated with big-city liberalism had failed as well. For the backlash politics emerging at the moment, residing comfortably in suburbia, Pruitt-Igoe demonstrated that the city could not be saved, and it was wasteful folly for the federal government even to try.

The implosion of those apartment blocks in St. Louis gave the national press the excuse to look at what had become of the whole public housing enterprise, and they found it discouraging. Although Pruitt-Igoe might have been a particularly gruesome example of everything wrong with public housing, in fact, its problems—the chronic poverty of its residents, the chronic lack of funding for basic maintenance and competent management—could be found in almost all of the large-scale projects that resulted from urban renewal. Pruitt-Igoe stood as a symbol for the failure of public housing. *Time* took the occasion to pass this judgment: "cities suffer from the good intentions of urban planners."[88]

Sally Thran, who watched the demolition of Pruitt-Igoe as a reporter for the *St. Louis Post Dispatch,* thought that the episode raised the very largest question: "The central issue is whether there is still a definite commitment to the concept of low-income housing supported in part by federal funds."[89] Almost twenty-five years after Congress and the president called for "a decent home and a suitable living environment for every American," and with Pruitt-Igoe standing, and falling, as a metaphor for the failure of public housing, that commitment was anything but "definite," either in Washington or among a growing number of Americans generally.

The year 1972 was also when the interstate highway system was to have been completed. It was not, and though people groused about cost overruns and construction delays, the program continued to roll ahead. In fact, part of the reason completion was late was because in 1968, Congress had added an additional 1,500 miles to the whole system, bringing the total to 42,500 miles. Even as urban renewal came to be seen as central to a disgraced liberalism and to the view that government did not solve problems effectively, the highway projects were being expanded. It was money well spent for roads people needed.

Highways represented a successful program of the federal government to reshape the environment and engage in a massive social engineering experiment, because few people saw the enormous extent to which the roads were federally subsidized in the first place, and because few made the connection between publicly funded roads and the private profit of suburban development. Successful, because at 65 miles per hour, on a sunken or elevated expressway, people could drive on past all the problems of a decaying city and hardly even notice.

Nowhere was that juxtaposition between the promise of the suburban frontier and the failures of the city, between escaping and being trapped, more easily seen than on the Near West Side of Chicago. There, late in 1962, the "55-mph miracle" opened for business. Or, rather, to traffic. A north–south expressway about 11.5 miles long and 14 lanes wide, connecting one freeway with another. In tribute to a recently deceased Cook County commissioner, they called it the Dan Ryan Expressway.

A week after it opened, *Newsweek* crowed about its success: "After seven days of service, traffic was moving and the critics who had warned of massive tangles were forced to eat their words of doom." Illinois state highway engineer Roger Nusbaum was similarly smug. "It was a sad day for the pessimists," he told the press, "Over-all, it worked like a charm."[90] The charm did not last long. Within a year, the Dan Ryan was experiencing traffic "overloads," which led the *Chicago Tribune* to call for swift construction of another north–south highway, this one farther west.[91]

Earlier in the same year that motorists began speeding along the full length of the Dan Ryan, Chicago officials cut the ribbon on another massive project, the Robert Taylor Homes. Stretched out over more than two miles between 39th Street and 55th Street, the "homes" consisted of twenty-eight apartment buildings, each sixteen stories tall. All together, the roughly 4,400 apartment units in the project made the Robert Taylor Homes the largest public housing development in the nation. At the peak of its occupancy, it housed 27,000 Chicagoans— considerably more than originally intended –more than 20,000 of them children. In 1963, a year after Robert Taylor had opened, three of those children died in a fire, allegedly because the elevators had already broken down and firemen had to walk up to the fourteenth floor.

By 1965, conditions had deteriorated to such an extent at Robert Taylor that the *Chicago Daily News* devoted a multi-part investigative series to them. What the *Daily News* found only got worse over the next ten years. As areas of the project, including the gallery spaces in the buildings themselves, were fenced off, the whole place came to resemble a prison, a bitter irony since gang- and drug-related violence went on largely unabated. By 1975, the Chicago Housing Authority reported that more than 10 percent of the units at Robert Taylor were vacant and that an astonishing 92 percent of the remaining residents received some form of government assistance. With Pruitt-Igoe reduced to rubble, the Robert Taylor Homes competed with Chicago's Cabrini Green for the dubious distinction of being the worst housing project in the nation, and the symbol of everything that had failed in urban America.[92]

The Robert Taylor Homes occupied a narrow strip between the Bronzeville neighborhood and the Dan Ryan Expressway. In fact, they formed almost a curtain wall on the western edge of the historic center of Chicago's black population. They literally cast a shadow over that neighborhood as the sun sank in the west. Those with apartments facing west could watch the traffic on the Dan Ryan whiz by. For drivers, the experience must have been jarring—as these towers loomed into view, they looked bleak and forbidding, and positively Soviet. Slab after identical slab, in that version of modernism that made "cheap" its first and last design priority. The image was jarring—but only briefly. As long as the traffic was moving, the Robert Taylor Homes and the 27,000 people who tried to eke out a life there went by in about two minutes. Then they were gone.

If drivers never quite noticed the people living in the projects as they drove by, the residents of the Robert Taylor Homes and the other public housing projects certainly noticed the drivers. Delores Watkins had come to Chicago from the South shortly after the Second World War, married another southern transplant, and raised her family through the 1960s in the public housing development called the Brooks Extension, a few blocks west of the Dan Ryan and north of Robert Taylor. Built in 1959, the Brooks buildings were already falling apart ten years later; the cinderblock walls were crumbling and permeable, enabling smoke from a nearby incinerator to come through the walls so thickly it sometimes drove the Watkins family out. As Delores Watkins noted in 1970, "They haven't done one thing to this building. But you go down Dan Ryan and they're always fixing on it. We don't have a new tree here. We don't have grass. On Dan Ryan they have pulled and put down new trees two or three times."[93]

Building the Dan Ryan Expressway and the public housing projects that ran alongside it involved tearing down an enormous number of old buildings, though some of the Dan Ryan was also run on top of a railroad right of way. In the case of the Robert Taylor Homes, few were sorry to see that area go. The Robert Taylor Homes replaced what had been referred to since the 1930s as the Federal Street slum, and it was acknowledged as just about the worst, most dilapidated section of the city. Even by the 1940s, running water was still a luxury in certain blocks of the Federal Street area. When Martin Luther King Jr. came to Chicago in 1966, he did so to launch a campaign for open housing and to eliminate the slums. He moved into a tenement apartment to underscore just how bad conditions were for those living in those old, run-down buildings. As one of his aides declared at the time, "The days of the slums are numbered."[94] Even by 1966, slum clearance had an appeal for those who experienced them daily.

Heading north, after skirting Bronzeville and leaving the Robert Taylor Homes behind, the Dan Ryan swings west and then resumes north, pointed toward perhaps the most well-known of all Chicago's neighborhoods. By the time the curve reaches Cermak Street, it straightens back out, and the Dan Ryan parallels Halsted Street as it runs toward the Congress Expressway. Jane

Addams's Halsted Street. Through the neighborhood that she had made her life's work.

In some ways, the Near West Side in 1962 still resembled the place Jane Addams moved to in 1889. It remained an immigrant destination—though now Mexicans and African Americans had joined the Greeks and the Italians—and was yet among the poorest sections of the city; the Near West Side remained rough, dirty, and crowded. "Look down," M. W. Newman told readers in 1959, "and you see garbage-strewn streets, gaping slums, big-eyed kids shuffling among the fishbones and filth in soiled alleys." "A patchy mixture," he called it, "of vile slums and good old homes." A 1951 survey found that fewer than half the houses in Jane Addams's neighborhood had their own bathroom. South of Roosevelt Road, things were even worse: only 12 percent of the houses there had central heat, and people in those blocks had to contend with Chicago winters as best they could. To walk the streets around Halsted in the 1950s was to see "all of Chicago's best hopes and worst nightmares, in one overpowering chunk." There were 55,000 heterogeneous people crammed into less than two square miles.[95]

In fact, the bulldozers had been closing in on the neighborhood from several directions. The surrounding area was already the site of several public housing projects, the first of which—fittingly enough called the Jane Addams Homes—opened in 1938. That project was joined by the Robert Brooks Homes (1943), Loomis Court (1951), and the Grace Abbot Homes (1955). The Congress Expressway (later expanded into I-290) ran just to the north, crossing Halsted Street just north of Harrison, and had been built in pieces during the 1950s. "It's being torn down and rebuilt," Newman continued about the area, "Parts of it look as if it had been bombed."

The announcement of the route of the Dan Ryan Expressway caused the predictable upheaval along the Halsted Street corridor. The expressway gobbled up "many a store front and evicted many a family" before the concrete was poured. And then in February 1961, the board of trustees of the University of Illinois announced plans to build a new campus for the University of Illinois, Chicago (UIC), directly on top of Hull House and its surrounding property. Mayor Daley had been urging that the campus be put on that Near West Side site as part of a large urban renewal project, but neither he nor anyone else bothered to consult Hull House about it. The Hull House trustees met on February 10, and a majority voted to oppose the plan, though they had little leverage to put behind that vote.[96]

Those two announcements were related, and by more than the fact that federal money would make both projects possible. The UIC board envisioned its "urban campus" in entirely anti-urban terms. With highway access on two sides and thus in all directions, it built a "commuter university, said to be singular in the United States and certainly in the Middle West," according to the *New York*

Times.[97] A suburban campus populated with modernist buildings set in plaza spaces and surrounded by oceans of parking, right in the middle of what had been one of the densest, most dizzyingly diverse neighborhoods in the nation.

Hull House workers had turned that diversity into a colorful map in 1895. Nearly half of the neighborhood those Hull House workers mapped was torn out by the expressway project. In the end, the original Hull House was spared demolition, as the university was built around it, and it still sits at 800 South Halsted, a nineteenth-century Italianate anachronism perched on the eastern edge of campus, now a museum of itself. Its social service functions were moved out of the Near West Side in the mid-1960s to the Uptown section of Chicago. Its big front porch opens out onto the chasm created by multiple lanes of highway and access ramps. Big Dan Burnham wanted to bury the neighborhood under civic buildings in his 1909 plan for the city. Instead, the Dan Ryan buried it under traffic.

The End of the Age of Planning?

When William Whyte published *The Exploding Metropolis* in 1958, he did so to offer an alternative view of the city to the one guiding the work of urban renewal. The last essay in *The Exploding Metropolis* came from Greenwich Village resident Jane Jacobs. Three years later, Jacobs would publish her own book and change fundamentally the debate over cities and the practice of city planners.

The Death and Life of Great American Cities created a stir when it appeared in 1961, and a half-century later it stands as undoubtedly the most influential book about cities to appear in America after the Second World War. If William Whyte was angry with what city planners—"a surprising number of whom like to live in suburbs," he wrote accusingly—were doing to the American city, Jacobs spent more than 400 pages denouncing the entire profession. She made that absolutely clear from the book's very first line. "This book," she began, "is an attack on current city planning and rebuilding."[98]

Jacobs wanted to present a view of how the city actually worked from the level of the street and the sidewalk, not from the aerial view or from the aggregate metropolitan statistics preferred by the "orthodox planner." Where planners saw "problems," Jacobs saw vitality; what planners wanted to destroy, Jacobs insisted be kept. Density, diversity, mixed use, variety, bustle, all the things planners wanted to eliminate from the city—these were the things that made cities work, and Jacobs celebrated them all. The table of contents sketched an anatomy of the city: sidewalks; parks; neighborhoods; small blocks, old buildings; diversity; concentration. Her point of view, unorthodox to the point of contrariness in 1961, has itself now become the conventional wisdom for city planners, even if sometimes more in word than in deed.

So given how canonical *The Death and Life of Great American Cities* has become, it is worth remembering that when the book appeared, both it and its author got badly panned. In 1961, it was easy to dismiss Jane Jacobs herself. After all, for chauvinists of the day she was only a woman—a housewife, at that—and seemed to lack any professional credential. (She was, in fact, an editor at *Architectural Forum*.) Lewis Mumford's *New Yorker* review of *Death and Life* drips with that sort of nasty sexism. He summed up the book as a "mingling of sense and sentimentality, mature judgments and schoolgirl howlers." He titled his review of this "schoolgirl's" efforts "Mother Jacobs' Home Remedies" for urban problems. Arthur Row called her a "screeching critic."[99]

Others noted that the "orthodox planner" Jacobs complained about was really a straw man. The book included no specific names or projects or theories, Lafayette College professor Paul Pfretzschner pointed out, but plenty of "vituperation" and "unlikely stories." And since the book's great strength lay in its fine-grained observations of New York City, some asked whether the book had any relevance outside of Gotham, or indeed outside of Greenwich Village. "Her book is not about Toledo or Akron," Pfretzschner wrote, "it is about New York and Chicago and Los Angeles—but especially New York."[100]

That charge, in turn, pointed to a larger one. By 1961, many people felt, the nation had finally achieved some level of consensus that urban problems required large-scale solutions. Arthur Row, a city planner at Yale and thus presumably one of those "orthodox" planners against whom Jacobs railed, defended the entire endeavor of urban renewal when he wrote: "America has entered upon a great task—the purposeful rebuilding of its cities.... [T]he task is now being undertaken as major public policy with the purpose of raising our urban environment to a level commensurate with both the potentials of our economy and the ideals of our society." In the face of that, in the face of the vast scale of urban problems and the resources required to address them fully, Jacobs offered only "over-simplified solutions" and "palliatives." "In effect," Row continued, "she advocates a retreat into accepting the present development pattern of our cities...a multiplicity of small efforts scattered in space to provide gradual improvement." As such, Row concluded, "although many of her criticisms are valid in themselves, her solution is no solution."

Lewis Mumford leveled the same charge: "Mrs. Jacobs' most original proposal then, as a theorist of metropolitan development, is to turn its chronic symptom of disorder—excessive congestion—into a remedy, by deliberately enlarging the scope of the disease."[101] In effect, she had taken more than a half-century's worth of conventional planning wisdom and dismissed it out of hand.

Here was the contradiction of *The Death and Life of Great American Cities*. The book amounted to a long indictment of the practice of urban planning.

Given that, Jacobs certainly did not want to offer herself as a planner. What, then, did she propose as the alternative to urban renewal?

At one level, she offered a faith in the small and incremental, though the urgency to deal with urban problems wholesale would only grow during the decade. Harlem was not Greenwich Village, after all, nor was Watts, Newark, North Philadelphia, Detroit, or Chicago's South Side.

At another level, she offered urban laissez-faire, and her book can be read as an indictment of the government power that enabled those planners to do their damage in the first place. She described government as a Kafkaesque experience: "too labyrinthine even to be kept mapped and open, let alone serve as reliable and sensitive channels...of action for getting things done. Citizens and officials both can wander indefinitely in these labyrinths, passing here and there the bones of many an old hope, dead of exhaustion."[102] Jacobs, writing three years before Martin Anderson condemned the "federal bulldozer," had come to the same conclusion: the urban crisis was being made worse, not better, by government programs. She ended her book by asserting that "lively, diverse, intense cities contain the seeds of their own regeneration, with energy enough to carry over for problems and needs outside themselves."[103]

In 1961, Jane Jacobs offered a vision of positive urbanism rather than anti-urban renewal. Of all the things she believed contributed to the vitality of the city, perhaps the most intriguing was continuity, both physical and social. Old buildings and street patterns, yes, but also long-time residents and rooted people. She saved particular vitriol to describe the effect of the car on the city.

Perhaps the most provocative critique Jacobs made in her book, however, was to argue that the problem of the slums was not a problem of economics but of mobility. "The key link in a perpetual slum," she wrote, "is that too many people move out of it too fast—and in the meantime dream of getting out." Neighborhoods that function retained their residents, who in turn made it possible for those neighborhoods to continue functioning.[104] In this, she echoed some of the Progressives who fretted over the rapid turnover of city neighborhoods in the teens and twenties.

Yet if Jacobs offered a vision of what made a city work, she really did not offer a way either to preserve it or to restore it. Clearly, urban renewal and urban highways only made things worse for city residents. But to cross one's fingers and wait for the seeds of regeneration to take root seemed either naïve or obtuse, especially in the face of job losses, racial tensions, and federally sponsored suburbanization. In fact, Catherine Bauer, whom Jacobs dismissed out of hand as another of the planners she despised, pointed the way to a new urbanism when she suggested that planners and architects work in collaboration with neighborhoods to shape their future together. But that kind of planning process would have to wait another generation.

Paul Pfretzschner predicted that *The Death and Life of Great American Cities* would be "useful only to laissez-faire extremists"; in 1970, William F. Buckley included a section of the book in his anthology of conservative thought.[105] By that time, after the long hot summers, the declining populations, and the disappearing jobs, neither the federal government nor the private market seemed to offer any real solutions for the American city, and Jane Jacobs had relocated to Canada.

In 1969, New Yorkers held a fortieth anniversary celebration of sorts, but that was only an attempt to put a happy face on an otherwise embarrassing situation. In that year, the New York City Planning Commission issued its long-awaited *Plan for New York City*, forty years after the Regional Planning Association had published its great plan, and thirty years after the city charter had called for such a document.

After thirty years—after a world war, after Robert Moses, after white flight and racial violence, and after the departure of old ethnic groups and the arrival of new ones—it was a long time in coming and its publication was indeed an event. The thing itself seemed to underscore the anticipation: six oversized volumes, each measuring 17 inches square; 300,000 words; thousands of maps, charts, graphs, and images. Before it was released, the commission estimated that it would weigh 22 pounds. As a physical object, it is simply magnificent.

Impressive without question, but what was it, exactly? Certainly, it was not a comprehensive plan in the conventional sense of that term. It was so unconventional, in fact, that Planning Commission member Beverly Spatt wrote an angry dissent to the plan that was published at the end of the introductory volume: "Thirty years of labor," he complained, "have delivered a mouse." It was a "non-plan," he went on, because it did not do what a comprehensive city plan needs to do: "A comprehensive plan…must set forth policies and it must indicate the means, time, and cost of implementing them." Long on discussions of the city's problems and challenges, the plan was short on offering specific solutions to any of them, and as a result, Spatt charged, it "reads like a *New York Times* editorial rather than either a Plan or even a program."[106]

New York Times architectural critic Ada Louise Huxtable was more charitable than the commissioner. She noted that the six volumes represented a "break with tradition," but she was more enthusiastic about the results. She acknowledged that "its renewal strategies are not the familiar redevelopment schemes in which the city is divided into neatly mapped areas with before and after pictures of blight and beauty." Instead, she remarked that "these strategies deal with the renewal of people—their education, job opportunities, standards of living, participation in the governing process." Spatt complained that the document read more as a social service manual than a guide to how the city ought to rearrange its physical environment; Huxtable recognized that people, not buildings or roads or zoning codes, ought to be at the center of any plan for the city. Besides, she wrote, "experience shows that the master plan, as a physical plan, based on land use, zoning and specific renewal is an obsolete concept." [107]

Jane Jacobs was about to leave town when *The Plan for New York City* thumped onto people's desks. But her ideas run beneath the surface of these volumes. Cities are for people, not for planners. And attention to public safety and health rather than proposals to ease traffic congestion. Even the suggestion that density might be an urban virtue, which Commissioner Spatt found particularly galling. Jacobs is not in the index, but much of the text was written by William Whyte.

The Plan for New York City appeared forty years after the Regional Planning Association's attempt to give the entire region a blueprint. But it also marked the sixtieth anniversary of Daniel Burnham's plan for Chicago. Sixty years later, the kind of brash confidence Burnham exuded, and which Robert Moses embodied, was harder to find. The Big Plans, the large-scale projects that remade American cities with federal money, were now linked to the urban crisis of the 1960s. In 1969, the New York City Planning Commission reflected this ambivalence, confusion, and disappointment. Its huge plan could not simply recycle ideas and programs so obviously in disgrace, but it wasn't sure exactly what to do instead. The influence of Jane Jacobs may run throughout the plan but the tension in it harkens back to that lunch Daniel Burnham had with Jane Addams. Do we understand the city from the sky or from the sidewalks?

In 1972, the year Pruitt-Igoe came down and the year the interstate highway system was due to be completed, the Rand Institute published a collection of essays looking at the state of the American city. As befits a product of Rand, the book was filled with technocratic language, charts, graphs, and steely-eyed policy analysis. The book concluded with an interview with George Sternlieb, a well-known and well-published urbanist. The exchange he had with his interviewer is a nice measure of the attitude toward the American city held by the experts who knew best:

Q: Is there any way to stop the flight of people and business out of the cities and into the suburbs?

A: I don't think so.... [T]he crisis of the city is not a crisis of race.... The problem of the city is a crisis of function. What is left to the city that it does better than someplace else?... What actually does the city have to offer to keep people? The answer today is: very little.[108]

In 1972, virtually everyone had given up on the American city because few had a compelling answer to those questions. It is easy to blame modernist architects or urban renewal administrators or politicians for the absence of an urban vision, but it had been more than a half-century since the Progressives viewed American cities as the hope for the future. Americans did not talk about their cities like that anymore, and they had not done so for a long time.

7 THE TRIUMPH OF THE DECENTRALIZED CITY

At some point in the summer of 1954—the Chamber of Commerce reckoned it was on July 3—the city of Houston welcomed its one millionth resident. There was no brass band in a hospital delivery room or a big banner across the highway exit to identify the individual; it was one of those predictions based on demographic inevitability. But the arrival of Houstonian no. 1 million provided an excuse for the city to take stock of itself, and for the rest of the nation to do so as well.

Houston sits midway, give or take, along the "Sunbelt," roughly one-third the way between Atlanta and Los Angeles. In the postwar years, the Sunbelt boomed as jobs, people, and investment shifted from the Northeast and Midwest to the South and West. Those areas had not experienced urbanization to nearly the same extent as the industrial heartland had before World War II, but after the war was over, Sunbelt cities drove the Sunbelt boom. By 1981, the Commission on the Future of the South surveyed the region and announced that the "future of the South cannot be separated from the future of Southern cities."

Americans noticed that these were not simply fast-growing urban centers but also fundamentally new kinds of cities. They embodied a fresh notion of urbanism altogether, one that seemed poised to supplant the old version, and they appeared to point the way to the future. Of the ten largest American cities in 1950, only Los Angeles was located west of the Mississippi River. By 2010, seven of the ten largest cities basked in the Sunbelt.[1]

These new American cities emerged at exactly the same moment as the older industrial cities began their decline. The dichotomies between them are easy enough to draw: North and East versus South and West; Rustbelt versus Sunbelt; old economy (steel, cars, heavy machinery) versus new economy (aerospace, IT, service); shrinking and dying versus growing and prosperous. Those descriptors contain a measure of truth as far as they go, but they do not tell the whole story. After all, "old city" Boston had certainly become a hub of the postindustrial "knowledge economy," and New York came to dominate international finance even more after the war. Seattle and San Francisco, both older, nineteenth-century cities though located on the Pacific coast, emerged from their shipping pasts to be centers of the digital revolution.[2] The Sunbelt cities did not spring up entirely new, either, but it is fair to say that their postwar growth was astonishing.

Neither geography nor economic base explains the physical shape these new cities took. Instead, we can see them as creations of the anti-urban impulses that began in the early twentieth century. Spatially, these cities are less dense than their older urban cousins, thus more horizontal than vertical, with residential patterns that rely more on single-family detached houses, often sitting on generous lots, rather than the row-house, semi-detached, or apartment pattern found in older cities.

Most significantly, the difference between older kinds of cities and the newer ones can be summarized in another dichotomy: those built before the automobile, and thus having to accommodate it after the fact, and those that grew up around the car.[3] As early as the 1920s, decentralizers had argued that the car would decrease urban density and thus eliminate the problems associated with it. Futurama, the General Motors exhibit at the 1939 World of Tomorrow fair, made the point powerfully to the millions who saw it. More than anything else, the demands of the car have determined the shape of these places, from the off-street parking in residential neighborhoods to the commercial strips on major arterials to the freeways that connect the increasingly far-flung sections of the city, even as they bisect urban space, creating physical and psychological barriers between adjacent areas. In their dependence on cars, they substituted the convenience of personal mobility for physical proximity.[4] Futurama went on display in New York City, but what it foreshadowed, with its sleek towers set between freeways and interchanges, was Los Angeles. Or Phoenix. Or Houston. Because these cities had been relatively small to begin with, it proved easier and less destructive to build them in the image of Futurama than it was for New York or Chicago to redesign themselves that way.

Their growth came in part because their populations increased and in part because their boundaries kept expanding. We tend to measure the size of a city by its population, but many of these new Sunbelt cities are bigger geographically than their eastern counterparts. New York City's 300-square-mile area ranks twenty-fifth in the nation; Phoenix's 500 square miles ranks eleventh.

In other words, these were, finally, decentralized cities, and they certainly astonished the intrepid who came to explore them from the outposts of older urbanism. As they emerged in the postwar years, they appeared to have "solved" the problem of density—concentration—and they accommodated themselves to the automobile, the latter enabling the former. Writing in *Harper's* in 1949, Carey McWilliams described Los Angeles as having finally solved the problem of urban congestion. "If Los Angeles had been a compact, centralized city," he wrote, "the migration of the past eight years would have had a devastating impact." Happily, he continued, "the newcomers simply fill up the vacant spaces" in a region with "space to burn." For this reason, he announced, Los Angeles stood as "the first modern, widely decentralized industrial city in America."[5] The vision of a decentralized city of tomorrow that Americans saw in New York in 1939 had come to life 3,000 miles away, and only ten years later.

These cities do not just present a contrast to the older cities of the nation's Northeast and Midwest; they also represent a radical departure from the patterns of roughly 6,000 years of urbanism. They are not necessarily located because of older kinds of physical advantages, like rivers and harbors. Los Angeles is to some extent, Dallas less so, though in 1932 the writer Morris Markey found himself wondering about Los Angeles: "It struck me as an odd thing that here, alone of all the cities in America, there was no answer to the question 'Why did a town spring up here, and why has it grown so big?' " Ten years later, journalist Roger Butterfield told readers of *Life* magazine that Los Angeles was simply "the damnedest place."[6] And although they concentrated people and activity in a particular region, they decentralized that activity across a wide area.

In these cities, space and politics have worked in mutually reinforcing ways. Through their arrangement of space and the way people would occupy it, those who built the new cities favored the private over the public. As the architect Charles Moore explained in 1965: "The most evident thing about Los Angeles, especially, and the other new cities of the West, is that in the terms of any of the traditions we have inherited, hardly anybody gives anything to the public realm."[7] And without any of those inherited urban traditions, many feared, millions of private individuals could not become a collective public. The boom cities of the Sunbelt, therefore, embodied both parts of the anti-urban equation: they were decentralized in their physical arrangement and their people were suspicious of government in their political outlook.

Thus, although these cities felt many of the same growing pains as their Northeast and Midwest predecessors had in an earlier generation—strains on infrastructure, housing shortages, and friction between different kinds of people—they believed that the market, not government, would solve those problems. As a consequence, whereas cities like Phoenix and Dallas grew just as astonishingly after the Second World War as Chicago and Philadelphia had before the First World War, that growth did not, in turn, generate a similar kind of "progressive" response.

Here, then, was another difference between the old and the new cities. The older ones had a physical shape that reflected and fostered a sense of the public and the idea that government could promote the common good, while the new cities emerged as decentralized spaces, reflecting a basic distrust of government and the public altogether. In this sense, the physical shape of these cities reflected an ideology. Their combination of decentralization and anti-statism made Phoenix and Dallas and the others the first outposts of a new decentralized urban form, places where the conservative politics of the New Right was given physical shape.[8]

The Biggest, Boomingest City of Them All

Sunbelt cities may not have sprung from nothing after 1945, but they did to a remarkable extent emerge from their own Platonic conception of themselves, to borrow the phrase F. Scott Fitzgerald used to describe Jay Gatsby.

In the case of Houston, real estate speculators from New York started staking out Buffalo Bayou as early as 1836. By the time the Civil War broke out, about 5,000 intrepid people had settled in that swampy area. The city prospered throughout the nineteenth century as a cargo transit point connecting the nation's railroad network with the Gulf of Mexico, about fifty miles away. Houston's geographical location puts it at the point where the South meets the West. Cotton and timber were the first, most important commodities to be moved through the channel port from the East Texas cotton fields and forests in the city's hinterland. Next came cattle from ranches that grew to Texas-sized magnificence. Even today, Houston's George Bush Intercontinental Airport is bounded on one side by FM 1960, as in "Farm to Market" Route 1960, a nice juxtaposition of the city's old-economy past and its new-economy present.

But Houston's location also put it on top of the richest single oil deposit in the nation. Once those wells started to pump, oil became the city's primary cash crop. By mid-century it was no exaggeration to say that more wealth came out of the ground within 200 miles of downtown Houston than from any other location of equal size anywhere in the world.[9] It might have been the luckiest place to put a city in the history of city making.

Luck, of course, is a combination of what happens to you and what you make happen. In 1910, less than a decade after the Spindletop well in Beaumont became the international symbol of the Texas gusher, Harris County commissioners voted overwhelmingly to spend $1.25 million (nearly $30 million in current dollars) to dredge a proper shipping channel from Houston out to the Gulf. President Woodrow Wilson came down from Washington to open the channel in November 1914. All that oil coming out of the ground in the flats around Houston, the petrochemical plants that sprung up along the channel, and the demand nationally and internationally for it all made the Port of Houston very busy, indeed.

When World War II started, the city had grown to 385,000. So it was no wonder that many Americans were taken by surprise to learn just fifteen years later that this bayou upstart of a city had already joined the million-resident club. They also noticed that by the time Jane or John One Million arrived in Houston, its port was second only to New York's in the tonnage it handled each year. Even more than Los Angeles, which had been the stuff of national fantasy since Hollywood took over the movie business, many Americans were not sure what to make of Houston.

It was easy enough for the East Coast smart set to chuckle condescendingly at the place—even Hubert Mewhinney, editor of the *Houston Post*, called the city "a whiskey-and-trombone town"—and that was right after the war was over. It was viewed as "the land of the big rich," to borrow the title of George Fuerman's 1951 portrait of the place: a city where wealth had come so spectacularly and so fast that there were more millionaires per capita in Houston than in any other city in the country. There were so many millionaires that a class structure had emerged among them: a "rich millionaire" was worth $100 million or more; between $30 and $100 million, one could be considered an "average millionaire"; at the low end, "poor millionaires" had accumulated only $3 to $30 million. Below $3 million, of course, was not worth bothering about because that fortune might disappear quickly.[10]

A class structure, perhaps, but in the eyes of many it was no class at all. New Yorker Horace Sutton published a dispatch from his visit to Houston that began by reporting how he had to "slough my way through the knee-deep nap of the Warwick [Hotel]'s carpets, and had got past the Aubussons and the imported French paneling in the lobby" before he could actually find the city. Once he did, the writer, "brought up in the country ways of mid-Manhattan," found much to "boggle the eye" and found himself "altogether awed" by things like bank lobbies resembling "elongated versions of the Taj Mahal."[11] How could you not snigger at a town where many among the power elite walked around in ten-gallon Stetsons and cowboy boots, and where one of the doyens of society was named Ima Hogg?

Underneath a number of those Stetsons in the postwar period were men not many years removed from two-dollar-a-day jobs digging ditches or cutting lumber. They had parlayed their own hard work, their business acumen, and their great good luck to be in the right place at the right time, into huge fortunes. They saw themselves as frontiersmen, though the frontier now extended down into the East Texas oil deposits rather than across the continent; rugged individuals and self-made men who brought those nineteenth-century virtues of independence and self-reliance into the twentieth century, and had supercharged them, Texas style.

They built Houston in their own image. What emerged after the Second World War, perhaps more than in any other Sunbelt city, embodied many of the anti-urban ideals of the period. It was decentralized rather than dense; it accommodated the automobile, now the central fact shaping the postwar American landscape. And above all, it rejected the "collective" impulses of older cities in favor of urban privatism. Houstonians even resorted to the language of pioneer individualism when they described the place: "This is the last frontier," one oil executive exulted.[12] The frontier is a place free of government, at least in the minds of those who mythologized it. Houston's new generation of frontiersmen wanted their city to grow without any interference from government—local, state, or federal. And so it did. A city built entirely by private enterprise, not shaped by public control.

As the 1950s ended, few could argue that Houston was thriving, though some pointed out that the way the city was growing threatened its future. The bumptious physical growth of the city, according to its own planning department, had created a situation where

> without correction and guidance of future growth, there is indicated a rapid blighting and extremely rapid growth of slum areas, a questionable successful future for many commercial and industrial areas, an urban area that will become more inefficient in serving the various needs of the people.[13]

The writing was not elegant, but the warning was clear: bumptious was quickly turning chaotic.

Its detractors pointed to a single reason. As Houston leapfrogged older cities to rise on the list of the nation's largest, as its port jostled with New York and New Orleans and Los Angeles as the nation's busiest, it did hold an undisputed number 1 ranking: Houston was far and away the largest city in the country without any zoning code.

Zoning was one of the great inventions of the Progressive urbanists. Through zoning, cities could improve the living conditions of their residents by segregating the multiple functions of industrial cities. Zoning could forbid industrial areas in residential neighborhoods; it could regulate commercial activities and protect public assets like open space or waterways. It could limit the height of buildings in cities rapidly moving vertical, in order to ensure adequate light fell on the streets. And it did so through public mechanisms: legislation or regulation. In short, a zoning code enabled the public to shape the physical space of the city.

More than the newness of the wealth or the speed of the growth, what baffled visitors to Houston was the chaos as it was inscribed on the unzoned physical landscape. They simply found the place visually incomprehensible, and they reported back the results of a city growing without any controls. *Life* magazine provided readers in 1946 with a photo essay of "Booming Houston," but noted that Houston was a "city proceeding with plans for a $100 million medical center, but it still dumps its garbage out on the edge of town." The photo essay in *American City* was even more to the point in answering the question "What has happened in an unzoned city?" What happened was used-car lots next to houses, and similar things. Writing for the *New York Times Magazine*, Stanley Walker described a city where "Unkempt blocks, decayed houses and unsightly parking lots are located among the finest buildings."[14] It just did not make sense, at least not for those accustomed to an older urban model.

Even *Business Week*, which otherwise celebrated the wild-west capitalism of the city, chided Houston for its lack of zoning, calling it "one of the biggest headaches" for the city. As a consequence, according to the magazine, Houston "has grown in crazy-quilt fashion, without rhyme or reason. It's hard to know who your neighbor will be from one day to the next—a warehouse, a fertilizer plant, or a barbershop." *Business Week* went on to quote a local realtor who made Houston sound more like frontier homesteading than a proper city: "Most Houstonians would rather make a potful by selling out their home to a filling station than worry about the residential values of the neighborhood."[15] Houston was what happened when cowboy rugged individualism got into the real estate development business.

Houstonians wanted no part of zoning. As the city's planning director put it, perhaps a bit wistfully, Houston "is the last stronghold and concentrated seat of rugged individualism."[16] And just after the war, zoning caused a clash between two of the city's titans.

Jesse Jones—Mr. Houston, to many people—was born in 1874. He had come to Houston by way of the Tennessee tobacco fields and got into the lumber business, where he did quite well. Quickly, however, he moved into banking and real estate as his adopted city began its remarkable period of growth. By the time he died in 1956, locals estimated that he owned half of downtown Houston.

No one in Houston was more civic-minded than Jesse Jones. His opinion carried a great deal of weight, and his network of friends and associates—known as the Suite 8F Group, after the suite in the Lamar Hotel where they met—carried at least as much influence. After the war, Jones returned to the city after serving in the Roosevelt administration as head of the Department of Commerce and the Reconstruction Finance Corporation, and he began to advocate for a zoning code.

Hugh Ray Cullen, his antagonist, made his money in oil. Born on a Texas ranch, Cullen played the part of Texas oilman as if sent from central casting. Brash, often obnoxious, Cullen began work on his lavish Houston mansion in

1933, the very worst year of the Great Depression. By mid-century, he might well have been the city's wealthiest man, the biggest of the big rich. And he gave his money away just as flamboyantly as he made it. He donated to hospitals and to the symphony, but most significantly, this elementary school drop-out was the primary benefactor of the University of Houston. In 1954, he made a spontaneous gift of $2.5 million ($21 million today) after the football team won an upset victory.[17]

Cullen jumped into the fight against zoning, annoyed that Jones seemed intent on foisting it on the city. Zoning, Cullen wrote to the *Houston Post*, gave bureaucrats "more power over the individual than any government should have over its citizens." And in case anyone missed the larger implications, Cullen went on, "This very condition had led to most of the ills of regimentation in the totalitarian governments of Europe." Elsewhere, Cullen made the fight intensely personal: "Jones has been away from here for the last twenty-five years," Cullen complained, "and has come back to Houston and decided, with the influence of a bunch of New York Jews, to run our city."[18]

Cullen did not fight alone, of course. A group of influential businessmen calling themselves the Committee to Present the Negative Side of Zoning issued a lengthy and thorough critique of the city's proposed zoning plan. In its prefatory remarks, the committee noted that zoning first came to the United States from Germany, with the stated purpose of controlling density and land use. "Its hidden purpose," however, "is the substitution of political control for the economic principles that determine value."[19] Whether or not the proposed zoning plan was a good one, this is what galled opponents of zoning: that public politics might infringe on private economics. When Houstonians went to the polls in 1948, zoning lost by a margin of two to one.

Here, then, was a more fundamental distinction between new cities and old ones than geographical location or economic base. Older cities, more compact, more dense, and controlled to a greater or lesser degree by zoning codes, were legible—comprehensible—to people in ways that the new cities were not, especially when experienced on a pedestrian rather than vehicular level. The freeway systems built after World War II in Los Angeles, Phoenix, or Houston might have a logic of their own, but once you stepped out of the car, places like those became difficult to read. "Houston is not an easy city to assess because unlike the older cities of the East or South, it hasn't as yet developed a full personality of its own," as one writer put it in 1949. "Well there she sits," wrote Stanley Walker about Houston, "or squats, or sprawls, or festers, or blooms, depending upon how one looks at it. The city is quite vigorous, quite messy, and full of apparent contradictions. Not even its leading residents can agree on what is good about the place and what is wrong with it."[20]

Yet what seemed chaotic, accidental, and thoroughly unplanned about Houston resulted from a political ideology, as the fight over zoning made abundantly clear. Hugh Roy Cullen's rhetoric as he led the charge against zoning was not simply inflammatory, Texas-sized hyperbole. He articulated as colorfully as anyone else that underneath the opposition to zoning lay a deep suspicion about the role of government. Cullen genuinely believed that a zoning code designed to protect residential neighborhoods from, say, chemical refineries was the first step taken by overweening government on the road to communist totalitarianism. That Cullen blamed the very idea of zoning Houston on "New York Jews" was a nice touch, especially right after the war. After all, for men like Cullen that phrase was really a redundancy. The anti-Semitic slur certainly underscored how some Houstonians saw the difference between New York and their hometown.

In fact, during his public career Cullen had held press conferences to denounce the New Deal, and then Harry Truman's Fair Deal, so frequently that a local paper assigned a beat reporter to him just to report on his tirades. Fresh from vanquishing zoning in Houston, Cullen joined the Dixiecrat movement in 1948 and worked with dogged energy to unseat Texas's Democratic delegates who had already committed to President Harry Truman. He invited Strom Thurmond to speak in Houston in front of a big crowd, and he organized another big rally for Thurmond just two weeks before the election.[21]

Cullen was already an important player on the national political scene, and though things did not work out for the Dixiecrats, he stayed involved in national politics through his enthusiastic support of Senator Joseph McCarthy. He contributed locally to the anti-communist crusade by having the chancellor of the University of Houston fired, though in the end he turned out not to be a communist after all.[22]

Before the 1950 midterm elections, Cullen invited journalist John T. Flynn to Houston. Flynn stands now as one of those lesser-known characters who moved from the left to the right of the political spectrum because of what he saw as the dangers of the New Deal. After the war he joined his anti-government views with anti-communism and continued to publish widely. Cullen had read Flynn's 1949 book *The Road Ahead* (spoiler alert: it leads to socialism) and was so impressed with it that he had thousands of copies mailed to people around the country with the hope of influencing the congressional elections. Introducing Flynn to the gathering in Houston, Cullen said: "This book may be one of the principle weapons we have in our fight to prevent the converting of our Government into a welfare state ... and lessening the tragedy of our country, helping to prevent it from going down the road toward socialism."[23]

The Road Ahead belongs to that group of anti-communist jeremiads that appeared in the 1940s and '50s. It is not a particularly gripping read, and from this vantage its arguments feel faded and almost quaint. The "real enemy," Flynn began, was not the Communist Party, traitorous though its members are, but those New Deal liberals who have taken over American institutions intent on turning the nation socialist. "We are following, not in the footsteps of Russia," Flynn warned, "but in the footsteps of England. We are being drawn into socialism on the British gradualist model." He devoted an entire chapter to "The War on the South," by which he meant Truman's push for a civil rights agenda. Yes, Flynn acknowledged, "sooner or later this country must face the problem of the Negro," which he also called a "perpetual irritant," but Negroes were making progress and their plight was entirely exaggerated. More to the point, it was exaggerated by communists. The focus of Flynn's chapter was to demonstrate that the entire civil rights movement was nothing more—and nothing less—than a front for communist agitation. He listed eighty-seven civil rights organizations that had been "organized and promoted and in many cases originally financed by Communists or left-wing groups," including the Association for the Study of Negro Life and History and the Harlem Christian Youth Council.

Flynn did not focus on urban questions as such; he had bigger fish to fry, though he did note that the drift of politics in New York City perhaps best illustrated his "down the English road" thesis. There, "following precisely the British example, the Socialist groups threw their strength to the Democrats in some districts while in other districts the Democrats nominated men satisfactory to the Socialist groups."[24]

But Flynn's rhetoric does help us understand how anti-urbanism fit so neatly with a larger anti-statist political point of view in the postwar period. More than anything else, Flynn told his readers to beware of "planning"—and by extension, planners—because it and they constituted a dangerous fifth column: "Socialism itself is never called socialism," Flynn revealed. "It is National Planning."[25]

Several dozen times in this slim paperback Flynn railed against planning. "What do they mean by planning?" Flynn asked and then explained: "The central idea in the minds of all the Planners is a great National Economic Board." Drawing again from the English experience, he went on to say: "This is precisely what the Economic Planners had in mind and this is precisely what the Fabian Socialists aimed at and succeeded in producing in England." Flynn focused on economic planning, and his equation was straightforward. Any attempt at planning, as far as Flynn was concerned, was necessarily an encroachment on individual liberty and therefore socialist.[26]

In fact, Americans never went down the road of large-scale national economic planning—except during war—but where "planning" had been more fully embraced was in the American city. City planning emerged as a profession during the Progressive era as a way of responding to the urban crisis of that moment. For many Americans, therefore, city planning was simply of a piece with the larger socialist conspiracy of planning. Meredith James, veteran of the anti-zoning campaign of 1947 and a member of the anti-zoning committee, drew a direct line from Marx to zoning in an essay he wrote in 1961. According to James, one of the primary goals of "rabid socialists is the abolition of private ownership of land.... Obviously," he concluded, "the control of land uses through zoning laws which place control of private property in the hands of a central committee meets these requirements, and it is only under-informed, short-sighted people who will brush zoning off as 'no different from traffic controls.' The dedicated socialists are opportunists who will seize on any measure that furthers their cause." Likewise, Vernon Elledge, one of Cullen's anti-zoning allies, made the dangers of zoning quite clear: "It just goes back to the idea of Joe Stalin, that one man can figure out everything—the whole plan."[27] Zoning was part of a transitive property that led straight to Moscow: zoning = planning = government interference = Stalinism.

Houstonians showed their phobia of government again in the mid-1950s. Houston, like so many of its Sunbelt sisters, faced a set of strains on municipal services as the metropolitan area grew quickly and chaotically. How to deliver clean water, dispose of the garbage, and keep the roads paved across a metropolitan area

"Lady, I don't need a search warrant. I'm from Zoning Headquarters."

In Houston, zoning was portrayed by its opponents as the first step onto the slippery slope toward Stalinism. Even the dogs would be regulated. *Photo by author, courtesy of the Houston Metropolitan Research Center*

made up of two dozen different municipal governments, even as the demands on those systems grew dramatically every year?

Those strains came in two forms: demographic and geographic. Houston's population exploded after the war from an influx of people that seemed to have no end. At the same time, Houston kept moving out, swallowing its surroundings voraciously. It almost resembled one of those amoebas you can watch under a microscope, gobbling up everything around it, only on an enormous scale. At war's end, Houston was a modest 80 square miles; in 1949, it doubled itself to 162 square miles; in 1956, it doubled again, adding nearly 190 square miles. By 1960, Houston's footprint was larger than New York's, roughly 50 percent larger than Chicago's, and almost three times the size of Philadelphia's. *U.S. News & World Report* predicted that soon "Houston could end up larger in area than Rhode Island."[28] More people, therefore, needed water, roads, and police and fire protection, and they needed those services spread across an ever-expanding sprawl. Houston's infrastructure could not keep up, and everyone knew it.

In 1955, state legislators in Austin thought they had come up with the answer. They created the Harris County Home Rule Commission, charged with looking at what to do with this mess. Two years later the commission recommended that the county assume responsibility for many of these public services as a way of operating them more efficiently and in a more coordinated way. That modest proposal was rejected because it smelled too much like government intrusion on people's freedom. As *Time* magazine put it in a profile of the city, "as a result of its citizens' almost anarchic individualism, Houston is probably the nation's most lightly governed big city." The city had gone as far as banning smoking on the buses, but "passengers puff away as they please—and so do bus drivers." A few years later, the editors of *Fortune* conducted a survey of twenty-three cities to grade them on their municipal services and governance. Houston failed to receive any "good marks" from the survey and finished dead last.[29]

Although the local fight over zoning in Houston might seem a long way from Capitol Hill, in fact by the mid-1950s the two had become close, indeed. As the federal government rolled out its urban renewal program, it funneled the money through city agencies. That, in turn, meant that city officials could decide whether or not to participate, and several of the new Sunbelt metropolises, including Dallas and Phoenix, chose not to. Phoenix rejected federal money in 1961, making it the first major city to "slap Uncle Sam's hand publicly." Dallas had used federal money for slum clearance in the 1950s, but in 1962 the city council voted to stop accepting any federal urban renewal money, and voters put a halt to the construction of any new public housing there.

Houstonians did not even have to confront the choice. Urban renewal funding required that the city have a code; without one, Houston was not eligible for many of the urban renewal programs, and through the 1950s the city took no federal urban renewal money. As one Houston official put it some years later, "Urban renewal was not even in our lexicon."[30] When the first round of urban renewal projects was announced in 1955, Houston was one of only four of the nation's biggest thirty cities not to participate, and certainly the largest. Dallas was another.[31]

In 1960 the city did receive $60,000 to survey the needs and possibilities of urban renewal. Announcing the grant, Mayor Lewis Cutrer told Houstonians that there "are two ways to go about urban renewal—the first being a private enterprise method…and the second being the federal government matching fund program."[32] Houston preferred the former. Several months later, the Houston city council again considered the question of zoning, and this time the federal urban renewal program was not far from people's minds. Mayor Cutrer reminded people that "there are areas in Houston which day by day and night by night present health, fire and police problems." He spoke to an angry crowed of roughly 100 demonstrators who made their opposition to urban renewal plain.

Demonstrator Robert Rowland insisted that urban renewal could not be discussed "without considering the teaching of Karl Marx." He insisted that zoning and urban renewal "were Communist-inspired devices which allowed federal intervention into local affairs." Rowland's father spoke to the council somewhat more apocalyptically: "I give this country two years at the most to go under—two years if we continue as we have in the past. It is time for us to wake up." Loud applause ensued.[33]

In November 1962, Houstonians had the chance to vote on zoning again. This time, a group called the Greater Houston Planning Association led the anti-zoning effort. The group published a small newspaper titled "Zoning Facts" and distributed it across the city. The headline of the fourth issue, which blared "Zoning Means 1-Man Rule," captures the tone of the four-page sheet. That same issue carried a "story" informing readers that "Zoning Opens Way for Urban Renewal Here." Whereas anti-zoning Houstonians had long believed that zoning was the first step on the slippery slope to socialism, the immediacy of federal urban renewal made their case that much easier to make. One of the campaign flyers read: FIGHT POLITICAL CONTROL OF PROPERTY.[34] On November 6, 1962, zoning lost in Houston again.

Phoenix followed Houston's lead in 1961 by repealing its housing code, effectively disqualifying it from any federal urban renewal money since, as mentioned earlier, those grants required such a code. As the *New York Times* noted, "repeal of the code means temporarily the city has no provision outlawing outhouses or unvented gas heaters." Instead, Phoenix decided to finance its public works project by issuing its own bonds because, as Republican Mayor Sam Mardian put it, "people here still like to do things for themselves." Tellingly, the committee of bankers, politicians, and businessmen that put the bond package together excluded any spending on housing, and rejected urban renewal funds because, as one of the bankers stated, "Urban renewal has a stigma attached to it, a bad image that somehow urban renewal is something evil, something undemocratic, something un-American."[35] The John Birch Society, active in Houston, and in Phoenix during these fights, also saw the straight line that connected urban renewal with creeping socialism. No less than Robert H. W. Welch himself delivered a series of speeches warning that urban renewal was a vast left-wing conspiracy. Early in 1964, the John Birch Society sponsored a large rally in Illinois that attracted nine influential congressmen to denounce urban renewal.[36]

As an alternative, Phoenix had its own cowboy in a white hat in the person of real estate developer Ralph Staggs, who promised to clear the slums and replace them with new housing, all without the benefit of tax revenues. The *Phoenix Republic* was beside itself, promising that, with the Staggs plan, "We hope to lay to rest the ghost of both urban renewal and public housing."[37]

Phoenix, of course, was Senator Barry Goldwater's hometown, and it would be easy enough to see his influence on the city's decision to snub urban renewal. Goldwater himself had named urban renewal in his litany of federal programs that should be shut down because the government had overstepped its "Constitutional mandate"—along with education, social welfare programs, and housing. Mayor Mardian was quick to correct that impression, and in so doing fell back on the now-predictable if utterly hackneyed antonym to "government": "Goldwater is not the cause of the conservative movement in Arizona," the mayor insisted, "He is the product of the conservative instincts of a pioneering people." For his part, Mayor Sam Mardian, a former radio talk-show host, described himself as a "reformed liberal."[38]

In these Sunbelt cities, conservatives successfully portrayed urban renewal as a burdensome imposition from Washington that violated the "pioneer spirit" central to the mythology of these places. The *Phoenix Republic* railed: "The Federal government will naturally call the shots if it pays the bills. Phoenix city officials will find themselves under the domination of Washington bureaucrats."[39]

Conservative leaders in Phoenix, Dallas, and Houston saw urban renewal as the vanguard in Washington's march toward socialism; in all three cities, rejecting urban renewal was the way they could man the barricades against the invasion. Fighting urban renewal became a central cause for the anti-government urbanites of the South and West, who wanted their cities run entirely by private enterprise, even if it meant rejecting federal assistance. In this sense, the New Right scored some of its earliest victories in the cities of the Sunbelt.

Except that none of these places actually did forgo all federal money. Call it "situational small government." Even while leaders in Phoenix, Dallas, and

Houston rallied against the "big government" tyranny of urban renewal, all three cities eagerly accepted federal highway money, and they did so without question or qualms, though it meant acceding to control from Washington.[40] After all, places like these could not function without automobiles, and those automobiles, in turn, could not traverse the huge expanses of these cities efficiently without large-scale, high-speed roads. Public housing would lead to socialism (and public transportation would take us there even faster), but federally funded roads—that just made sense. In this, the Sunbelt cities were no different from other cities, except in the disconnect between their anti-government rhetoric and the eagerness with which they cashed federal checks.

Houston was a railroad city in the first half of the twentieth century—a place where, as the boosters crowed, "seventeen railroads met the sea." After World War II, local leaders worked hard to transform it into an automobile city, and they did so with extensive federal help. The Gulf Freeway—the city's first—opened for traffic in 1948. In 1952 alone, Houston received nearly 53 percent of all the federal highway money allocated to the state of Texas—a whopping $235 million. By the 1980s, more than three-quarters of a billion federal dollars had helped created a freeway system of 210 miles in and around Houston. Of course, if Houstonians knew their history, they recognized that federal largesse was no stranger to Buffalo Bayou. When President Wilson came to open the ship channel in 1914, he did so because it was an event of national significance and because the federal government had picked up half the tab for that project, too. The $1.25 million that Congress sent to Houston represented the largest federal grant ever made to a municipality.[41]

As it was designed, the radial-and-spoke highway system in Houston, as in many other places, served two functions. First, it both enabled and drove the ever-expanding, centrifugal sprawl of the city in a reinforcing, city-planning feedback loop. The relationship between highway projects and real estate development was obvious from the very beginning. When the Gulf Freeway reached as far as Galveston in 1952, land values along the right-of-way had jumped as much as 67 percent, by one estimate.[42] And as Houston annexed its surroundings, it needed new and expanded roads to accommodate the increased traffic moving across greater distances; as those roads were built and enlarged, it enable development to move outward even farther.

No wonder, then, that as early as 1954 Houston's commuter statistics mirrored the national figures in reverse: whereas 70 percent of American commuters took some sort of public transit to work in that year, in Houston 70 percent of commuters drove to work.[43] In 1954, as it happened, the Gulf Freeway recorded its 500 millionth vehicle mile. In 1955, as the state commission worked on its proposal to improve Harris County services, which Houstonians would shortly

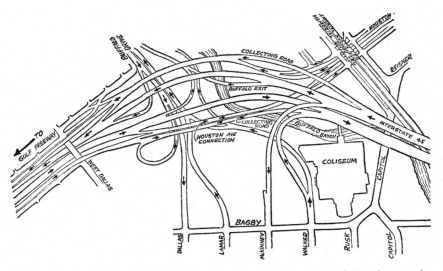

When Houstonians built their freeway system after the Second World War, they put the "spaghetti bowl" right in the center of the city, on top of Buffalo Bayou, where the city had been founded before the Civil War. *Photo by author, courtesy of the Houston Metropolitan Research Center*

reject, Houston voters approved a vehicle registration tax to enable the county to issue bonds to acquire highway right-of-ways. As a slick pro-tax pamphlet published by the Harris County Freeway Committee put it, the new highway construction unleashed by these bonds "will break the crippling traffic jams now threatening our continued growth."[44] Houston had planned a highway system running 238 miles divided among a dozen different roads; by 1957, 85 miles of the system had been completed or were under construction; right-of-ways for an additional 115 miles had already been acquired.[45]

At the same time, road construction accomplished at least one part of what Houston had passed up by not pursuing urban renewal projects. Highway construction could be an even more effective and efficient way to get rid of deteriorating neighborhoods and their residents, without the bother of having to build any new housing or provide any relocation assistance. So, for example, a chunk of the mostly black Fifth Ward, north of downtown, now lays buried under a stretch of I-10.[46] (Things went a little less smoothly in Dallas. William Adkins, of the Texas Transportation Institute, reported happily in 1957 that a Dallas expressway had already attracted new businesses along its corridor. The only exception, he complained, was where it skirted "a large residential area for negroes" where people would not leave because of "the old settlement's resistance to change."[47] Adkins seemed oblivious to the fact that these troublesome residents would be displaced without any of the relocation assistance that would have been provided by urban renewal.)

But perhaps the most poignant example of this urban-renewal-by-freeway means in Houston took place on the eastern side of the city's Fourth Ward. That neighborhood abuts Houston's downtown, just a mile or so west of City Hall. It had been established by freed slaves after the Civil War and had become the center of the city's African American life—its Harlem, as people had referred to it in the 1920s, by which time the ward was home to about one-third of the city. It was also where the city's first Jewish community had laid its dead to rest.

The Fourth Ward had produced many of Houston's prominent African American citizens and the city's first black church, but after the Second World War it was surely what many Houstonians had in mind when they thought of "blight" in their city. So when work began on what would become I-45, the first section to be cleared was through Freedman's Town. Demolition began in the early 1950s, and that first section of road opened to traffic in 1955.

Interstate 45 destroyed a substantial part of the neighborhood, but just as important, it cut off the area from the rest of the city and from sections of itself. What had been a poor but lively section of town began to stagnate. As the *Houston Chronicle* put it in 1971, this "gloomy" area is "a neighborhood waiting for something to happen." By that time, the population was in steep decline and roughly half of the original section had been razed, replaced by the highway and by downtown skyscrapers. It had become, in the words of a local resident, "nothing but an old folks home, compared to the 1930s and '40s." Though he surely did not mean to extend this metaphor, in 1976 State Representative Ron Waters implored the city to do something about the neighborhood. Citing the area's "rapid disintegration," Waters called the Fourth Ward "a living coffin." In response, Mayor Fred Hofheinz delayed, countering, "People are moving out of the area. It's one of several pockets of poverty with very serious problems. It would be unintelligent for us to put the area at the top of our list of priorities." In the early 1980s, when activists and academics put together an application to place Freedman's Town on the National Register of Historic Places, the nomination included almost entirely residential buildings—a local variation of the wood-framed shotgun shacks found in other parts of the South. By that time, though, most of the neighborhood's institutional buildings and its life—schools, churches, libraries, and commercial establishments—were already gone. A study commissioned by the city in 1980 suggested simply razing the entire area "so that it can be redeveloped for residential us by middle and upper income families as well as low income persons such as those now living in the area."[48]

In his thoroughly celebratory history of Houston's freeways, Erik Slotboom writes about the construction of I-45 that "there were generally no objections to the displacement of residences in the neighborhoods around downtown."[49] That is not entirely true, of course. And it may be just as much of an exaggeration to say that I-45 exclusively caused the demise of the Fourth Ward. But the highway project did set in motion the erosion of Houston's most historically resonant neighborhood. If the slums were not exactly renewed, then at least they were walled off from the rest of downtown, and drivers could zip past the sight of them in less than two minutes.

Since 1914, therefore, the federal government had played a central, if offstage, role in Houston's development and prosperity, even while Houstonians extolled the virtues of their own hard work and pioneer spirit. By funding the basic transportation infrastructure of the city, the federal government made it possible for Houston to exploit its abundant natural resources. In 1961, however, the federal government assumed a more direct part in the city's economic success when Congress awarded Houston the National Aeronautic and Space Administration's Manned Space Center.

In competing for this plum, Houston's boosters promoted the city's infrastructure and low cost of living, its universities, and its population of skilled workers; it lobbied for the Space Center, and beat out places like Cambridge, Massachusetts. All of this was, no doubt, very persuasive to the chair of the House Appropriations Committee, Albert Thomas. That he was also Houston's own representative in Congress might have played a part, too, as did the fact that Vice President Lyndon Johnson was in the city's corner. Thanks to the federal government, the oil town would become Space City. Where better than in America's last frontier town to locate the facility to explore space, the final frontier?

Two years later, Lyndon Johnson triumphed in the presidential election in one of the largest electoral landslides in American history. He received more than 63 percent of the vote in his home state, while small-government crusader Barry Goldwater did not quite reach 36.5 percent. Even as federal money poured in to build the Space Center, however, in Houston's Harris County, Goldwater did almost 4 percentage points better than he did nationally.

Technically, the Space Center—which would later be named for President Johnson—was located just next to Houston's city limits, as was Clear Lake City, the development that popped up to serve the new residents and jobs that the center would attract. But in 1967, *U. S. News & World Report* predicted that the city would "swallow up Clear Lake City in its determined drive to become America's largest metropolis." In 1977 that prediction proved partially correct when Houston annexed much, though not all, of Clear Lake City. Some anticipated that NASA's new settlement would grow to 200,000 people, but just as important, the big federal facility attracted a whole new genus of businesses to Houston. Now Boeing and Lockheed joined the oil refineries and chemical plants to form the core of Houston's economy, the "old" economy blending seamlessly with the "new."

Houston, Do We Have a Problem?

In the same year that Goldwater ran for president, Morris W. Lee, a mortgage broker and real estate appraiser who had played a central role in defeating zoning every time it came up in the city, published an essay entitled "Zoning: Myth or Magic," and it circulated widely among property-rights advocates. Throughout the rest of the 1960s and into the 1970s (he died in 1974), Lee received dozens of letters from around the country asking for help in either defeating zoning ordinances or repealing them. Writing from Seattle, real estate broker Vick Gould ranted to Lee that zoning "is outright socialism and economic dictatorship." For people like these, Houston became the model of what a city could be if left entirely to the market.[50]

In response, Lee was only too happy to crow that "Houston enjoys a unique position today and is considered to be a model for growth industry, culture, development, and certainly an excellent place in which to live and enjoy the use of one's property." Mayor Louis Welch concurred, writing to Lee that "zoning has not worked in cities where it has been in effect for a long time. And you cannot argue with results. I believe that the growth of Houston has been more orderly without zoning than has the growth of many other cities which are zoned."[51]

Not everyone, however, agreed with that rosy assessment. Even as construction proceeded on the Space Center, the latest achievement of Houston's can-do, free-enterprise, federally assisted culture, people noticed many things in this "new" city were no better, and arguably worse, than they were in the older cities of the Midwest and North. *Newsweek* commented that "much of the city remains behind the times on such matters as public welfare, urban planning and integration." In 1965, Texas State Senator George Parkhouse asked incredulously, "What kind of a city can spend $31.6 million for a baseball stadium and not give proper care to the patients at its charity hospital?"[52] What kind of city, indeed? But of course, Parkhouse was from Dallas.

In fact, Houston had been plagued with a variety of urban ills for quite some time. In 1948, a Houston survey found nearly 26,000 families were living in inferior housing; 20 percent of the city's housing stock was classed as inadequate. At that moment, and faced with that situation, the city did decide to take advantage of federal assistance to build four modest public housing complexes. Nevertheless, in 1950—after the war and the New Deal were over—a proposal to create more public housing was defeated by Houston voters. In 1959, the city's own Planning Commission estimated that 100,000 to 120,000 Houstonians lived in "residential structures which are either completely sub-standard or are rapidly approaching that condition."[53]

Marian Hiller's seventh-grade students saw these statistics up close when she sent them out to map and study certain Houston neighborhoods. The seventh graders were stunned by Houston's slums. Helen Baird, for instance, reported that she "found one house with sewage right in front and children playing in it." She probably expressed the view of many Houstonians when she told a *Time* magazine reporter that she had thought that slums "were all in the East." After all, Houston was not like those older cities, was it? Economic growth, spectacular though it was, did little to alleviate this situation. By 1967, with the Space Center up and running, the city's housing authority operated 2,500 units of subsidized housing, and 21,000 families still lived in slum conditions.[54] Allowing developers to operate without the restrictions of zoning and rejecting federal urban renewal money did not mean that Houston solved its housing crisis more effectively than other cities—it simply allowed Houstonians to ignore it.

Marian Hiller taught at the Stonewall Jackson Junior High School, a nice reminder that while the cowboy hats and cattle pens made Houston a western city, its race relations were entirely southern. In the Fourth Ward, the hospital that served the poor and indigent had been named after Jefferson Davis, and it remained a place where "segregation and Jim Crow reign supreme." In fact, Houston is closer geographically to Jackson, Mississippi, than it is to Amarillo, Texas. After the Supreme Court's *Brown v. Board* decision in 1954 declaring segregated schools unconstitutional, Houston schools promptly integrated the school system's phone directory. This, like the people themselves, had been racially segregated, but the board actually reversed that bold step forward in 1957. In 1955, just a year after *Brown*, Houston School Board member Dallas Dyer requested that, as a way to cut costs, only rice and beans be served at the Mexican American school. In fact, the district did not accept federal money to subsidize school lunches for poor students until 1967 because it equated federal aid with federal control.[55]

Just after the war, Mexican Americans and African Americans constituted roughly 25 percent of the city's population, living in what *Life* magazine called "bitter slums."[56] That situation had not changed appreciably by the mid-1960s, but Houston's African American and Latino population did not get swept up in the current of civil rights until as late as 1965. Only in that year did the city witness its first demonstration, in which 2,000 African Americans marched to demand faster school integration.

Texas Southern University (TSU), the city's historically black college, had been viewed by civil rights leaders as "a campus so somnolent that [they] wrote it off as a 'hot-bed of apathy.'"[57] Then, on April 13, 1967, Stokely Carmichael of the Student Non-Violent Coordinating Committee (SNCC) came to town. His speech touched off a race riot. Or at least that is how many Houstonians saw it. By the time it was over, 144 TSU classrooms had been trashed, nearly 500 students had been arrested, and one Houston police officer was dead. It took a while, but even Houston now had to acknowledge that it had a race problem.

The city responded the following year with a series of community meetings and dialogues between the police and the black community that were designed to foster understanding and reduce tensions. Police chief Herman Short was not romantic about the program. "This wasn't intended to be any love-in," he said, but conceded, "I think a lot of good is coming out of it." Not so much because these conversations might relieve Houston's racial tensions but "because it is an all-local program with nobody from the Federal Government butting in."[58] Houstonians filtered all their local problems through the lens of their anti-government animus.

Housing and race were not the only issues Houston's "pioneer spirit" failed to solve. Throughout the 1950s and '60s, Houston had one of the highest murder rates in the country and, perhaps not coincidentally, one of the smallest police forces per capita. That reflected the city's reluctance to pay for public services. Houston had also become an environmental mess, a consequence of the city's aversion to regulation and zoning.

By the mid-1960s, nearly 100 million gallons of sewage flowed into Buffalo Bayou every day, and in 1967, James Quigley of the Federal Water Control Administration opined about Houston's ship channel that "on almost any day this channel may be the most badly polluted body of water in the entire world."[59] For those downwind of any refinery or chemical processing plant, the air was not much better. And, of course, without any zoning or effective city planning, who knew when a chemical plant might open up next door?

In the postwar period, Houston and its Sunbelt sisters served as laboratories for a new kind of urban growth, and they created a new kind of urban form. That form resulted from a celebration of free enterprise and the market and a bellicose, if selective, hostility toward government of all kinds. Houstonians did not want the federal government meddling in their race relations, or their socioeconomic suffering, but they were happy to use government money to build the infrastructure that the private sector required but would not build on its own. "Houston was built by men of vision," trumpeted one J. G. Miller, "not by slide-rule experts with an omniscient egotism and a pocket full of silly statistics," and most Houstonians truly believed it.[60] That vision was a deeply conservative one—part Old South, part Wild West, part John Birch Society. Stirred together, Houston became the physical embodiment of anti-urbanism and of the New Right.

Most Houstonians might have been taken by that vision, but not all of them, by any means. Corresponding with anti-zoning crusader M. W. Lee, Mrs. John

Mason, an otherwise unidentified writer, challenged his Panglossian vision of the city. "I was unaware," she wrote somewhat sarcastically in 1967, "that unzoned Houston is without slums, traffic congestion, juvenile delinquency, or tax problems." But then she went directly to the heart of the matter:

> I feel that the right of private ownership is not absolute. If we own property on a desert island then this would be different. No one else is affected by our actions. But when you live in a community what you do affects the other guy. In order to have your own personal rights protected, there must be laws that restrict the other person. And you are also the other person in a community.[61]

The latter-day pioneers who built Houston in the twentieth century championed the unbridled rights of private property, but they did not pay much mind to what might happen to "the other guy."

If You Can't Beat 'Em...

By the 1970s, Houston's leadership had decided that federal money for projects other than canals, roads, and space centers might not be such a bad idea, after all. During that decade, federal grants to cities increased almost eightfold nationally, and Houston decided it was time to get its share. In fact, between 1973 and 1978, the amount of money Houston received from Washington increased a Texas-sized 600 percent. According to a Brookings Institution study, Houston turned to the federal government to clean up the messes its unregulated, unplanned growth had created. Houston's "fight for federal dollars," the report concluded, "has come about largely *because* of its economic boom." Acknowledging, finally, that public services, especially on the urban edges and recently annexed areas, were inadequate, "Houston leaders came to see the economic and political benefits of using federal aid."[62]

Phoenix had come to that conclusion a few years earlier. Five years after rejecting urban renewal money, the business elites in Phoenix were having serious second thoughts. By 1966, that city of roughly 500,000 up-by-their-bootstraps pioneers had failed to confront the problem of urban blight, and things were only getting worse. Nothing had come from Ralph Staggs's market-based project because he found himself hamstrung by the local enthusiasm to abolish all forms of government meddling. "We have to have a housing code," he pleaded, "without it areas can continue to deteriorate into slums." Those with south-facing offices in one of the city's shiny downtown skyscrapers could look out on a shantytown of nearly one square mile, serviced by about 800 privy pits. For those executives, the slums seemed to be creeping closer and closer to their buildings. In other words, Phoenix's choice to solve its housing problem by thumbing its nose at the federal government had failed. As one of the city's worried business leaders put it, "much as it was desirable to go it alone, the economics of life today [are] such that we must use the tools provided by the Federal Government or take the consequences."[63]

Besides, Ralph Staggs could not acquire much property because he lacked the power of eminent domain, and also because many property owners refused to sell out to him. They expected the price of their land to go up because of a proposed highway extension. Which is a nice encapsulation of the irony that Phoenix embraced federal highway money with open arms even though it rejected it for housing.

The urban crisis in the older industrial cities fueled a backlash against New Deal and Great Society liberalism. That crisis resulted from the combustible mix of faltering urban economies and racial animosities. But the crisis was exacerbated by the essentially anti-urban vision that shaped the response to it. That response—the destruction of neighborhoods and public spaces by highways or urban renewal projects—tore literally and figuratively the fabric of those cities in the first quarter of the twentieth century.

With their booming economies and burgeoning populations, the newer cities of the South and West seemed to many to have escaped the urban crisis of the mid-twentieth century. Those cities extolled the virtues of the private market (even though that market was supported and stimulated by public investment). These Sunbelt cities did not reject merely the programs of the Great Society. With their entirely privatized notion of urbanism and their deep-rooted hostility to government, they neglected the public functions of the city altogether—the public realm necessary for successful urbanism. In this sense, although Houston's leading figures wanted no part of Lyndon Johnson's liberalism, and though some of them had denounced Franklin Roosevelt's liberalism, they even rejected the kind of city that the Progressives imagined at the turn of the twentieth century, back when Houston was still an inconsequential town on a fetid bayou.

Sparkle on the Rustbelt

Here's a bit of trivia. Since the end of World War II, as the factory cities of the Midwest started to rust, and as people and jobs packed up and moved out to the suburbs and down to the Sunbelt, only two older cities in this industrial heartland continued to grow and expand: Indianapolis, Indiana, and Columbus, Ohio.[64]

The two share much in common. Both serve as state capitals, and each was founded early in the nineteenth century, Columbus in 1812 and Indianapolis in 1820. Both cities were sited to be roughly in the middle of each state, rather than for their proximity to transportation or natural resources. As a consequence, both largely missed the era of industrialization, though the steel, auto, and other heavy industries thrived not very far away. And as a consequence, neither city experienced the waves of immigration from Eastern and southern Europe. In 1900, for example, less than 10 percent of Columbus's residents were foreign born, and the natives were proud of that fact.[65] You can get a good cannoli in Cleveland, but not in Columbus.

Nor did either city attract large numbers of migrants from the American South during the period of the Great Migration. Both cities remain roughly two-thirds white. Cleveland, by contrast, now has a black majority. When manufacturing did gain a foothold in Columbus during and after the Second World War, the labor force remained less unionized than in other midwestern cities, and consequently wages remained lower, by an average of 5 to 15 cents per hour.[66]

And while Cleveland and Gary have been contracting, Columbus and Indianapolis keep growing. Since 1950, both cities have roughly doubled their population. Indianapolis grew from about 425,000 to approximately 830,000 in 2010. Columbus expanded from 375,000 to 760,000 in the same sixty years. While that was happening, Cleveland has lost fully 50 percent of its population, dropping from a city of just over 900,000 people to one of fewer than 450,000. Most people register surprise when they learn that Columbus is now, and by a wide margin, the largest city in Ohio.

In a host of ways, therefore, Columbus and Indianapolis are Sunbelt cities, only without the sun. Service sector and other postindustrial jobs form the core of their economies, and they have developed spatially in the way that characterizes cities of the South and West. Columbus's population density, at about 3,400 people per square mile, is half that of Cleveland's and about the same as the density of Dallas. Indianapolis is less dense still, about 2,200 per square mile, lower even than Phoenix. To put those figures in perspective, Chicagoans inhabit their city at a density of about 12,000 people per square mile and in San Francisco at an average of 16,500 per square mile.

Columbus and Indianapolis, therefore, serve to underscore for us that the original new urbanism, created by the decentralizing, anti-urban, and politically conservative ethos that built Houston, was not confined to a particular region of the country or to a specific economy. Neither announced itself with the brashness (crassness?) of Houston—their midwestern manners would not allow that— but these cities are of a piece with Houston, Phoenix, and the rest. Both cities expanded physically along the same decentralized, automobile-centric patterns of the Sunbelt, and politically, private enterprise trumped public well-being. "Profit is *not* a dirty word" in Columbus, according to an ad placed in *Business Week*, suggesting that in other places it was.[67] Purely coincidentally, the ad ran right next to a story about Houston.

So let's take a quick tour of Columbus, where the contrast between the old and new urbanism is most proximate, where the Sunbelt-like success of that city sits less than 200 miles from the rustbelt symbol of Cleveland. After the Second World War, this nineteenth-century midwestern capital transformed itself into a Sunbelt city; and far more so than Los Angeles or Atlanta, Columbus has been known since the mid-twentieth century as the most "American" of American cities, with the most "average" demographic. Since at least World War II, Columbus has served as the test market for everything from new frozen foods to ATM machines. It was the corporate home to Wendy's and its late founder Dave Thomas, that hamburger-eating everyman. Forget New York; in America's postwar consumer economy, if you can make it in Columbus, you can make it anywhere.

In 1977, journalist Betty Garrett described the city as pervaded by "a wonderful, godawful irritating solidity, productiveness, conservatism, and smugness." Twenty-five years later, not much had changed. A *USA Today* article summed it up this way in a 2003 profile of the city: "Columbus *is* America."[68]

Columbus did undertake four urban renewal projects in the 1950s and '60s, in and around the historic core of the city, and a number of other municipal improvements besides. This marked a new era for the city whose conservative voters, before the war, had resolutely rejected any attempted to tax themselves for civic improvements. During World War II, "the city was in a state of ramshackle disrepair," according to a profile of Columbus that appeared in the *Saturday Evening Post*, a town "busted and bewildered." The city's water system was so inadequate that during a drought in 1944 the city ran out of drinking water. After the war, the mayor and a coalition of business leaders sold the voters on the need for large-scale civic projects "like Heinz sells ketchup," and it worked. [69]

In 1956, voters overwhelmingly approved $48 million in bonds which, in turn, leveraged over $120 million federal dollars for slum clearance, school construction, hospital expansion, and airport modernization. And for highways— mostly for highways. Of the nearly $172 million for these projects, $112 million was allocated for highway construction to run a beltway around downtown. It was a triumph of the business and political coalition led by the Metropolitan Columbus Committee.[70]

Although this coalition of businessmen and city politicians made it possible to rebuild the core of the city, the city's growth came for a different reason. Columbus's expansion resulted because it continued to annex its surroundings, just as aggressively as Houston had. Annexation turned out to be another difference between the older cities of the Northeast and Midwest and the newer cities of the South and West. The first great wave of urban annexation took place in the last half of the nineteenth century, starting with Philadelphia's consolidation in 1854 and it reached a culmination of sorts with the union of the five boroughs of New York City in 1898. After that, by and large, city boundaries around the older cities have remained fixed. As the postwar suburbs developed with astonishing speed around those fixed urban boundaries, it became clear, just as quickly, that those suburbs were taking population, jobs, and commerce away from their cities. Many mid-century urban planners believed that annexation would cure what ailed the older cities.[71]

Things were different in the Sunbelt, however. Houston was certainly not alone in expanding by swallowing up outlying towns, townships, and suburbs. So did Dallas, Albuquerque, and Memphis. Atlanta added 83 square miles and roughly 100,000 residents when it reinvented itself as the major urban center of the Old South.[72] For urban experts, annexation explained why the new cities thrived while the old cities faltered.

To suggest that Detroit or Chicago could solve many of its urban woes by annexing its suburbs might well have been persuasive around a seminar table or in a neighborhood bar. Politically, however, the idea was laughable, especially in the 1950s and '60s. Those older cities, after all, were—and still are—surrounded by well-established suburbs that grew and defined themselves precisely as "not the city." Those suburbs, and the politicians who represented them, would never have permitted themselves simply to be swallowed by the big city. Never.

Columbus, like its Sunbelt cousins, however, had the advantage of being less "urban" in the first place—fewer smokestacks, fewer immigrants, fewer black people—than Cleveland or Pittsburgh. Its population density was low, and thus it was hard to see or feel the difference when you crossed the border between city and suburb. City politics also corresponded to the politics of the region more than in other metropolitan areas. Columbus, like much of central Ohio, has been run by small-town Republicans rather than big-city Democrats. All members of the Columbus City Council are elected "at large," meaning that individual neighborhoods do not have their own representatives in city hall. This may have helped Columbus avoid the problems associated with machine politics, but it has also meant that for those looking to advance neighborhood agendas in the City Council, the buck stops nowhere, giving business leaders a free hand to set the political agenda.

More than all of that, Columbus—much like Los Angeles—annexed surrounding areas by controlling access to the water and sewer systems of the region. In this way, the city grew horizontally because it could more or less force the outlying areas to be annexed or face the prospect of building an infrastructure on their own. It was a deal few suburban areas could afford to refuse. When in 1954, for example, voters in adjacent Marion Township turned down the annexation of 168 acres on which sat "the county's richest industrial section," county commissioners met and overruled the vote.[73]

And the pattern continued unabated through the rest of the twentieth century. Columbus encompassed a mere 40 square miles in 1950; by 1985, that had grown to 189 square miles.[74] During the 1990s, Columbus added nearly 35 square miles more to its domain through annexation. At 217 square miles, Columbus now occupies more than twice the land that Cincinnati does, and is considerably bigger than Detroit or Philadelphia.

All of which has made Columbus, like Houston, a postwar urban success story, at least looked at in the aggregate. Columbus did not lose residents, jobs, and revenue to the suburbs because it simply added those suburbs to the city. After the war, as reports began to trickle in about the impending crisis in American cities, the *Saturday Evening Post* told its readers that Columbus "approaches, almost as nearly as any in the land, the common-sense ideal of a fruitful, decent, comfortable, enlightened and well-governed city."[75]

But despite the upbeat postwar attitude about the city's future, like other Sunbelt cities Columbus had not avoided many of the problems facing urban America. In the postwar period, the social geography of the city arranged itself in a familiar set of concentric circles: the central city was generally poor and inhabited by older people and singles, few of whom were raising children; the area also had the highest concentration of black residents anywhere in the city. Around the central city an inner city ring was similarly poor, though more racially mixed. Farther out, the city had already developed a ring of affluent, nearly all-white suburbs. Finally, the metropolitan area included a ring ever farther out of what was still farm country.[76]

In 1959, the City Planning Commission described Columbus in a way and with an attitude that might have described almost any city in America at that moment: "If we were to draw a circle around the heart of the city, approximately three miles out from Broad and High [the Ohio State Capitol sits at that intersection], we would encircle tens of thousands of buildings ranging in age from 40 to 100 years old. Many of these structures, which represent the city of yesteryear, have become dilapidated and completely substandard."[77] Even as it annexed new suburbs, the dispersal of population and services across the landscape meant that the central parts of the city suffered. In 1960, six census tracts in the central city area had reported rates of dilapidated and deteriorating housing from 60 to 100 percent.[78]

Looked at in the changed political environment of the 1960s, and from a slightly different political perspective, the happy, all-American town that the

Saturday Evening Post found in 1952 now seemed insidious. "Columbus by and large remains a soggy, reactionary Middle Western town," Journalist James Ridgeway wrote in 1966; "the John Birch Society fits easily into the atmosphere of Columbus and is said to prosper there." Columbus continued to be dominated by a few old families, the Wolfes first and foremost, who not only controlled the city's biggest bank but also owned its troglodytically right-wing newspaper, the *Dispatch.* Whether or not Columbus really was just a big John Birch Society clubhouse—and that is probably unfair—it certainly was the case that in the 1960s African Americans, who constituted roughly 20 percent of the population, were not represented in city government.[79]

So when Columbus experienced its own racial violence in 1969, the real surprise was that it took so long to arrive—two years later than it did in Jim Crow Houston. But arrive it did, in July in the black neighborhood a mile or so from the state capitol. "Monday, July 21, 1969, promised to be a special day in Columbus," begins a report to Columbus Police Chief Robert Baus. The mayor had declared a holiday to observe the moon landing. But, the report continued, "Monday July 21, 1969, was a special day in Columbus for another reason; this was the day that violence and rioting began on Columbus's near East side."

The violence lasted for several days. When it was over, dozens had been arrested, two men had been killed, and the Ohio National Guard—not yet nationally infamous for killing four students at Kent State University—had to be called out. In trying to assess why the riot happened, the report to Chief Baus laid blame squarely on the black leaders of the neighborhood. After quoting several statements sharply critical of the police that had appeared in the neighborhood newspaper, the report concluded: "If unrealistic statements such as these are indicative of the attitude and direction that responsible Negro leadership is taking in our community, then the riot of July 21–27 did not make any sense; and we can begin preparing for the next one."[80]

The following year the city's Department of Development issued a twenty-year master plan for the downtown area. To judge from its focus, the problems of deteriorating neighborhoods, racial segregation, and the rest were not high on the agenda of those who planned for the future. Instead, "insufficient parking" ranked first on its list of eight problems facing downtown; next came "rush-hour traffic jams." In fact, as the report noted, economic growth in the city—as state government continued to grow and companies like Nationwide Insurance expanded—had produced "one of the more economically healthy central cities in the nation." The report estimated that $100-million worth of new office construction was either underway or on the drawing boards.[81]

Columbus had indeed completed the inner beltway project voters had approved back in the late 1950s, "one of the nation's few completed freeways

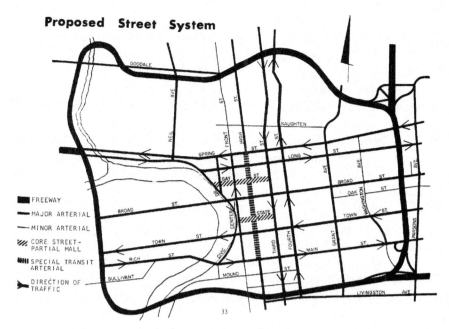

The triumph of the beltway. Columbus, Ohio, boosters were very proud of the beltway they built around the central city. They built an outer beltway, too, and that hastened the decline of downtown as a residential and commercial area. *Downtown Area Plan, Planning Division, Department of Development, City of Columbus, 1970*

encircling the entire downtown," the report boasted. Not surprisingly, planners who saw downtown primarily through the vantage of their windshields also saw the future in terms of their cars. Downtown would need 20,000 additional parking spaces, as well as wider streets and a system of arterials to accommodate an expected doubling of rush-hour traffic to 220,000 cars.

Encircling is perhaps not the right word. *Girdling* might be more apt. The beltway that ringed downtown was a marvel of automotive efficiency—at least initially—but it cut off the center of the city from the neighborhoods that once bordered it. It created a circular chasm of dead space in the heart of the city, a vehicular moat which turned downtown into something like an office-tower island.

The 1970 master plan recognized some of the symptoms, even if it could not quite figure out the cause. Also on the list of eight primary problems was the "erosion of small-merchant retailing and services," the "decline of the metropolitan focus for culture," and "an 8-6 community only."[82] Creating an inner beltway around the central urban core, along with the urban renewal projects, had deliberately and successfully evacuated downtown of its residents. It had cleared downtown of much of its older fabric to make room for new office buildings, and it surrounded those shiny new edifices with parking lots. And in 1970, the city's planning division began to wonder where all the people had gone.

The answer to that question was obvious: they kept moving out. Without a different vision of what the city might be, city leaders kept doing what they had been doing since the 1950s. The residential growth continued to move outward in all directions from the center like ripples in a pond, and with it followed retail and commercial growth and eventually the development of large office parks as well. By 1975, Columbus residents could move around the hinterland on I-270, the newly completed outer belt—a 55-mile loop that helped make the central city increasingly irrelevant.

Ten years after that, city officials announced the construction of yet another inner-city freeway. The 5.7-mile stretch of I-670 connects the center of the city with the outer belt and takes traffic to the airport. "It's more than a high-speed route between the airport and Downtown," explained Mayor Dana Reinhart, "It's an economic development tool as well." Of course, mayors had been saying that about freeway projects for thirty years, and the fact that Reinhart could still parrot the sentiment was remarkable. This time, at least, the promise of economic development was greeted with a little skepticism. City Council President Jerry Hammond responded by saying, "The question is whether it will have a positive economic impact. I'm not so sure."[83]

Skepticism, but not much more. The 100+ families and businesses evicted along the 5.7-mile stretch greeted the project with resignation rather than with anger or with organizing. After all, without a locally based councilperson to plead their case, how would those families make their voices heard? A federal district court agreed that planners had not consulted with black residents during the early planning stages, and the court noted that the citizens advisory council set up to guide the project was stacked with business interests and government officials. But, the judge decided, c'est la vie. Neighborhood residents did not force the issue through a citywide referendum because, as the Dispatch reported, "they could not have mustered enough support outside their own area, at least partly because the project will be a convenience to everyone else."[84] That turn of phrase encapsulated a political shift quite nicely: once cities embarked on civic improvement projects to expand the common good; now they were supported because they catered to individual convenience.

By the end of the 1980s, downtown Columbus had been so thoroughly evacuated that even city leaders recognized the need for a large-scale project to reverse the trend. The result of those efforts opened in 1989. They called it Columbus City Center, and it sat just a few blocks south of the capitol.

The urbane-sounding name aside, City Center was a 1.2-million-square-foot shopping mall entirely of the suburban kind. It amounted to a three-level retail box, self-contained and enclosed. It did not even have windows that might offer shoppers a view of the city outside. City Center had ambitions of attracting high-end shoppers, and to lure them the architects attached the mall to a Hyatt hotel and to parking garages with pedestrian bridges. Suburban shoppers could drive into the city on one of those freeways, park their cars in the garage, shop in the mall, and never would they have to set foot on a city sidewalk or street.

High-end ambitions faded quickly. Business at City Center went well for about three years, with 144 tenants filling most of the square footage. Then things took a bad turn. By the mid- and late 1990s, City Center reeled from the opening of two new extravagant malls out in the suburbs. Its death knell came in 2007 with the opening of yet another suburban mega-mall. By 2009, there were only eight small stores left occupying just 5,000 square feet. Many of the new McMansions built out by those new malls were bigger than that. City Center closed that year.

Even during its brief heyday, City Center loomed as a forbidding, impenetrable block in the section of downtown Columbus it dominated, an ugly, ill-fitting anachronism in the nineteenth-century street grid. It had no street presence, nor did it make any attempt visually or architecturally to engage with the city around it. Designed as it was to be a fortified retail bunker, it was the very essence of anti-urban planning in the very center of the city.

By the turn of the millennium, Columbus stood as the most economically prosperous city in the state, but growing numbers of people recognized that its brand of urbanism could not be sustained. The relentless horizontal expansion of the city (and contiguous suburbs) ate up some of the most productive farmland in the Midwest—35,000 acres of it alone between 1965 and 1985.[85] Its low density and its reliance on highways for transportation have also left it among the most automobile-dependent cities in the nation. Columbus is the largest city in the United States without any passenger rail service at all. Even Phoenix now has a light-rail system. So does Houston, and it has Amtrak service to boot, whereas all that passes for public transit in Columbus is a sad and shabby bus service.

The patterns of economic and demographic growth have come with another cost, as well. Beneath the sunny boosterism that has been a hallmark of city leaders since the 1950s lies the uneasy sense that Columbus lacks any real civic identity. In 1952, the *Saturday Evening Post* ended its puff piece on Columbus by saying that "Columbus discovered America and now America is discovering Columbus." Yet by 1989, the city was still being described as "250,000 people who came to the Ohio State Fair and stayed," and *Newsweek* reported that the "city fathers are waiting for America to discover Columbus."[86]

The All-American city. Columbus grew much like a Sunbelt city in the postwar years. Yet despite its economic success, Columbus was once described as a place where several thousand people came for the Ohio State Fair and stayed. It struggles still to find some sense of civic identity. *Library of Congress HAER OHIO, 25-COLB, 49—15*

Twenty years later, they wait still. Early in this century, city leaders undertook a three-year effort to find a slogan for the place. Some pithy way to capture Columbus's identity and to give its residents a sense of connection to the place. As of yet, they have had no luck. As Paul Astleford, director of Experience Columbus, told the *New York Times,* "Columbus has not had a bad image. It has just had no image in the national marketplace."[87]

After the Second World War, Columbus transformed itself from a small, compact nineteenth-century midwestern city into a sprawling Sunbelt-style metropolis, but along the way it lost track of its soul.

New Cities and the Past

If ever passenger rail service were to resume through Ohio, the trains would have no place to stop in Columbus. In 1979, the city's *burghermeisters* demolished Union Station, a lovely if small Beaux Arts building from the early twentieth century. No station, no trains. The symbolism of that demolition was hard to miss. Columbus staked its future on its cars and private transportation; it wanted nothing to do with public transit. Cars were the new city future, and for a city like Columbus, trains represented the old city past.

The demolition of Union Station points to another difference between the new urbanism and the older version. Beyond expressing their contempt for trains, those who ordered the building torn down expressed their contempt for Columbus's past. Part of creating the new urban form in Columbus involved tearing down much of the physical remains of the city's own history. Walk around the nineteenth-century core of Columbus and you are struck, not by the new office towers which rise as monuments to banking and insurance and state government, but by how much of downtown has been torn down and left vacant—or replaced with parking lots. Union Station, fittingly enough, fell to make way for vehicular access for the convention center.

Lewis Mumford, in his magnum opus *The City in History*, wrote that one crucial function of a city is to serve as a living museum of human history. Within what he called "the historic city" can be found evidence of "every variety of human function, every experiment in human association, every technological process, every mode of architecture and planning."[88] In the mid-twentieth century, many cities erased significant pieces of their past in the name of urban renewal, urban highways, or of progress more broadly. But it is probably fair to say that cities like Houston and Columbus have been more energetic than most in tearing down the past and less attentive to the civic importance of their own history.

And that history is important. It is directly connected to the identity crisis that keeps Columbus officials wringing their hands. Civic identity springs from two sources in conversation with each other: on the one hand, the city is shaped by those who live and work in it at any given moment; on the other hand, those lives are given their particular urban texture by the histories of all those who have occupied the place in the past. This effortless, ongoing dialogue between past and present is what gives each city its particular flavor, and it is what gives the people in those cities their special connection to it.[89] Unless, that is, you tear it all down and replace it with sterile sameness. It is no coincidence that the two neighborhoods most trumpeted in Columbus these days are revived and restored nineteenth-century ones. The Short North and the German Village sit on the north and south edges of downtown, respectively, and both were damaged significantly by highway projects before people recognized their urban potential.

A few of the finest buildings from Houston's Fourth Ward still stand, but they do so nowadays along a little walking path in the middle of Sam Houston Park. Removed from their people and from their physical context, these structures do not so much preserve the past in any meaningful way as remind people of what's been lost. Walking through the park is a mournful experience. Likewise, there is one small piece of Union Station remaining. A pair of columns topped with an arch occupies a small green space in a district by the hockey arena in downtown Columbus. Few people notice this remnant as they go into the arena or stumble out of the sports bars. In its loneliness and disconnection, that arch captures nicely Columbus's difficulty in finding itself.

8 SMALL TOWN, NEW TOWN, COMMUNE

For millions of Americans in the second half of the twentieth century, decentralization meant moving to the suburbs. For a number of writers, critics, and influential intellectuals, however, the suburb seemed to mock the very purpose of decentralizing the city. Umbilically attached as they were to metropolitan centers, these suburbs did not produce their own economic lives, did not generate much in the way of their own cultural lives, and, perhaps most damningly, substituted single-family housing for a more expansive sense of community. They were ridiculed as banal, homogenizing, and, more insidiously, as places that produced a dangerous conformity.

In the decades after World War II, Americans across a wide swath of the political spectrum tried to build alternatives both to urban life, which so many in the postwar years saw as being in irreversible decline, and to those conventional suburbs that sprouted so quickly on the landscape. In imagining these alternatives—the small town, the new town and the commune—those who created them put the formation of community at the center of their anti-urban agendas, and all looked to the past to achieve it.

The Small Town's Last Stand

Today he is the answer to a trivia question: Who was Franklin Roosevelt's first chairman of the Tennessee Valley Authority? Answer: Arthur Ernest Morgan.

To look at photos of Arthur Morgan is to stare into the stern face of the nineteenth century. Unsmiling, Morgan looks lean and tough and formidable, high starched collar and all. Born near Cincinnati in 1878, raised largely in St. Cloud, Minnesota, Morgan absorbed the rigid Baptist moralism of his mother Anna. As a young man, Morgan went west, as so many ambitious children of that age did, and taught himself to be a hydraulic engineer. Just before the First World War he returned to the region of his birth, more specifically to Dayton, Ohio.

The Great Flood of 1913 brought him there. In the aftermath of that devastation, Morgan proposed a system of earthen dams, levees, and other flood-control measures to tame the Great Miami River and its tributaries. City leaders followed his plan and built the dams, and with that Morgan made his reputation. The Miami Valley Conservancy District became the model for other such water management projects that Morgan designed around the country, and by 1920 he was probably the best dam-builder in the nation.

Morgan's success as an engineer brought him to the attention of the Roosevelt administration roughly fifteen years later, when the TVA was being established. But when the call from Washington came, Morgan was already deep into his second career as president of Antioch College, about twenty miles east of Dayton in the tiny town of Yellow Springs.

When Morgan took over the presidency of the college in 1920, it was just about dead. Its enrollment had dwindled, and it was broke. The year he arrived, a grand total of four seniors graduated. Very rarely in the life of an institution is it possible to restart from scratch, but Morgan saw his opportunity and seized it. He fired many of the faculty—there were hardly any left anyway—and replaced the board of trustees, some left over from Antioch's more evangelical Protestant past, with figures from the world of business and industry, most importantly Dayton industrialist Charles Kettering.

Morgan's most famous educational innovation was to bring "co-op" education, until then the preserve of aspiring engineers, to the liberal arts curriculum. Morgan made sure that every Antioch student, from art majors to zoology majors, spent time working out in the real world. In a very direct way, therefore, intellectual life enriched the work, and the work enriched the intellectual life. It is no exaggeration to say that Morgan's Antioch became the most interesting, most innovative, most dynamic small college in America during the middle years of the twentieth century, producing graduates as diverse as Coretta Scott (later King), Leon Higginbotham, Rod Serling, Clifford Geertz, Mark Strand, and Stephen J. Gould.

The TVA originated in Roosevelt's "first New Deal" along with the National Recovery Agency and the Agricultural Adjustment Agency, and was its largest attempt to build the infrastructure of decentralization. In fact, it provides another connection between the New Deal and the regional planners of the 1920s. At the last meeting of the Regional Planning Association of America (RPAA), held in 1931, discussions included a hypothetical project that in retrospect looked a great deal like the TVA. New York Governor Franklin Roosevelt attended that meeting.[1]

In retrospect, it seems almost inevitable that Morgan's tenure at the TVA would be an unhappy one. Morgan, progressive as he was as an educator, remained

Arthur Morgan came to Yellow Springs, Ohio, to rescue Antioch College, and he created for students like these one of the most dynamic liberal arts institutions in America. He also brought nineteenth-century midwestern values to the task of saving the American small town. After his term as president of Antioch College, and after he served as director of the Tennessee Valley Authority, Morgan returned to Yellow Springs and wrote about small towns and about the nature of "community." *Courtesy of Antiochiana, Antioch College*

a child of the nineteenth century, committed to its values and verities, particularly about private enterprise. The TVA was perhaps the closest thing to socialism that the Roosevelt administration ever undertook. It was a bad fit from the start.

Morgan had been brought into the TVA to pour concrete, to design and manage the construction of the dams and other flood-control devices that would rationalize this vast watershed. David Lilienthal, another TVA director, was appointed by FDR to create the electrical grid that would result from all the new hydroelectric power those dams would generate. The two clashed almost immediately.

In summary, Morgan believed that private utilities and public power ought to co-exist peacefully. In a memo written in the summer of 1933, Morgan revealed his midwestern sense of doing business. "I think we should assume," he told Lilienthal, "reasonableness, fair play and good will on the part of the utilities unless experience in *our own* relations with them demonstrates the contrary."

Lilienthal, a veteran of fights with private utility companies, must have chuckled at this naiveté. He wanted the TVA to neuter private power companies even if it meant driving them out of business.[2]

Tensions between Morgan and Lilienthal simmered through FDR's first term, and they came to a boil during his second. The proverbial last straw involved a deal Lilienthal brokered with Tennessee Senator George Berry for a $5 million purchase of land. Morgan thought the amount and the deal itself smelled bad. According to the *Chicago Tribune*, Morgan "insisted that the claim [of value] was made in bad faith, with the intent to defraud the government, and that the land had been procured for that purpose and none other."[3] In 1938, Morgan called on Congress to launch an investigation into the TVA's finances and into Lilienthal's use of money more specifically.

FDR had been trying for nearly five years to massage the feelings and egos of his TVA directors, but with little success. To have one of them accuse the other of fraud forced the issue. From the administration's point of view, Morgan and his rectitude meant he simply could not play well with others. The merits of the case hardly mattered. By the end of the year he had been sacked. Sixty years old, he came back home to Yellow Springs and settled into the final act of his remarkable career. He embarked on a campaign to save the American small town.

When Arthur and Lucy Morgan moved their household to Yellow Springs in 1920, the town they intended to live in was not much better off than the college he had come to lead. There were 1,300 people, give or take, living in the village. Which was respectable enough for a midwestern small town, but many of those people were elderly farmers who moved into town when they could no longer farm. The economic life of the town consisted, Morgan recalled, of "an ancient sawmill, a nearly defunct canning plant, a grain elevator, and a nursery which propagated evergreens from cuttings." Together these employed maybe twenty people.[4]

Morgan came to Yellow Springs to revive Antioch College. Almost immediately he realized that he had the opportunity to revive the town as well. In fact, in Morgan's mind the two would rebuild each other. And it worked. Thirty years after Morgan arrived like a Protestant force of nature, the population of Yellow Springs had doubled (not even counting the college students) and the economy had blossomed to include a new precision foundry, a medical instrument manufacturer, an auto-parts designer and manufacturer, and the Antioch Bookplate Company. All of these enterprises, and several others as well, had their roots in the work Antioch students did while on campus.

Morgan scarcely took time to catch his breath after his dismissal from the TVA and his return to Yellow Springs. In 1940 he founded Community Service, Inc., and he used it as the pulpit from which he preached the gospel of small-town revival to a national audience. Community Service saw itself as promoting "the interests of the community as a basic social institution and concerned with the economic, recreational, educational, cultural and spiritual development of its members." It did this through publishing books about the small community, sending out lecturers and consultants, and sponsoring conferences. In its first quarter-century, Community Service had done work in thirty-seven states, as well as in India, Ghana, and Mexico; and it could report that "several American Indian tribes appealed to Community Service for advice and professional help in maintaining their autonomy."[5]

Morgan began his mission to save the small town by issuing a jeremiad. He published it in 1942 and called it *The Small Community: The Foundation of Democratic Life*. He minced no words, from the very first page: "In modern times the small community has played the part of an orphan in an unfriendly world. It has been despised, neglected, exploited, and robbed. The cities have skimmed off the cream of its young population." If this sounded slightly aggrieved, Morgan continued "Yet the small community has supplied the lifeblood of civilization, and neglect of it has been one of the primary reasons for the slowness and the interrupted course of human progress." He concluded this opening salvo by trumpeting "It is high time that the fundamental significance of the small community be recognized."[6]

The American nation, in Morgan's view, sprang from its small towns. "The American Constitution...was the product of a nation of villagers, and reflected their temper," he wrote, perhaps stretching things just a little. And yet, he asked, "what have we in America done with community? We have taken for granted intimate human culture, without realizing its need for an abiding place." Morgan recognized that "in recent times economic forces have had disastrous effects on village communities," but he insisted that this amounted to an aberrant pathology. "Many of the social ideals which the Western world values most highly have been preserved from ancient times in small communities," he reminded readers, warning that "The progressive disappearance of the village community in America constitutes a serious departure from the general course of human history."[7]

Face-to-face community; face-to-face democracy. That was what Morgan saw as the foundation of a better society, and that was what he wanted to promote. He also insisted that a real community encompassed the totality of people's lives—economic, cultural, educational—and was therefore more holistic than a mere interest or affinity group: "A stock breeders' organization, a co-operative creamery, a trade association, or a church...scarcely deserves the name of community."[8] One can only imagine how he would have reacted to the proliferation in our digital age of "virtual communities" that now masquerade as genuine communities.

In an urbanized nation that would soon suburbanize rapidly, the small town stood as a place apart. What happened in a small town, therefore, became the basis for building the rest of society. "The small community," Morgan wrote, "can be the testing laboratory and the nursery for society. There, on a small scale, men can actually live by the good will, mutual respect and confidence, helpfulness, tolerance, and neighborliness which are the ideal of all human societies."[9] In his own way, Morgan imagined utopia not as a place in some hypothetical future but as the most cherished American place of the American past: the small town.

Morgan was not alone in reasserting the cultural, social, and political central- ity of the small town after World War II. Indiana newspaperman H. Clay Tate published an ode to the small town in 1954, calling it "the balance wheel of our economic, social and cultural order. It is the insurance policy against the loss of the individual's ability to determine his own destiny." Clay dedicated it to "the intelligent young people who are beginning to turn away from centralization to the non-metropolitan areas of the United States in quest of the good life. They are the guardians of the American dream."[10] The following year the Russell Sage Foundation published *Studying Your Community*, a how-to guide for conduct- ing surveys designed to improve the quality of small-town life. Fittingly, the book carried a lengthy epigraph from philosopher Josiah Royce: "I believe in the beloved community and in the spirit which makes it beloved, and in the commu- nion of all who are, in will and in deed, its members. I see no such community as yet, but none the less my rule of life is: Act so as to hasten its coming."[11] For many Americans, it could come only in a small town.

Morgan, as an accomplished man of the world, understood full well that the beloved community could not exist purely on its own good vibrations. Small communities needed a solid and diversified economic base. Historically, at least as Morgan saw it, small towns began as single-industry places: a mining town, a farming town, a timber town. This meant the fate of the community was tied dan- gerously to the health of a single economy. In 1953, Morgan published *Industries for Small Communities* to tackle that problem head on.

Morgan was bullish on small business. He related a conversation he had had with the president of a big New York bank. The choice for America, Mr. Banker boomed, "is between big business and peanut stands." That conversation took place just before the crash of 1929, and writing twenty-five years later, Morgan could triumphantly point to all sorts of studies, reports, and statistics demon- strating that small business was alive and thriving. "Those who see big business as coming to have a monopoly of our economic life," Morgan wrote, sounding truly progressive, "are living in the economic climate of decades past."[12] Small business was the future.

The problem for small-town economic life, as Morgan saw it, might be described as directional. Fretting about shrinking income, the loss of jobs and people, local leaders tended to look out. They searched for a business willing to relocate, and sometimes this worked. "Frequently," Morgan pointed out, "such incentives are provided as free location, remittance of local taxes for five or ten years, or the purchase of a block of stock. Hundreds, perhaps thousands, of American small towns have records of securing industries by such enticements." In the end, however, businesses left anyway.[13]

Morgan suggested that leadership ought to look inward, to develop new businesses from the talents, interests, and resources already available. The real issue wasn't size—small was not inherently better than big in Morgan's view—but, rather, diversity. "Unless there are reasonable chances for making their livings near home," Morgan warned, "young people will leave for the city, and with their leaving the home town loses some of its vigor and attractiveness."[14] Diversified small industry was Morgan's answer to the dilemma that had plagued America since the nineteenth century: how to keep young people from moving to the city.

The subtitle of Morgan's treatise on small-town industry revealed a central problem with his analysis, however. He organized his book around cases from Yellow Springs. On the face of it, why not? Morgan had been instrumental in revitalizing Antioch College and Yellow Springs. But he seemed reluctant to acknowledge just how unusual the place really was. Yellow Springs, after all, was a college town, and not just any college town, but home to the most innovative educational experiment being carried out in American higher education.[15] A very few small towns might have a college to support them—H. Clay Tate spent fully half of his paean to the small community talking about his own hometown of Bloomington, Indiana—but many of those colleges were still wallowing in their denominational mediocrity and were hardly places of economic and cultural innovation. Yellow Springs was no more a model for most American small towns than Harvard was a model for the small liberal arts college.

Indeed, toward the end of *Industries for Small Communities* Morgan discussed what he saw as "serious problems ahead for our village." In a word, growth. Morgan predicted that "several of the industries may double or triple their employees in a few years, and the village may grow accordingly." And he wondered, "Then what will become of its small-community characteristics? Already the size is about the maximum for a face-to-face community."[16]

In 1953, when Morgan wrote that, many small towns wished they had such problems. In fact, they were experiencing exactly the opposite. Tate pointed out in 1954 that in the previous decade, 116,000 "units" of local government— roughly 25 percent of the total—had disappeared through consolidation or evaporation, and he predicted that hundreds of communities would die in the next quarter-century. Max Lerner, writing in 1957, was even more definitive. "In the quarter century between 1930 and 1955," he offered, "the decisive turn was made, away from small-town life." A survey conducted by the state of New York found conditions in small towns to be "as bad or worse than those found in big city slums."[17]

Although Morgan saw small industries of the future as a way of reviving the small town, Lerner saw what was destroying it in the present. The fragility of the American small town could not withstand "the big changes in American life," including "the auto and super-highway, the supermarket and the market center, the mail-order house, the radio and TV." In other words, it was threatened by modern, mass society as it exploded in the postwar period.

Lerner was right to put the automobile at the top of his list, but he misspoke slightly to put it next to the superhighway. He should have said the superhighway and the bypass. Certainly, interstate highways did their damage to local landscapes and local economies as they snaked all over the map. The commerce necessary for interstate travelers, the restaurants, motels, and gas stations, clustered near the on and off ramps, forcing the equivalent businesses in nearby towns to close. Often the interstates ran parallel to older, local roads, enabling drivers to take the same journey but skip the towns entirely. Thus, they simply pulled traffic out of those towns and accelerated the pace with which people moved through and moved out.

Perhaps more commonly, however, state highways were responsible for sucking the economic life out of American small towns. The process went something like this: A network of roads developed across the map of nineteenth-century America, linking small towns. Those inter-town connectors usually ran along the main business corridor, along Main Street or Broad Street or First Avenue, as they went through towns. In the twentieth century, those roads were taken over by states and given route numbers. Then, as car traffic increased on those numbered routes and Main Streets, states decided to widen the roads so that some allowed speeds as fast as those on the highways. Then state highway planners took aim at the slow spots on their newly speedy roads: small towns.

Take a drive almost anywhere in the country, off the interstates, on the local roads, through the land of small-town America. The pattern is the same. Roll down a state route, through farm fields, or woodland, or even suburban developments, and as you approach an older small town you get a choice. Exit and head into town, or maintain speed and bypass the town.

Take that "business" route into town and you are liable to find Main Street a shadow of its former self. Commercial spaces are now empty or filled with antique and second-hand stores, the last refuge of the small-town economy. Often the surrounding residential real estate is not in much better shape. Take the bypass, on the other hand, and at one end of it or the other you are liable to find a shopping center, with the big-box stores that have put the local ones out of business and the Cinema One Too Many that has replaced the town's old movie theater. State departments of transportation destroyed large sections of America's cities by plowing through them. They ruined countless small towns by going around them.

Camden, Ohio, sits about five miles from the Indiana state line and about fifty miles from Yellow Springs, west by southwest. When Arthur Morgan was writing about the industries of Yellow Springs and wondering what would happen to the town if they grew too big, Camden's leaders were worried about State Route 127.

State highway planners had announced that they would reroute and expand that road, which runs north and south from suburban Cincinnati to the Michigan border. The initial plans called for the road to bypass the towns of New Miami, Seven Mile, and Somerville, all to the south of Camden. In 1959, however, the Ohio Department of Transportation announced that the rebuilding project would indeed be extended north. Route 127 would skip Camden by swinging to the west of town. The road opened in 1961. Almost immediately, several restaurants closed in the center of town, as did several cabins and motels catering to tourists, who now just drove past and skipped the town altogether. Ray O'Dell moved his gas station out to be closer to the new road.

Whatever hope Camden might have had for health and stability in the postwar boom left when the bypass opened. By the end of the twentieth century, Camden had lost most of its employers and most of its institutions. In 1988, a fire tore through City Hall, and though it left the building standing, the town did not have the money to tear the gutted hall down. And in a cruel coincidence, 1988 also saw a fire destroy the Dearth Building. A handsome nineteenth-century brick structure, it had anchored the commercial district, though by that point it was home to a pizza joint. After this fire the building did come down, replaced—fittingly enough—with a parking lot. People know each other in Camden in that small-town, friendly way, but that is largely because people there did not have anywhere else to go. This was small-town America since the end of World War II.[18]

Morgan, not unlike New England enthusiasts Bernard DeVoto, Edward Chapman, and the rest, saw the small town as the antidote to urban civilization and all its discontents. What they failed to see was that the forces threatening their communities were the same as those tearing American cities apart in the age of urban renewal. And with many of the same results, only in microcosm.

Small towns, many of them, have seen their populations shrink and their schools suffer. They have lost jobs in the Great Deindustrialization. In big cities, job loss came from the closing of hundreds of factories and workshops; in the small towns, it often meant the closure of one or two businesses. As a result, small-town America, much of it anyway, is also like big-city America because it has become poor.[19] The city did not kill the small town, as so many including Morgan believed it would. Rather, the centrifugal forces of deindustrialization and suburbanization did.

Arthur Morgan and the rest did not make that connection. Their conception of the small town remained rooted in the anti-urban rhetoric and traditions that reached back into the nineteenth century. Morgan believed that America had created "true unified communities" back in the "pioneer period." The fall from that moment of grace came with what Morgan called "technical society" eroding any sense of real community. Instead, in a technical society, people group themselves around "special interest."[20]

Indeed, Morgan's conception of community did not cling to the nineteenth century abstractly, but sprang to life in 1895 quite specifically. As a seventeen-year-old on the cusp of his adulthood, he had a vision:

> I had a picture of a little community. . . . We'd be making our living. . . . We'd be selling things so we'd be independent. . . . The teachers would have their families there and the pupils would be living in the teachers' houses with them. . . . There would be nothing that we wouldn't be talking about . . . trying to invent new industries, new ways of making money. It would be a community of explorers and inventors and teachers and students. . . . I remember just being so taken up with that picture that I stood there on the footpath in the hazelbrush for possibly an hour.[21]

It is a moment both Roycian and Emersonian, and almost utopian.[22] A vision of a beloved community that struck him, bolt out of the blue, while hiking. Plenty of people in the first half of the twentieth century imagined a retreat from the city and a return to the small-town community of the nineteenth century. More than any of them, Arthur Morgan succeeded in creating such a place.

I say that because I live in Arthur Morgan's Yellow Springs, and I can attest to the remarkable vitality of this village even today. Only 4,000 people live here, and for better or worse we do all seem to know one another. It is indeed a face-to-face community. Through what seems like a collective act of will, we have held on to many of our important small-town institutions. We still have our (prize-winning) weekly newspaper, a grocery store, our own repertory movie theater, and a small hardware store. Added to that, we have several coffeehouses and restaurants that function not simply to keep us fed but also to keep us conversing with each other. Yellow Springs has succeeded in developing an ethos of the "local" that many other places would find enviable. I write this sitting at a desk made for me by one of my neighbors, and I eat my meals on plates made in a wood-fired kiln by another of my neighbors. I have the very great luxury of knowing many of the people who produce the food that I put on those beautiful plates.

Living here as I do, however, I can say with confidence that Yellow Springs is no ordinary place; it is certainly not like the rest of small-town America. Antioch College over the years has contributed its share to all this, but there is more to it than that.[23] Call it the politics of the place, broadly defined, a politics of tolerance that in turn has created a socioeconomic diversity that people here prize. Historically, Yellow Springs has been a haven for those on the margins of American society. The college brought abolitionism to town before the Civil War; the local lore has it that Yellow Springs was an underground railroad stop for escaped slaves who crossed the Ohio River and made their way north, moving through the town on their way to Michigan and Canada. Later, Yellow Springs was among the few racially integrated places in a region in the heart of Klan country. My children attended the school where Coretta Scott King did her student teaching. No other school in the area would accept a black teacher.

Arthur Morgan leads a civil rights march down the main street of town to mourn the assassination of Martin Luther King Jr., in April 1968. Small though it is, Yellow Springs has thrived in part because of its openness and tolerance. *Courtesy of Antiochiana, Antioch College*

Through much of the twentieth century, it was a place where interracial couples could raise their families without fear. More recently still, Yellow Springs has welcomed gay couples and their children, and it has a disproportionate number of artists, artisans, and other creative types. It is an island of thoughtfulness surrounded by a reactionary sea.[24]

In other words, Yellow Springs has continued to survive and flourish precisely because it embraced certain urban values—tolerance and diversity foremost among them, and all that comes with them. It welcomed the social changes of the postwar period whereas so many small towns have resisted them and wilted as a consequence. It works because it has managed to be both small and remarkably cosmopolitan. It is not uncommon for people to describe Yellow Springs as a funky big-city neighborhood, only without the rest of the city.

The village is certainly not immune to what Sinclair Lewis wonderfully called "the village virus"—a smug, provincial self-satisfaction that often infects small-town life. Nor is it without its more significant problems and serious challenges. The small-scale industry that Arthur Morgan watched grow has contracted, like industry across much of the Midwest. It has been replaced with a tourist economy. Thousands of people come from great distances every year to "experience" the town, walk its streets, listen to some music, patronize its stores. They come, in other words, because Yellow Springs is resolutely not a shopping mall or a suburban development or a "planned community." What many of them probably do not recognize is that underneath the eclectic shops and creative free spirit is a widely shared commitment to the public good—to the village, the nation, and even the world. For a town of 4,000 people, Yellow Springs has an absurd number of nonprofit organizations and volunteer groups that work on everything from preserving local farmland to training subsistence farmers in Ethiopia. That insistence that we all share in the commonweal makes this small town seem much bigger. The tourists may recognize that this is a different place, but one wonders how many of them understand why.

Since the mid-1960s, Americans have proved remarkably consistent about at least one thing. In 1966, the Gallup organization started asking people "If you could live anywhere in the United States that you wanted to, would you prefer a city, suburban area, small town, or farm?" In that first survey, the winner, if that's the right way to put it, was the small town, with 31 percent of respondents. The results of that 1966 survey have stayed more or less the same: about one-third of us would prefer to live in a small town, though fewer than 20 percent want to live in a city, the lowest result from all these polls.[25]

That preference expressed over and over again in fourteen separate polls bears no relation to where Americans actually live, needless to say. Only a tiny fraction of Americans live in a small town today, and very few ever have.[26] Those poll numbers express a nostalgia one step removed—not a longing for something we once knew, but a yearning for a life as we imagine it must have been. Max Lerner understood this when he observed in 1957: "The fact that the small town is dwindling in importance makes Americans idealize it all the more."[27]

Those poll numbers show Americans in mourning, not quite for the small town itself but for something at once more specific and more ineffable. They represent the desire Americans have for "community" and the absence of it they feel in their own lives. Unable to conceive that urban life might provide opportunities for fulfilling community, Americans during the 1950s and 1960s committed themselves to a suburban future and pretended that they could find what they sought there. Those survey results remind us that they have not.

The most idealized small town anywhere in America, of course, opened on July 17, 1955. On that day, on 160 acres of Orange County, California, walnut groves and orange trees, Walt Disney invited thousands into his Disneyland. They walked from the parking lots through the gate on to Main Street. Disney built Main Street as his shrine to the small-town America he grew up in, a fantasy of Victoriana complete with all the things Americans thought belonged in a small town, including a city hall and a train station. That last touch was particularly ironic since the only way to get to Disneyland was on US Route 101. The road was widened by two lanes to accommodate the expected crush of traffic. The millions of Americans who come every year to Walt Disney's shrine to small-town life, and all the conservative small-town values Disney clung to, travel on a road paid for by the federal government.

From Urban Renewal to Urban Tragedy: The Kerner Commission Report and Its Aftermath

Even before the acrid smoke had cleared from the city of Detroit late in July 1967, President Lyndon Johnson established the National Advisory Commission on Civil Disorders. The president wanted answers. He told the commission to figure out: "What happened? Why did it happen? What can be done to prevent it from happening again and again?" He appointed Illinois governor Otto Kerner to chair the commission.

On the face of it, what happened hardly required a commission. In the early morning hours of Sunday July 23, Detroit police raided a speakeasy in a black section of town and began arresting people more or less indiscriminately. Such police actions were not uncommon in black Detroit or in the black sections of most American cities. On July 23, however, the patrons of the "blind pig" reacted, resisted, and rebelled. Thus started the 1967 Detroit riot, and by the time it was over, after the National Guard had been called out and Army troops had been sent in, more than 7,000 people had been arrested, more than 450 people had been hurt, and 43 Detroiters were dead. When it was over, Jerome Cavanaugh, the mayor who watched his city go up in flames, reached for the only comparison he could find: "It looks like Berlin in 1945."

It was the deadliest, most destructive urban riot of the twentieth century, a tragedy that would have warranted a federal investigation all on its own. But the Detroit riot had followed the riot in Newark a week earlier. Newark had followed Buffalo, where a riot had broken out late in June. The riot in Buffalo was serious enough to bring Martin Luther King Jr. to town. By the end of the July, Detroit and Newark made Buffalo look tame. In fact, by the end of the summer 1967, the longest and hottest of them all, riots had broken out in more than 100 places around the country. And 1967 had outdone 1966, when riots had torn apart neighborhoods in thirty-eight cities.

This is what Johnson charged the Kerner Commission with figuring out, and on March 1, 1968, it released the results of its research. The report ran more than 500 pages. Even so, it was issued as a trade paperback that sold nearly a million copies, and for those Americans who read the report, its upshot was captured by one attention-grabbing line: "Our nation is moving toward two societies, one black, one white—separate and unequal." The report went on even more unsparingly:

> Segregation and poverty have created in the racial ghetto a destructive environment totally unknown to most white Americans. What white Americans have never fully understood but what the Negro can never forget—is that white society is deeply implicated in the ghetto. White institutions created it, white institutions maintain it, and white society condones it.[28]

It was a stark and chilling equation: white racism equals black riots.

Needless to say, that formulation generated immense controversy. Some on the left chuckled bitterly at the verb phrase "is moving toward." How about "is and always has been" separate and unequal across the entire span of American history? But a larger number of white Americans balked at somehow being blamed for the random violence and wanton destruction of the urban riots that they watched on TV.

The report, commissioned by a Democratic president, presented a dilemma for the Democratic Party as it approached the 1968 election. For his part, LBJ received the report coolly; he certainly did not rush to act on any of its recommendations. Understandably, perhaps, because just as the report came out, Johnson was coming to his own stunning decision to withdraw from the presidential race in order to focus on the Vietnam War for the remainder of his term. In advance of what would turn out to be the ill-fated 1968 Democratic National Convention, Oklahoma Senator Fred Harris, who chaired Vice President Hubert Humphrey's presidential campaign, called on the Democratic Party platform committee to endorse the findings and recommendations of the Kerner Commission. That might have been a bit self-serving since Harris had been a member of the commission, but he pointed out that the Oklahoma Democratic Party had already given its support to the commission.

The editors of the *Chicago Tribune*, in the city where the Democrats would shortly convene, thought this was a terrible idea. "It would be hard to think of a more efficient way of sabotaging the chances of the Democrats," the editors wrote, "than to adopt as part of their platform a report which blames the riots primarily on 'white racism' and which proposes to appease the rioters with a variety of new and expanded programs."[29]

The party tried to split the difference. The platform delegates in Chicago included this plank: "We acknowledge with concern the findings of the report of the bi-partisan National Advisory Commission on Civil Disorders and we commit ourselves to implement its recommendations and to wipe out, once and for all, the stain of racial and other discrimination from our national life." The party "acknowledged" the Kerner Commission, but hardly endorsed it. By extension, that equivocation represented the fact that, by the end of the 1960s, the party did not really know what to do with the American city.

The politics of the moment constituted only half of the problem for the Democrats as they tried to figure out how to handle controversy that the Kerner Commission had created for them. The other half lay in finding which recommendations, precisely, to endorse. There were plenty of specifics, of course; probably too many. Taken as a whole, however, the recommendations struck many as the same old same old. On the right, *National Review* had its own ideological axe to grind when it complained that

> most notable about the report ... is the fact that not a single fresh idea or proposal has been discovered in that gigantic text. ... The recommendations are, needless to say, that the government should spend more money, billions and billions more, on exactly the same projects that have brought zero or below-zero results from the billions spent on them in the past.[30]

That probably overstated the case, especially given that the commission had made the "law and order" proposal that police departments develop intelligence units and make more use of informants and undercover officers in black neighborhoods.

But when Kenneth Clark, the renowned African American social psychologist, testified before the commission, he captured a genuine sense of sad exhaustion. In the commission's work he saw only "the same moving pictures re-shown...the same analysis, the same recommendations."[31]

Events only hardened the positions of those on opposite sides of the Kerner Commission report. A month after its release, riots erupted in more than 100 cities in the wake of Martin Luther King Jr.'s assassination; two months later, Robert Kennedy's assassination prompted another "blue ribbon" presidential panel to examine violence in America. Writing in the *New York Times*, Victor Navasky denounced this as

> a cruel, inappropriate and meaningless way to mark Senator Kennedy's tragic death. A more fitting gesture would involve some action to implement the Kerner Commission's report, which called for faster residential integration, including into all-white suburbs, and increased employment programs for African Americans. [32]

The Democratic Party convention itself exploded in violence and mayhem at the end of the summer. Whether or not the Kerner Commission report offered any solutions for the America of 1968, it certainly risked being crowded out of sight by the very sorts of civil disorder it attempted to address.

Whatever else might be said about the commission's recommendations, they attempted to confront a particular problem. The commission concluded that the urban riots of the 1960s represented the confluence of the colossal failure of American race relations and the corrosive, debilitating effects of urban poverty. It thus offered solutions—coercive or courageous or simply naïve, depending on your point of view—to fix that problem: more racial justice, more social welfare.

In this sense, the report cemented in the public's imagination the union of "urban" problems with "black" problems. With its stress on black poverty as a cause of the riots, the report also underscored the three-part union of black with poor with city.

In other words, the Kerner Commission Report took for granted that the "civil disorders" occurred in American cities, and thus did not address urban policy as separate and apart from civil rights policy. That is perfectly understandable, given the circumstances of those riots and the politics of that moment. But just as urban renewal failed too often to see beyond the question of urban housing, so too the Kerner Report lost sight of larger urban dynamics in its focus on black despair and white racism. Amid the hundreds of pages dealing with issues like policing, the criminal justice system, unemployment, and family structure, the report devoted a scant twenty pages to "The Future of the Cities."

Even here, it confined itself to predictions about the growth of "Negro ghettos"—underscoring that the black cities of the future would be poor cities of the future, and as such would likely generate more violence. The report predicted, with some accuracy, when specific cities would become majority black, and noted "as Negroes succeed whites in our largest cities, the proportion of low-income residents in those cities will probably increase."[33] Tellingly, the brief nod that the 1968 Democratic Party platform gave to the Kerner Commission Report came under the heading "Toward a Single Society," not under the heading "Inner City." There, the Democrats simply promised to continue with the Model Cities program.

By 1968, then, the American city was perceived as increasingly poor, increasingly black, and largely hopeless. By the end of the 1960s, American cities seemed to have fallen entirely out of step with mainstream American life, and they made easy targets for the backlash politics ushered in by Richard Nixon.

New Towns to Save Old Cities

As 1968 rolled on and Americans lurched from assassination to urban violence to anger and desperation about Vietnam; and as Johnson studiously avoided the Kerner Report he had commissioned; and with the mood of voters increasingly turning against any large-scale urban programs, enthusiasm did begin to grow for a different federal response to the perceived implosion of the American city. An old solution, actually: to build new cities on the periphery of the old ones, Garden Cities, and new towns, updated for the 1970s. The urban renewal and interstate projects had frayed and fractured the city in order to save it. With major parts of major (and smaller) cities increasingly in ruins, it was time to leave them.

With the urban riots explicitly on his mind, former President Dwight Eisenhower offered his own response to the Kerner Commission Report by sketching a program "to insure domestic tranquility" in the spring of 1968. It came in three parts: housing, education, and job training. Eisenhower minced no words describing the housing situation in urban America. "We shall never solve this problem," he wrote, "simply by tearing out vast areas of substandard dwellings and stacking people vertically in new high-rise apartment complexes. We have tried this before, and such new housing swiftly and inevitable degenerates into just another slum." This was quite an admission from a man who presided over exactly such efforts during his two administrations.

Instead, Eisenhower continued, "we must provide room to breathe in the inner cities." To achieve that breathing space, "the first essential of any realistic housing plan is to reduce the density of population by encouraging large numbers

of people to relocate in new, more wholesome communities." Echoing the planners of earlier generations, Eisenhower saw urban problems as rooted in urban
"congestion." These new towns, Eisenhower proposed, would be self-sufficient
communities with shopping, schools, and an economic base. And in a nod to
the civil rights movement, Eisenhower insisted that "these new areas must not
become just added enclaves of segregation. They must be open, and made inviting
to decent people of all races."[34] For those looking for a way out of the contemporary city, both literally and metaphorically, Eisenhower took people back—back
to the 1939 World's Fair, back to the Regional Planning Association, back to the
Garden City ideal.

A week before the Democratic National Convention opened in Chicago,
the *Tribune* picked up on Eisenhower's new town proposal and called for the
creation of just such places as a way to solve what they believed to be the problem underlying American cities, and thus solve the urban crisis; it sounded
awfully familiar, indeed. "Too many people are crowded into big cities, where
they breathe polluted air, pay high prices for everything they buy, fray their
nerves in a daily battle with traffic congestion, and generally get in each other's
way," the *Tribune* wrote.

The flip side of this maldistribution of people, of course, was that "Too few
people live in small towns and open countryside, where air is clean, prices are
more reasonable, traffic is light and neighbors are friendly." The *Chicago Tribune*
pointed out that the rural-to-urban migration in the United States had slowed
for the first time since the 1930s, and offered as an explanation that the trend
might reflect "a growing feeling among city-dwelling Americans that it's a whole
lot safer, more convenient, and more pleasant to live in a small town or the open
countryside."[35] New towns, deliberately planned and built from scratch, would
capitalize on this sentiment and offer the best of city life without any of its
problems.

Just a few days later, Republican Vice Presidential candidate Spiro Agnew
called for the same thing. Speaking in the friendly confines of a VFW convention
in Detroit, Agnew called for a new federal program to support the creation of
new towns in order "to relieve congestion in city ghettoes." Agnew subtly posi-
tioned this idea as an alternative to "open housing" and integration, which had
been the focus of so much civil rights activity in northern cities. "You must face
the fact," Agnew told Vets, winking and nodding to the segregationists, "that well
into the foreseeable future many black Americans will want to continue living
right where they are now. But they won't want to live in houses they don't own.
They won't want to continue to live in a neighborhood in which they have no
personal financial stake."[36] Essentially Agnew suggested the African Americans

ought to own the ghetto rather than rent it, and that the federal government ought to fund new towns for white people who wanted to leave the city.

Agnew wasn't alone. Although he was courting the VFW vote with this plan, Democratic presidential candidate Eugene McCarthy also called for a "new towns" program. On both side of the political divide in 1968, the only way forward for the American city was to build a way out.[37]

If the decentralists of the interwar period did not anticipate the way decentralization would actually occur after the war, then certainly by 1968 the suburban sprawl had become a major political concern. Critics of one sort or another had been complaining about suburbia since the very first Levittown home went up, deriding it as a place where alienated organization men and their wives afflicted with the feminine mystique retired every night to self-medicate.

By the mid-1960s, these critics had been joined by architects, planners, and environmentalists who decried the aesthetic and ecological impacts of sprawl. New towns, therefore, would be the antidote to suburbia as well as the solution to urban America. As Kansas City real estate developer William Haas put it, "Don't you agree that it would be preferable to have a Nation dotted from coast to coast with new cities, each one distinct and self-contained, than filling areas of our country with massive concrete and steel nightmares where everyone and his individuality are lost in the shuffle?" Another "new town" enthusiast agreed, writing "By thoughtful planning new towns seek to avoid contributing to suburban sprawl and to prevent forever within their own borders the multiple disasters that are now overwhelming so many older cities." *Washington Post* columnist Wolf von Eckardt concurred: "We desperately need 'new towns'…to save the existing big city." And making the equation between urban problems and "new town" solutions, he continued, "The big city, as we all know, is exploding and this centrifugal explosion scatters the taxpaying middle-class, the new jobs and the new wealth all over the landscape and leaves only the poor and the problems of poverty behind."[38]

This resurrection of the "new town" idea, born out of the urban riots, reached its legislative apotheosis in 1970, when Congress passed the Urban Growth and New Community Development Act. What Agnew had described in Detroit in 1968 became Nixon administration policy. The act called for "the orderly development of well-planned, diversified, and economically sound new communities, including major additions to existing communities," and it hoped to foster "desirable innovation in meeting domestic problems whether physical, economic or social."[39] Through the early years of the 1970s, the federal government would sponsor a dozen or so "new towns," with nearly $1 billion authorized in the 1970 legislation, as refuges from cities now seen as increasingly hopeless. For the first time since the New Deal the federal government promised to fund the creation of new towns.

HUD Secretary George Romney, who oversaw the beginning of the federal new town program, had a prototype in mind. It amounted to,

> what the great monuments of this century must be...a place for man to live, a decent happy place, with air to breathe, with a place to stand in the sun, and place for children to run and play and learn—a place where people of all ages can become lifelong learners—a place where black, brown, white, yellow, red people from all economic and ethnic segments of our society can live together in peace and harmony.[40]

That dreamy utopia was called Columbia, Maryland.

Those who wanted to seize this moment of urban collapse to build new cities pointed over and over again to Columbia (and to a lesser extent, Reston, Virginia) as the model for a brave new post-urban future. Columbia stood as the antithesis of banal postwar suburbs, and it was designed precisely to address the complaints that had accumulated about them.

James Rouse created Columbia. It sprang from his vision and from his previous experience as a successful developer of shopping centers.[41] In the early 1960s, Rouse began buying up property in Maryland's Howard County, roughly halfway between Washington and Baltimore. Relatively quickly, he put together a holding of about 15,000 acres, and he began construction of his new town in 1966. The first residents moved in a year later.

The original plan envisioned seven villages of roughly 15,000 people each (a city, therefore, of about 100,000); each of those villages in turn would be divided into three or four "neighborhoods." In designing Columbia, Rouse had taken to heart the emerging consensus that new town planning had to be done comprehensively, reflecting the influence of the academic planners who saw space and sociology as intimately connected. As Edward Eichler, a California counterpart of Rouse's, put it, "future developments should be conceived in terms of wholes—they [should] be determined on the basis of essential physical, social, economic, and human needs."[42] Rouse's schematics for Columbia included a variety of residential options—to fit different incomes and different lifestyles: space for commercial and industrial development, shared facilities, open spaces, and even public transit, an amenity that seemed anathema to the new suburban ethos. Rouse had read Jane Jacobs, and he was a fan.

Although Columbia received a great deal of attention as a new alternative to suburbia, Rouse held on to an older faith. Planners and dreamers as far back as Ebenezer Howard believed that the right planning of physical space would restore a sense of community that had been destroyed, first by urban growth and more recently by suburban sprawl. Rouse was clear about his goal in a 1966 speech he gave to a group of bankers:

> The task is to produce community—community in which a man, his wife, and children are important, come first—ahead of buildings, streets, and automobiles—a community in physical form, they can identify; find boundaries to; feel responsible for; be proud of—a community which in human terms cares about them.[43]

In a 1963 speech at Berkeley, Rouse described new towns in a way that made them sound less like real estate ventures and more like California self-actualization centers. These new towns, he told the crowd, "will release among the people in them the potential for the noblest civilization the world has ever known."[44]

Creating a genuine sense of community was as much the grail of new town developers as it had been in the 1930s. As Samuel Jackson diagnosed the problem at a 1971 American Institute of Architects conference,

> The greatest tragedy of current growth patterns is not the physical form of that growth but the fact that it has polarized Americans by race and class. Bankers, real estate brokers, homeowners, and unfortunately even governments seem to have conspired to zone out the poor and exclude racial minorities.[45]

To understand just what "community" really meant, organizers of a "new towns" conference held in Los Angeles in 1972 invited none other than Margaret Mead to speak. She described a community as

> a group of people with ties to each other, ties of kinship and friendship, ties of shared work and shared responsibility and shared pleasure. The nucleus of any community is people who know and value each other. Therefore the first requirement for constructing a new community is to devise a way in which people who already know each other can form the nucleus.[46]

That might well be right from an anthropological perspective, but it certainly was a tall order for a real estate development.

To help him achieve his goal of community and of human growth at Columbia, Rouse looked to Yellow Springs, Ohio, to Arthur Morgan's town and to his Antioch College. In 1967, Rouse began negotiations with Antioch College to establish an outpost in Columbia. In 1968, the college approved the idea of setting up a "field studies center," making it sound more like a research station in some remote wilderness than an educational project in suburban Maryland. Rouse had approached Antioch because educational experimentation and building a self-governing community lay at the heart of what the college was all about. Rouse wanted to bring that experience to Columbia.[47]

For its part, many at Antioch saw in Columbia the opportunity to study the process of community creation from its very beginning. "It is a random, amorphous place," College vice president Morris Keeton told his colleagues, "not yet a community." The college offered five specific reasons to support the partnership, but the larger goal was that Antioch could help make Columbia a community and study the process of that creation at the same time.[48] The creation of this partnership demonstrated Rouse's insistence that Columbia really would be different and bold.

It wasn't an altogether happy collaboration. Antioch students, left wing even by the standards of the era, complained about the presence of defense contractors in Columbia's industrial zones, and they chided Columbia for solving urban problems by abandoning the city altogether.[49] And maybe that wasn't so far off.

The enthusiasm that greeted Columbia as it was opened gave Rouse and others reason to hope that the new town really might be the prototype the nation was looking for to solve its urban problems and to stem an ever-spreading tide of sprawl. Indeed, in its first several years, Columbia successfully attracted a number of black families, making good on the promise that it would be an interracial development. With federal money, the American landscape could be remade in Columbia's image. James Rouse was certainly enthusiastic about the new towns program. Testifying before Congress, he said of Columbia: "It can and should be replicated and vastly improved upon in smaller and larger communities over and over again throughout America."[50]

When HUD Secretary George Romney announced the first project—Jonathan, Minnesota—the *Chicago Tribune* predicted enthusiastically: "By the turn of the century, just 30 years away, as many as 30 million Americans may be living in 'new towns' built either in open rural land or redeveloped sections of decaying cities." Dutifully repeating the rationales that had been offered since at least 1968, the *Tribune* continued "Many urban planners believe careful construction of completely new communities is the only answer to a growing problem of urban sprawl and a deterioration of the quality of city life."[51] These places would save cities from the effects of too much poverty and rescue suburbia from the banality of too much affluence.

Shortly afterwards, the *Chicago Tribune* could report on a new town project even closer to home. Park Forest, a suburb south of Chicago, had been built as a classic suburb of the 1940s and '50s variety; now developer Lewis Manilow, son of developer Nathan Manilow, promised a new town "suburb" of that suburb, which he called Park Forest South. As he explained it: "If Park Forest was the home of the organizational man, then Park Forest South will be the home of the community oriented family man."[52] The homes for those community-oriented family men would be subsidized by the federal government, to the tune of $30 million in loan guarantees.

The language here repeats the language of the original legislation. The federal government would facilitate the creation of new "communities," or additions to existing "communities"; Park Forest South was intended for the "community-oriented family man." In fact, the act funded projects to build small cities, usually within close proximity to even larger cities—outside New York, Chicago, Minneapolis, Houston, San Antonio. But the word *city* now had such a bad odor that it was not even used. Once again, the word *community*, with all of its warm and wholesome connotations, stood as the antonym of *city*.

In 1974, two years after the demolition of Pruitt-Igoe, the Nixon administration cancelled the Model Cities program. Twenty-five years after the federal government endeavored to rebuild the American city, the squalid and dangerous public housing projects, sterile downtown office-plaza blocks, and neighborhoods that continued to deteriorate as people and capital left them all stood as physical testimony to the failure of those efforts. In the face of that, the federal government decided that the most effective immediate response to the urban crisis was to hasten the escape from the city.

The New Town that Wasn't

When First Street in downtown Dayton, Ohio, crosses the Great Miami River, it becomes Salem Avenue, and it bends northwest on a diagonal through the gridded streets of some of Dayton's finest neighborhoods. Some have aspirational names like Princeton Heights and University Row, though others, like Greenwich Village, remind you of the connection Dayton's elite felt to the East Coast. The Wesleyan Hills neighborhood is bounded on the south by Cornell Drive and on the east by Philadelphia Drive. Just beyond Wesleyan Hills, Salem Avenue passes by the Miami Valley Golf Club. Farther out, Salem intersects Shiloh Springs Road, and if you turn left and head west, in a few miles, just as you cross Diamond Mill Road, you will find yourself on the site of Don Huber's dream.

Huber was already a rich and influential man by 1970, and he and his family were the largest suburban developers in the Dayton region during the postwar period. They named their largest venture Huber Heights to honor the patriarch of the family. But by the early 1970s, Don Huber had grown weary of the very suburbs he had built. He had his epiphany, he claimed, on a 1957 trip to Europe, where he saw innovative town building. That trip, he said, made him realize that "in Huber Heights we were just building houses, building shelters."[53] He itched to do a project along European lines in the Dayton area. Nearly fifteen years after that eye-opening European tour, Huber saw his chance through the federal new towns program.

Dayton had experienced its own urban unrest in the summer of 1966, although in the larger, sadder scheme of things it didn't amount to much. Yet as a small manufacturing city overreliant on the auto industry, Dayton and its economy began to slide during the decade, and with it much of the city's health and vitality. In 1960, Dayton recorded the largest number of residents in its history—just over 260,000. By 1970, twenty thousand of them had left, making the 1960s the first time in its history that the city experienced a population loss. By 1970, those grand buildings on and around Salem Avenue were already being subdivided into rooming houses, their striving families beginning to be replaced by prostitutes and junkies.

Don Huber saw himself as heir to America's "pioneer spirit." A puff piece about him, issued by his own company, began: "If Donald Huber had been born in the 18th century, chances are he would have been one of Ohio's early pioneers—pushing boundaries westward, establishing new settlements." Having missed his eighteenth-century chance, Huber instead would pioneer "a new era of development."[54] He called it, fittingly enough, "Newfields."

Huber amassed roughly 4,000 acres for his Newfields, some of it agricultural, some of it still wooded. The land lay out in the country, beyond the edge of Dayton's northern and western sprawl. Its remote feel belied what Huber gambled would be a good location. It was still an easy shot, back down Salem Avenue, to downtown Dayton. It takes about fifteen minutes if you hit all the lights right. Those acres also sat just south of I-70 and not too far west of I-75. Huber hoped Newfields would prosper because of that easy highway access. In this sense, Huber took advantage of one federally subsidized project and hoped that another would fund the building of his new town. His plan was to build Newfields over a period of twenty years, and he predicted it would eventually house 40,000 people. He submitted his proposal to HUD on March 22, 1973.

Huber liked to talk about the European inspiration behind Newfields, but closer to home he took Columbia and Reston as his models. And like the others, he incorporated the latest academic ideas about planning to make sure his development would harmonize with, rather than ignore, the natural surroundings. Wolf Creek meanders through those acres on its way to the Great Miami, and Huber insisted that its flood plain would be preserved, along with other natural aspects of the site. He hired ecologist Ralph Scott to develop a natural management and assessment program for Newfields.[55]

In addition to his environmental sensitivity, Huber wanted to do Columbia and Reston one better in the way he organized Newfields's social planning. "Newfields is unique," his company claimed, "in that for the first time the entire community will be planned and developed by dual-developers." He would be one of those dual developers, handling the "land use planning, and residential, commercial and industrial development and marketing." A separately consti-tuted "Community Authority" would provide "residents with the opportunity to establish their own government which will be responsible for developing, maintaining and operating community facilities and more than 800 acres of open space." Huber called this Community Authority "perhaps the most outstanding innovation in community development."[56]

The Ohio New Communities Act made such a partnership possible, and in pursuing it Huber clearly tried to address one of the critiques already emerging about Columbia, Maryland. Although the physical design of Columbia, Reston, and some other places represented a vast improvement over the off-the-rack sub-divisions still preferred by most sprawl developers, there was a growing skep-ticism whether even these improved physical forms had fostered an improved social landscape. At the same moment that Huber planned his Newfields, criti-cism mounted that there was "a lack of democratic participation among the residents" of Columbia and the other new towns. A 1974 study of Columbia concluded that "competing values, differing beliefs as to the appropriateness and legitimacy of the developer-sponsored social planning effort, and patterns of institutional independence Balkanized any genuine effort to engage in com-munitarian social planning." Columbia had "failed to realize this citizen par-ticipation ideal."[57] Huber believed that with a Community Authority, Newfields would be different.

Different, perhaps, but Huber and St. Louis planner Gerwin Rohrbach, whom Huber had hired to oversee the work of planning Newfields, turned to exactly the same place as Rouse had to help shape the nature of citizen par-ticipation, of democratic planning, and the role of the Community Authority. Rouse had brought Antioch College to Columbia. Rohrbach simply went down Dayton-Yellow Springs Road to Yellow Springs to enlist Griscom Morgan and Community Service, Inc.

Arthur Morgan's son was, according to those who remember him, one of those proverbial village "characters." As head of the organization his father founded, he continued its work promoting the ideals of the face-to-face community. He had tried to live those beliefs as well. When he married, he and his wife moved to a forty-five-acre property just outside of town and called it The Vale. There they invited other families to join them in a cooperative of sorts, coining the term "intentional community" in the process.

Morgan also disliked cities to such an extent that his view of them verged on the apocalyptic. He was convinced that urban population density was the cause of virtually every social malady, and that the creation, or restoration, of small communities was the corresponding cure-all. According to Morgan, "an important cause of harm from large city density is its disintegration of small community associations that give individuals healthy social contacts, security, social control, personal identification and stability of culture." Morgan drew his conclusions primarily by analogy. In an almost Malthusian way, he quoted from studies of animal behavior—though he did like to cite a study of Manhattan residents that revealed a whopping 80 percent of them "had detectable psychiatric disorders"—demonstrating that when animals are crowded together beyond a certain point they begin to fight, kill each other, and otherwise disintegrate socially.

After twenty-five years of studying "the problems associated with urban densities, and particularly causes of harm from large city living," Morgan wrote in the early 1970s, he believed "good social policy would develop a stable and wide distribution of population in smaller cities widely distributed over the land."[58] After the riots of the long, hot summers, the federal government had come to the same conclusion.

Rohrbach wanted Morgan's help in figuring out just how the Community Authority would work, how it would create citizen participation and democratic governance in Newfields. Quickly, however, Rohrbach and Huber began to disagree over the role of the Community Authority. Rohrbach quit the whole project late in 1972, and the idea of genuine citizen participation left Newfields with him. The following year, Huber wrote to county commissioners clarifying the role of the Community Authority. Although he still imagined it operating as a small municipal government, he described its most important role as the ability to promote the town and protect it from undesirable development. He went on that "although the Community Authority has no police powers...it does possess the ability to require a high level of maintenance, rigidly control the visual landscape, and protect the environment."[59] Which sounds less like an innovative experiment in civic engagement and more like a standard, suburban homeowners' association.

The experience of driving out Salem Avenue to Newfields today is dispiriting compared to what it must have been when Don Huber began putting together his 4,000-acre parcel. Downtown Dayton is a shadow of what it was then, and the grand Dayton neighborhoods, already in decline by 1970, have become altogether less than what they once were. Jewish Dayton, which had clustered along Salem Avenue by the 1960s, has dispersed, and the avenue itself mostly looks like any suburban strip mall, down at the heels for much of its length.

When you do arrive at Newfields, you haven't really arrived anywhere. There simply is not much there: a cluster of "townhouses," without any town; a handful of small apartment units; a lot of empty, unplanned space. In fact, what is there is not Newfields at all. It is the residential miscellany that washed up on the site after Don Huber's dream died.

He was still fighting for Newfields as late as 1975, when he sued a local township over a zoning dispute. But the project was already lost by that point. In a 1976 status report on Newfields, HUD concluded, "A market for a new town does not exist. HUD's plans call for the acquisition of the project and build-out of a limited planned residential development of up to 500 acres. Excess land would be sold off."[60] The 40,000 people Huber predicted would move to his new town never came. However, between 1970 and 1980 the city of Dayton did see its population decline by 50,000.

Don Huber should not have taken his failure personally. The air went out of the new town balloon fairly quickly. In 1974, reports began to circulate that the new town projects were in financial trouble: "Almost all of the 15 federally assisted 'new town' projects in various stages of development around the country under an ambitious plan to create orderly, imaginative communities instead of haphazard growth," the *Washington Post* reported, "are in serious financial difficulty. Some of the projects appear to be on the brink of outright financial failure." The next year HUD announced that it would not be funding any more new town proposals, leading architect John Schmidt to say "The era of the large-scale developer is over. New town projects are as dead as a doornail."[61]

It remained for *Time* magazine to write the program's obituary. "They are an urban planner's dream," *Time* began its look back on the brief, sad life of the new towns program, "new cities carved out of the raw earth, self-contained, self-sufficient and carefully designed to avoid all the problems that afflict older, unplanned urban centers." But less than a decade later, "the planner's dream has become HUD's nightmare." HUD was pulling up its financial stake in these projects and would attempt to sell them off to recoup whatever money it could.[62]

Failure, however disappointing, could be easily explained. Launched at the very end of the great boom economy of the postwar period, the new towns could not achieve lift-off velocity when that economy slumped into the nasty recession of 1973. In Park Forest South, for example, land costs wound up nearly 90 percent higher than anticipated, though sales during its first five years were nearly 60 percent lower than projected. Other projects suffered because the developers guessed wrong about the first rule of real estate: location. They sited their projects where the metropolitan growth was not. Had Don Huber located Newfields to the south or east of Dayton, where the most explosive growth in the region occurred, rather than to the northwest, things might have turned out differently.

Beyond the financial technicalities and logistical problems, however, a number of skeptics wondered whether the goals of these new towns could ever be achieved. Could "community" really be engineered and planned? There was, after all, something marvelously utopian about these new town dreams that could only disappoint in reality. As one critic quipped, "the ballyhoo surrounding "New Communities"... implies that American technology has accomplished the unprecedented feat of locating the Garden of Eden within one-hour commuting time of Sodom and Gomorrah."[63]

Even the new town projects that started as private developments before the federal subsidies became available had fallen on hard times.[64] Robert Simon, scion of New York real estate barons, came to the fox-hunting country west of Washington, D.C., to build Reston, Virginia, in 1962. His town got high marks for planning and for its architecture, but it quickly ran into financial trouble. By 1967, the project had been taken over by Gulf Oil Corporation.

Five years after that, the *Washington Post* ran a wistful story about Reston's "loss of innocence." Within the previous two years, the paper reported,

> Reston has weathered a major crisis of teen-age drug use, survived sporadic bouts of vandalism, had one of its 14-year old girls found dead of a heroin overdose and—last month—recorded in 17-year old Gwen Ames a homicide that stunned the community. Fairfax County police say that problems or crime, drugs and death are no different in Reston than elsewhere in the county, but that statement itself is for some Restonians a betrayal of expectations.

Reston resident Mike Horwatt summarized this fall from grace simply: "In many ways we're just like any other suburb now."[65]

HUD, for its part, was left scratching its departmental head. As the federal new towns program wound down, HUD undertook a study of the experience. It concluded that in addition to a bad financing model, the recession, poor site selection, and the rest, "government at all levels failed to use new town development as a high priority tool for controlling and channeling urban growth." This struck HUD as baffling since "The new communities experience has shown that well-planned development results in cost savings to both the private and public sectors." Despite that, HUD had to acknowledge, "The fact remains that urban areas are still growing and unplanned development, both urban, suburban and exurban, is still the order of the day."[66]

At the beginning of the 1970s, new towns had been "one of the most widely publicized Government social experiments," promising to relieve the urban crisis and tame the ceaselessly expanding suburban frontier. By the end of the decade,

American cities remained just as desperate socially and financially and that suburban frontier continued to move into the exurban horizon.

In 1970, with the enthusiasm for new towns still growing, *Business Week* decided to send a reporter to visit the original American new town: Radburn, New Jersey. It had aged "awkwardly," the magazine told its readers, swallowed up really by the suburban sprawl of subsequent years. The irony, as *Business Week* noted, was that "Radburn was billed as 'The Town for the Auto Age,' but the age has outrun it."[67]

Leave the City and Head Back to the Garden

Suspicion of government constituted a central part of the anti-urban ethos, and cities were thus among the first places where the political agenda of the New Right emerged. Urban renewal soured many African Americans and others on the other side of the political spectrum, on Johnson's Great Society, and on liberalism more broadly. In the 1970s, anti-urbanism grew further on the political left in the form of two related phenomena: the commune movement and the environmental movement. The rise of both signaled a retreat from urban issues, and they were essentially different versions of white flight.

Population exodus from America's urban areas had created what musician George Clinton humorously called the chocolate cities and the vanilla suburbs. Among those millions, however, were a small number of urban refugees with very different politics who also rejected and left the city, but for very different places and for very different reasons. They went to places with names like Total Loss Farm in Vermont; Drop City, Colorado; and The Farm in Tennessee. Rather than moving to new suburbs within a metropolitan region, these people established communities in the country; rather than pursuing a set of middle-class aspirations, they were downwardly mobile; rather than valorize the nuclear, property-owning family, they celebrated the communal and the tribal. They headed for the hills and went back to the land.

In 1969, the same year that *Business Week* extolled the federal proposals to sponsor new towns, *Newsweek* magazine declared 1969 the "Year of the Commune." If that seems a tad overblown given everything else swirling in 1969, consider that according to one sympathetic observer at the time, as many as 500,000 people moved into communes between 1965 and 1970. "By the late 1960s," one estimate had it, "the United States was well into the greatest epoch of commune-building in its history."[68] Whether or not *Newsweek* was hasty in its declaration, by 1969 communes seemed like the next big thing.

A handful of these communes have proved remarkably enduring, though many were momentary and ephemeral. These were the places where the counterculture fled, refugees from Haight-Ashbury and the East Village after those urban enclaves became toxic with drugs and violence. By 1970, Taos, New Mexico, had become known as Haight-Ashbury East. They ran from the Chicago riots, from the Columbia "uprising," from The Movement itself, as it descended increasingly into its own apocalyptic and fratricidal fantasies of violence and terrorism. A farm in Vermont seemed a better place to ride out the coming collapse of American society than Manhattan or San Francisco, and a better place to build a New Age out of the ashes.[69]

Whereas many hippie communards headed to the country in search of a certain kind of peace and quiet, they did not go quietly or unnoticed. Looking back on it all now, it is not hard to feel that the hippies who moved from metropolitan centers into rural communes were followed by an almost equal number of journalists and commentators, sociologists and anthropologists, who reported back to the nation on this grand social experiment almost in real time. Some commune members, like those in Drop City, felt that all the attention they were getting only made their lives more difficult. Members of the Hog Farm commune put out a bulletin pleading with people to stay away: "Any more people could easily kill us."

Add to all this the books and essays written by commune participants themselves, and it becomes clear that however consequential these communes may have proved to be in the long term, they certainly occupied an important space in the national imagination at the time. In an essay on the commune movement in which she tried hard to restrain her disdain, Sonya Rudikoff pointed out the ironies of all this for readers of *Commentary*: "No longer an underground or secret society, the counter-culture and its 'life-style' have pervaded American society, making their experience known to millions.... Seldom have 'revolutionary ideas,' as they are called, spread with such ease, publicity, and widespread acceptance."[70]

By this time hippies, initially dismissed as drop-outs and ne'er-do-wells, had been recast as living on a cultural and political cutting edge, and they had been given their own social theory. The year 1969 also saw Theodore Roszak's avuncular and largely sympathetic book *The Making of a Counter-Culture,* and the following year Yale professor Charles Reich published his entirely enthusiastic *The Greening of America*. Both books received wide attention and readership. Roszak sketched out the creation of the hippie counterculture in ways that took it quite seriously and made their response an understandable one in that social and political climate. Reich's book was a bold attempt to portray American history in terms of three great "consciousnesses." The first was that of the farmer and small entrepreneur; the second, of industrial, organizational society. The third, Consciousness III as he called it, described a "transcendence" of these previous eras and mindsets. "To survive, to regain power over our own lives," Reich prophesized, "we must transcend the machine.... Consciousness III is an attempt to gain transcendence."[71]

The anonymous author of a pointed and prescient notice in the *Antioch Review* wrote of Reich's book, "This book will be remembered as either the most over-praised or the most over-killed publication of 1970," and predicted that its future would be as "a stimulating if rather obvious cultural artifact." Certainly, Reich's title entered the common usage at the level of cliché, used in any number of contexts. In 1979, *Black Enterprise* magazine published a story about black-owned banks and S&Ls titled "The Greening of Black America."[72] Still, all the reportage, all the sociological studies, and the work of scholars like Roszak and Reich remind us just how seriously countercultural communes were taken at the time. In 1969, Consciousness III really was just on the horizon, and it was forming in hundreds of communes in rural America.

Just as the exodus to the communes took the nation by surprise in the late 1960s, so too the environmental movement seemed to spring fully formed onto the national stage. In his State of the Union address in 1970, Richard Nixon asked the nation, in terms that sound positively crusading today, "Shall we surrender to our surroundings or shall we make peace with nature and begin to make reparations for the damage we have done to our air, to our land and to our water?" The next month, *Time* put scientist and environmental activist Barry Commoner on its cover with an article entitled "Fighting to Save the Earth from Man."[73] On April 22, 1970, an estimated 20 million Americans participated in the first Earth Day. All of a sudden, and apparently out of nowhere, at least in the perception of many, the environment had become the issue of the day. Needless to say, the environmental movement did not come from nowhere. It had deep roots—in the writings of Rachel Carson and the research of Aldo Leopold, in the farming experiments of J. I. Rodale and even earlier of Sir Albert Howard.[74] Carson's book *Silent Spring* had been a best-seller in 1962, after all, but I think it is fair to say that although the conservation movement had started at the turn of the twentieth century, by mid-century it remained largely in the realm of academics, policy experts, and resource managers. What were new by the end of the 1960s were the mass demonstrations and local mobilizations that replaced esoteric publications and professional conferences in shaping public policy.[75]

The connections between communes and the environmental movement are indirect and at the level of sensibilities and shared concerns rather than actual alliances. Both sometimes resorted to the language of impending apocalypse. Communard Steve Diamond believed that what was important about the commune movement was that young people "decided to take matters—the matter of their own existence—into their hands." Likewise, environmental activist Tony Wagner warned "The most fundamental question facing us today is whether or not life will continue on this planet."[76] Both attempted, with varying degrees of depth and seriousness, to reorient people's relationship with the environment on a daily level.

According to Hugh Gardner, "As many as 500,000 Americans are estimated by *Organic Gardening and Farming* magazine to be serious about building new lives on small farms. There can be little question that the rural communes of the 1960s played a major *avant-garde* role in these developments." He went on: "Between 1970 and 1973, the period during which so many rural communes failed, there was a net migration of over 1 million people from cities *and* the suburbs into sparsely populated rural areas."[77] Insofar as the environmental movement of the 1970s placed an emphasis on consumer choices and lifestyle questions, the communes can be said to have helped foster those developments.

They also shared in common a reflexive, almost visceral reaction against the city, against the long, hot summers, and thanks to urban renewal and Vietnam, against government as well.

New Communes, Old Pastoralism, and the Anti-Urban Impulse

By 1972, "Aaron" had found himself by moving to a commune, fulfilling his "dream to belong to a tribe, where the energies flow among everyone." He explained his decision to social researcher Keith Melville:

> I was living in Los Angeles, and every day I felt one step closer to cracking up and landing in a mental hospital, totally isolated from other people and their lives....Like it was insane, it was a pressure cooker, and I had to get out....Finally, I decided that I would have to live in the country and work closely with my brothers and sisters. What was there to choose from in the city? City life offered me a trivial job I didn't want, a prison, or a mental hospital.[78]

Aaron's version of his journey echoed many who wrote about their experiences or were interviewed by that small army of journalists and social scientists who followed these hippies out into the country. A nineteen-year-old woman, writing with poignant desperation from Muscoda, Wisconsin, to a commune she hoped to join, confessed "The uptightness and the hustling of the city is not what I want, and for sure not what I need." Likewise, "Allen," a resident of a commune outside of Taos, New Mexico, reported:

> The city was a really bad place for me. I was allergic to it, but it really took me a long time to admit it....For a while when we first came here, we

were like a bunch of city kids at summer camp. Everyone was just amazed that they could actually make it in the country.... You should have seen us when the first crops started to come up.

Some were even more vague in their anti-urban yearnings. Complaining about what he called his "Big City Complacency," one letter writer to *WIN* magazine announced that although he had often visited the country, he had always come back to New York, "Until this year. Whatever it is the country has it, and the city doesn't."[79]

Counterculture icons also felt the pull. On one coast, the Grateful Dead and Janis Joplin, who had helped define Haight-Ashbury as The Haight, moved up into the hills of Marin County; on the other coast, Bob Dylan left the tight musical world of Greenwich Village (where he shot the wonderful cue-card sequence in his movie "Don't Look Back,") and went up the Hudson River valley to a farmhouse near a place called Woodstock.

We do not know how many of those hippies who joined communes actually came from cities. Most, I suspect, had probably been raised in the new suburbs, had spent some time in an urban setting, either as college students or as members of the diffuse counterculture, and then completed their migratory path to the country.[80] At least one woman living in a Taos commune fretted that an impending influx of city hippies would doom this experiment: "First we were chased out of the cities, then from the coast to more isolated areas like this one. Now we're being mobbed by the fugitives from the city insanity."[81]

Histrionic language to one side, there is no doubt about the genuine and powerful appeal these rural retreats had for this generation—and indeed, have always had in American life. The search for simplicity, for a more authentic connectedness both to the natural world and to other people, for an alternative way of living, was for many a real pursuit, and its attractiveness cannot be denied. It is also a quest rooted entirely in the American tradition. Nor should the desperate language about the city obscure the fact that urban America was in crisis during these years. However, whether this pilgrim's progress from city to country accurately reflects the demographic reality of commune dwellers is not the point. That journey served as a narrative to explain the meaning of the commune phenomenon.

By the late 1960s, the left was spinning apart centrifugally as different groups pursued more and more issues, each with its own goals and tactics. Whatever the issue, however, all were dedicated to destroying an abstract enemy: "'The Establishment,' an oppressive conspiracy led by government and corporate leaders."[82] At an equally abstract level, The City became, especially for those who fled it to join communes, the place where The Establishment lived, worked, and made its mischief.

Steve Diamond, a member of the Montague Farm in western Massachusetts, captured the symbolic distance between his commune and the city in a passage from his 1971 book *What the Trees Said*. Forced to go back to New York City to attend to some business, Diamond and a few friends piled into his old car and drove: "We stole bravely across the Mass-Conn border though there was no noticeable difference in terrain, no difference in the road, the billboards." As they got closer to their destination, however, "you could feel yourself approaching the Big C (City, Civilization, Cancer) itself, deeper and deeper into the decaying heart."[83]

The metaphor is overwrought and hyperbolic, but it remained effective nonetheless. In the most frightening organic terms, Diamond called the Big C diseased. The City was the same as American civilization was the same as cancer, and it was all rotting. The car trip from the farm to the city is a journey from all that is good and healthy and natural to all that is decaying. Cast this way, Diamond's decision to abandon it all for an old farmhouse in Montague made perfect sense.

That farmhouse dates back to the nineteenth century, a wonderfully rambling piece of New England vernacular. It fronts on a narrow gravel road on the southern slope of Chestnut Hill. Across the road sits a truly magnificent New England barn, a postcard-perfect scene of rural New England. The house, the barn, and the surrounding forty acres were bought by Marshall Bloom to establish a commune in 1968.

As an actual farm, however, Montague was always a challenge. The property sits on a rocky hillside with the parsimonious soil that makes farming in so much of New England difficult. Montague itself is an old jurisdiction, and much of it lies in the flat and fertile Connecticut River valley. By the time people starting settling up on the hill, however, all the good land was taken. You can pasture some animals on parts of the Montague Farm but you cannot do much else.

Sometime in the middle of the nineteenth century, so the story goes, people on the hill woke up one morning to find snow and frost and biting cold. In the middle of July. It broke the backs and the spirits of some of those people and they left, a small part of the larger out-migration from New England towns that was discussed earlier. Walk the woods around the Montague Farm and you will come across the remnants of old stone walls marking the fields that used to be.

So by the time Marshall Bloom came looking for a farm, the area had slipped into the kind of poverty endemic to much of rural New England. Mainstream American life had largely passed it by. Those natives who remained were a hardy bunch for sure, but underneath the sinew and toughness, many of them struggled to survive. Bloom, therefore, was able to buy forty acres very cheaply.

I have sat on the back porch of Montague Farm to watch the sun go down. A friend of mine calls this "the greatest show in Montague" and he is right. I lived at the farm for short periods over several years, in its last iteration as a collective. I helped give the house a new coat of paint, and I stacked some of the cords of wood necessary to heat the place through a Massachusetts winter. More than that, I formed a deep connection with the others living there as we shared our meals, took walks in those woods, and helped take care of each other's small children. I felt the appeal of communal life first-hand and can testify to its power.

When I first came to Montague, however, I did not realize that Montague Farm holds a special place among the communes of the late 1960s. Marshall Bloom and several of his friends established the commune to be the new home of the Liberation News Service (LNS). Bloom had started LNS with Ray Mungo in 1967 in Washington, D.C., as a clearinghouse of sorts for campus and alternative presses. By 1968, it had been relocated to New York City and those who ran it quickly devolved into factional fighting. Bloom, Mungo, and several others then engineered an audacious "liberation" of the printing press to Montague Farm on a Sunday morning while the militant SDSers were still sleeping off Saturday night.

The story turns quickly from comic to tragic. The angry New Yorkers, even more angry now that the press and LNS's money had disappeared, found Bloom in Montague, laid siege to the farmhouse, and held its residents hostage for several hours. They beat Bloom savagely, demanding to know where the press had

The Montague Farm, Montague, Massachusetts, became well known among the counterculture communes of the late 1960s and 1970s because it was home to several writers who described their experiences. Many communards fled the cities to find refuge in organic farming and collective living. *Photo by author*

been stored. He never told them, and the New Yorkers, exhausted apparently from the beating they gave Bloom, went back to New York. Several months after that, Bloom killed himself.

The sad story of LNS and Montague Farm sits at the center of Mungo's 1970 book *Famous Long Ago*. Written with all the wisdom and world-weariness that a twenty-three-year-old could muster, *Famous Long Ago* is Mungo's long, disillusioned farewell letter to The Movement. What sent him to the farm, Mungo writes, was not the forces against which he had been fighting, but the allies whom he thought were his brothers and sisters in the struggle. The assault on Bloom and then his suicide stand as a summary indictment of everything that had gone wrong with The Movement by the late 1960s.

As Mungo tells the story, it played out as an anti-urban morality tale. When Bloom initially floated the idea of Montague Farm, Mungo expressed a great deal of skepticism. "But Marshall insisted on a farm," Mungo reports, "said it was high time to abandon the urban nightmare anyway."[84] The Montaguans, called by Mungo "The Virtuous Caucus," had tried to preserve the integrity and idealism of LNS, and thus The Movement as a whole, by moving out of the city and into the country. The city, in the form of "The Vulgar Marxists," however, hunted them down and brought all their urban corruption and violence with them. They were thugs, as cancerous as Steve Diamond said, and they stood for the loss of innocence that comes from life in the city. Virtue vs. Vulgarity.

Plenty of observers at the time noticed the anti-urban impulse behind the commune movement. Albert Norman reviewed Mungo's book for *Newsweek* and described Mungo's story this way: "In frustration, without ideology or a plan to save the world, he deserts the hollow cities." Jack Newfield gave the book a warm review in the *New York Times* despite disagreeing "temperamentally and politically...with Mungo's solution" because Newfield identified himself "as an activist and incurable city head."[85]

As Mungo went, many predicted, so would The Movement. Norman, for one, believed that "Mungo and his nine disaffected farmers are among the first to take the Movement permanently out of society. The revolution has grown so far afield that part of it isn't coming back." Keith Melville believed that "those who were serious about finding a place for the new culture realized that it was much too fragile to survive in the city. If there was any place left where people could get by with a little help from their friends, where they could escape reporters and harassment, it was the country." The *New York Times* reported Marshall Bloom's suicide in an article suggesting that more activists like Bloom would move to rural communes because, as the *Times* quoted him, "the city burns people out."[86]

In a wonderful irony, the anti-urban discourse that lay underneath the commune movement helped domesticate it for the American mainstream. Though communards routinely talked in almost apocalyptic terms about escape, exodus, retreat, and isolation, they used The City as a foil for the commune. That certainly resonated with many Americans who were themselves fed up with or terrified by the condition of American cities, but who chose to move out of them into places with more reliable plumbing than communal farmhouses tended to have.[87]

Sociologist Bennett M. Berger identified the connections between hippie communes and older American traditions. "Instead of seeing the commune movement as a 'revolt,' by the children of the affluent against the 'suburban values' of their parents," Berger suggested, "it can be understood in part as an extension of some of those values." The connection, Berger believed, is what he and others have called the enduring pastoral myth in American life. That myth, "the vision of a simple rural life in harmony with nature, connects the rural communards of today with the suburbanites of the 1950s and with the more distant American past."[88]

Certainly, many of the communards borrowed from the American communitarian past with varying degrees of self-awareness. They came to those communes with copies of Thoreau or B. F. Skinner's *Walden II* in the pockets of their denim overalls, sometimes reciting Jack Kerouac or Robert Frost. They celebrated and romanticized the agrarian, pre-industrial, pre-urban past, finding a more congenial set of values in the traditions of Native American groups or salty New England farmers. Communard Martin Jezer believed "The Indians were very wise about living close to the land. We can learn from them, as we can learn from other more 'primitive' cultures and societies."

Mungo announced that "the New Age we were looking for proved to be very old indeed," and saw the past as a refuge from the future. "I've often wondered aloud at my luck," he continued, "for being 23 years old in a time and place in which only the past offers hope and inspiration; the future offers only artifice and blight." Similarly Steve Diamond ended his book with a dewy-eyed invocation of the coming New Age: "we've barely begun this voyage, the ocean liner bravely making its way through the storms and brilliant sunny days of the New Age, though everyone knows it's as old as the hills."[89] If hippies saw the world in Day-Glo colors in 1967, now they saw it in sepia tones. In 1969, Bob Dylan put out a country album. For these seekers, like those who offered New England or the Southern Appalachians as a living alternative to urbanized America, the past was a place where humans lived in balance with nature and where the bonds of community nurtured everyone. Looking backward, they found inspiration and validation in their retreat from urban America.

Mungo, for one, put his actions and motivations squarely in the American mainstream, in a wonderfully dissonant moment, in his book *Total Loss Farm*: "Culture-hero Steve McQueen has said 'I would rather wake up in the middle of nowhere than in any city on Earth.' Naturally, I second that."[90] The pastoral myth with its inherent anti-urban impulse joined together communards with suburbanites, Mungo with McQueen.

Communes, the Environment, and Race

By the end of the 1960s, any number of African American voices began to question whether the American city was the best hope for black America any longer. Floyd McKissick of the Congress of Racial Equality (CORE) doubtlessly spoke for many when he reminded a crowd in 1973, "In the late 1960s we looked at the cities and we saw welfare; we saw crime in the streets; we saw poor and inadequate housing; we saw discrimination, a lack of job opportunities, and a high job-migrations rate; and we decided that we must concentrate on one area: the city." But, he went on, "I raised my voice to say, 'No!' "[91]

McKissick made those comments at a conference promoting new towns held in New York, and he was there touting his own new town project in Warren County, North Carolina. It had been described in the press as a black new town—McKissick called it "Soul City"—but McKissick insisted that it too would be a racially integrated development. "We do not intend to adopt the white man's racism," he told the *New York Times*. But clearly he wanted to build Soul City because he believed that African Americans, too, had been betrayed by the American city. "The black man has been searching for his identity and destiny in the cities," he went on, "He should be able to find in on the plains of Warren County."[92] McKissick brought in James Rouse as a consultant, and Soul City was among the first new towns to received funding from HUD.

Other African American activists held on to the belief that the problems of African America were urban problems and they needed urban solutions. The back-to-the-land movement and the new enthusiasm for environmental issues caused considerable anger among some in the black power movement, and even among those who remained with the older civil rights movement.

In 1970, with Spiro Agnew serving as vice president, with Strom Thurmond and John Stennis in Congress, and with George Wallace gearing up for a presidential run, few would have nominated Ralph Nader as "the biggest damn racist in the United States." But so spoke Douglas Moore of the Washington Black United Front. The reason for Moore's vitriol was straightforward: Nader was "more responsible than any man for perverting the war on poverty to the war on pollution," and Moore threatened, "we will deal with him—that's right!"[93]

Moore's comments strike us now as buffoonish, but they were merely an extreme variation on a more common theme, and they underscore the link between the civil rights agenda and the urban agenda in the late 1960s and early 1970s. By that time, the two had become more or less synonymous. Urban renewal and the War on Poverty were both seen as largely urban projects benefiting largely black residents. Environmentalism seemed to pull the nation's attention away from those issues.

As the focus of the civil rights movement shifted out of the South and into the urban North, those cities represented two sides of the civil rights struggle. On the one hand, some of the most intractable and crushing poverty could be found in America's inner city (read: black) neighborhoods; on the other, they were places where black political organization was having some of its greatest success. Carl Stokes became the first black mayor of a major city when in 1967 he was elected in Cleveland. (Fellow Ohioan Robert Henry may have been the first black mayor of any northern city when he took the job in Springfield in 1966; Henry, as it happened, was a life-long Republican.) Stokes was followed by Richard Hatcher in Gary, Indiana, and by Coleman Young in Detroit.

Black militants and mainstream black politicians reacted suspiciously to the new environmental movement because they worried it would divert attention and resources from the black/urban agenda. For his part, Stokes insisted that cleaning up pollution could wait until urban residents lived in adequate housing; Mayor Hatcher sounded more like Douglas Moore when he reacted to the arrival of the environmental movement onto the political stage: "The nation's concern with the environment has done what George Wallace was unable to do: distract the nation from the problems of black and brown Americans." Six months after Earth Day, a reporter for *Business Week* filed a report headlined "To Blacks, Ecology Is Irrelevant." The story ran under *Business Week*'s "Cities Commentary" section. All of this was summarized in an exchange between a black activist in Chicago and a reporter from *Time*: "Ecology?" the activist balked, "I don't give a good goddam about ecology!"[94]

While racial segregation was being inscribed in the landscape of the metropolitan North one subdivision at a time, the rural communes were just as racially homogenous. Almost no African Americans joined communes, and many who studied them made this observation. For Benjamin Zablocki, this fact was "a matter worth speculating about in the search for a cultural etiology of communitarianism." Zablocki took as a given that "black culture in America is often so different from white culture," and then noted:

> For what it is worth, those few blacks in the communitarian sample often appeared to be among the most cynical and marginal members of their communes. Blacks in predominantly white communes often seem uninterested in consensus, cool to the joys of communion, and immune to the charms of white charismatic leaders.

Zablocki acknowledged that young black communards appeared "just as alienated from the larger society as the white members were," but he concluded "black communitarians were perhaps less confused about what they wanted."[95]

One explanation, which does not seem to have occurred to commentators of the day, might be rooted in the symbolic importance the American city held for black Americans in the mid-twentieth century. White, middle-class communards—most of them, at any rate—were at least a few generations removed from rural life. Far enough away from it that they could romanticize it and play at farming. Agricultural life, with all its backbreaking work, grueling routine, and economic cruelty was still a living memory for many American blacks, and the city represented an escape from it. Though the promise of urban life, which had drawn black Americans from the rural South since the First World War, remained too often unfulfilled by the 1960s, it existed in the collective memory. For many African Americans in the 1960s, forty acres and a mule was a bitter broken promise, not a slogan for the future.[96]

Whatever the explanation, very few young black Americans joined communes. In 1970, *Ebony* magazine printed a report about hippie communes by veteran newspaperman Louie Robinson. "Life Inside a Hippie Commune" focused on Robinson's own daughter Toni, a University of Chicago graduate who had moved to rural Colorado with her white husband and Robinson's two inter-racial grandchildren. "Toni...is something of a phenomenon," Robinson acknowledged, "even among today's far-out youth." He described his daughter as "one of only a handful of blacks who have fled the cities and what to them are the terrors of federal and local government for a life of fresh air, hard work, chemical-free vegetables and considerable deprivation."

Some of Robinson's article focused on the vexing question of how Toni could maintain her racial identity. Bemused and perhaps a bit wary, as a reporter and more as a parent, Robinson quotes his daughter as having a vital "appreciation" of her blackness, but feeling as well that this is not necessarily the central part of her life in the commune. Robinson was clear with his readers that this commune was "not the kind of white world seen by a ghetto or Southern rural black. The whites who inhabit Toni's world are about as far removed from the power-prejudice orientation of Caucasian America as it is humanly possible to be." Still, Robinson acceded, "Toni's world today is basically all white."[97]

Robinson's deeply personal article underscores the racial dilemma confronted, or not, by the new communes. On the one hand, black Americans might very well feel the anti-urban impulse even more than whites. The poverty and violence of the American city affected black Americans disproportionately—why not flee the "terrors" of urban life? Robinson insisted to his readers that these communes, genuinely free of the "power-prejudice" of white America, welcomed his daughter as an equal. In other words, for disaffected black youth in the late 1960s and early 1970s, living in a rural commune would seem to make all kinds of sense.

In the end, however, it did not. Taken in aggregate, the new communes might well have been more lily-white than the suburbs in which many of the communitarians were raised. If suburban segregation resulted from redlining, mortgage discrimination, and white resistance to black neighbors, the segregation of communes resulted from something else. When one New Mexico commune member did talk about race, his vision was steeped in nostalgia for a mythic, pre-industrial past. "The work," he wrote, "is to restore the communal basis for life which prevailed among both the Indian and the Chicano peoples before the White Man came."[98] Perhaps we can see in the demographics of hippie communes the self-selecting and melancholy result of a generation increasingly disillusioned with the integrationist hopes of the 1950s and early 1960s, a resignation on the part of young people both black and white that the divide between them would never be overcome.

Causally or coincidentally, hippies left the city at exactly the moment when civil rights and urban issues became virtually synonymous. Those who went to the new communes turned their backs, either deliberately or indifferently, on both. "A Grand Master Plan" developed by communard Patsy Sun inadvertently gives some sense of how far the communes had removed themselves from the urgent issues of race and poverty in the American city. She advised people looking to lead a more fulfilling life:

> Dig your toes in the warm dirt. Pick a tick off your friend's neck. Have a few stupid arguments. Write to the urban poor telling them you'd like to help families get out of the city if they want. Go out and plant a row of carrots. Make a mistake. Roll in the grass and begin again.[99]

Ms. Sun probably meant to sound insouciant and not dismissive, but it is hard to imagine a more flippant trivialization of the problems facing urban America than that.

The Environment and the City: Common Cause or Natural Enemies?

For their part, many of the new environmentalists and communards had little use for the New Left. As environmentalist Tony Wagner sketched it, with his own sanctimonious impatience, "we can argue the merits of third party politics, coalition movements, and student-worker alliances until doomsday, but in the coming years there is only going to be one meaningful alliance—the grouping together of people who are totally committed to the affirmation of all life on this planet." Counterculture theorist and celebrant Charles Reich saw the New Left rapidly growing old:

> The New Left is still fighting the battle against capitalism and imperialism.... But if we think of all that is now challenged—the nature of education, the very validity of institutionalism and the legal system, the nature and purposes of work, the course of man's dealing with environment, the relationship of self to technology and society—we can see that the present transformation goes beyond anything in modern history.[100]

More puckishly, in 1969, the Twin Oaks commune in Virginia published a small booklet entitled "The Revolution Is Over: We Won!"[101] Given the angry earnestness, and frequency, with which New Leftists and black power advocates invoked the word *revolution*, one can only imagine how infuriated the subscribers of *Ramparts* must have been.

So although New Leftists accused communards and environmentalists of being politically naïve, or of ignoring politics altogether, the communards did not necessarily disagree. Keith Melville approvingly called Ray Mungo's *Famous Long Ago* a manifesto for "this communal strategy...a brightly written statement of the case for dropping out of politics."[102] For their part environmentalists and communards had grown weary of and disaffected by the shrill dogmatism of the New Left and its growing fascination with violence. Ray Mungo and Marshall Bloom tried to keep the Liberation New Service publishing from the commune in Montague, but to no avail. As Mungo described it: "By February of 1969 and without any kind of public notice to the subscribers or the readers, LNS in Montague quietly died." Struggling to survive their first winter on the farm, "everybody had better and more useful things to do." From the vantage of their farm commune, the hothouse politics of SDS and LNS seemed suddenly small and insignificant.

Or comical. In the spring of 1969, Mungo went to visit the LNS crew in New York and found this LNS headline tacked to the office wall: "LNS Backs Stones in Ideological Rift with Beatles." Mungo and the others wiped their hands of LNS and of all it represented without regret: "LNS was one of those things we had left behind when we came over to the New Age."[103]

In fact, Mungo was wrong that communes turned their back entirely on politics as they cultivated their gardens. True, many communes did not survive past their first few growing seasons, but among those that did, some played important roles in local political struggles over logging, watershed protection, the development of organic farming, and the local food movement. And the Montague Farm became central to the anti-nuclear organizing of the Clamshell Alliance. Much of the book *No Nukes!* was written on the farm's kitchen table.[104]

Some voices in the New Left certainly saw a set of common purposes. The underground newspaper *Rat* ran a column declaiming: "revolutionaries must begin to think in ecological terms.... [A]n attack against environmental destruction is an attack on the structure of control and the mechanisms of power within a society." For the most part, though, the New Left eyed the environmental movement and the communitarians with a mixture of distrust and disdain.

Perhaps that is because, despite all of their analytic flourish, the New Left could not quite acknowledge the potential represented by the environmental movement. Could not or would not. They may have recognized that the environmental movement stood as a rejection of much of what the New Left now represented. Though it clearly grew out of the energies of the 1960s, it was a different sort of beast. The civil rights movement had a history and a trajectory that SDS both understood and tried to emulate. SDS took much of its original inspiration from the lunch-counter sit-ins, and thus SDS grew more and more militant, tracking the path of black power and the Black Panthers. The environmental movement, on the other hand, seemed to follow a different course. As historian of the movement Robert Gottlieb has noted, amid the great media swirl around it, "environmentalism became a movement without a history, with an amorphous social base, and with a clean slate on how best to proceed."[105]

In 1972, Richard Gale attempted a comparison between the civil rights movement and the environmental movement in an essay he clumsily titled "From Sit-In to Hike-In." In comparing the tactics used by each, Gale was most concerned with whether the environmental movement would eventually head down the path of violence. But he did note that two important things differentiated the two movements. First, environmentalism was not built on charismatic leadership the way civil rights had been. Second, it could build more readily into existing organizational structures—chapters of the Audubon Society, the Sierra Club, and the like—whereas civil rights activists, and the New Left, he might have added, distrusted existing organizations and tried to build their own.[106]

In the end, the communes and the environmental movement emerged at the moment the New Left had hit its peak and when the energy of the civil rights movement began to dissipate. And, in a demonstration of how close the far right and far left have always been in American political life, their attacks on the environmental movement sounded remarkably similar to those made by William F. Buckley and the Daughters of the American Revolution, one of whose members called environmentalism "one of the subversive element's last steps," and complained that "they have gone after the military and the police, and now they're going after our parks and playgrounds." Several conservative newspapers pointed out, conspiratorially, that April 22—Earth Day—was also Lenin's birthday.[107] Both left complicated legacies that continue to unfold, but among them was the charge that the environmental movement, with its emphasis on endangered species, wilderness protection, and personal behavior, was really a movement of the anti-urban elite, and crypto-racist to boot.[108]

Indeed, Douglas Moore's angry condemnation of Ralph Nader has more recently been echoed by Roy Innis, executive director of CORE. Innis took over CORE in 1968 when he was a radical black power advocate. He quickly became a Nixon supporter, then a Reaganite and NRA Board member. Joining forces with ExxonMobil and others opposed to environmental protections, Innis recently vowed to fight listing the polar bear as an endangered species because it would make oil drilling in the Arctic more difficult. He called those who cared about endangered species "modern day Bull Connors and George Wallaces, who are standing in the door, trying to prevent poor Americans from achieving Martin Luther King's dream of equal opportunity and true environmental justice."[109]

Some critics did point out that the environmental movement and the back-to-the-land communes fed the anti-urban impulse in American life. When *Time* magazine wrote in the 1970 issue, with Barry Commoner on the cover, that "water, air and green space know no class or color distinction," the implication, at least for some left activists, was that the environmental movement thus did not have to confront race or class, two of the most pressing urban issues. The two, as we have already discussed, had become synonymous in American political discussion.[110]

When environmental activists included population control in their list of concerns, New Leftists saw something suspiciously like eugenic social engineering of poorer, darker-skinned people. When Earth Day organizers stressed the role of individual behavior in solving environmental problems, some New Leftists heard the sound of the victim being blamed. Besides, some on the left themselves simply couldn't see that city and country had anything politically in common. Jim Bennett saw environmentalism as the province of "scientist-professionals." "Mother Nature has really little bearing on the urban young left....We are all ecologists in a nostalgic sense but we are not professionals. Nor do we live out in Mother Nature, we live in those messes called cities."[111]

It would take some years for Americans to come to a broader recognition of the relationship between poverty and environmental issues. It would also take time for people to recognize that good urbanism and environmental stewardship serve the same ends. The provocative sociologist Paul Goodman, for one, recognized these connections and cautioned those headed back to the land, "Mere esthetic and philosophical motives for rural reconstruction urge withdrawal from the urban mainstream," which he regarded as an unpromising solution to the problems of the day. Instead, he challenged people to create a better balance between the city and the country; but then Goodman himself was a city kid, born in and educated by New York.[112]

It was more than pure happenstance that the rise of the communes and the environmental movement, which each played on America's pastoral, anti-urban tradition, coincided with this moment of greatest urban despair. But the failure of environmentalists to develop and articulate a clearer urban agenda, and the failure of urban activists black and white to recognize their stake in environmental issues, helped neither cause through the 1970s and '80s. Progressive urbanites could not see past the anti-urbanism of the communes and the environmental activists, nor could the anti-urban progressives see beyond their disdain of the city as the source of all environmental ills.

In his Earth Day speech on the campus of the University of Pennsylvania in 1970, Senator Edmund Muskie tried to bridge the problems of the city, which had consumed the 1960s, with the problems of the environment emerging at the beginning of the 1970s:

> Those who believe that we are talking about the Grand Canyon and the Catskills but not about Harlem and Watts are wrong. And those who believe that we must do something about the SST and the automobile, but not about ABMs and the Vietnam War are wrong.[113]

That Muskie had to say this at Earth Day, however, reveals that as the 1960s turned into the 1970s, many believed Harlem really was a long way from the Catskills.

The City on the Screen

There is a scene in Woody Allen's 1977 film *Annie Hall* where Alvy Singer (Allen) is talking to his friend Max (Tony Roberts). Alvy has blamed anti-Semitism for the nation's failure to rally around New York in its hour of financial need. He explains, "Don't you see the rest of the country looks upon New York like we're left-wing, communist, Jewish, homosexual pornographers? I think of us that way sometimes and I live here." It's a funny line because it exaggerated, but only slightly. Had Alvy included "black" in his list of American pariahs, he would have completed the portrait of the American city that many people saw in the 1970s.

This was certainly the case for the Americans who took their image of the city from what played on their local movie theater screens. Throughout the decade, and certainly into the 1980s, Hollywood presented Americans with a dark, dys-topian version of the American city, a place of danger, violence, and loss. The *Godfather* saga, whose story takes place largely in the postwar period, makes one feel nostalgic for the good old days when New York was run by the Sicilian mob. Susan Sarandon and Burt Lancaster played out their odd, poignant relationship against the backdrop of an old, shabby Atlantic City literally being demolished to make way for shiny new casinos. Rocky came from one of those white, ethnic, working-class enclaves in Philadelphia whose way of life was fast dissolving. And he lost the big fight.

If the small-town boosters and new town builders traded on the pioneer myth to promote their visions, then Hollywood's American city as it appeared in a number of films relocated another piece of nineteenth-century mythology. The city became an updated Wild West, whose lawlessness and corruption could only be redeemed by a lone and lonely gunslinger. This motif runs through Al Pacino's *Serpico* (1973), who faced down an NYPD portrayed as entirely on the take; and through Clint Eastwood's *Dirty Harry* franchise, where San Francisco cop Harry Callahan had to take the law into his own hands because liberal laws simply coddled the bad guys. Richard Roundtree's *Shaft* (1971) demonstrated that the story worked just as well with a black man in the lead role, especially if he could crisscross New York to the beat of an Isaac Hayes soundtrack. It reached a climax of sorts in Paul Newman's *Fort Apache, The Bronx* (1981). The title of that popular movie made the analogy between the nineteenth-century West and the late-twentieth-century city explicit. And in case you still did not get it, the advertising campaign for the movie included this tag: "No Cowboys. No Indians. No Cavalry to the Rescue. Only a Cop."

Those movies, made with the bitter taste of Vietnam still in the nation's mouth, strived for contemporary urban realism. Frank Serpico really was a clean cop who with great courage blew the whistle on police corruption in New York; the South Bronx really had deteriorated into one of the most violent and desper-ate places in the nation. This was Hollywood's attempt to capture the story of urban America unvarnished and without sentimentality. Like John Shaft, these movies promised to tell it like it is, though sometimes they veered into a kind of urban voyeurism.

Just as fascinating is how often Hollywood has returned, almost nostalgically, to that moment and those places since. *Goodfellas* (1990) was Martin Scorsese's version of the mafia epic, based on real events that happened in New York in the 1950s, '60s, and '70s. In 2007, Denzel Washington played the real-life drug kingpin Frank Lucas, and Russell Crowe played Richie Roberts—the detective who brought him down—in *American Gangster*. Both movies brought viewers back to a New York where the cops were crooked, the mafia operated more or less unfettered, and heroin could be found on almost any street corner.

The appeal of these movies, then and now, is almost prurient—a romanticized fascination with urban violence and the mean streets where it took place. But those images, as is the case with so much hip-hop music which glorifies the gangsta myth, are consumed from a safe suburban distance. Those who watch the movies or listen to the music get to participate in a set of fantasies about the ghetto, but most of them do not have to live there. If they did, or if they bothered even to visit those neighborhoods, they would be chagrined to find life disappointingly mundane: people struggling to live decent lives, to raise their kids under difficult circumstances, and to hang on to their own dignity. They would also discover that there is nothing heroic about urban violence, nor is there anything romantic about being poor.

Beneath Woody Allen's joke lay another truth about the city in the 1970s. It remained a refuge for those who could not conform to American conformity. From the Stonewall Inn in the West Village, to the Castro in *Dirty Harry*'s San Francisco, cities provided some measure of liberation or simple relief for America's gay citizens. The city served as the best place for African American economic and political opportunity, since blacks remained effectively redlined out of most of suburbia. The city continued in its role as the engine of the nation's cultural and intellectual life, as when a collection of artists began to occupy vacant industrial space in lower Manhattan and filled it with their art, and Soho was born. And although hardly communists, those who chose to remain in the city during that desperate decade tried to uphold notions of the commonweal and the public good. All of those people deserve credit for holding together urban civilization at a time when other Americans routinely talked about abandoning their cities altogether.

They were able to hold that civilization together because the city—not the farm, nor the small town, nor the suburb—provided the room for them to express themselves as individuals. Although anti-urbanists, as we have seen, have insisted that the city life inevitably means a loss of freedom and liberty, they have failed to recognize the role of the city in allowing those not necessarily in the mainstream to breathe a little more freely. They have not acknowledged what sociologist Robert Park did a century ago: that in the city,

every individual, no matter how eccentric, finds somewhere…an environment in which he expands and feels at ease; finds, in short, the moral climate in which his peculiar nature obtains the stimulations that bring his innate qualities to full and free expression.…A smaller community sometimes tolerates eccentricity, but the city often rewards it.[114]

Two years after *Annie Hall*, Woody Allen released *Manhattan*. In that film, despite, or perhaps precisely because of, all the left-wing, communist, Jewish, homosexual pornographers, his character says, "Boy, this is really a great city. I don't care what anybody says." It's a romantic moment in the film, but in 1979 it also rang with a certain defiance.

9 NEW COMMUNITIES, NEW URBANISMS

By the last quarter of the twentieth century, Americans had succeeded in building an alternative to the dense central city, and the anti-government politics of the New Right had triumphed on the national stage. Roughly three out of every four of us live in large metropolitan regions, but the large cities that anchor those regions do not house a majority of those metropolitans. The greater Philadelphia region, on the East Coast, counts a population of just under 6 million, the city itself only 1.5 million; on the West Coast, the city of Los Angeles is home to nearly 4 million people, but the Los Angeles "metroplex" has grown to nearly 13 million. Hence the paradox: we are a nation clustered around our major cities, we rely on their infrastructure—transportation networks, education and research facilities, cultural institutions—and we remain deeply ambivalent about the city and city-ness itself.

At the same time, despite the flight from the city after the Second World War, despite the proliferation of physical environments shaped primarily by the automobile and private housing, Americans seemed no closer to solving the question of how to live the good life than they had been at the beginning of the century. Indeed, to judge by any number of sociological studies, public opinion surveys, and news reports, they were arguably further from finding that grail than ever before. A country of exiles, bowling alone, inhabiting a geography of nowhere. "At the conclusion of the 20th century," sociologist Robert Putnam concluded, "ordinary Americans shared [a] sense of civic malaise."[1] The longing to belong that underscored the twentieth century had not been satisfied, the beloved community that Josiah Royce had anticipated had not yet come to pass.

Into that loneliness and alienation emerged two movements promising to heal what ailed us. One was made up of a loose assemblage of sociologists, philosophers, lawyers, and public policy types who called themselves "communitarians." They have attempted to formulate an ethos to navigate between an excessive individualism and an overbearing state. The other was a group of planners, designers, and architects who called themselves the "new urbanists." These new urbanists believe that America's sterile built environment has contributed mightily to that civic malaise, and that with better planning we can create meaningful communities.

Though each had its own roots, the two movements converged in the 1990s. The communitarians offered a bracing critique of the nation's social ills, and they argued that a revived "community" would fill its void of values. The new urbanists envisioned landscapes that would facilitate exactly the ethos the communitarians advocated. Space could be reshaped into meaningful places, which in turn would foster the community at the heart of communitarianism. Both groups came to national prominence in the last decade of the twentieth century, both diagnosed the same ailment in American life, and both have been ambivalent about the role of the city in curing the "crisis of community" and have been largely silent on the larger issue of how to invigorate our public sphere.

A Philosophy of Community?

For a brief period in the 1990s, George Washington University sociology professor Amatai Etzioni enjoyed a kind of rock star status, at least in certain circles. In 1993, Etzioni founded the Communitarian Network, the purpose of which was to bring a set of sociological and philosophical discussions out of the seminar room into a wider sphere. The Communitarian Network describes itself as "a coalition of individuals and organizations who have come together to shore up the social, moral, and political environment. We are a nonpartisan, nonsectarian, transnational association."[2] Etzioni became the public face of the communitarian movement.

In their attempt to "shore up" those environments in contemporary America, communitarians necessarily wrestled with the tension between individual liberties and larger social obligations. In that sense, as some critics pointed out, they were doing nothing new. Whether or not this charge is fair, it is certainly true that communitarianism was entirely of its moment. It grew out of the soil of post-1960s, post-Cold War America, and it tried to resolve the welter of contradictions presented by that moment. Regardless of where one resided on the political spectrum, communitarians believed, everyone felt an emptiness. "People feel alienation," Etzioni told an interviewer, "that we are atomized, all living separately without enough common bonds. This creates a void. They say, 'We are supposed to have a community, but we don't, and we want to do something about it.'"[3] The communitarian movement offered itself as the answer for those who yearned for meaningful community.

Communitarianism attempted to intersect the increasingly shrill right–left spectrum of American politics somewhere in the middle and at 90 degrees, in an effort to intervene in the culture wars of that decade, which they saw in ideological fights over museum exhibits and school curricula. Communitarians decried both the "I'm okay, you're okay" easing of traditional moral strictures and structures that many viewed as the legacy of the 1960s left, and the dog-eat-dog, social Darwinian economics fostered and celebrated by the Reagan right. As presented by Etzioni, communitarianism resonated beautifully with the "third way" politics embraced by British Prime Minister Tony Blair and by the centrist Democratic Leadership Council. Rumors swirled that senior members of the Clinton administration were reading Etzioni's 1993 book *The Spirit of Community*.

The Spirit of Community is not a difficult book, as philosophical tomes go, and it was clearly written to engage a wide public, filled as it is with chirpy bromides and commonsensical assertions. Nor is it difficult to see why some liberals found a less-than-subtle reactionary agenda in the book. Although Etzioni and the other communitarians wanted to cast a pox on the houses of both political right and left, *The Spirit of Community* spends more of its time blaming the erosion of the institutions of community on the agencies of the liberal state than on the corrosive effects of laissez-faire economics. Here is a typical complaint:

> More and more people have been gobbled up by the economy—which is taxed to pay for hired hands to accomplish what people used to do as volunteers. Where we had ethnic groups taking care of new immigrants (which some still do), we now have a U.S. Refugee Resettlement Agency and a plethora of government-run welfare agencies. Where once we had families attending to their elderly, now we see families otherwise occupied and many of the elderly are institutionalized in nursing homes (which are often heavily subsidized by the government, which in-community care is not). And so it goes.[4]

And so Etzioni goes, substituting the idea of the private realm of community for the public realm of the state, never mind that many families are simply not equipped to handle the care of their elderly relatives.

Community required a set of institutions—family first and foremost—in order to function in any effective way. But Etzioni's suspicions sounded a great deal like the anti-government activists ascendant on the political right. Etzioni described it this way in *The Spirit of Community*:

> It is widely recognized that communities provide the social base of the mediating institutions that stand between the individual and the state, protecting the individual from excessive encroachment by the state. For these mediating institutions to be able to discharge this important

function they themselves must be shielded from the government. Such protection is high on the agenda of the Communitarian movement.[5]

The public sphere had emerged in the eighteenth century to play that mediating role between people's private lives, intensely local and inwardly focused, and the state, which otherwise might act oppressively. The communitarians elided the idea of community with the idea of a public.

To his credit, Etzioni addressed people who wanted a greater sense of community by reminding them that it came with hard work, obligations, and perhaps even some restrictions. As one journalist summarized the concept, "Would you like a nation where people cared more for each other but divorces were legally difficult? Welcome to communitarianism."[6] But sometimes Etzioni sounded like a scold, or worse. In one provocative essay, for example, he called for a return to public shaming. Shaming substituted the authority of the community for the authority of the state, and thus "it is deeply democratic. Shaming reflects the community's values and hence cannot be imposed by the authorities against a people."[7] He did not fully explain how this "deeply democratic" process would not simply become the tyranny of the majority.

He could also be a tad defensive when people pointed out that community could be exclusive and oppressive as well as warm and welcoming. "Listen, I know that the KKK was a community of sorts," he told an interviewer. "So was Salem at the time of the witch-hunts. The cult in Waco was a community. So was Jonestown. I think we can guard against the excesses and still move forward, to more authentic ways of relating and joining together on projects to make life better for us all."[8]

The communitarians did not or could not see the central problem with that kind of easy formulation. The only way for people to join "together on projects to make life better for us all" is if there is some consensus about what constitutes "better," about what "projects" might achieve that better, and who the "us" is who gets to decide. Communities tend to function precisely because there is very little internal debate on those questions, especially about who might belong. In a large, complicated democracy, however, those questions can be answered only in the public space of politics, not in the more intimate sphere of "community."[9]

Etzioni and his fellow communitarians provided a compelling diagnosis of the national illness, and they formulated a prescription to cure it, bad-tasting though some might find the medicine. For that they deserve a great deal of credit. But in addition to the conceptual problems of their notion of community they did not attend much to the question of where, exactly, community could be rebuilt. Etzioni fully understood that Americans move nearly every five years and thus no longer derive their identities from the places they live. He expressed some enthusiasm about communities that did not require physical proximity. One critic noted that what made Etzioni's conception of community new was precisely that it did not require any physical location or geographic boundaries.

When Etzioni did address the physical nature of community, he walked in a circle. "To make our physical environment more community-friendly," Etzioni explained, "our homes, places of work, streets, and public spaces—whole developments, suburbs, and even whole cities—need to be designed to enhance the Communitarian nexus."[10] Thus in order to foster community, our physical environment needs to be built to foster community.

In fact, Etzioni's suspicion of the state and the dichotomy he saw between government and community put him squarely in the twentieth-century tradition of anti-urbanism. And when Etzioni stopped talking about community in the abstract and imagined it as a place, he saw a small town. When he proposed a return to public shaming, for example, he pointed out that the communities of eighteenth-century New England were "much smaller, more tightly knit, and more moralistic than any here today." When he published *The Spirit of Community* in 1993, he saw "a welcome return to small-town life." But by 1993, unlike, say, 1933, few could argue seriously for a return to the American small town in a nation so thoroughly dominated by metropolitan regions. Etzioni reassured his readers that "although not all suburbs, which attracted millions of city dwellers, make for viable communities, as a rule the movement to the suburbs has enhanced the Communitarian nexus."[11] Since real small-towns in America have been suffering for at least half a century, Etzioni hoped that some suburban areas would fill the bill.

In this sense, the communitarians of the 1990s sounded much like the anti-urbanists of the 1920s or of the 1970s. They believed that Americans needed "community" of some sort as the mediator between alienating individualism and an oppressive state. And like their anti-urban predecessors, they were suspicious of the role of government in people's lives, and they saw the city as antithetical to their notion of community.

The Newer New Urbanism

Perhaps Etzioni did not feel it was necessary to be more specific about the physical shape and location of his community. His fellow communitarian Robert Putnam was not sure that mattered much, as he believed that sprawl "might account for . . . 10 percent of the problem" of community.[12] By the time the communitarians began to attract public attention, however, other people were busy planning the shape of community.

In 1993, the same year Etzioni published *The Spirit of Community*, a group of planners, architects, policy advocates, and others came together to found the

Congress for the New Urbanism. The Congress was founded on the principle that physical space really does structure the quality of human experience and interaction, and it has dedicated itself to promoting design and development (and policy) that foster community.

In its charter, ratified in 1996, the Congress announced: "We stand for the restoration of existing urban centers and towns within coherent metropolitan regions, the reconfiguration of sprawling suburbs into communities of real neighborhoods and diverse districts, the conservation of natural environments, and the preservation of our built legacy." More specifically, the Congress committed itself to a set of principles that included neighborhoods that were diverse socially and

SUBURBAN SPRAWL

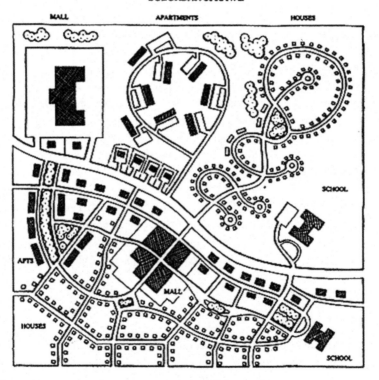

TRADITIONAL NEIGHBORHOOD

Traditional neighborhoods versus suburban sprawl. The former creates denser, mixed-use, pedestrian-friendly environments while the latter segregates uses and forces people to drive everywhere. Much of the "new urbanism" has not been that new at all but, rather, a reinvigoration of older forms of urban planning and land use. *Courtesy of Duany Plater-Zyberk & Company and the Congress of New Urbanism* economically; spaces that catered to pedestrians and public transit in addition to cars; public spaces that served a wide range of publics; and design that was sensitive to local history, local climate, and local ecology. Those principles stand as a succinct critique of roughly fifty years of American development and a reassertion of the value of urbanism.

Andres Duany and Elizabeth Plater-Zyberk, Miami-based architects and planners, have been the most visible driving force behind the movement. They have become celebrities in the world of planning, architecture, and public policy. But they did not start out that way. After graduate school, the couple designed tall boxes in the modernist style in which they had been trained. Then, in the late 1970s, they were approached by a developer who wanted to build a new town on the Florida panhandle. From a combination of the developer's desire to evoke the "old" coastal towns of his youth and the architects' sense that conventional town planning had led to sterile architectural and social environments came Seaside, Florida. It opened in 1989.

Seaside appeared revolutionary to a society conditioned to planned obsolescence and suffering from historical amnesia. It was a town built from scratch, deliberately designed to look like a town that had always been there. This meant smaller building lots than in conventional suburban developments and more residential density; pedestrian-friendly streets; mixed-use spaces—the antithesis of most of the development that had taken place in the United States since the end of World War II.

The "new" in the label new urbanism was, therefore, something of a misnomer. One of the most striking things about new urbanism has been its embrace, driven by a sense of loss, of much that is old. Vincent Scully, perhaps the most influential architectural writer of the second half of the twentieth century, has been among the most enthusiastic supporters of new urbanism. "It now seems obvious to almost everyone... that community is what America has most conspicuously lost, and community is precisely what canonical Modern architecture and planning of the middle years of this century were totally unable to provide." For Scully, mid-century modernism of the sort that dominated urban revival after the war was the architectural analogue to the alienated individualism that Etzioni fretted over. These monuments, Scully wrote, "celebrated the individual free from history and time. One could not make a community out of them." To fix those mistakes, according to planner Todd Bressi, new urbanism aims to "revive principles about building communities that have been virtually ignored for half a century."[13] Not for nothing did *U.S. News* call the new urbanists "neo-traditionalists."[14]

The problem new urbanism proposed to fix was not new, either. Over and over again there has been a desire to use physical space to create meaningful community. Duany and Plater-Zyberk have been unapologetic in their goal to do just that. As they wrote in their exhortation *Suburban Nation*, "We believe more strongly than ever in the power of good design to overcome the ills created by bad design."[15]

Design, therefore, was a means to an end, not an end unto itself. The goal of design should not be architectural or aesthetic, or even about land use for its own sake, but about strengthening our social bonds. "Of course, the ultimate goal must not be limited to the cessation of sprawl," Duany and Plater-Zyberk wrote. "For our country to prosper, Americans must also concern themselves with the building of community.... [C]ommunity flourishes best in traditional neighborhoods. When this fact is widely acknowledged, government officials, designers, and citizens will begin to act with the confidence that what is good for neighborhoods is good for America." When they wrote "We Americans have been building a national landscape that is largely devoid of places worth caring about," they nicely echoed the way Josiah Royce extolled the importance of "provincialism" at the beginning of the century. [16]

If Royce saw the city as corroding the American community because of its anonymity, the mobility of its residents, and its sheer size, then the new urbanists saw the threat coming from exactly the opposite direction. For those at the beginning of the century, the problem was urban congestion and overconcentration; for those at the end of it, the problem was too much decentralization. In a word, sprawl.

"Automobile suburbia is a manifestation of the devolution of community from a shared realm with shared purpose to an amalgamation of closely bunched, independent mini-estates," wrote photographer and writer Richard Sexton, and in that intense focus on people's private spaces, "residents of suburbia try to own individually what a community once provided for all. They don't share, but hoard, as each homesite seeks to be a self-sufficient entity." In other words, they created the opposite of community.

Lest people think that new urbanism amounts to little more than the do-gooding social engineering dreamt up by architects, a growing body of evidence suggests that people would choose to live in a neo-traditional environment, if given the opportunity. In 1997, Vince Graham addressed the National Association of Home Builders and told them, in the most basic math of all real estate developers, "If what you are selling is privacy and exclusivity, then every new house is a degradation of the amenity. However, if what you are selling is community, then every new house is an enhancement of the asset." Likewise, Pulte Homes, one of the nation's largest developers, found that people in its surveys and focus groups consistently liked new urbanist designs and neo-traditional neighborhoods precisely because of their shared public spaces.[17] Higher density, mixed-use, and public amenities, it turned out, could be profitable, too.

New Urbanism? Or New Small-Townism?

In its reaction to sprawl, new urbanism has been seen as the savior not so much of cities proper but of their suburbs. By the end of the twentieth century, few people—except the big developers of sprawl and a handful of right-wing free-market fundamentalists—wanted to defend sprawl publicly. *U.S. News & World Report* defined sprawl as "those tracts of characterless split-levels, with no shops or businesses to walk to, only driveways connecting to streets connecting to rivers of highways," and it described new urbanism as "putting the brakes on suburban sprawl." Summing up the difference between sprawl and new urbanism, Amanda Hale, who had just moved her family into a neo-traditional development near Chapel Hill, North Carolina, told a reporter "We want our four children to grow up in a community, not at a highway exit."[18]

And there can be no question that new urbanism's principles and goals have been hugely influential. By the turn of the millennium, by *Time*'s reckoning, more than 100 neo-traditional developments had opened, and another 200 were in the planning stages. New urbanism seems to have succeeded in linking design and community in a way that Radburn, the New Deal new towns, or the Nixon-era new towns never did. But like those earlier experiments, new urbanist projects, more often than not, took place outside cities themselves. They tried to recreate the small town by bringing principles of urbanism out to the suburbs.

Still, it is useful to keep this influence in perspective. New urbanist projects remained a fairly small part of the new housing market. In 2000, the nation saw roughly 1.6 million new housing starts. Most were of the sprawling variety. Old land-use habits die hard. Just ask the developers who came to Middletown Township, Pennsylvania.

Middletown Township is located along Baltimore Pike as it angles south and west out of Philadelphia. You can still get to Baltimore along the old Baltimore Pike if you follow it carefully. These days, however, the trip probably takes only slightly less time than it did in the eighteenth century, when this road provided the main land connection between the two cities. Headed south, the stop-and-go traffic of Baltimore Avenue in Philadelphia yields to only slightly less stopping and going as the road meanders through the increasingly choked suburbs of Delaware and Chester Counties.

For years, the Franklin Mint, stamper of commemorative coins and molder of all manner of collectibles of the sort your aunt might keep on a mantelpiece, sat as a major landmark on Baltimore Pike in Middletown Township, Delaware County. The mint closed in 2004, shaking the QVC crowd to its core, and the site sat empty. Real estate developers abhor vacant land even more than nature dislikes a vacuum, and in the years after the mint ceased operations, developers purchased the campus and adjacent parcels, which eventually totaled 150 acres.

Then they unveiled their plans to the Township Council: 1.3 million square feet of retail space; 1,300 residential units; a 300-room hotel. Township residents balked and mounted a campaign to defeat the plan. They rallied under the slogan "No City!"

The residents won and forced the developers back to their drawing boards, only this time developers brought a number of township residents with them to participate in the planning process. In March 2009, they presented the results of their work. The new proposal was a classic example of new urbanist principles: the whole project was smaller and denser—fewer residences, fewer hotel beds, less retail space, but these elements were clustered to create open space. The developers also added green space buffers, particularly along busy Baltimore Pike. Most dramatically of all, the whole project would be anchored by a regional rail station. It was a pedestrian-friendly, transit-oriented development, dropped down in the middle of suburban sprawl.

Despite the inclusive planning process, some residents remained opposed to it. "We are a well-designed bedroom community," John Laskas testified; "We don't want to change the character of our town."[19] A strange complaint to make, given that there is neither any "town" nor any "character" to speak of in Middletown Township. Mr. Laskas did not seem to see that a "bedroom community" is a contradiction in terms, nor did he realize that it is a virtual antonym of the idea of a "town." But Laskas's concerns were entirely predictable and underscored a central conundrum facing new urbanist planners and architects. Americans may report that the "bedroom" suburbs they live in leave them feeling lonely, alone, and alienated, but any plans designed to change that by making their suburbs more "urban" invariably meet with stiff resistance. The anti-urban impulse runs deep in American life.

In fact, most of the influential new urbanist developments are really modeled on small towns, and in that sense they are the latest attempt to solve the "crisis of community" by returning to the small-scaled intimacy of the American small town, or at least what they thought it to be. New town dreamers of the early twentieth century imagined decentralizing the city to reduce its density. New urbanists propose to increase the density of the conventional suburb. Both groups wound up extolling the virtues of the small town, and those virtues are not without their complications.

Among other things, the small town—whether in its 1920s incarnation or in its more recent new urbanist phase—has not been able to sustain itself economically, apart from some larger urban center, nor has it been particularly welcoming of ethno-racial or socioeconomic diversity, though the Congress for the New Urbanism insists that communities ought to be "diverse." Small towns have stood as among the best examples of the fact that the notion of community is built on exclusion as well as inclusion.

Without question, the most famous and most scrutinized new urbanist project was launched in Osceola County, in central Florida, in the mid-1990s. Sitting on nearly 5,000 acres, the brand new town was designed by marquee architect Robert Stern. It features all the new urbanist elements: front porches and sidewalks; a mix of housing, both in style and in price; and an eighteen-acre commercial "downtown" easily accessible by foot or bike from the surrounding neighborhoods.

It was not the white picket fences or the post office designed by Robert Graves, nor even the town hall designed by Philip Johnson, that were responsible for all the attention. What brought the eyes of the nation to this new urbanist creation in central Florida was the force behind it: the Disney Corporation. Disney built the town, put it right next to Disney World, and called it Celebration. The first residents moved in during 1996; by the end of the decade Celebration had been written about in more than 2,500 news stories.[20]

Celebration has offered a target-rich environment for those who want to critique the neo-traditionalism of the new urbanist movement. Sponsored by Disney and located within ear-shot of Disney World's nightly fireworks display, and created out of whole cloth but designed to look as if it had been built in the 1920s, Celebration begged to be called *ersatz*.

Life for the several thousand people who live in Celebration is more mundane than some of the caricatures would suggest. As one resident put it, "We're not Stepford wives. We still have problems. It's just a nicer place to have problems." Initially it proved quite popular with the public: the housing units sold across all the price ranges and the commercial downtown was busy. Even more significantly, housing prices were higher than surrounding comparables—people seemed willing to pay a Celebration premium. To give Celebration its due, it did not look like a typical Florida subdivision, and the people who lived there inhabited their space differently, too. As anyone who has been to Florida knows, there are precious few places anywhere in the state where you can actually walk to get a cup of coffee.[21]

What the Celebration premium bought, however, was not simply good design and planning. For many residents, the attraction of Celebration was the promise that Disney would control the environment of the town just the way it had made its amusement parks the happiest places on earth. Residents contract privately for services, and the town's Architectural Review Committee strictly regulates the physical appearance of the place. "Most of us came here not because of Disney," resident Kathleen Carlson told the *Miami Herald*; "we came because we wanted that type of control over our neighborhood. You don't have to worry that your neighbor will suddenly start parking an old pickup on his front lawn." Celebration has substituted corporate control for democratic participation in the life of the town. It is hardly the sort of reinvigorated "community" new urbanists hoped they could create, but exactly the result one might expect, given the way "community" has been turned into a real-estate asset.

When the Great Recession settled into Florida, however, not even Disney could control real estate values inside its model town. By the end of 2010, property prices had dropped even more than they had in the rest of the state—in some cases as much as 60 percent—and foreclosures were happening more frequently as well. In the space of a week at the end of 2010, the town experienced its first murder and then the suicide of a resident who had barricaded himself in his home and held a SWAT team at bay for fourteen hours. Stunned, much like residents of Reston had been when drugs and violence had come to that model town a generation earlier, Celebrationites had to confront reality.[22]

Writing about Seaside, that first new urbanist experiment, Vincent Scully exulted that it "has...succeeded, more fully than any other work of architecture in our time has done, in creating an image of community."[23] "Image" is an interesting choice of word. I suspect Scully meant it in the sense of "template" or "model," but its meaning can also shade toward the two-dimensional, or the superficial, a meaning reinforced in this case because the movie *The Truman Show* was shot in Seaside. Architect Alex Krieger looked at Seaside and saw something more sinister. "The current rush of enthusiasm for the 'community' found in the traditional small town disregards the many anti-public predilections of small-town life," he wrote in 1995. "Reading the minutes of the Seaside homeowners association meeting, like re-reading Sinclair Lewis's *Main Street,* may temper some of the accolades for Seaside," he continued. The architecture was not at issue, he was quick to note, but he was skeptical that places like Seaside represented a "paradigm for democratic social exchange."[24]

The challenge for new urbanism, like the challenge faced by the communitarians, is whether members of these new communities wind up feeling trapped in Gopher Prairie and whether the idea of community itself opens up larger democratic vistas.

Putting the Urban in New Urbanism

On June 1, 2010, the housing authorities of Charlotte, North Carolina; Covington, Kentucky; Dallas, Texas; Jersey City and Trenton, New Jersey; and Memphis, Tennessee received the happy news that they had been awarded grants from the Department of Housing and Urban Development totaling $113.6 million. The money came through HUD's HOPE VI program (HOPE stands for Housing Opportunities for People Everywhere). HOPE VI had begun in 1993 as a Clinton administration initiative, and by 2010 HUD had granted 132 housing agencies over $6 billion to revitalize public housing projects.

HOPE VI represented the first large-scale, innovative attempt by HUD to put cities back on the national agenda. As president, Ronald Reagan barely hid his contempt for urban problems and his disdain for the American city. Plenty of commentators at the time noticed how so much of Reagan's rhetoric was thinly veiled racial code. But that rhetoric also included thinly veiled assaults on the city—from the attacks on public housing and his invocation of the fictitious "welfare queen" who lived there—and in that sense Reagan reinforced the equating of "black" and "urban" in the minds of white, suburban, and rural voters.[25] With few exceptions, American presidents have not come from American cities, but Reagan was among the most anti-urban of our chief executives.

He appointed Samuel Pierce, an African American and life-long Republican, as secretary of Housing and Urban Development. Whereas Robert Weaver's appointment as the first HUD secretary and first black cabinet member had the heady feel of a civil rights watershed, Pierce's selection carried the faint whiff of political tokenism. A man of a certain accomplishment, Pierce largely vanished from sight during Reagan's eight years, and HUD along with him. At a U.S. Conference of Mayors gathering in Washington, Reagan addressed Pierce by saying "Hello, Mr. Mayor," giving the impression that Reagan did not even know his own cabinet member.

Pierce was the only member of Reagan's cabinet to serve for all eight years. During those eight years, he saw a 50 percent reduction in funding for low-income housing and the virtual cessation of funds for the construction of new housing. Only after Pierce shook hands with Reagan as he left the White House in 1989, however, did the real scandal break. Investigators discovered that under Pierce's stewardship, HUD had engaged in a vast smorgasbord of corrupt activities, including rigging the bids for contracts to favor well-connected Republicans, one of whom was James Watt, Reagan's first Interior secretary. Indictments rained down, and eventually sixteen people were convicted. As it turned out, "Silent Sam" Pierce had presided over the most venal operation in Reagan's Washington.

Reagan's successor, George H. W. Bush, had taken some tentative steps toward reviving HUD. In 1989, he authorized a thorough review of the nation's public housing and called for recommendations to improve it. He appointed Jack Kemp, a football hero and conservative Republican from Buffalo, as HUD's secretary. Kemp should be credited with setting in motion the urban enterprise zone program. The program was designed to stimulate economic activity in targeted areas, and 800 of them are operating today. Kemp approached his work at HUD with an almost penitent enthusiasm, believing that economic and racial justice could be achieved in the American city. Though he was a member of the civil rights generation, he recognized that, like so many of his fellow conservatives, "I wasn't there with Rosa Parks, or Dr. King, or John Lewis." But through his work at HUD he went on, "I am here now, and I am going to yell from the rooftops about what we need to do." And Kemp's HUD should be credited with laying the foundations of HOPE VI. Nevertheless, by the time Bill Clinton moved to town, HUD was still largely a demoralized, battered, and irrelevant operation, and the problems of urban America had largely been ignored. HOPE VI was designed to reenergize HUD and to give new life to the federal role in the American city.

Under the leadership first of the Henry Cisneros, a rising star in the Democratic Party who became embattled in a personal scandal, and then the equally high-flying Andrew Cuomo, HUD set about to fix the mistakes of the past. Initially, HOPE VI targeted existing public housing projects for rehabilitation, but it evolved quickly into something much more sweeping. Rather than merely repair what had become dilapidated, HUD decided to tear down and start again. Just like the slum clearance that characterized the urban renewal era, by the late 1990s, HUD was engaged in wholesale demolition.

HOPE VI has become best known for tearing down the infamous "projects" built in the 1950s and '60s. A full 50,000 units of project housing had been demolished by 2000 in roughly eighty cities, and HUD had slated another 46,000 to go in subsequent years. The demolition of St. Louis's Pruitt-Igoe in 1972 proved to be just the opening salvo in a campaign to erase the "vertical ghettos" from the urban landscape.

There was a certain symbolism in the fact that Chicago embraced this demolition with greatest gusto. Chicago's public housing might have actually been the worst in the nation in some measurable sense, and it certainly functioned that way in the nation's imagination. When TV producer Norman Lear created a sitcom about a struggling black family, he set it in a Chicago housing project. By the time Henry Cisneros arrived at HUD, the Chicago Housing Authority (CHA) had become so dysfunctional that he had to take it over. So when the dynamite detonated at Cabrini Green, the Robert Taylor Homes, and some of Chicago's other "crime-ridden failures," more than mere buildings came down. There was an almost Oedipal quality to the drama: what Richard Daley the Father had put up with such enthusiasm, Richard Daley the Son tore down.[26]

All told, Chicago demolished (or significantly rehabbed) about 25,000 units of its public housing stock occupied by more than 130,000 people. This time around, city and federal officials paid much more attention to the problems of displacement. In theory, the CHA could only demolish a project after guaranteeing that there was alternative affordable housing for residents being displaced. The lessons of the 1950s and '60s had been learned, though whether displacement has been handled better this time around is still a matter of some debate.

As gratifying as it might have been for city mayors to tear down high-rise projects, the goals of HOPE VI are considerably much more ambitious than that. Its objectives included:

(1) changing the physical shape of public housing; (2) reducing the concentration of poverty that had occurred in the older projects; (3) combining housing options with a range of other services, including education and job training; (4) encouraging higher standards of "personal responsibility," including in some cases a path to homeownership; (5) forming "public-private" partnerships for the re-development of these neighborhoods.[27]

To accomplish these goals, HUD fully embraced the principles of new urbanism and put them to work to remake the landscape of public housing in cities across the nation.

Having torn down the modernist version of urban renewal, HUD used new urbanism to guide what would rise from the dust. Specifically, HUD drew a set of lessons from the new urbanist agenda. They included replacing large-scale vertical buildings with smaller-scale horizontal ones, with a concomitant shift from multi-family units to single-family ones. HUD also placed a new emphasis on ownership rather than renting. Gone were the "projects" replaced by neighborhoods of homes.

At the same time, HUD moved from the brutal mid-century modernism to more traditional kinds of architecture. The goal was not to stand out from—or loom over—the existing area but to blend in with it. In a further sensitivity to the existing neighborhood fabric, HOPE VI projects engaged the streets and sidewalks, sometimes including front porches on the new houses. If Le Corbusier and Futurama informed the postwar generation of project builders, Jane Jacobs was the required reading for those at the turn of the millennium.

Moving out from the housing unit itself, HOPE VI projects tried to create viable and lively neighborhoods by returning to the small-scale commercial and retail activity that had been effectively zoned out of most new developments. HOPE VI projects have often built such spaces into their projects from the outset, attempting to lure back the grocery stores, hardware stores, restaurants, and other amenities that had been disappearing from so many distressed urban neighborhoods since the 1960s.

If the primary social struggle over housing in the postwar period had been racial—about racial segregation and open housing—then new urbanism tried to shift the grounds of that debate. Mixed income, rather than mixed race, was the goal of new urbanist projects, and HOPE VI incorporated that ethos at the very

The new urbanism meets the new public housing. The HOPE VI program of the Department of Housing and Urban Development has brought the principles of new urbanism to a new generation of public housing, such as this project in Cincinnati, photographed in 2010. *Courtesy of Torti Gallas and Partners and the Congress for the New Urbanism*

center of many of its projects. Rather than replacing vertical warehouses of poor people with rowhouses of poor people, HOPE VI insisted that projects merge subsidized and market-rate housing. The goal has been both to end the isolation of poor people that had resulted from the old projects and to bring middle-class residents, with their buying power and, presumably, their aspirational values, back to those neighborhoods.

In other words, if new urbanist towns like Seaside tried to recreate the small town of the 1920s, then HOPE VI projects tried to recreate city neighborhoods before they were torn apart by high-rises, highways, and the flight of capital. By the end of the millennium, according to *New Urban News*, HUD had allocated nearly $4 billion to new urbanist-influenced projects through the HOPE VI program. *New Urban News* counted just over two hundred such projects either under construction or in the planning phases, from the tiny half-acre project in Dallas's Uptown neighborhood to the massive, nearly 3,000-acre infill project on the site of Denver's Stapleton Airport.[28]

Those who helped craft and implement that project have reason to feel proud about the program. A 2005 study found that people involved in the program experienced significant improvements in their quality of life. Other studies have demonstrated that crime rates have dropped dramatically in HOPE VI neighborhoods, and that income levels have risen much faster in those neighborhoods than in the city as a whole, presumably as poverty has been de-concentrated and more working- and middle-class residents have moved in. [29]

Clearly, it has been difficult to achieve the mixed-income neighborhoods originally envisioned, at least in many HOPE VI projects, and they have sometimes had difficulty attracting commercial development as well. At the same time, it is hard to deny that these neighborhoods are more hospitable and safer than the projects they replaced. Nor can it be denied that HOPE VI projects, in many instances, have served to stabilize city neighborhoods. That means not only that they have helped stanch the flow of people and money out of those neighborhoods, but also that they have returned some sense of order and calm to places that once seemed out of control. That, in turn, has encouraged private developers to invest in neighborhoods they would otherwise have written off as too risky. In cities around the nation this knock-on effect has been a significant success of HOPE VI.

In that sense, HOPE VI and new urbanism more generally have contributed to what many called the urban renaissance of the 1990s and early years of the twenty-first century. After the urban nadir of the 1980s, some cities, at least, began to rebound. They cut their crime rates—sometimes with considerable controversy; they got their budgets under control after years of lurching from one fiscal crisis to another; and people stopped voting with their feet by leaving town. Chicago even posted a modest population increase between 1990 and 2000. Between 2000 and 2010, Philadelphia did the same.

Much of the redevelopment of those cities, from Portland to Philadelphia, took at least some of its inspiration from new urbanism, with its emphasis on walkability, mixed-use development, and human-scale projects. Even in automobile-centered Columbus, Ohio, new urbanism has arrived downtown. During the first decade of this century, Mayor Michael Coleman has worked tirelessly to bring people back to the desolate downtown that was created in the previous generation. A new minor-league baseball stadium and a new professional hockey arena draw suburbanites in for games and for beer. And new housing has begun to pop up in and around the center of the city. Not all parts of downtown close at 5:00 P.M. anymore.

Gated Communities: Oxymoronic or Redundant

As if by some alchemy, revived hipster neighborhoods in Brooklyn and Chicago, and new urbanist projects in Columbus and Lexington, have been matched over the last few decades by their doppelgangers on the exurban frontier: gated communities.

Putting walls around human settlement goes back to the very origins of cities and civilizations; in the twentieth century, gated (or fortified) communities were a hallmark of the cheek-by-jowl inequalities of Third World cities, whether in South Africa or Sao Paolo. In the United States, however, they are a more recent phenomenon, becoming widespread only in the early 1980s.

By the turn of the millennium, according to a Census Bureau estimate, between 7 and 8 million American households lived behind gates, roughly 6 percent of the nation's population. Such developments were more common in the Sunbelt, but could also be found on the edges of most metropolitan areas, and increasingly within cities themselves.[30] As a category, gated communities probably represented the fastest-growing sector of the real estate market, at least until the collapse of 2007.

The idea is straightforward. In one way or another, gated communities restrict access in and out, and often around a residential development. Sometimes entrance requires a card or an electronic code; other developments are staffed by private security guards who screen every car at checkpoints. And there are only a few of those checkpoints. Gated communities, like medieval castles, are walled off from the rest of their surroundings. In other words, gated communities have taken the privatization of space to its logical extreme.

Inside the gates, most of these developments are unincorporated and thus usually governed by some sort of real estate association—a homeowners' group, or a body run by the developer or property manager—rather than by any elected public body. These entities provide some services, like trash collection, street repair, landscaping, and above all security, but they can also regulate life in these places to a remarkable extent. They might limit the number of visitor automobiles, or restrict the colors permitted on the exteriors of residents' houses, or forbid drying laundry outside.

Call it civitas by legal contract rather than social contract; this trend is quite revealing. If the allure of the postwar suburbs was the personal freedom that a single-family home with a front lawn and a back yard represented, then the popularity of these gated enclaves suggests that residents do not mind having their living spaces micro-managed by a private corporation.

In retreating through the gates and behind the walls, those who live in these places have withdrawn from a larger civic space and civic life. Cosseted in these enclaves, gated communitarians seem not to participate in the governance of their developments, leaving it instead to private extra-governmental organizations. Far from creating neighborliness, gated communities provide a private, third party you can call if you object to the music coming from next door. With their limited access, security checkpoints, and the rest, they are a mélange of the high tech, postmodern, and medieval.

Research also suggests that their residents act to fight any obligation placed on them by larger political entities—towns, counties, even states. Residents in gated communities have turned out to demand property tax rebates, since they provide certain services on their own, and to oppose environmental regulation or land-use restrictions that might impinge on their own properties. Some gated communities, especially in California where the legalities are easier, have seceded altogether to form their own, freestanding municipalities. In so doing they have seceded from any sense of shared public obligation, just as they have isolated themselves physically.[31]

Behind the gates people seem prepared to give up democratic control over the places they live in exchange for the promise of safe, secure "community." The larger question that arises is whether community in this twenty-first-century incarnation will prove to be the antithesis of democracy. The proliferation of gated communities also forces us to ask questions about how we measure and value economic growth. Without question, the development of gated communities added tens, perhaps hundreds of billions, to the GDP. In regions like Phoenix and southern California, gated communities being developed were even larger parts of the local economy. They represented thousands of jobs in the construction, real estate, and related industries.

At another level, of course, if we could put a price tag on all those developments (and it is difficult to do exactly) we could quantify the "civic malaise" Robert Putnam identified in his research. The real estate agents who sell these places pitch them as "lifestyles." "At Hampton Lake," the advertising for one gated community reads, "it's all about the water. Located in Bluffton, South Carolina, Hampton Lake is the Hilton Head area's premier private lake community."[32] Lovely as that sounds, it is not all about the water. People attracted to gated communities may be looking for a variety of things, but above all else they are looking for privacy and for protection from their fears. When Marcia Newton relocated to New Orleans, her first reaction was "Oh, my God, all the crime." She moved into the almost bizarrely named "The Lakes of Chateau Estates" gated community because "it feels clean and safe."[33]

But it is not necessarily the specific fear of crime that makes gated communities attractive to many. In addition, gated communities promise the broader sense of safety that comes from carefully controlled and regulated physical space. Once inside the gates, residents know they will not encounter tourists or transients or people simply traveling from one place to another. You will not cross paths with anyone who does not belong there. And given the socioeconomic segregation of most gated communities, you run little risk of chance encounters with people who are not just like yourself. Life inside the gates, in this sense, represents exactly the opposite of city life, and it bespeaks a society where social bonds have frayed, where we simply do not trust each other and do not even want to make the attempt. What's been good for the GDP, in other words, may be terrible for the polity.

Community—despite the cozy connotations the word brings to mind—necessarily involves exclusion: we are members of the community; they are not. But at its best, the ideal of community also demands a set of mutually reinforcing commitments—to people, to places, to principles—that enable those inside one community to connect in meaningful ways with those in other communities to shape a shared future. That is, after all, one definition of democracy.

Gated communities eliminate that second part of a functioning community and reduce the first part to a set of shared amenities: a swimming pool, a golf course, some tennis courts. Membership in that community requires nothing more than the purchase of real estate and the paying of annual fees. Civic life in these places, like so much else in the American economy during the last generation, has been outsourced or eliminated altogether.

So let's try a thought experiment: juxtapose in your head images of two kinds of residential landscapes. For the first, picture a reviving urban neighborhood in Denver or Chicago or Philadelphia or Brooklyn, and set it next to an image of any of the gated communities that have developed in places like Orange County, California, or around Naples, Florida. Now imagine the political landscape as it has changed since the 1980s: increasingly shrill and bitter and divided. It has seen an almost unrelenting attack not merely on specific programs or policies but also on the very notion that the government has any role to play in promoting the general welfare, except as it enhances private wealth.

Now put those two images next to each other. Not that they correspond in a strictly geographical sense, though there is a fair degree of overlap. In fact, the Republicans who crafted and approved their 2012 presidential campaign platform did not mention cities, much less their health and well-being, even once in a document that ran to 31,000 words. This led writer Kevin Baker to remark that the GOP, through a combination of its revived race-baiting and its anti-government hysteria, had well and thoroughly become the anti-urban party.[34]

More than that, those two images resemble each other—how the physical environment mirrors the political discourse, and vice versa. There is no strict causal connection—architecture is not destiny, after all. But a political rhetoric that plays on people's fears of others, on their selfishness toward those on the losing end of our economic system, and on a more diffuse anger at a changing world certainly rings inside the physical environments that allow us to retreat into our own paranoias, that shields us from our public obligations as citizens, and where everything is controlled for us because we pay for the pleasure.

These two landscapes, one political and one physical, are the twin legacies of the anti-urban impulse as it has shaped American life during the twentieth century.

URBANISM AS A WAY OF LIFE

DATELINE: Cincinnati, 1828. Frances Trollope was plagued by the pigs. Having come to the United States from England with her family, Trollope had landed in Cincinnati by 1828. Cincinnati was the largest city west of the Appalachians, gateway to the vast American interior, a bustling port on the Ohio River, linking the Midwest with the great watery spine of the Mississippi.

By the time Trollope arrived, Cincinnati was home to roughly 25,000 people and to an uncountable number of pigs. The pigs were only temporary residents, of course, because Cincinnati was the place they came to be slaughtered and processed. Trollope could not seem to escape them or the awful (offal?) reminders of them. "Our walks were," she complained, "curtailed in several directions by my old Cincinnati enemies, the pigs; immense droves of them were continually arriving from the country by the road that led to most of our favourite walks." They were inescapable, so much so that "the brook we had to cross, at its foot, [was] red with the stream from a pig slaughter-house...our feet...literally got entangled in pigs' tails and jaw-bones." They did not call it "Porkopolis" for nothing.

If Trollope could find no respite from the hogs out in the countryside surrounding the city, she had no better luck at home. Her "cottage" came equipped with "an ample piazza" which made "a delightful sitting-room." One day, however, she "perceived the symptoms of building in a field" nearby her home. When she rushed over to find out what was under construction, she was told, "Tis to be a slaughter-house for hogs." Incredulous, Trollope explained that there were "several gentlemen's houses in the neighborhood," and surely a hog butchery in the midst of them would be a "nuisance."

" 'No, no,' " was the reply; 'that may do very well for your tyrannical coun-try, where a rich man's nose is more thought of than a poor man's mouth; but hogs be profitable produce here, and we be too free for such a law as that, I guess.' "[1]

In 1828, in the burgeoning Cincinnati, Mrs. Trollope and this unnamed hog butcher dramatized a central tension in American life and the one that has played out most acutely in the city: freedom, in the form of putting an abattoir in the middle of an existing residential neighborhood and perceived tyranny, in the form of trying to restrain what a man might do to earn a living, in the name of the common good. That tension, between the desire of free individuals to pur-sue happiness in any way they choose and the need for communities to create frameworks, rules, and expectations to facilitate some sense of social cohesion and commonweal, stands at the center of the way Americans have reacted to our cities. It defines anti-urbanism.

Cities are necessarily public affairs. As more and more people come to live in greater density—and in closer quarters with people different from themselves—they discover that simply relying on the bonds of family or even of community does not suffice to make the complicated urban organism work. Achieving a greater measure of common good and aspiring to a greater sense of shared pur-pose can only come through the development of a civic, public sphere. Americans reacted against the urban form because of its density and heterogeneity, and against that sense of public that grows in urban soil.

The anti-urban impulse, deeply rooted in American life, has shaped the nation's two landscapes that this book has traversed. One is the physical shape of the city, with its density of people and activity; the other is political, defined as the deep-seated American suspicion of government as an agent of the collec-tive good. Both landscapes allow people to indulge in fantasies about individual autonomy and personal freedom, which ignore the costs associated with them and the larger obligations we all have as members of a society.

Good planning by itself cannot solve all of our problems, urban or political. Bad planning, however, can make many of those problems worse. Design is not destiny, contrary to what many have believed, and the relationship between phys-ical space and social relationships is a complicated, mutually reinforcing dance. Clearly, better buildings and better spaces will not make a better society by them-selves, without a host of other social reforms—some of those Progressive-era reformers and their successors were wrong about that. At the same time, the spaces we live in, work in, travel through, and otherwise occupy each week do structure our social interactions in all kinds of ways. A more humane physical environment will not in itself create a more humane society; but it is probably fair to say that we will not solve any of our problems without better spaces.

We surely need a new commitment to our cities, and some of that must take the form of policy. Rather than thinking strictly of a national "urban policy," we should start by undoing all of our "anti-urban" policies that have subsidized urban decentralization to such an extent that we have taken it to be inevitable. As the economist Edward Glaeser points out quite rightly, our housing and transportation policies seem "almost intentionally designed to hurt the cities."[2] Removing those subsidies would go a long way toward leveling the playing field and toward restoring the competitive advantage cities naturally enjoy.

Some of these policies are federal, like the subsidies we have provided to suburban real estate development and to the highways that make life in those places possible. Others are more local, like zoning codes that force separate uses and functions and mandate extravagant amounts of parking. The results of these kinds of policies are easy to see. In fact, the real genius of these private paradises may be how they conceal all the ways they have been propped up by the rest of us. In economics-speak, these are called "negative externalities." All the costs that one person runs up that get paid for by the rest of us. At the turn of the millennium, for example, journalist Jane Holtz Kay calculated that American drivers paid less than half of the real cost of driving.[3] Other costs are trickier to put a price tag on, such as the productivity lost because of car commuting, or the obesity caused by our suburban sedentariness, or the toxic run-off into our water from tens of thousands of chemically treated suburban lawns. Hard perhaps to figure with real precision, but they cost us all just the same.

Most urgently, we will need policies to deal with the costs of poverty. More than anything else, our cities have become home to a disproportionate number of our poor citizens. That much is obvious, whether you look from the high elevation of statistics and demographics or walk the streets of urban neighborhoods. That has always been the case, as Jacob Riis and Jane Addams well knew. Two things have changed since World War II, however. First, cities no longer provide the same ladders of economic opportunity for those at the bottom. As a consequence, too many of yesterday's urban poor will be tomorrow's urban poor as well. Second, the decentralization of urban populations has enabled many of us to escape and ignore the crisis of urban poverty. And as a consequence of that, for at least a generation, poverty has not been high on our national agenda, and cities have been left to deal with it more or less on their own. In a bitter irony, poverty turns out to be quite expensive—measured in lost productivity, in health-care costs, in educational costs, in the costs of crime, and a dozen other ways.

The failure to embrace the urban nature of American civilization has been a failure of imagination, rather than of policy. Edmund Bacon, the head of Philadelphia's Planning Commission in the middle years of the twentieth century, complained that "in the United States we are almost devoid of a generally accepted, constructive, tangible urban image." He wrote that in 1960, but it still rings true today.

Policies are merely tools we use to create the kind of society we want to inhabit. The larger question lies in the realm of national culture and identity. If we began to value the advantages of urban life and celebrate the possibilities that only come in the city, we would demand policies to foster it. If we could develop that "urban image," I have every confidence that we could craft policy to make it a reality.

Let me put that in the obverse: those who celebrate the suburbs see them as delivering the product people want. Subdivisions, in their thinking, sprout to satisfy rational economic actors operating in a free market. As we have already discussed, and others have explored exhaustively, the market at work here has hardly been "free." Postwar suburbia offered a burgeoning population a housing and neighborhood "choice" in the way that Henry Ford once offered people a choice in cars: you can live anywhere you want as long as it is in a subdivision, especially if you want to take advantage of FHA-subsidized mortgages. But as we have also discussed, the decentralization of central cities that the suburbs achieved was the product of our anti-urban impulse in the first place. As Bacon went on to write: "It can safely be said that the overwhelming majority of the American people operate on the basis of the suburban way of life as the only acceptable goal for all right-minded people." [4] In that sense, our policies have indeed reflected our image of ourselves.

Creating what Bacon called an urban image, a cultural ethos in which we enjoy the fruits of an urban civilization while taking collective responsibility for its care and maintenance, is crucial if we want to live in a more fulfilling physical landscape and if we want a more effective political environment.

We might start with recognizing that good urbanism fosters a more sustainable environment. Suburbia requires that individuals consume resources—energy, water, and land—at a rate that would have embarrassed Lorenzo di Medici. In some narrow economic sense, that consumption might be "good" for the gross domestic product, but it is hardly good in any larger sense, nor can it be sustained. The "acceleration of sprawl," concluded one report on the future of California in 1995,

> has surfaced enormous social, environmental, and economic costs, which until now have been hidden, ignored, or quietly borne by society. The burden of these costs is becoming very clear. Businesses suffer from higher costs, a loss in worker productivity, and underutilized investments in older communities....
> We can no longer afford the luxury of sprawl. [5]

The author of this report was not the Sierra Club, but Bank of America. Bank of America has made enormous profits selling the mortgages of suburban sprawl, and yet even it has concluded that we simply cannot afford our suburban landscape.

Cities—and by that I mean places of human density, diversity, and centralization, whether as big as New York or as small, say, as Asheville, North Carolina—turn out to be more efficient environmentally, as a number of economists have begun to demonstrate. They permit those who live and work in them to burn less energy and occupy less space. In so doing, urban patterns of living and working do a better job preserving open spaces and locally based agricultural economies than the sprawl which has dominated our ideas about development and growth for half a century. If New York City were a separate state, it would rank ninth in population and fifty-first in per-capita energy consumption. If Americans all lived at the density of Brooklyn residents, all 300 million of us would fit into a space the size of New Hampshire, leaving the rest of the country empty. Urban living, almost counter-intuitively, would help us save farmland and green space.

That more efficient use of resources is surely connected to the fact that cities are economically more efficient, too. Workers are more productive in cities, and they are more innovative and entrepreneurial as well. In part, that may result from the infrastructures that exist in cities, whether financial, intellectual, or cultural. Just as important, cities put people in closer proximity to each other which, in turn, facilitates economic activity and creative innovation. In an information age and a knowledge economy, cities generate new ideas and new networks. Jane Jacobs, having discredited the mid-century planners for their misunderstanding of how cities worked, devoted a later volume to the economic centrality of cities. She borrowed the title from none other than Adam Smith, and called the book *Cities and the Wealth of Nations*.

Because of the social and cultural environments they foster—that "meeting place" function I discussed at the outset of this book—cities attract the aspirational and the entrepreneurial. They are and always have been the places where things happen. The great architect Louis Kahn captured this wonderfully when he said "A city is a place of availabilities. It is the place where a small boy, as he walks through it, may see something that will tell him what he wants to do his whole life." Very few teenagers, I suspect, have found those "availabilities" while cruising the mall.[6]

Kahn's own story reminds us of the role cities play in fostering a democratic culture in our society. Kahn was born in Estonia and named Itze-Leib Schmuilowsky. He came with his family to Philadelphia in 1906, like so many millions of immigrants who came to American cities in the years surrounding 1900. They turned those cities into perhaps the most heterogeneous, polyglot, and culturally diverse places on the planet. They also recreated the meaning of the American experiment and the nature of American democracy.

The American promise was not always fulfilled, and certainly not without struggle and adversity. Still, figuring out how to negotiate that diversity stands as a major function of our cities, and as one of their important triumphs. William Whyte recognized as much in 1958 when he noted: "Despite the violence in many of its streets, many couples maintain that the city can be a *better* place to raise children than suburbia.... [I]t exposes children to all kinds of people, colored and white, old and young, rich and poor."[7] In a "globalized" twenty-first century, the role cities play in teaching children—all of us, really—how to get along with each other has become even more necessary. The cities of the early twentieth century were where Randolph Bourne first saw the virtues of a "trans-national" America, and in the 100 years since those virtues have only become more important.

My own sense is that the cities that will do well in the next generation have two things in common. First, they have a strong institutional foundation upon which to build a postindustrial economy, particularly the "meds and eds" economy. Second, they have not lost their essential "cityness"—they make room for new kinds of people, who come together in new kinds of ways, and they foster a sense of civic identity that transcends the boundaries of race or class or ethnicity or religion. Particularly, cities that have attracted new emigrants from Asia, Africa, Central and South America, and the Caribbean seem to be doing better than those cities that have not. That should come as no real surprise. They have transformed their new urban homes no less than those immigrants who arrived here at the turn of the twentieth century.

There may be some evidence that some Americans are developing that "urban image" Ed Bacon found missing in our culture. The late-twentieth-century "urban renaissance" is surely tentative and, all things considered, small, and it is far too early to predict whether it will last. But the baby boomers, now empty-nesters, who want to give up their driving commute and enjoy the cultural life of cities, and the 30-somethings who are feeding any number of creative urban endeavors, are clearly onto something. And the local food mavens who shop the farmers markets of New York and Philadelphia thereby supporting local farmers are finally linking city and country in mutually supportive ways.

Likewise, there are intriguing signs that the antagonism between city and suburb is mellowing at least a bit. As more and more Americans come to reside in metropolitan regions surrounding the central cities, many are beginning to understand that the futures of both city and region are fundamentally interconnected. Air and water quality, economic development, transportation networks—all of these and more are problems that crisscross the political boundaries that separate cities from suburbs. Metropolitan regions that succeed in the coming century will be those that recognize this shared destiny and develop a political agenda to foster it. As the Roanoke County Commissioners we met at the beginning of this book are attempting to do.

At the same time, the urban renaissance many have touted has been uneven, at best. The South Bronx may have been transformed from an urban wasteland into an urban oasis during the past twenty years, but Detroit continues to hemorrhage people and money. So does St. Louis. And Dayton. And Youngstown. For every revived neighborhood in Chicago or Philadelphia, there is another one that remains desperately poor and hopeless. That 2005 study that found residents of HOPE VI projects to have a higher quality of life also noted that the employment situation for these people had not improved, which only underscores a central problem reformers have been wrestling since the Progressive era: better housing alone cannot solve the larger array of socioeconomic problems faced by people at the bottom of the economic pyramid. The creative class economy chased by many cities, and with some success, does not necessarily construct the same ladder of economic opportunities that the older industrial economy did.

I do not want to pretend that cities have solved all of our socioeconomic divides. But because of their inherently public nature, expressed through public and quasi-public spaces, they provide what sociologist Eli Anderson has called "cosmopolitan canopies." Those canopies—parks, markets, shopping districts, among others—furnish the space for different kinds of people to come together. By allowing people to interact in civil or even friendly ways, these canopies help us "work toward a more cosmopolitan appreciation of difference.... The canopy," he concludes, "can thus be a profoundly humanizing experience."[8]

As it happens, Eli Anderson and I share an affection for one such cosmopolitan canopy: the Reading Terminal Market in Philadelphia. At lunch time, the Reading Terminal is packed with a remarkable cross-section of our urban diversity. Black, white, Asian, Hispanic, young and old, professionals and working class—standing on line together, sharing tables, making small talk. All those people buy their food from merchants whose products represent some of the city's rich diversity: German sausages, Italian pastries, African American soul food—take your pick. I have always found it a deliciously humanizing experience.

Those lessons in civility and diversity aren't simply feel-good exercises, either. They are essential for a functioning democracy. One of the real strains on our political system now is that, while Americans are mobile, or rootless, or disconnected (whichever you prefer), our political system is still structured geographically. We elect our representatives based on geographic boundaries—at all levels, save for the presidency. So it is worth asking: what happens to that system when fewer and fewer Americans feel any connection to those specific places? Does the

Lunchtime at the Reading Terminal Market in Philadelphia. Cities provide the social and physical opportunities for different kinds of people to mix and interact, though few of these "cosmopolitan canopies" promise this much good food. *Courtesy of Reading Terminal Market Corporation*

quality of our democratic engagement suffer because many of us have no particular investment in where we live, or, conversely, if so many of those places are not worthy of our investment?

Whyte reminds us of another important way cities function in a democratic society. The suburbanized landscape was created as a racially segregated place, and despite some shifting demographics, it remains largely so today. But suburbia has been just as rigorously graded by class as well, though this has not received the same attention. Since the vast majority of suburban residential developments are a kind of architectural monoculture with a narrow range of housing options, most of the people who live in them come from the same income group. The nearby retail centers, in turn, cater to whichever income groups live in the vicinity. Walmart in certain area shopping centers, Bergdorf's at other malls.

Cities, on the other hand, are home to a more representative cross-section of races and classes than most suburban areas. As a consequence, big city mayors and city councilors must appeal to a much wider range of voters than any suburban legislator, and must work to balance a much wider range of interests. That kind of compromise and pragmatism is the very essence of the democratic process. By contrast, in 1960 MIT economist Robert Wood wrote that "an American suburbanite feels politically safe only when his government resembles a fraternal order peopled by his brothers or when no government is involved in his affairs at all." Surely it is more than a coincidence that Newt Gingrich and Bob Barr, and their angry, intransigent brand of conservative politics, came out of the racially exclusive and affluent suburbs of Atlanta.[9]

I've borrowed the title of this afterword from an essay written by Chicago School sociologist Louis Wirth, published in 1938. In it, Wirth tried to give some sociological precision to the meaning of "urbanism." That definition included, quite imprecisely: size (big), density (denser than the surrounding countryside), and heterogeneity (also more so than the surrounding areas). But Wirth also noted that part of the urban way of life meant a set of human interactions that were impersonal, rather than intimate. [10]

Many of us, I suspect, would bristle at that. The American desire for "community" which we have explored throughout this book is a desire for those intimate connections that we feel have withered or disappeared altogether. *Community* is surely one of the most overused and overburdened words in our public discussions. As Eric Hobsbawm has archly and astutely put it, by the end of the twentieth century, the word *community* was "used more indiscriminately and emptily" even while "communities in the sociological sense [had become] hard to find in real life."[11] Never have there been so many "communities"; never have Americans ached so much to belong to a real one. As we have seen, many Americans have believed that such community was impossible to find in the city. It can be, of course, and I know this from my own lucky experiences. Still, the widespread belief that city and community are antithetical may be the largest failing of our urban vision.[12]

Wirth, however, tried to describe, not to pass judgment, when he saw those impersonal relationships. One positive consequence of them, he noted, was a breakdown in traditional hierarchies and a realization that individuals could better pursue their interests as part of larger groups. In other words, those impersonal relationships, those affinities expressed through institutions and organizations, are necessary to create the "public" and to separate it from the "private."

The very notion of a democratic "public" grew up in the urban centers of the eighteenth century. It has eroded across the twentieth century as we have let our cities fall into dysfunction. If we want a democracy that works more effectively to define and then address our common good, then we need to recognize the ways in which cities function to foster that.[13] Frederic Howe was right a century ago. Our cities really are our best hope for democracy. So here's a variation on the prediction made by Josiah Strong with which I began this book: the problem of the twenty-first century will be how we re-urbanize, of how we fix the mistakes of our anti-urban twentieth century.

NOTES

INTRODUCTION

1. See a series of newspaper stories, op-eds, and letters to the editor in the *Roanoke Times*, July 2011. This was reported nationally in the *New York Times* by Leslie Kaufman and Kate Zernike, "Activists Fight Green Projects, Seeing U.N. Plot," February 4, 2012. The U.N. plot refers to "Agenda 21," a nonbinding resolution approved by the U.N. in 1992 that calls for more sustainable development around the world.

2. Max Weber, "The Nature of the City," in Richard Sennett, ed., *Classic Essays on the Culture of Cities* (New York: Meredith, 1969), pp. 23–46. The essay originally appeared in Weber's book *The City*

3. Langston Hughes, "City," in Arnold Rampersad, ed., *The Collected Poems of Langston Hughes* (New York: Vintage Classics, 1995), p. 602.

4. Margaret Mead, *Some Personal Views* (New York: Angus and Robertson, 1979), p. 118.

5. The most influential discussion of the public sphere today comes from the work of German philosopher Jurgen Habermas, and especially his book *The Structural Transformation of the Public Sphere*. The American philosopher John Dewey also wrestled with many of the same questions in his book *The Public and Its Problems* (New York: Henry Holt, 1927).

6. This is a point explored by Richard Sennett in his still-provocative book *The Fall of Public Man* (New York: Knopf, 1977). See esp. part I and ch. 13.

7. Lisa McGirr's important study of the rise of the New Right focuses on Orange County, California, perhaps the archetypical example of postwar suburbia. See Lisa McGirr, *Suburban Warriors: The Origins of the New American Right* (Princeton, NJ: Princeton University Press, 2001).

8. Americans have been more enthusiastic about creating utopian experiments than any other people in the world. These experiments, religious or secular, were intended to be places apart. Whether the Owenites or the Shakers in the early nineteenth

century, or the Amish who still farm in Pennsylvania, Ohio, and Iowa, these were communities of retreat, literally and figuratively—places separate and safe from the ills of the rest of American society. Notice, however, that when Americans have imagined utopia, their vision is always rural. It is surely the case that American utopias came from many of the same anti-urban impulses that will concern us here, but those utopias have been well studied and I won't spend too much time with them in this book. See, for example, Robert Fogarty; and Timothy Miller, *The Quest for Utopia in Twentieth-Century America, 1900-1960* (Syracuse, NY: Syracuse University Press, 1998). Fogarty has also edited the *Dictionary of American Communal and Utopian History* (Westport, CT: Greenwood, 1980). Fogarty, *All Things New: American Communes and Utopian Movements, 1860-1914* (Chicago: University of Chicago Press, 1990).

9. There is a rich historical literature about both, including Arnold Hirsch and Raymond Mohl, eds., *Urban Policy in Twentieth-Century America* (New Brunswick, NJ: Rutgers University Press, 1993).

10. Thomas Bender's book *Community and Social Change in America* (Baltimore: Johns Hopkins University Press, 1978) remains perhaps the best consideration of the tension between these two things and about the meaning of community in American life.

11. Josiah Strong, *The Twentieth Century City* (New York: Baker and Taylor, 1898), p. 53.

CHAPTER I

1. Much has been written about the American attitude toward government, especially in the founding era. But the best survey of this attitude across a broad sweep of the nation's history is Gary Wills, *A Necessary Evil: A History of American Distrust of Government* (New York: Simon & Schuster, 1999).

2. Thomas Jefferson, *Notes on the State of Virginia* (Boston: Wells and Lilly, 1829), p. 173. This quote comes in response to Query XIX, Manufactures.

3. Cited in Peter Katz, *The New Urbanism: Toward an Architecture of Community* (New York: McGraw-Hill, 1994), p. xxxv. The remaining 81 percent of Americans broke down this way: 34 percent wanted to live in a small town; 24 percent in a suburb; 22 percent imagined they would be happiest on a farm. My thanks to Tracey Sugar of the Gallup organization, who provided me with data from these surveys going back to 1966.

4. My colleague Angela Brintlinger reminds me that Peter the Great built his capital on a swamp as well. St. Petersburg did grow into a magnificent city much faster than Washington, D.C., did, but only after thousands of people died during its construction. At least at the turn of the eighteenth century, Peter could justify needing access to the sea; Americans had ports available in New York, Philadelphia, and Baltimore.

5. For a nice summary of the history of redistricting, see David Stebenne, "Re-Mapping American Politics," in "Origins: Current Events in Historical Perspective," http://origins.osu.edu/article/re-mapping-american-politics-redistricting-revolution-fifty-years-later.

6. Julian Ralph, "Colorado and Its Capital," *Harper's New Monthly Magazine* 86 (1893): 935–48.

7. Walt Whitman, *Song of Myself* (Mineola, NY: Dover, 2001), p. 43.

8. Morton and Lucia White, *The Intellectual versus the City* (Cambridge, MA: Harvard University Press and MIT Press by arrangement with Mentor, 1962). As they wrote in the book's introductory chapter: "the growing city became the bête noir of our most distinguished intellectuals rather than their favorite," p. 14.

9. Quoted in Philip Gura, *American Transcendentalism* (New York: Hill and Wang, 2007), p. 201.

10. Henry Adams, *The Education of Henry Adams* (Cambridge, MA: Riverside Press, 1918); see chs. 1 & 2.

11. Josiah Strong, *Our Country: Its Possible Future and Its Present Crisis* (New York: Baker & Taylor, 1885), pp. 179–80.

12. Quoted in Richard Hofstadter et al., *The United States*, 4th ed. (Englewood Cliffs, NJ: Prentice-Hall, 1976), p. 397.

13. This oft-reproduced speech can be found in Daniel Boorstin, ed., *An American Primer*, vol. 2 (Chicago: University of Chicago Press, 1966).

14. My gloss on populism as essentially nostalgic disagrees with some of the more recent work on the phenomenon, including that of Charles Postel, *The Populist Vision* (New York: Oxford University Press, 2007).

15. Frederick Jackson Turner, "The Significance of the Frontier in American History" (Ann Arbor, MI: University Microfilms, 1966), p. 217.

16. John Higham, "The Divided Legacy of Frederick Jackson Turner," in John Higham, *Writing American History: Essays on Modern Scholarship* (Bloomington: Indiana University Press, 1970), p. 121.

17. I have borrowed this phrase from Raymond Williams in his book *The Country and the City*.

18. Andrew Cayton and Susan Gray, "The Story of the Midwest: An Introduction," in Andrew Cayton and Susan Gray, eds., *The American Midwest: Essays in Regional History* (Bloomington: Indiana University Press, 2001), p. 11. For more on Turner, see John Mack Faragher, *Rereading Frederick Jackson Turner* (New York: Henry Holt, 1994); Allan Bogue, *Frederick Jackson Turner: Strange Roads Going Down* (Norman: University of Oklahoma Press, 1998); James Bennett, *Frederick Jackson Turner* (Boston: Twayne, 1975).

19. Josiah Royce, *The Hope of the Great Community* (New York: Macmillan, 1916), p. 43.

20. "Words of Professor Royce," in *Papers in Honor of Josiah Royce* (New York: Longmans, Green, 1916), p. 282.

21. Royce, *Hope of the Great Community*, pp. 39, 42, 50.

22. Josiah Royce, *The Feud of Oakfield Creek: A Novel of California Life* (Boston and New York: Houghton Mifflin, 1887), pp. 20–21.

23. Royce, *Hope of the Great Community*, p. 37.

24. Royce, "Words of Professor Royce," in *Papers in Honor of Josiah Royce*, pp. 279, 282.

CHAPTER 2

1. Dana White makes a similar point in *The Urbanists, 1865-1915* (New York: Greenwood, 1989), p. 116.

2. Frank T. Carlton, "Urban and Rural Life," *Popular Science Monthly* 68 (1906): 255.

3. Carlton, "Urban and Rural Life," p. 255; "The Commission on Country Life," *World's Work* 17 (1908): 10861.

4. See John Higham, "The Reorientation of American Culture in the 1890s," in *Writing American History: Essays on Modern Scholarship* (Bloomington, IN: Indiana University Press, 1970), p. 89.

5. Figures from Max Page, *The Creative Destruction of Manhattan, 1900-1940* (Chicago: University of Chicago Press, 2000), pp. 31–32.

6. "The Overcrowded City," *Outlook*, 97 (1911): 626–27.

7. Marsh's biography comes from a Cornell University Library website: www.library. cornell.edu/Reps/DOCS/marsheco.htm, accessed May 2011.

8. Benjamin Clarke Marsh, *An Introduction to City Planning: Democracy's Challenge to the American City* (New York: B. C. Marsh, 1909), p. 11.

9. "Report of the New York Congestion Commission," *Survey* 25 (1911): 977–79.

10. "The Municipal Problem: The Ideal City," *Outlook* 93 (1909): 141.

11. "Overcrowding Must Stop," Editorial, *Survey* 25 (1911): 989–90.

12. Daniel T. Rodgers, *Atlantic Crossings: Social Politics in a Progressive Age* (Cambridge, MA: Belknap, 1998), p. 172.

13. Benjamin Clarke Marsh, "City Planning in Justice to the Working Population," *Charities* 19 (1908): 1514; Marsh, *Introduction to City Planning; Washington Post*, May 22, 1909.

14. See Rodgers, *Atlantic Crossings*, p. 152; Marsh, *Introduction to City Planning*, p. 39. On the use of government power in European and American cities, see Andrew Lees, *Cities Perceived: Urban Society and American Thought, 1820-1940* (New York: Columbia University Press, 1985), p. 255.

15. See Rodgers, *Atlantic Crossings*, p. 169, for a discussion of this episode. Rodgers also thoroughly traces this transatlantic exchange of city planning ideas.

16. Rodgers, *Atlantic Crossings*, pp. 186–96.

17. Marsh, *Introduction to City Planning*, p. 39.
18. Frederic Howe, *The City: The Hope of Democracy* (New York: Scribner's, 1913), p. 287; Marsh, *Introduction to City Planning*.
19. *Washington Post*, May 22, 1909.
20. Marsh, *Introduction to City Planning*, p. 39.
21. "Settlers in the City Wilderness," *Atlantic Monthly* 77 (1896): 118.
22. Agnes Sinclair Holbrook, "Map Notes and Comments," in *Hull House Maps and Papers* (New York: Thomas Y. Crowell, 1895), pp. 11–12.
23. Holbrook, "Map Notes and Comments," p. 11.
24. Holbrook, "Map Notes and Comments," pp. 5–6.
25. Jane Addams to Richard Ely, October 31, 1894, Jane Addams letters, Special Collections, Richard Daley Library, University of Illinois, Chicago. Holbrook, "Map Notes and Comments," p. 13.
26. Holbrook, "Map Notes and Comments," p. 13.
27. Robert A. Woods and Albert J. Kennedy, *The Settlement Horizon: A National Estimate* (New York: Russell Sage, 1922), pp. 305–306.
28. This episode is recounted in Thomas S. Hines, *Burnham of Chicago: Architect and Planner* (New York: Oxford University Press, 1974), pp. 324–25.
29. Hines, *Burnham of Chicago*, p. 331.
30. See Victoria Bissell Brown, *The Education of Jane Addams* (Philadelphia: University of Pennsylvania Press, 2004), pp. 275, 279.
31. Quoted in Hines, *Burnham of Chicago*, pp. 343–44.
32. Quoted in Charles Moore, *Daniel H. Burnham: Architect Planner of Cities* (Boston: Houghton Mifflin, 1921), 2: 102.
33. Quoted in White, *The Urbanists*, p. 142.
34. Quoted in Mel Scott, *American City Planning Since 1890* (Berkeley: University of California Press, 1969), p. 108.
35. Quoted in Moore, *Daniel H. Burnham*, 2: 102.
36. See Carl Smith, *The Plan of Chicago: Daniel Burnham and the Remaking of the American City* (Chicago: University of Chicago Press, 2006), pp. 45–47; see also Robert Hunter, *The Tenement Conditions in Chicago* (Chicago: City Homes Association, 1901).
37. See Scott, *American City Planning*, p. 108.
38. Scott, *American City Planning*, p. 99.
39. J. Horace McFarland, "The Growth of City Planning in the United States," *Charities* 19 (1908), p. 1523.
40. See Stephen Crane, *George's Mother* (New York: E. Arnold, 1896); Jacob Riis, *How the Other Half Lives* (1890); Upton Sinclair, *The Jungle* (New York: Grosset & Dunlap, 1906).
41. Robert A. Woods, ed., *The City Wilderness: A Settlement Study* (New York: Arno Press, 1970), p. 1 [first published, Boston: Houghton Mifflin, 1898].

42. "Settlers in the City Wilderness," pp. 118–23.

43. Bacon's quote from the *Oxford English Dictionary Compact Edition* 1979 reprint. The quote comes from the 5th definition of the word.

44. Robert Woods, "The Neighborhood in Social Reconstruction," *American Journal of Sociology* 19 (1914): 586.

45. For more on the role of the "small community" in the thinking of Progressive intellectuals, see Jean B. Quandt, *From Small Town to the Great Community: The Social Thought of Progressive Intellectuals* (New Brunswick, NJ: Rutgers University Press, 1970).

46. Woods, "Neighborhood in Social Reconstruction," pp. 577–91.

47. Woods, "Neighborhood in Social Reconstruction," p. 579; Walter Laidlaw, "The Church and the City Community," *American Journal of Sociology* 16 (1911): 578–79.

48. Woods, "Neighborhood in Social Reconstruction," p. 579.

49. For examples of Perry's ideas, see Clarence Perry, *The Rebuilding of Blighted Areas: A Study of the Neighborhood Unit in Replanning and Plot Assemblage* (New York: Regional Planning Association, 1933); and "City Planning for Neighborhood Life," *Social Forces* 8 (1929): 98–100. For more on the history of this idea, see Donald Leslie Johnson, "The Origin of the Neighborhood Unit," *Planning Perspectives* 17 (2002): 227–45.

50. I have taken all these quotes from Robert Woods, "Neighborhood in Social Reconstruction," pp. 577–91.

51. Robert Park, "The City as a Social Laboratory," in T. V. Smith and Leonard D. White, eds., *Chicago: An Experiment in Social Science Research* (Chicago: University of Chicago Press, 1929), p. 1.

52. For a further discussion of this, see Fred H. Matthews, *Quest for an American Sociology: Robert E. Park and the Chicago School* (Montreal: McGill-Queen's University Press, 1977), p. 120. See also Sudhir Venkatesh, "Chicago's Pragmatic Planners: American Sociology and the Myth of Community," *Social Science History* 25 (2001): 277.

53. Don Martindale, "Prefatory Remarks: The Theory of the City," in Max Weber, *The City*, ed. and trans. by Don Martindale (New York: The Free Press; London: Collier, 1968), p. 23.

54. Robert Park, Ernest Burgess, and Roderick McKenzie, *The City* (Chicago: University of Chicago Press, 1925), p. 1.

55. Park, "City as Social Laboratory," p. 1.

56. In a caustic aside about the ongoing influence of the ecological model, Martindale pointed out that if the city had changed as little as the interpretations of it, all its problems should have been solved already. See Don Martindale, "Prefatory Remarks: The Theory of the City," p. 26.

57. Park quote appears in Venkatesh, "Chicago's Pragmatic Planners," p. 283.

58. For more on this, see Venkatesh, "Chicago's Pragmatic Planners," pp. 276–98.

59. Josiah Strong, *Our Country: Its Possible Future and Its Present Crisis* (New York: Baker & Taylor, 1885), p. 189; the Bryce reference is from Weber, *The City*, p. 12.

60. A number of historians have written about this phenomenon and have pointed to the irony of trying to fix urban problems in ways that were anti-democratic. Daniel Rodgers, for example, points out that "American municipal progressives rarely admitted that the broad range of services they admired in European cities might have been dependent on the European city elites' success in staving off formal democracy so long." Rodgers, *Atlantic Crossings,* p. 158. More recently, see also Jackson Lears, *The Rebirth of a Nation: The Making of Modern America, 1877–1920* (New York: HarperCollins, 2009), p. 199. There was also no end of books published at the time preaching the gospel of Progressive municipal reform. See Richard Ely, *The Coming City* (New York: Thomas Y. Crowell, 1902), and Morris Llewellyn Cooke, *Our Cites Awake: Notes on Municipal Activities and Administration* (Garden City, NY: Doubleday, 1918), for examples.

61. "The City and the Citizen," *Outlook* 74 (1903): 109–111.

62. Charles Hatch Sears, *The Redemption of the City* (Philadelphia: Griffith & Rowland, 1911), pp. 19–23.

63. Howe, *The City*, pp. 7, 43; Frederic C. Howe, *The British City: The Beginnings of Democracy* (New York: Charles Scribner's, 1907), p. 362.

64. Frederic Howe, "In Defense of the American City," *Scribner's Magazine* 51 (1912):484–85.

65. Howe, *The City*, p. 164.

66. Howe, *The City*, p. 7.

67. Howe, *The British City*, pp. 362–63.

68. Park, quoted in Maurice Stein, *The Eclipse of Community* (New York: Harper & Row, 1960), p. 26.

69. Addams, quoted in Lewis Feuer, "John Dewey and the Back to the People Movement in America," *Journal of the History of Ideas* 20 (1959): 546; for more about the relationship of ideas between Park and the settlement houses, see Park Dixon Goist, "City and 'Community': The Urban Theory of Robert Park," *American Quarterly* 23 (1971): 58; Jane Addams, "The Subjective Necessity of Social Settlements," which appears as a chapter in her *Twenty Years at Hull House* (Boston: Bedford/St. Martin, 1999).

70. Laura E. Baker has examined the way the promotion of Burnham's plan was built around the idea of civic loyalty. See Laura E. Baker, "Civic Ideals, Mass Culture, and the Public: Reconsidering the 1909 *Plan of Chicago*," *Journal of Urban History* 36 (2010): 747–70. Merriam quote from Baker, "Civic Ideals," p. 753.

71. Josiah Royce, *The Philosophy of Loyalty* (New York: Macmillan, 1924), pp. 229–30.

72. Royce, *Philosophy of Loyalty,* pp. 211–48, and Josiah Royce, "Provincialism," *Putnam's Magazine* 7 (1909): 232–40.

73. See Mary Jo Deegan, *Jane Addams and the Men of the Chicago School, 1892-1918* (New Brunswick, NJ: Transaction, 1988), p. 253. See Royce's celebration of provincialism as being part of the anti-urban intellectual tradition, in Morton and Lucia White, *The Intellectual Versus the City* (Cambridge, MA: Harvard University Press, 1962), pp. 181–85. I don't disagree, but I think Royce can be read in a more expansive way. The case can be made that at least some of the positive virtues Royce called for could be found in the city, and that he hoped they might pervade the village in the future.

74. Cecil North, "The City as a Community: An Introduction to a Research Project," in Ernest W. Burgess, ed., *The Urban Community: Selected Papers from the Proceedings of the American Sociological Society, 1925* (Chicago: University of Chicago Press, 1926), pp. 233–36.

75. Cecil North, "The City as a Community," p. 234

76. Cecil North, "The City as a Community" p. 234. For more on the question of community, see R. Jackson Wilson, *In Quest of Community: Social Philosophy in the United States, 1860-1920* (New York: John Wiley, 1968).

77. Randolph Bourne, "Trans-National America," *Atlantic Monthly* 118 (July 1916): 86–97. In recent years Bourne has been "rediscovered" as the grandfather of multiculturalism and as a prescient critic of modern war for his opposition to WWI. See, for example, Bruce Clayton, *Forgotten Prophet: The Life of Randolph Bourne* (Columbia: University of Missouri Press, 1998) and David Hollinger, *Postethnic America: Beyond Multiculturalism* (New York: Basic Books, 1995).

78. "The Municipal Problem," p. 142.

CHAPTER 3

1. Louis Wirth, "Urbanism as a Way of Life," *American Journal of Sociology* 44 (1938): 2.

2. Ralph L. Woods, *America Reborn: A Plan for Decentralization of Industry* (London: Longmans, Green, 1939), p. 113.

3. These figures come from Daniel Amsterdam, *Building a Civic Welfare State: Businessmen's Forgotten Campaign to Remake Industrial America* (Philadelphia: University of Pennsylvania Press, forthcoming). Thanks to the author for giving me a preview of this data.

4. Jon Teaford has made this argument for the late nineteenth century as well. See *The Unheralded Triumph: City Government in America, 1870-1900* (Baltimore: Johns Hopkins University Press, 1984).

5. Woods, *America Reborn*, pp. 50, 90.

6. Woods, *America Reborn*, pp. 89–90.

7. Woods, *America Reborn*, pp. 89–90, 95, 97, 269.

8. See Edward S. Shapiro, "Decentralist Intellectuals and the New Deal," *Journal of American History*, 58 (1972): 940.

9. Patrick F. Quinn, "Agrarianism and the Jeffersonian Philosophy," *Review of Politics* 2 (1940): 94; see also William Leverette Jr. and David E. Shi, "Herbert Agar and 'Free America': A Jeffersonian Alternative to the New Deal," *Journal of American Studies* 16 (1982): 189–206.

10. Brownell, quoted in "Pioneer Spirit Revival Is Aim On N. U. Parley," *Chicago Daily Tribune,* April 11, 1937; Woods, *America Reborn,* pp. 77, 270–71.

11. Holt, quoted in Jacob Dorn, "The Rural Ideal and Agrarian Realities: Arthur E. Holt and the Vision of a Decentralized America in the Interwar Years," *Church History* 52 (1983): 59.

12. For a history of the magazine, see Leverette and Shi, "Herbert Agar and 'Free America,'" pp. 189–206.

13. Emerson Hynes, "Fascists Please Copy," *Free America* 2, no.8 (1938): 20.

14. Angeline Bouchard, "Metropolis versus Province," *Free America* 2, no. 9 (1938): 9.

15. Nor did Joseph McCarthy, George Wallace, or Sarah Palin in subsequent years. In her equation between cities and collectivism, Bouchard echoed the sentiments of Spanish fascists who railed against "red" Madrid.

16. Bouchard, "Metropolis versus Province," p. 10.

17. Clarence Stein, *Toward New Towns for America* (Liverpool: University of Liverpool Press, 1951), p. 21.

18. See Roy Lubove, *Community Planning in the 1920s: The Contribution of the Regional Planning Association of America* (Pittsburgh: University of Pittsburgh Press, 1963). See also Edward K. Spann, *Designing Modern America: The Regional Planning Association of America and Its Members* (Columbus: Ohio State University Press), p. 55.

19. Annie Diggs, "The Garden City Movement," *Arena* 28 (1902): 632; quoted in Spann, *Designing Modern America,* p. 42.

20. For a thorough consideration of Geddes's influence on Mumford, see Casey Blake, *Beloved Community: The Cultural Criticism of Randolph Bourne, Van Wyck Brooks, Waldo Frank, and Lewis Mumford* (Chapel Hill: University of North Carolina Press, 1990), pp. 192–201; see also Robert Casillo, "Lewis Mumford and the Organicist Concept in Social Thought," *Journal of the History of Ideas* 53 (1992), pp. 91–116.

21. See Casillo, "Lewis Mumford and the Organicist Concept," p. 105; Lewis Mumford, "Regions—To Live In," *Survey* 54 (1925): 152.

22. Quoted in Spann, *Designing Modern America,* pp. 37–38.

23. Clarence Stein, "Dinosaur Cities," *Survey* 54 (1925): 138.

24. Mumford, "Regions—To Live In," p. 151.

25. Lewis Mumford, "The Plan of New York," *New Republic* 71 (June 15, 1932): 122.

26. Quotes are from Mumford's "The Plan of New York," *New Republic* 71 (June 15, 1932): 121–126 & "The Plan of New York II," *New Republic* 71 (June 22, 1932): 146–54.

27. Mumford, "Regions—To Live In," p. 152.

28. Quoted in Spann, *Designing Modern America,* p. 165. Park Dixon Goist feels that it is "misleading and inaccurate" to characterize Mumford as "anti-urban." See Park Dixon Goist, "Lewis Mumford and 'Anti-Urbanism,'" *Journal of the American Institute of Planners* 35 (1969): 340–47. But there are aspects about Mumford that are clearly "anti-urban," though I recognize that he is a complex, complicated, and sometimes maddening figure and that labels like these risk being too reductive.

29. Quoted in Spann, *Designing Modern America,* p. 121.

30. Quoted in Spann, *Designing Modern America,* p. 59.

31. See Mark Luccarelli, *Lewis Mumford and the Ecological Region: The Politics of Planning* (New York: Guilford, 1995), p. 146.

32. Mumford, *The Culture of Cities* (New York: Harcourt, Brace and World, 1938), p. 364

33. For the most complete discussion of this topic, see Blake, *Beloved Community,* ch. 6.

34. Bauer's letter, quoted in Donald Miller, *Lewis Mumford: A Life* (New York: Weidenfeld & Nicolson, 1989), p. 334.

35. Luccarelli, *Lewis Mumford and the Ecological Region,* pp. 148–49.

36. Stein to Mumford, October 22, 1967, Mumford Papers, Rare Books and Manuscripts, Van Pelt Library, University of Pennsylvania, Folder 4664.

37. Quoted in Spann, *Designing Modern America,* p. 111.

38. "A Town for Moderns," *Survey* 59 (1927–28): 621.

39. Tracy Augur, *Radburn—The Challenge of a New Town* (New York: City Housing Corporation, 1931), n.p. This little booklet reprinted two articles by Augur that appeared originally in *Michigan Municipal Review.*

40. Augur, *Radburn.*

41. Mumford, "Plan for New York," *New Republic* 71 (June, 22, 1932): 153.

42. See David Ward, "Social Reform, Social Surveys, and the Discovery of the Modern City," *Annals of the Association of American Geographers* 80 (1990): 491; Ernest W. Burgess, "Can Neighborhood Work Have a Scientific Basis?" *Proceedings of the National Conference of Social Work* 51 (1924): 410.

43. Jesse Frederick Steiner, "An Appraisal of the Community Movement," *Social Forces* 7 (1929): 338.

44. "Community Life in Radburn," *Survey* 66 (1931): 99–100; Stein, *Toward New Towns,* p. 225. For a more thorough consideration of Radburn, see Daniel Schaffer, *Garden Cities for America: The Radburn Experience* (Philadelphia: Temple University Press, 1982).

45. Robert Hudson, *Radburn: A Plan for Living* (New York: American Association for Adult Education, 1934), pp. v, vi, 2, 8.

46. " 'Town for the Motor Age' Finds Public Ready for Innovation," *Business Week,* July 9, 1930, p. 19.

47. Geddes Smith, "A Town for the Motor Age," *Survey* 59 (1928): 697; Hudson, *Radburn: A Plan for Living,* p. 7.

48. Hudson, *Radburn: A Plan for Living*, p. 85.
49. Stein, quoted in Spann, *Designing Modern America,* p. 115; Elbow, quoted in Schaffer, *Garden Cities for America*, p. 169.
50. Ralph Borsodi, "Dayton, Ohio, Makes Social History," *Nation*, April 19, 1933, p. 448.
51. Ralph Borsodi, *This Ugly Civilization*, 2nd ed. (New York: Harper Brothers, 1933), pp. 1, 165, 414.
52. Bernhard Stern, Review of Borsodi's *Ugly Civilization, Social Forces* 9 (1930): 135.
53. Ralph Borsodi, *Flight from the City: The Story of a New Way to Family Security* (New York : Harper Brothers, 1933), p. 171.
54. "Away From The City But Not From Machines," *New York Times*, September 3, 1933; Catherine Bauer, "Swiss Family Borsodi," *Nation*, October 25, 1933, p. 489.
55. Bauer, *Swiss Family Borsodi,* p. 489.
56. Borsodi, "Dayton, Ohio, Makes Social History," pp. 447.
57. Borsodi, "Dayton, Ohio, Makes Social History," pp. 447–48.
58. "Colonizing Of Idle On Farms Is Urged," *New York Times,* June 1, 1933.
59. Borsodi, "Dayton, Ohio, Makes Social History," pp. 447–48. I have drawn on Jacob Dorn, "Subsistence Homesteading in Dayton, Ohio 1933-1935," *Ohio History* 78 (1969): 75–93, for the specific details of the Dayton project. Dona Brown discusses Borsodi's Dayton project in her book *Back to the Land: The Enduring Dream of Self-Sufficiency in Modern America* (Madison: University of Wisconsin Press, 2011), pp. 167–71. For a concise overview of Borsodi's career and the Dayton project, see William Issel, "Ralph Borsodi and the Agrarian Response to Modern America," *Agricultural History* 41 (1967): 155–66.
60. Bauer, "Swiss Family Borsodi," p. 489.
61. Quoted in Dorn, "Subsistence Homesteading," p. 84.
62. Borsodi, "Dayton, Ohio Makes Social History," p. 448.
63. See Dorn, "Subsistence Homesteading," p. 86.
64. Borsodi, *Flight from the City*, p. 9.
65. Quoted in Dorn, "Subsistence Homesteading," p. 84.
66. Quoted in Dorn, "Subsistence Homesteading," p. 84; Borsodi, *This Ugly Civilization*, p. 430.
67. For more on the Division of Subsistence Homesteads, see Paul Conkin's *Tomorrow a New World: The New Deal Community Program* (Ithaca, NY: Cornell University Press, 1959); and Robert M. Carriker, *Urban Farming in the West: A New Deal Experiment in Subsistence Homesteads* (Tucson: University of Arizona Press, 2010). Carriker's book focuses primarily on the four western homestead projects.
68. "Dayton Projects Additional Homes," *New York Times*, April 1, 1934.
69. Quoted in Dorn, "Subsistence Homesteading," p. 92.
70. Quoted in Dorn, "Subsistence Homesteading," p. 89.
71. "Dayton Projects Additional Homes," *New York Times*, April 1, 1934.

72. Stein to FDR, March 1, 1933, Mumford Papers, Rare Books and Manuscripts, Van Pelt Library, University of Pennsylvania, Folder 4664; see Jeffrey Marlett, "Harvesting an Overlooked Freedom: The Anti-Urban Vision of American Catholic Agrarianism, 1920-1950," *U.S. Catholic Historian* 16 (1998): 88–108; E. Shapiro, "Decentralist Intellectuals," p. 944; Woods, *America Reborn*, p. 297.

73. Borsodi, quoted in Shapiro, "Decentralist Intellectuals," p. 955.

74. Borsodi, quoted in Leverette and Shi, "Herbert Agar and 'Free America,'" p. 202.

75. John Evans, "Pioneer Spirit Revival Is Aim Of N. U. Parley," *Chicago Daily Tribune*, April 11, 1937.

76. Brownell brought people back to Northwestern again the following year, and Borsodi spoke again, complaining, on the one hand, about federal housing and agricultural policies and extolling the possibilities of a modern agrarian life, on the other. This time, Borsodi stressed outlawing absentee ownership of land, "thus making it possible for the city millions as well as the tenant farmer to own a plot of land." Philip Kinsley, "N.U. Conference Tackles Issues Of Agrarian Life," *Chicago Daily Tribune,* April 6, 1938.

77. Frank Lloyd Wright, *When Democracy Builds* (Chicago: University of Chicago Press, 1945), p. 9; quoted in *New York Times,* November 27, 1956. For more on the anti-urbanism that informed Wright's planning ideas, see Robert C. Twombly, "Undoing the City: Frank Lloyd Wright's Planned Communities," *American Quarterly* 24 (1972): 538–49.

78. Wright to Kimball, April 30, 1928. Bruce Brooks Pfeiffer & Robert Wojtowicz, eds., *Frank Lloyd Wright & Lewis Mumford: Thirty Years of Correspondence* (New York: Princeton Architectural Press, 2001), p. 50.

79. See Donald Leslie Johnson, "Frank Lloyd Wright's Community Planning," *Journal of Planning History* 3 (2004): 3–28.

80. Frank Lloyd Wright, *The Disappearing City* (New York: William Farquhar Payson, 1932), p. 21.

81. Wright, *Disappearing City*, pp. 49, 74–75.

82. Wright, *Disappearing City*, pp. 19, 64, 88; Wright, *When Democracy Builds*, p. 113.

83. Wright, *Disappearing City*, p. 19; Wright, *When Democracy Builds*, p. 41.

84. Lewis Mumford, "The Sky Line: Mr. Wright's City—Downtown Dignity," *The New Yorker,* April 27, 1935, pp. 79–80.

85. The letter was written July 9, 1936. Pfeiffer and Wojtowicz, p. 168.

86. Mumford to Wright, June 25, 1935, *Frank Lloyd Wright & Lewis Mumford: Thirty Years of Correspondence*, pp. 165–66.

87. *Orlando Evening Star,* c. 1947.

88. Quoted in Richard C. Crepeau, *Melbourne Village: The First Twenty-Five Years (1946-1971)* (Orlando: University of Central Florida, 1988), pp. 15, 16.

89. "New Village Is A Planned Community…For Creative Living," *Miami Herald,* March 28, 1948.

90. Robert Bird, "Homestead Snarl Puts Theorist Out," *New York Times,* May 5, 1940.

91. William Tucker, "Out In Suburbia, The Frontier Spirit Isn't What It Was," *New York Times*, March, 6, 1977.

92. Tucker, "Out in Suburbia."

93. Borsodi, *Flight from the City*, p. xiii.

94. Leverette and Shi, "Herbert Agar and 'Free America,'" pp. 204–205; *Washington Post*, May 18, 1947.

CHAPTER 4

1. Quotes are from Mark Gelfand, *A Nation of Cities: The Federal Government and Urban America, 1933–1965* (New York: Oxford University Press, 1975), pp. 24, 55. Rexford Tugwell, *In Search of Roosevelt* (Cambridge, MA: Harvard University Press, 1972), p. 62. See *The Public Papers and Addresses of Franklin D. Roosevelt*, compiled by Samuel Rosenman (New York: Harper Brothers, 1938–1950), vol. 13; John T. Flynn, *Country Squire in the White House* (New York: Doubleday, Doran, 1940).

2. Tugwell, *In Search of Roosevelt*, p. 82.

3. For the most thorough explanation of this story, see Gail Radford, *Modern Housing: Policy Struggles in the New Deal Era* (Chicago: University of Chicago Press, 1996).

4. James Moffett, "Vast Federal Housing Program Set Out," *New York Times,* August 5, 1934. Figures cited in Roger Biles, *A New Deal for the American People* (DeKalb: Northern Illinois University Press, 1991), p. 209.

5. "Home Building Up 109.5 Percent In October," *New York Times,* November 11, 1935.

6. Arthur M. Weimer, "The Work of the Federal Housing Administration," *Journal of Political Economy* 45 (1937): 483.

7. See data in Weimer, "Work of the Federal Housing Administration," p. 472; Moffett, "Vast Federal Housing Program Set Out."

8. Redlining has been well-documented by historians. See, for example, Kenneth T. Jackson, *The Crabgrass Frontier: The Suburbanization of the United States* (New York: Oxford University Press, 1985).

9. Stein to FDR, March 1, 1933, Mumford Papers, Rare Books and Manuscripts, Van Pelt Library, University of Pennsylvania, folder 4664.

10. Rexford Tugwell, *Democratic Roosevelt* (Garden City, NY: Doubleday, 1957), p. 207.

11. Rexford Tugwell, "Problems And Goal Of Rural Relief," *New York Times,* December 15, 1935. I consulted Bernard Sternsher, *Rexford Tugwell and the New Deal* (New Brunswick, NJ: Rutgers University Press, 1964), for my summary of the RSA's objectives.

12. Jonathan Mitchell, "Low-Cost Paradise," *New Republic* 84 (September 1935): 152–55.

13. For a complete examination of the New Deal new town programs, see Joseph Arnold, *The New Deal in the Suburbs: A History of the Greenbelt Town Program, 1935-1954* (Columbus: Ohio State University Press, 1971), and Paul Conkin, *Tomorrow a New World: The New Deal Community Program* (Ithaca: Cornell University Press, 1959). See also Gelfand, *A Nation of Cities*, ch. 2.

14. Henry Churchill, "America's Town Planning Begins," *New Republic* 87 (1936): 96–98. For a thorough, if largely celebratory, history of Greenbelt, Maryland, see Cathy Knepper, *Greenbelt, Maryland: A Living Legacy of the New Deal* (Baltimore: Johns Hopkins University Press, 2001). In 1936, the Resettlement Administration published a booklet detailing the ideas of the greenbelt towns complete with inviting illustrations. See *Greenbelt Towns* (Washington, DC: Resettlement Administration, 1936).

15. Mumford, "Introduction," in Clarence Stein, *Toward New Towns for America* (Liverpool: University of Liverpool Press, 1951), p. 15.

16. Mitchell, "Low-Cost Paradise," p. 152.

17. Mitchell, "Low-Cost Paradise," p. 152; Churchill, "America's Town Planning Begins," p. 96.

18. Mitchell, "Low-Cost Paradise," p. 152.

19. See Conkin, *Tomorrow a New World*, p. 150.

20. "Greenbelt Goes Completely Co-operative," *Reader's Digest* 33 (1938): p. 36 (originally from *New York Herald Tribune*); "Co-op Stores Grow in Greenbelt," *Business Week*, May 14, 1938, pp. 17–18.

21. Hugh Bone, "Greenbelt Faces 1939," *American City* 54 (1939): 59–61.

22. Churchill, "America's Town Planning Begins," p. 98; Mitchell, "Low-Cost Paradise," p. 154.

23. From "Report on Cincinnati, Ohio and the Selection of a Site for Suburban Resettlement," unpublished manuscript, Research Section, Division of Suburban Resettlement, Resettlement Administration, 1936, Greenhills Historical Society.

24. FSA Press Release, January 26, 1938, Greenhills Historical Society; "'Green Belt' Towns Solve Slum Problem," *Decatur Herald and Review*, c. 1937, Greenhills Historical Society.

25. "Greenhills: Second Anniversary, 1940, A Community for Wholesome Living," n.p., Greenhills Historical Society.

26. "'Green Belt' Towns Solve Slum Problem."

27. "'Green Belt' Towns Solve Slum Problem."

28. From an unidentified clipping at the Greenhills Historical Society; the resident quoted was Valeria Goetz.

29. From "The City of Greenhills: Past/Present/Future," n.p., c. 1980, p. 21, Greenhills Historical Society.

30. Greenhills Manual, n.p., c. 1938, Greenhills Historical Society; "Greenhills, Cincinnati Ohio" (Washington, DC: Resettlement Administration, c. 1938).

31. " City of Greenhills."

32. "Greenhills: Second Anniversary"; "Report on the Planning of Greenhills" Resettlement Administration, typescript, 1937 Greenhills Historical Society.

33. "Greenhills: Second Anniversary,"; the school teams are still called The Pioneers.

34. In 1988, fifth-graders at Greenhills elementary school interviewed first residents and transcribed the interviews into a book, Greenhills Historical Society.

35. Rexford Tugwell, "The Meaning of Greenbelt Towns," *New Republic* 90 (1937): 42–43

36. "Greenbelt Goes Completely Co-operative," p. 33.

37. Transcript of the Hearings Before the House Committee on Banking and Currency, House of Representatives, March 18 and 24, 1949, Library of Congress, pp. 21–37. For more on the way this episode played out in Greenbelt, Maryland, see Knepper, *Greenbelt, Maryland: A Living Legacy of the New Deal* (Baltimore: Johns Hopkins University Press, 2001), ch. 4.

38. Philip S. Brown, "What Has Happened at Greenbelt?" *New Republic* 105 (1941): 184.

39. For the story of how Greenhills turned into Forest Park, and then how Forest Park evolved, see Zane Miller, *Suburb: Neighborhood and Community in Forest Park, Ohio, 1935-1976* (Knoxville: University of Tennessee Press, 1980).

40. "City Of Tomorrow Shown In Sphere," *New York Times*, April 27, 1939.

41. For an account of how the film was made, and of the tensions between the filmmakers and the planners, see Howard Gillette, "Film as Artifact: *The City*," *American Studies* 2 (1977): 71–85. George Weller, "The City: America's First Decentralist Film," *Free America* 3, no. 8 (1939): 18–19.

42. I have transcribed the text here from my own viewing of the film.

43. Weller, "The City," p. 18.

44. "Futurama Is Voted The Most Popular," *New York Times,* May 17, 1939. Thomas Hewes, *Decentralize for Liberty* (New York: E. P. Dutton, 1947), pp. 51, 145.

CHAPTER 5

1. Louis C. Jones, *Three Eyes on the Past: Exploring New York Folk Culture* (Syracuse: Syracuse University Press, 1982), p. xix. For a consideration of the intellectual origins of this folk discovery, see Robert L. Dorman, *Revolt of the Provinces: The Regionalist Movement in America, 1920-1945* (Chapel Hill: University of North Carolina Press, 1993), ch. 3.

2. For a thorough consideration of this "discovery" of the Southwest, see Sherry L. Smith, *Reimagining Indians: Native Americans Through Anglo Eyes, 1880-1940* (New York: Oxford University Press, 2000). Lummis quoted on p. 124.

3. Ruth Benedict, *Patterns of Culture* (Boston: Houghton Mifflin, 1934), pp. xiii, 51.

4. Collier, quoted in Dorman, *Revolt of the Provinces*, p. 67.

5. To situate Collier in the world of Progressive-era and New Deal reform, see Stephen J. Kunitz, "The Social Philosophy of John Collier," *Ethnohistory* 18 (1971): 213–29. Collier quoted on p. 215. For more on Collier's work with Native American issues, see Kenneth R. Philp, *John Collier's Crusade for Indian Reform, 1920-1954* (Tucson: University of Arizona Press, 1977).

6. For a history of folklore studies, see Simon J. Bronner, *American Folklore Studies: An Intellectual History* (Lawrence: University of Kansas Press, 1986), and Don Yoder, *Discovering American Folklife: Studies in Ethnic, Religious, and Regional Culture* (Ann Arbor, MI: UMI Research Press, 1990).

7. John A. Lomax and Alan Lomax, *American Ballads and Folk Songs* (New York: Macmillan, 1934), esp. Introduction, pp. xxv–xxxix.

8. The intellectual history of interwar regionalism has been best discussed by Robert Dorman in his book *Revolt of the Provinces*. He sees Americans as reacting against modernity broadly defined, though he does not focus specifically on their complaints about the city.

9. For more on the complicated, back-and-forth relationship between American and European "modernism," see Richard Pells, *Modernist America: Art, Music, Movies & the Globalization of American Culture* (New Haven, CT: Yale University Press, 2011).

10. Grant Wood, *The Revolt Against the City*, (Iowa City, IA: Clio Press, 1935), pp. 9, 16–17, 22–23.

11. Grant Wood, *The Revolt Against the City*, pp. 9, 16–17, 22–23.

12. Donald Davidson, *The Attack on Leviathan: Regionalism and Nationalism in the United States* (Chapel Hill: University of North Carolina Press, 1938), p. 216. A nice touch, too, that Davidson's book has been reissued as part of the Library of Conservative Thought, edited by Russell Kirk.

13. Patrick F. Quinn, "Agrarianism and the Jeffersonian Philosophy," *The Review of Politics* 2 (1940): 87–104.

14. Edward M. Chapman, *New England Village Life* (Cambridge, MA: Riverside, 1937), p. 213.

15. Bernard DeVoto, "New England, There She Stands," *Harper's Monthly* 164 (1932): 406; Chapman, *New England Village Life*, pp. 230–32. Edward E. Whiting sounded many of the same notes in his book *Changing New England* (New York: Century, 1929). While the surface appearances might change, the "eternal things" about New England don't.

16. For the best account of the "invention" of New England, see Joseph A. Conforti, *Imagining New England: Explorations of Regional Identity from the Pilgrims to the Mid-Twentieth Century* (Chapel Hill: University of North Carolina Press, 2001), esp. pp. 263–64.

17. DeVoto, "New England, There She Stands," p. 411.
18. Conforti, *Imagining New England*, p. 300. Van Wyck Brooks, in his classic work, *The Flowering of New England* (New York: E. P. Dutton, 1952), p. 539, wrote "here we have a homogenous people," and did not think that was a bad thing necessarily.
19. Clarence M. Webster, *Town Meeting Country* (New York: Duell, Sloan & Pearce, 1945), p. 3.
20. Lewis Mumford, *Sticks and Stones* (New York: Boni and Liveright, 1924), pp. 29–30. The "invention" of New England and the New England town, of course, had been going on for some time, as Stephen Nissenbaum describes in his provocative essay "Inventing New England," in Charles Reagan Wilson, ed., *The New Regionalism* (Jackson: University of Mississippi Press, 1998), pp. 105–34. Among other things that historians and archeologists have discovered is that actual 18th-century New England towns were usually not like the 20th-century versions of the towns we imagined them to be.
21. See small note in the *Nation* 71 (1900): p. 331; "Whither New England?" *New Republic* 57 (1928): 58; Louis Adamic, "Tragic Towns of New England," *Harper's Monthly* 162 (1930–31): 748–60; Harold Fisher Wilson, *The Hill Country of Northern New England* (Montpelier: Vermont Historical Society, 1947), esp. pp. 346–50.
22. Jonathan Daniels, *A Southerner Discovers New England* (New York: Macmillan, 1940), p. 378.
23. Quoted in Edward K. Spann, *Designing Modern America: the Regional Planning Association of American and Its Members* (Columbus: Ohio State University Press, 1996), p. 114.
24. Webster, *Town Meeting Country*, p. 3.
25. Webster, *Town Meeting Country*, p. 208.
26. Webster, *Town Meeting Country*, pp. 175, 215–16.
27. Webster, *Town Meeting Country*, pp. 3, 228; Chapman, *New England Village Life*, p. 225.
28. Chapman, *New England Village Life*, p. 218.
29. Webster, *Town Meeting Country*, pp. 189, 231.
30. Webster, *Town Meeting Country*, p. 235.
31. DeVoto, "New England, There She Stands," p. 407.
32. DeVoto, "New England, There She Stands," p. 408.
33. DeVoto, "New England, There She Stands," p. 407.
34. Louise Dickinson Rich, *We Took to the Woods* (Philadelphia: J. B. Lippincott, 1942), p. 306.
35. DeVoto, "New England, There She Stands," p. 414.
36. Webster, *Town Meeting Country*, p. 241.
37. Conforti, *Imagining New England*, ch. 6.
38. Chase, quoted in Bronner, *American Folklife Studies*, p. 107.
39. "Melbourne Village," promotional brochure, c. 1940s. Available on the Village's website http://www.melbourne-village.com, accessed July 2010.

40. Collier talked a little bit about this in his memoir *From Every Zenith* (1963). See also Kenneth Philp, *John Collier's Crusade for Indian Reform*, pp. 5–7.

41. List taken from David Whisnant, *All That Is Native and Fine: The Politics of Culture in an American Region* (Chapel Hill: University of North Carolina Press, 1983), pp. 7–8.

42. See Whisnant, *All That Is Native and Fine*, pp. 10–11.

43. Richard B. Drake, *A History of Appalachia* (Lexington: University of Kentucky Press, 2001), p. 121.

44. For a more thorough discussion of this, see Henry D. Shapiro, *Appalachia on Our Mind: The Southern Mountains and Mountaineers in the American Consciousness, 1870-1920* (Chapel Hill: University of North Carolina Press, 1978), esp. pp. 242–59.

45. Olive Campbell to John Glenn, April 6, 1925, Russell Sage Foundation Archives, Early Office Files, Box 37, Folder 303, Rockefeller Archive Center (RAC).

46. Figure in Jane S. Becker, *Selling Tradition: Appalachia and the Construction of an American Folk, 1930-1940* (Chapel Hill: University of North Carolina Press, 1998), p. 49.

47. Olive Campbell to Lee Hanmer, February 26, 1925, Russell Sage Foundation Archives, Early Office Files, Box 37, Folder 303, Rockefeller Archive Center (RAC).

48. Olive Campbell to Olive March, September 5, 1924, Russell Sage Foundation Archives, Early Office Files, Box 37, Folder 303, Rockefeller Archive Center (RAC).

49. Olive Campbell to John Glenn, January 6, 1925, Russell Sage Foundation Archives, Early Office Files, Box 37, Folder 303, Rockefeller Archive Center (RAC); Lula Weir, "Folk School in Mountains," *Sentinel*, July 30, 1933.

50. John Glenn to Olive Campbell, n.d., Russell Sage Foundation Archives, Early Office Files, Box 37, Folder 304, Rockefeller Archive Center (RAC).

51. Daniel Rodgers discusses Campbell's folk school and its relation to Danish models in *Atlantic Crossings: Social Politics in a Progressive Age* (Cambridge, MA: Belknap Press, 1998), pp. 359–61.

52. Fundraising brochure, October, 1939, Russell Sage Foundation Archives, Early Office Files, Box 37, Folder 303, Rockefeller Archive Center (RAC).

53. Olive Campbell to John Glenn, December 5, 1927, Russell Sage Foundation Archives, Early Office Files, Box 37, Folder 303, Rockefeller Archive Center (RAC).

54. Fundraising brochure, October 1939, Russell Sage Foundation Archives, Early Office Files, Box 37, Folder 303, Rockefeller Archive Center (RAC); Trustee Minutes, March 24, 1928, Russell Sage Foundation Archives, Early Office Files, Box 37, Folder 304, Rockefeller Archive Center (RAC); Olive Campbell to Mrs. John Glenn, January 13, 1926, Russell Sage Foundation Archives, Early Office Files, Box 37, Folder 303, Rockefeller Archive Center (RAC).

55. Olive Campbell to John Glenn, March 7, 1928, Russell Sage Foundation Archives, Early Office Files, Box 37, Folder 303, Rockefeller Archive Center (RAC).

56. For more detail on the commodification of Appalachian craft, see Becker, *Selling Tradition,* quote on p. 167.

57. Olive Campbell, Grant Proposal, c. 1943, Russell Sage Foundation Archives, Early Office Files, Box 37, Folder 303, Rockefeller Archive Center (RAC).

58. Olive Campbell, "Agricultural Cooperation in the Southern Highlands of the United States," n.d., Russell Sage Foundation Archives, Early Office Files, Box 37, Folder 304, Rockefeller Archive Center (RAC). See also Shapiro, *Appalachia on Our Mind,* pp. 216–21.

59. Excerpt of a speech in the journal *Mountain Life and Work* v (1929): 1–3

60. For the most complete account of Benton MacKaye's life, see Larry Anderson, *Benton MacKaye: Conservationist, Planner, and Creator of the Appalachian Trail* (Baltimore: Johns Hopkins University Press, 2002), MacKaye quote on p. 193. For an interpretation of the trail project, see Mark Luccarelli, "Benton MacKaye's Appalachian Trail: Imagining and Engineering a Landscape," in David Nye, ed., *Technologies of Landscape* (Amherst: University of Massachusetts Press, 1999), pp. 207–17. MacKaye wrote his own vision of regional planning in his book *The New Explorations: A Philosophy of Regional Planning* (New York: Harcourt, Brace, 1928). In it he extolls the virtues of New England and Appalachia and proposes planning to control the "metropolitan invasion."

61. Quoted in Spann, *Designing Modern America,* p. 19.

62. Quotes from Anderson, *Benton MacKaye,* pp. 187, 238.

63. MacKaye's essay has been reprinted in Anderson, *Benton MacKaye,* pp. 371–79, quotes are from there.

64. MacKaye, quoted in Spann, *Designing Modern America,* pp. 29.

65. MacKaye, quoted in Anderson, *Benton MacKaye,* p. 225.

66. Quoted in Anderson, *Benton MacKaye,* p. 5.

67. The film is available on the Library of Congress website.

68. See Becker, *Selling Tradition,* pp. 220–21.

69. For a history of Cades Cove, see Durwood Dunn, *Cades Cove: The Life and Death of a Southern Appalachian Community, 1818-1937* (Knoxville: University of Tennessee Press, 1988).

CHAPTER 6

1. Dolores Hayden provides a useful overview of the first generation of postwar suburbs—what she wonderfully calls "sitcom suburbs"—in her book *Building Suburbia: Green Fields and Urban Growth, 1820-2000* (New York: Pantheon, 2003), ch. 7.

2. Figure from Bernard Sternsher, *Rexford Tugwell and the New Deal* (New Brunswick, NJ: Rutgers University Press, 1964), p. 301.

3. From the on-line edition of the *Encyclopedia of Chicago,* available at http://www.encyclopedia.chicagohistory.org/pages/335.html, accessed January 2013.

4. To this day, my mother still hates the suburban upbringing she had; as a teenager she snuck off regularly to Greenwich Village.

5. See *Look* magazine, September 21, 1965. *Look* claimed a circulation of over 7.5 million readers. Jon Teaford's *Rough Road to Renaissance: Urban Revitalization in America, 1940-1985* (Baltimore: Johns Hopkins University Press, 1990) is a useful overview of this period.

6. The anecdote is cited in Robert Twombly, "Undoing the City: Frank Lloyd Wright's Planned Communities," *American Quarterly* 24 (1972): 541. I haven't been able to find the original source.

7. For the most thorough overview of the urban renewal era, see Teaford's *Rough Road to Renaissance*. See also Arnold Hirsch, *Making the Second Ghetto: Race & Housing in Chicago, 1940-1960* (Chicago: University of Chicago Press, 1983); John Bauman, *Public Housing, Race, and Renewal: Urban Planning in Philadelphia* (Philadelphia: Temple University Press, 1987); Zane Miller and Bruce Tucker, *Changing Plans for America's Inner Cities: Cincinnati's Over-the-Rhine and Twentieth-Century Urbanism* (Columbus: Ohio State University Press, 1998). The best overview of federal urban policy is in Mark Gelfand, *A Nation of Cities: The Federal Government and Urban America, 1933-1965* (New York: Oxford University Press, 1975).

8. For the best consideration of the legal meanings of "blight," see Wendell Pritchett, "The 'Public Menace' of Blight: Urban Renewal and the Private Uses of Eminent Domain," *Yale Law & Policy Review* 21 (2002): 1–52.

9. For more on this see Christopher Klemek's excellent study *The Transatlantic Collapse of Urban Renewal: Postwar Urbanism from New York to Berlin* (Chicago: University of Chicago Press, 2011), esp. pp. 52–61.

10. For the most thorough consideration of Le Corbusier's American influence, see Mardges Bacon, *Le Corbusier in America: Travels in the Land of the Timid* (Cambridge, MA: MIT Press, 2001), pp. 282–311. The traffic in architectural ideas moved in both directions across the Atlantic. For more on this, see Richard Pells, *Modernist America: Art, Music, Movies and the Globalization of American Culture*, (New Haven, CT: Yale University Press, 2011), ch. 3.

11. See Bacon, *Le Corbusier in America*, pp. 296–97.

12. Quoted in Owen Gutfreund, *Twentieth-Century Sprawl: Highways and Reshaping of the American Landscape* (New York: Oxford University Press, 2004), pp. 40–41.

13. For a comparison of Howard, Frank Lloyd Wright, and Le Corbusier, see Robert Fishman, *Urban Utopias in the Twentieth Century: Ebenezer Howard, Frank Lloyd Wright, and Le Corbusier* (New York: Basic Books, 1977).

14. William Whyte, ed., *The Exploding Metropolis* (Garden City, NY: Doubleday Anchor, 1958), p. vii.

15. Catherine Bauer, "The Architect's Role in Urban Renewal," *Journal of Architectural Education* 10 (Spring 1955): 37.

16. Catherine Bauer, "The Architect's Role in Urban Renewal": 37–38.

17. Whyte, *Exploding Metropolis,* p. xi.
18. William Whyte, "The Anti-City," in Elizabeth Green, Jeanne R. Lowe, and Kenneth Walker, eds., *Man and the Modern City* (Pittsburgh: University of Pittsburgh Press, 1963), p. 52.
19. In 1958, the *Chicago Defender* editorialized about the urban renewal program in the Hyde Park section of the city, saying that the University of Chicago was "more interested in Negro clearance than in land clearance." See "Urban Renewal for Whom," *Chicago Defender,* May 26, 1958. Observations of contemporaries like these have largely been ratified by historians. See, most importantly, Hirsch, *Making the Second Ghetto.*
20. The figures are from Bernard Frieden, *The Future of Old Neighborhoods: Rebuilding for a Changing Population* (Cambridge, MA: MIT Press, 1964), ch. 1. A number of historians have documented the phenomenon of white flight. See, for example, Kenneth T. Jackson, *The Crabgrass Frontier: The Suburbanization of America* (New York: Oxford University Press, 1985); Tom Sugrue, *The Origins of the Urban Crisis: Race and Inequality in Post War Detroit* (Princeton, NJ: Princeton University Press, 1996); Ronald H. Bayor, *Race and the Shaping of Twentieth Century Atlanta* (Chapel Hill: University of North Carolina Press, 1996).
21. See Hirsch, *Making the Second Ghetto,* for the most comprehensive study on the relationship between race and urban renewal. Hirsch argues in particular that Chicago's public housing projects were created to preserve and contain racially segregated ghettos, thus "protecting" downtown interests from expanding black neighborhoods. His work focuses on Chicago, but it has justly become a classic for understanding urban renewal more widely.
22. B. T. McGraw, "Urban Renewal in the Interest of All the People," Phylon 19 (1958): 45–46.
23. Robert C. Weaver, *Dilemmas of Urban America* (Cambridge, MA: Harvard University Press, 1965), pp. 57–59.
24. Martin Anderson, *The Federal Bulldozer* (New York: McGraw-Hill, 1964), p. vii.
25. Rand's work has been described as "Nietzsche for dummies," an assessment which may be unfair to Nietzsche.
26. Anderson, *Federal Bulldozer,* p. 5.
27. Anderson, *Federal Bulldozer,* p. 184.
28. McGraw, "Urban Renewal in the Interest of All the People," p. 48.
29. Anderson, *Federal Bulldozer,* p. 6.
30. This has been well documented by historians of suburbia, starting with Kenneth Jackson's influential *Crabgrass Frontier.* See, for example, Thomas W. Hanchett, "The Other 'Subsidized Housing': Federal Aid to Suburbanization, 1940s-1960s," in John Bauman, Roger Biles, and Kristin Szylvian, eds., *From Tenements to the Taylor Homes: In Search of an Urban Housing Policy in Twentieth-Century America* (University Park: Pennsylvania State University Press, 2000).

31. Herbert Gans, "The Failure of Urban Renewal: A Critique and Some Proposals," *Commentary* 40, no. 4 (1965), p. 29.

32. See Weaver, *Dilemmas of Urban America*, p. 40.

33. George Raymond, Malcolm Rivkin, and Herbert Gans, "Urban Renewal," *Commentary* 40, no. 1 (July 1965): 73. This is a roundtable discussion of Gans' article which appeared in *Commentary* a few months earlier.

34. Herbert Gans, "The Failure of Urban Renewal," *Commentary* 39, no. 4 (April 1965): 29–37.

35. Quoted in Hirsch, *Making the Second Ghetto*, p. 210.

36. Martin Meyerson, "Urban Policy: Reforming Reform," in Martin Meyerson, ed., *The Conscience of the City* (New York: George Braziller, 1970), p. 365.

37. Jon Teaford makes this point in his *Rough Road to Renaissance*. See also "Pittsburgh Comes Out of the Smog," *Newsweek*, September 26, 1949, pp. 25–29, for an example of the press attention these efforts garnered.

38. Mark Gelfand suggests that cities might have been worse off without urban renewal/Great Society programs. See Gelfand, *Nation of Cities*, p. 389.

39. For more on Hyde Park, see LaDale Winling, "Students and the Second Ghetto: Federal Legislation, Urban Politics, and Campus Planning at the University of Chicago," *Journal of Planning History* 10 (2011): 59–86.

40. Tom Sugrue has noted that the role of hospital complexes and universities in urban change remains an understudied issue. See Thomas J. Sugrue, "Revisiting the Second Ghetto," *Journal of Urban History* 29 (2003): p. 282.

41. Frieden, *Future of Old Neighborhoods*, p. 35.

42. Taft, quoted in Russell Kirk and James McClellan, *The Political Principles of Robert A. Taft* (New York: Fleet Press, 1967), p. 151.

43. Quotes from Kirk and McClellan, *Political Principles of Robert A. Taft*, pp. 151–52; and James Patterson, *Mr. Republican: A Biography of Robert A. Taft* (Boston: Houghton Mifflin, 1972), p. 317. Patterson's book provides a full discussion of Taft's role in public housing; the Kirk and McClellan biography is largely hagiographic fluff.

44. Weaver, *Dilemmas of Urban America*, p. 47.

45. I have taken this data from Niles Craig Schoening, *The Effects of Urban Renewal on the Pattern of Racial Segregation in Columbus, Ohio,* MA thesis, Ohio State University, 1969.

46. Quoted in Hirsch, *Making the Second Ghetto*, p. 209.

47. Raymond, Rivkin and Gans, "Urban Renewal," p. 74.

48. Quoted in Wendell E. Pritchett, *Robert Clifton Weaver and the American City: The Life and Times of an Urban Reformer* (Chicago: University of Chicago Press, 2008), pp. 255–56, 284.

49. A number of excellent studies demonstrate the connection between racial segregation and housing in the urban north, including Sugrue, *Origins of the Urban*

Crisis (Princeton, NJ: Princeton University Press, 1996) and *Sweet Land of Liberty*; Beryl Satter, *Family Properties: Race, Real Estate, and the Exploitation of Black Urban America* (New York: Henry Holt, 2009); Matthew Lassiter, *The Silent Majority: Suburban Politics in the Sunbelt South* (Princeton, NJ: Princeton University Press, 2006); Kevin Kruse, *White Flight: Atlanta and the Making of Modern Conservatism* (Princeton, NJ: Princeton University Press, 2005).

50. Alison Isenberg discusses this confluence of race and urban problems in her book *Downtown America: A History of the Place and the People Who Made It* (Chicago: University of Chicago Press, 2004), p. 192. She quotes the editors of *Fortune,* who wrote in 1962: "the Negro problem is what city planners and officials are really talking about whey they refer to The City Problem."

51. Quoted in P. J. Madgwick, "The Politics of Urban Renewal," *Journal of American Studies* 5 (1971): 267.

52. Quoted in Pritchett, *Robert Clifton Weaver and the American City,* p. 278

53. C. A. Doxiadis, *Urban Renewal and the Future of the American City* (Chicago: Public Administration Service for the National Association of Housing and Redevelopment Officials, 1966), p. 9.

54. Interview with David Rockefeller, *U.S. News and World Report,* June 7, 1971, pp. 50–51.

55. This point is made most astutely by Robert Fishman, *Urban Utopias: The Rise and Fall of Suburbia* (New York: Basic Books, 1987), p. 260.

56. "Motor Traffic and Tomorrow's Cities," *Better Roads* 9 (1939): 19.

57. Quoted in Gutfreund, *Twentieth-Century Sprawl,* p. 48.

58. See Frederic Paxson, "The Highway Movement, 1916-1935," *American Historical Review* 51 (1946): 236–53; see also Gutfreund, *Twentieth-Century Sprawl,* ch. 1.

59. Enfield, quoted in Richard Weingroff, "The Greatest Decade, 1956-1966," Federal Highway Administration, Highway History, available at http://www.fhwa.dot.gov/infrastructure/50interstate.cfm, accessed October 2010.

60. Quoted in Ben Kelley, *The Pavers and the Paved* (New York: Donald W. Brown, 1971), p. 4.

61. There are a number of overviews of the interstate program, including Jane Holtz Kay, *Asphalt Nation: How the Automobile Took Over America and How We Can Take It Back* (New York: Crown, 1997); Mark Rose, *Interstate: Express Highway Politics, 1939-1989* (Knoxville: University of Tennessee Press, 1990); Tom Lewis, *Divided Highways: Building the Interstate Highways, Transforming American Life* (New York: Viking, 1997); and James Flink, *The Automobile Age* (Cambridge, MA: MIT Press, 1988). For a more popular account, see Earl Swift, *The Big Roads: The Untold Story of the Engineers, Visionaries, and Trailblazers Who Created the American Superhighways* (Boston: Houghton Mifflin Harcourt, 2011).

62. Report of the Philadelphia Planning Commission, 1950.

63. Of course, highway boosters were similarly obtuse about the benefits of the interstate to rural, underdeveloped sections of the nation. They imagined these places would be "opened up" for economic development by the new highways; it apparently didn't occur to them that the new roads would make it easy for people in those forgotten corners of America to leave for a job in the nearest city and a house in the suburbs, or that many drivers would speed right by those rural towns and villages without stopping to spend a dime. For a nice essay on this see David Holwerk, "Interstate 75: A Morality Play," *Nation* 215 (November 20, 1972): 492–95.

64. McGraw, "Urban Renewal in the Interest of All the People," p. 46.

65. Kelley, *Pavers and the Paved*, p. 3; see also Raymond A. Mohl, "Planned Destruction: The Interstates and Central City Housing," in Bauman, Biles, and Kristin Szylvian, *From Tenements to the Taylor Homes*, p. 227.

66. Figures cited in "In the Path of Progress: Federal Highway Relocation Assurances," *Yale Law Journal* 82 (1972): 373; Kelley, *Pavers and the Paved*, p. 145; Mohl, "Planned Destruction," p. 240.

67. Chester Hartman, "Relocation: Illusory Promises and No Relief," *Virginia Law Review* 57 (1971): 787.

68. *Business Week,* May 2, 1970.

69. For more on the opposition to road projects, see Klemek, *Transatlantic Collapse of Urban Renewal*, esp. pt. 3. He argues that the opposition to urban renewal generally started with these fights against road projects. I am drawing a sharper distinction between highway projects and the urban renewal program than Klemek does. My argument is that the question of race and housing generated earlier and more opposition to urban renewal. For a specific analysis of the prolonged fight over the "Three Sisters Bridge" project, see Zachary M. Schrag, "The Freeway Fight in Washington, DC: The Three Sisters Bridge in Three Administrations," *Journal of Urban History* 30 (2004): 648–73. For a broad overview of opposition to highways projects, see Raymond A. Mohl, "Stop the Road: Freeway Revolts in American Cities," *Journal of Urban History* 30 (2004): 674–706. Mohl acknowledges that widespread protests didn't really erupt until later in the 1960s.

70. Hartman, "Relocation," p. 765.

71. Quote from Hartman, "Relocation," p. 809.

72. "Fighting the Freeway," *Newsweek,* March, 25, 1968, pp. 64–65. For more on the anti-highway movement that gained momentum in the late 1960s and 1970s, see Teaford, *Rough Road to Renaissance,* esp. pp. 232–36.

73. See F. James Davis, "The Effects of a Freeway Displacement on Racial Housing Segregation in a Northern City," *Phylon* 26 (1965): 209–15. Davis found, interestingly, that while the displacement concentrated racial segregation, this did not result from outright discrimination: "Direct discriminatory action does not appear sufficient to account for the increase in racial housing segregation after the freeway clearance. Much of the increased concentration of nonwhites was evidently due to

fear of discrimination outside of the nonwhite area, and the in-group cohesiveness in the face of potential discrimination" (p. 215); Mohl, "Planned Destruction," p. 238. Mohl stresses the racial aspect of how highways were planned and built.

74. See Bernard J. Frieden and Robert Morris, eds., *Urban Planning and Social Policy* (New York: Basic Books, 1968).

75. "Highway Boom or Bust?" *U.S. News and World Report*, May 25, 1959, p. 55.

76. Figures cited in Kelley, *Pavers and the Paved*, p. 3.

77. See Kelley, *Pavers and the Paved*, p. 93.

78. "Fighting the Freeway," p. 64. Wise, quoted in Toni Anthony, "Road Will Oust Residents In Five Areas," *Chicago Defender*, April 25, 1970.

79. "Checking The Flight To The Suburbs," *Chicago Tribune*, May 17, 1958.

80. Quoted in Gutfreund, *Twentieth-Century Sprawl*, p. 95.

81. Figures from Gutfreund, *Twentieth-Century Sprawl*, pp. 57, 165.

82. Quoted in Daniel Patrick Moynihan, "New Roads and Urban Chaos," *Reporter* 22 (April 14, 1960): 13.

83. "In the Path of Progress," pp. 374–400.

84. *U.S. News and World Report*, October 8, 1962, p. 55.

85. Quoted in Moynihan, "New Roads and Urban Chaos," p. 19.

86. See *Forum*, April 1951; James Bailey, "A Case History of Failure," *Architectural Forum* 23 (1965): 22–25. A great deal of ink has been spilled debating Pruitt-Igoe. Much of the discussion revolves around the question of whether the architecture and design of the project bears primary, secondary, or less responsibility for the social failures of the project. Many have pointed out that the bad design choices were forced on the architect by cost consideration and PHA demands; others insist that the demographics of Pruitt-Igoe meant social dysfunction no matter what the design. More recently, people have pointed to some of what went right at Pruitt-Igoe, insisting that the story of the project was at least as much a myth created for ideological purposes as a fair analysis of what took place there. For one particularly good obituary, see Jane Holtz Kay, "Architecture," *Nation*, September 24, 1973, pp. 284–86.

87. Charles Jencks, *The Language of Post-Modern Architecture* (New York: Rizzoli, 1977), p. 9. That quip has had a remarkable staying power and has been quoted countless times. David Harvey also pointed to Pruitt-Igoe's demolition as the moment when modernism died. See his *The Condition of Post-Modernity: An Enquiry Into the Origins of Cultural Change* (London: Wiley, 1989).

88. "The Tragedy of Pruitt-Igoe," *Time*, December 27, 1971, p. 38.

89. Sally Thran, "No Room for the Poor," *Commonweal* 97 (1973): 293.

90. "55-mph Miracle," *Newsweek*, December 31, 1962, p. 12.

91. "North-South Expressway," *Chicago Tribune*, May 26, 1963.

92. For a thorough review of the history of Robert Taylor Homes, see D. Bradford Hunt, "What Went Wrong with Public Housing in Chicago?" *Journal of the Illinois State Historical Society* 94 (Spring, 2001), pp. 96–124.

93. Quoted in "Ecology of a Ghetto," *Time,* April 6, 1970, p. 48.

94. "Gamble in the Ghetto," *Newsweek,* January 31, 1966, pp. 24–25.

95. I have taken these quotes and the data about the Near West Side neighborhood from an unpublished, undated (c. 1960) report titled "A History of Near West Side Planning," prepared, I think, by people associated with Hull House. See Hull House Association Collection, Box 11, Folder 116.

96. "Plan to Raze Hull House Is Hit By Board," *Chicago Tribune,* February 11, 1961.

97. Illinois U Unit All Set To Move," *New York Times,* February 14, 1965.

98. Jane Jacobs, *The Death and Life of Great American Cities* (New York: Random House, 1961), p. 3.

99. Lewis Mumford, "Mother Jacobs' Home Remedies," *The New Yorker* 38 (December 1, 1962): 148ff; Arthur T. Row, review of Jane Jacobs, *Death and Life of American Cities, Yale Law Journal* 71 (1962): 1597–602.

100. Paul A. Pfretzschner, "Panning the Planners," *Antioch Review* 22 (1962): 130–36.

101. Mumford, "Mother Jacobs' Home Remedies," p. 148; and Row, 1597–602. See also Robert Fishman, "The Mumford-Jacobs Debate," *Planning History Studies* 10 (1996): 3–11.

102. Jacobs, *Death and Life of Great American Cities,* p. 413.

103. Jacobs, *Death and Life of Great American Cities,* p. 448.

104. See Jacobs, *Death and Life of Great American Cities,* p. 271.

105. See William F. Buckley Jr., *Did You Ever See a Dream Walking?: American Conservative Thought in the 20th Century* (Indianapolis: Bobbs-Merrill, 1970).

106. "Dissenting Report of Commissioner Spatt," in *Plan for New York City* (New York: New York City Planning Commission, 1969), pp. 174–75.

107. Ada Louise Huxtable, "Plan Is Regarded As Break With Tradition," *New York Times,* November 16, 1969.

108. Robert K. Yin, *The City in the Seventies* (Itasca, IL: F.E. Peacock, 1972), p. 263.

CHAPTER 7

1. In point of fact, the 1960 Census lists Houston as having just under 1 million people, so those announcements in 1954 might have jumped the gun. Either way, by 1960—the first time it appeared in the top ten—Houston was the seventh largest city in the United States.

2. Carl Abbott notes that urban theorists disagree about the effects of the post-industrial economy of the spatial development of cities. See "Through Flight to Tokyo: Sunbelt Cities and the New World Economy, 1960-1990," in Arnold Hirsch and Raymond Mohl, eds., *Urban Policy in Twentieth-Century America* (New Brunswick, NJ: Rutgers University Press, 1993), p. 199.

3. Many people have made this observation. See, for example, Randall M. Miller, "The Development of the Modern Urban South: An Historical Overview," in Randall M. Miller & George E. Pozetta, eds., *Shades of the Sunbelt: Essays on Ethnicity, Race, and the Urban South* (Boca Raton: Florida Atlantic University Press, 1988), p. 2.

4. Robert Fishman and Kenneth Jackson also stress that the automobile created an entirely new urban form.

5. Carey McWilliams, "Look What's Happening to California," *Harper's Magazine,* October 1949, pp. 21–29.

6. Morris Markey, *This Country of Yours* (Boston: Little, Brown, 1932); Roger Butterfield, "Los Angeles is the Damnedest Place" *Life* 15 (1943): 102–18.

7. Charles W. Moore, "You Have to Pay for Public Life," *Perspecta* 9–10 (1965): 58.

8. The most complete study of Phoenix's growth and its politics in the postwar era is Elizabeth Tandy Shermer's *Sunbelt Capitalism: Phoenix and the Transformation of American Politics* (Philadelphia: University of Pennsylvania Press, 2013).

9. "Southern City, Northern Pace: How Long Can It Last?" *Business Week,* January 24, 1953, p. 78.

10. George Fuermann, *Houston: Land of the Big Rich* (Garden City, NY: Country Life Press, 1951), Mewhinney quote on p. 14; Horace Sutton, "Things Are Looking Up in Houston," *Saturday Review,* November 14, 1964, p. 44.

11. Sutton, "Things Are Looking Up," p. 42.

12. *Time,* April 12, 1963, p. 27.

13. *Comprehensive Plan—Houston Urban Area; 1c Population, Land Use, Growth* (Houston: Houston City Planning Commission, 1959), p. 98.

14. "Booming Houston," *Life,* October 21, 1946, pp. 108–17; "What Has Happened in an Unzoned City?" *American City* 68 (March 1953): 93; Stanley Walker, "Houston, Texas: A 'Yes, But—' Town," *New York Times,* August 1, 1954, p. 16ff.

15. "Houston, Texas: What It's Like to be New," *Business Week,* January 24, 1953, p. 98.

16. Quoted in Willie Morris, "Houston's Superpatriots," *Harper's Magazine,* October 1961, p. 55.

17. That story is part of the Cullen lore and appears in a number of sources. See "Philanthropist Hugh Roy Cullen Enjoyed Giving His Money Away," *Houston Business Journal,* July 13, 2009.

18. See Cullen quotes in Ed Kilman and Theon Wright, *Hugh Roy Cullen: A Story of American Opportunity* (New York: Prentice-Hall), p. 243; and Fuermann, *Houston,* p. 115. For more on the zoning fight, see "Houston Millionaire Beats Jones on Zoning," *Business Week,* February 14, 1948.

19. "Report of the Committee to Present the Negative Side Effects of Zoning," unpublished report, September 17, 1947, Houston Metropolitan Research Center, M. W. Lee Collection, Ms. 58, Box 1, Folder 1.

20. Sam Boal, "Treatise On Texas And The Texans," *New York Times Magazine,* May 15, 1949, p. 57; Walker, "Houston, Texas," p. 16.

21. See Fuermann, *Houston,* p. 115; Kilman and Wright, *Hugh Roy Cullen,* pp. 258–62.

22. See Joe R. Feagin, *Free Enterprise City: Houston in Political-Economic Perspective* (New Brunswick, NJ: Rutgers University Press, 1988), p. 129.

23. Quoted in Kilman and Wright, *Hugh Roy Cullen,* p. 284.

24. John T. Flynn, *The Road Ahead, America's Creeping Revolution* (New York: Devin-Adair, 1949), p. 96.

25. Flynn, *Road Ahead,* p. 41.

26. Flynn, *Road Ahead,* p. 62

27. Meredith James, *Zoning—A New Frontier?,* unpublished manuscript, Houston Metropolitan Research Center, M. W. Lee Collection, Ms. 58, Box 1, Folder 2; *Houston Post,* January 28, 1948.

28. See "Houston's Texas-Size Land Grab," *Business Week,* July 23, 1960, p. 54; "On a Texas Prairie—Space City for 200,000," *US News & World Report,* February 18, 1967, p. 69.

29. *Time,* April 12, 1963, p. 27; see also Robert Connery and Richard Leach, "Southern Metropolis: Challenge to Government," *Journal of Politics* 26 (1964): 60–81; "Best Run U.S. Cities Give Most Service," *Los Angeles Times,* November 17, 1958.

30. Quoted in Beth Ann Shelton et al., *Houston: Growth and Decline in a Sunbelt Boomtown* (Philadelphia: Temple University Press, 1989), p. 43.

31. "U.S. Aiding In Drive To Erase Slums," *New York Times,* November 13, 1955.

32. "City Gets $60,000 For Urban Renewal Survey," *Houston Chronicle,* August 29, 1960.

33. See "Urban Renewal Hit By Demonstrators," *Houston Post,* January 5, 1961; "Group Protests Urban Renewal," *Houston Press,* January 4, 1961.

34. See Houston Metropolitan Research Center, M. W. Lee Collection, Ms. 58, Box 1, Folders 2–4 for more material on the anti-zoning campaign.

35. "Phoenix Scorns U.S. Assistance For Its Slum-Clearance Project," *New York Times,* May 13, 1961.

36. See "Welch Hits Renewal," *New York Times,* October 10, 1961; Jack Eisen, "City Renewal Foes List Birchers As Sponsors," *Washington Post,* March 1, 1964.

37. Quoted in Richard L. Gilbert Jr., "Phoenix Unreborn," *The Reporter* 29 (November 21, 1963): 48–49.

38. "Phoenix Scorns U. S. Assistance For Its Slum-Clearance Project," *New York Times,* May 13, 1961. See Barry Goldwater, *The Conscience of a Conservative* (Shepardville, KY: Victor Publishing Co., 1960), p. 47.

39. Quoted in Gilbert, "Phoenix Unreborn," pp. 48–49.

40. All the construction and design standards for interstate highways were set by Washington, which explains among other things why the signage is uniform from Maine to San Diego. For more on this, see Zachary Schrag, "Transportation and the Uniting of the Nation," in Steven Conn, ed., *To Promote the General Welfare: The Case for Big Government* (New York: Oxford University Press, 2012), pp. 21–43.

41. See Shelton et al., *Houston,* p. 46; Feagin, *Free Enterprise City,* pp. 181–85; William B. Angel Jr., "To Make a City: Entrepreneurship on the Sunbelt Frontier," in David Perry and Alfred Watkins, *The Rise of the Sunbelt Cities, Urban Affairs Annual Review* 14 (1977): 119.

42. Stephen Spacek, *The State-Maintained Houston Freeway System*, unpublished manuscript, Houston Metropolitan Research Center, vertical files H-Freeways.

43. "Solving Houston's Parking Jam," *Business Week*, October 9, 1954, p. 103.

44. "Traffic Jams…or Freeways," unpublished manuscript, Houston Metropolitan Research Center, vertical file H-Freeways–1950s.

45. "Where Do We Stand?" *Houston Magazine,* July 1957, p. 68.

46. Feagin, *Free Enterprise City,* p. 184.

47. Quoted in Louis Ward Kemp, "Aesthetes and Engineers: The Occupational Ideology of Highway Design," *Technology and Culture* 27 (1986): 765.

48. See Mimi Crossley, "Fourth Ward: A Gloomy Area With An Air Of Expectation," *Houston Chronicle,* April 25, 1971; Claudia Freeman, "Historic Fourth Ward Called 'Living Coffin,'" *Houston Chronicle,* September 23, 1976; Fred Haper and Raul Reyes, "4th Ward Is Obsolete," *Houston Chronicle,* April 1, 1980; "Freedman's Town Historic District, Houston, Texas," submitted to the National Register Department, Texas Historical Commission, 1984 Houston Metropolitan Research Center. The area was put on the National Register in 1985.

49. Erik Slotboom, *Houston Freeways: A Historical and Visual Journey* (Cincinnati: C. J. Krehbiel, 2003), p. 2003.

50. See Vick Gould to Lee October 1, 1964, Houston Metropolitan Research Center, M. W. Lee Collection, Ms. 58, Box 2, Scrapbook 1.

51. Lee to J. B. Harris, October 26, 1967; and Welch to Lee, January 5, 1966, Houston Metropolitan Research Center, M. W. Lee Collection, Ms. 58, Box 2, Scrapbook 1.

52. "And now…Over to Houston," *Newsweek,* June 14, 1965, pp. 34–36.

53. Houston City Planning Commission, "Condition of Residential Structures Survey," 1959, p. 7.

54. David McComb, *Houston: The Bayou City* (Austin: University of Texas Press, 1969), pp. 224–25; "Civic Experiment," *Time,* May 22, 1950, p. 56.

55. "Houston, Texas: What It's Like to be New," *Business Week,* January 24, 1953, p. 98; Ronald Moskowitz, "Education and Politics in Boomtown," *Saturday Review,* February 17, 1968, p. 53.

56. "Booming Houston," *Life,* October 21, 1946, p. 113.

57. "The Stokely Generation," *Newsweek,* May 29, 1967, p. 24.

58. See "And now…Over to Houston," *Newsweek,* June 14, 1965, p. 36; "The Stokely Generation," *Newsweek,* May 29, 1967, pp. 24–25; "Black Power Explodes Again— Policeman Slain," *U. S. News & World Report,* May 27, 1967, p. 10; "One City's Try at Racial Amity," *U. S. News & World Report,* May 20, 1968, pp. 16–17.

59. See McComb, *Houston: The Bayou City*, pp. 209–15.

60. Quoted in McComb, *Houston: The Bayou City*, p. 218.

61. Mason to Lee, September 18, 1967, Houston Metropolitan Research Center, M. W. Lee Collection, Ms. 58, Box 2, Scrapbook folder.

62. Susan A. MacManus, *Federal Aid to Houston* (Washington, DC: Brookings Institution, 1983), pp. xi–5.

63. For more on these cities, see Robert B. Fairbanks, "The Failure of Urban Renewal in the Southwest: From City Needs to Individual Rights," *Western Historical Quarterly* 37 (2006): 303–25. Quotes from Ed Meagher, "Phoenix Shifts For U.S. Renewal Aid," *Washington Post,* April 14, 1966.

64. *Newsweek* featured Columbus as a "Gleam Along the Rust Belt" in a special issue devoted to "hot" cities. *Newsweek,* February 6, 1989, pp. 48–49.

65. See Paul David Horton, *A Study of Administrative and Planning Deficiencies,* MA thesis, Ohio State University, 1964, p. 8.

66. Horton, *Study of Administrative and Planning Deficiencies,* p. 19.

67. See ad in *Business Week,* November 19, 1966, p. 138.

68. See "Why Columbus?" *Saturday Review,* April 30, 1977, p. 14; Haya El Nasser, "Columbus, Ohio: The 'Everyman' Of America," *USA Today,* December 17, 2003.

69. George Sessions Perry, "Columbus, Ohio," *Saturday Evening Post,* May 3, 1952, pp. 22–23ff.

70. See "Columbus, Ohio Starts Big Physical Improvement Program," *American City* 72 (February, 1957): 112.

71. See, for example, Thomas and Doris Reed, "Does Your City Suffer from Suburbanitis?" *Colliers,* October 11, 1952.

72. For more on annexation in Atlanta, and the racial dynamics of it, see Kevin Kruse, *White Flight: Atlanta and the Making of Modern Conservatism* (Princeton, NJ: Princeton University Press, 2005), ch. 9.

73. See *Business Week,* January 8, 1955, p. 56.

74. See Michael Lafferty, "City Plows Under Farmland," *Columbus Dispatch,* December 15, 1985.

75. Perry, "Columbus, Ohio," p. 100.

76. For this data, see Paul Esmond King, *The Spatial Aspects of Social Area Change: Columbus, Ohio 1950-1960,* MA thesis, Ohio State University, 1969.

77. Quoted in Horton, *Study of Administrative and Planning Deficiencies,* p. 2.

78. See Horton, *Study of Administrative and Planning Deficiencies,* map p. 43.

79. James Ridgeway, "Missionaries in Darkest Ohio," *New Republic* 154 (February 5, 1966): 9–10.

80. See "The Columbus Riot," unpublished manuscript, Columbus Planning and Research Bureau, 1969.

81. See "Downtown Area Plan," report prepared by the Planning Division, Department of Development, City of Columbus, 1970.

82. See "Downtown Area Plan."

83. Alan Johnson, "It's Really Happening: I-670 Connector Under Way," *Columbus Dispatch,* August 18, 1985.

84. "Neighborhoods Have to Fend For Themselves," *Columbus Dispatch,* September 8, 1985.

85. Michael Lafferty, "City Plows Under Area Farmland," *Columbus Dispatch,* December 15, 1985.

86. "America's Hot Cities," *Newsweek,* February 6, 1989, p. 42.

87. Erik Eckholm, "There May Be 'No Better Place,' But There Is A Better Slogan," *New York Times,* July 31, 2010.

88. Lewis Mumford, *The City in History: Its Origins, Its Transformation, and Its Prospects* (New York: Harcourt, Brace, and World, 1961), p. 562.

89. Dolores Hayden makes this point in her book *The Power of Place;* see especially chs. 2 and 3.

CHAPTER 8

1. David Schaffer, *Garden Cities for America: The Radburn Experience* (Philadelphia: Temple University Press, 1982), p. 224.

2. The most thorough work on Morgan and the TVA is Roy Talbert Jr., *FDR's Utopian: Arthur Morgan of the TVA* (Jackson: University of Mississippi Press, 1987) Morgan quoted on p. 139. For Morgan's view of utilities in the heat of this moment, see, for example, "Dr. Morgan Pleads For Cooperation With The Utilities," *New York Times,* January 17, 1937.

3. "Scandal In The TVA," *Chicago Tribune,* March 5, 1938.

4. These are Arthur E. Morgan's recollections in his *Industries for Small Communities* (Yellow Springs, OH: Community Service, 1953), p. 19.

5. "About Community Service Incorporated," undated brochure (c. 1965), Community Service Inc., Box 6, Folder "About Community Service," Antiochiana Collection, Olive Kettering Library, Antioch College.

6. Arthur E. Morgan, *The Small Community: Foundation of Democratic Life* (Yellow Springs, OH: Community Service, 1942), p. 3. That same year Morgan published an article in *Free America* using almost exactly the same language. See Morgan, "Design for the Small Community," *Free America* 6 (1942): 3–6.

7. Morgan, "Design for the Small Community," p. 4; Morgan, *The Small Community,* pp. 42, 43, 54, 57.

8. Morgan, *The Small Community,* p. 25

9. Morgan, *The Small Community,* p. 86.

10. H. Clay Tate, *Building a Better Home Town* (New York: Harper Brothers, 1954), p. 31.

11. Ronald Warren, *Studying Your Community* (New York: Russell Sage Foundation, 1955).

12. Morgan, *Industries for Small Communities,* pp. 5, 7.

13. Morgan, *Industries for Small Communities,* p. 3. This remains an urgent issue for localities. In 2012, the Pew Charitable Trusts issued a study to chart the effects of tax breaks and other incentives on luring employers from one state to another.

14. Morgan, *Industries for Small Communities,* p. 15.

15. Antioch features prominently in Burton Clark's *The Distinctive College* (New York: Aldine, 1970).

16. Morgan, *Industries for Small Communities*, p. 106.

17. Tate, *Building a Better Home Town*, pp. 41, 46; Max Lerner, "The Decline of the Small Town," in Suzanne Freeman and Morrow Wilson, eds., *Rural America* (New York: H. H. Wilson, 1976), p. 123. David Russo largely agrees with Clay's observation. Russo writes, "After World War II it was quite clear that by itself town government could not serve the needs of the people within its jurisdiction. Thus many of the functions of local governments were gradually assumed by county, state, and federal governments." Russo, *American Towns: An Interpretive History* (Chicago: Ivan R. Dee, 2001), p. 112; "Small-Town Slums Found Bad As City's," *New York Times*, October 24, 1958.

18. Richard Davies has written a moving, elegiac history of Camden, Ohio. It is the birthplace of Sherwood Anderson, and Davies's hometown as well. *Main Street Blues: The Decline of Small-Town America* (Columbus: Ohio State University Press, 1998). See also Russo, *American Towns,* p. 85.

19. See Davies, *Main Street Blues,* Prologue.

20. Morgan, *The Small Community*, p. 94.

21. Quoted in Talbert, *FDR's Utopian,* p. 46.

22. Morgan published a history of utopia in which, with his engineer's enthusiasm, he declared, "Utopias are as essential to human society as plans are essential for building bridges." *Nowhere Was Somewhere: How History Makes Utopias and How Utopias Make History* (Chapel Hill: University of North Carolina Press, 1946), p. 3.

23. The heyday of the college lasted until the early 1970s, at which point it began a slow spiral of decline. It was closed in 2008, but after a heroic effort by dedicated alumni and others it reopened in 2011 with a new board of trustees and a new faculty.

24. My neighbors and friends also include a best-selling author, a beloved NPR voice, a pair of Academy Award–nominated documentary film makers, and an internationally famous entertainer. When our town paper did a piece on the 40th anniversary of Woodstock, it ran an interview with one of my neighbors who played at Woodstock.

25. Many thanks to Tracey Sugar of the Gallup office, in Princeton, New Jersey, who provided me with this data, November 2010.

26. See Russo, *American Towns,* p. 292.

27. Max Lerner, *America as a Civilization: Life and Thought in the United States Today,* (New York: Simon and Schuster, 1957), p. 125. That idealization remains quite common. Nostalgia suffuses Richard Lingeman's 1980 book *Small Town America: A Narrative History, 1620-present* (New York: G. P. Putnam's, 1980).

28. I have taken these quotes from the executive summary of the *Report of the National Advisory Commission on Civil Disorders* (New York: E. P. Dutton, 1968).

29. "Bum Tip for the Democrats," *Chicago Tribune,* July 4, 1968.

30. "Guest Editorial," *Chicago Tribune,* March 17, 1968. The piece originally appeared in the *National Review Bulletin.*

31. Clark quoted in Drew Pearson, "Pessimism Over Riots," *Washington Post,* March 10, 1968.
32. Victor Navasky, "Futility of Panel," *New York Times,* June 10, 1968.
33. *Report of the National Advisory Commission on Civil Disorders,* p. 399.
34. Dwight Eisenhower, "To Insure Domestic Tranquility," *Reader's Digest,* May 1968, pp. 56–57.
35. " 'New Towns' Idea Seen As City Space Aid," *Chicago Tribune,* August 18, 1968.
36. "Agnew Offers Plan To Build New Towns," *Chicago Tribune,* August 22, 1968.
37. McCarthy made the speech on May 28, 1968, at the University of California, Davis. See Jeremy Larner, *Nobody Knows: Reflections on the McCarthy Campaign of 1968* (New York: Macmillan, 1970), pp. 107–109.
38. "New Towns Seen Solving Sprawl And Rural Waste," *Washington Post,* May 11, 1968; Gurney Breckenfeld, *Columbia and the New Cities* (New York: Ives Washburn, 1971), p. 13; Wolf von Eckardt, "Building 'New Towns' To Save The Old Cities," *Washington Post,* February 22, 1970. See also "The City: Starting From Scratch," *Time,* March 7, 1969, pp. 7–8.
39. Letitia C. Langord and Gwen Bell, "Federally Sponsored New Towns of the Seventies," *Growth and Change* 6, no.4 (1975): 24.
40. Romney, quoted in Breckenfeld, *Columbia and the New Cities,* p. 16.
41. For more on Rouse's career, see Joshua Olsen, *Better Places, Better Lives: A Biography of James Rouse* (Washington, DC: Urban Land Institute, 2003); and Nicholas Dagen Bloom, *Merchant of Illusion: America's Salesman of the Businessman's Utopia* (Columbus: Ohio State University Press, 2004). Ann Forsyth has compared Columbia with two other large-scale planned developments—Irvine, California, and The Woodlands in Texas. See her *Reforming Suburbia: The Planned Communities* (Berkeley: University of California Press, 2005).
42. See Edward Eichler and Marshall Kaplan, *The Community Builders* (Berkeley: University of California Press, 1967), pp. 8–9.
43. Rouse quoted in Richard Oliver Brooks, *New Towns and Communal Values: A Case Study of Columbia, Maryland* (New York etc: Praeger Publishers, 1974), pp. 10–12.
44. Joseph Rocco Mitchell and David L. Stebenne, *A New City Upon a Hill: A History of Columbia, Maryland* (Charleston: History Press, 2007), p. 59. Mitchell and Stebenne provide a detailed, almost year-by-year account of Columbia's development.
45. Samuel Jackson quoted in James Bailey, ed., *New Towns in America: The Design and Development Process* (New York : John Wiley, 1973), p. 115.
46. Margaret Mead, "New Towns to Set New Life Styles," in Harvey S. Perloff and Neil C. Sandberg, eds., *New Towns: Why—And for Whom?* (New York: Praeger, 1973), p. 120.
47. Rouse also approached the new Dag Hammarskjold College, though it did not have accreditation. There was tension in the partnership with Antioch from the

outset. Rouse found his motives attacked by a number of Antioch's increasingly self-righteous radicals, and many on the faculty worried about the financing and the administrative arrangements, while some blanched at participating in a project sponsored by a private corporation.

48. See documents from the Administrative Council, December 4, 1968, Antiochiana, Antioch College.

49. See Olsen, *Better Places, Better Lives,* p. 202.

50. See Brooks, *New Towns and Communal Values,* p. 15. Rouse, quoted in Olsen, *Better Places, Better Lives,* p. 212.

51. "All-New Towns and Cities Seen Housing 30 Million," *Chicago Tribune,* May 23, 1970.

52. "New Town Begun in South Suburbs," *Chicago Tribune,* July 12, 1970.

53. Huber referred to this trip often. See "Statement of Donald L. Huber," unpublished manuscript, Wright State University Special Collections, Charles Simms Papers, Box 5, File 7; Jim Nichols, "Huber Inherited Bug," *Dayton Daily News,* April 1, 1973.

54. "Donald Huber, 20th Century Pioneer," Wright State University Special Collections, Charles Simms Papers, Box 5, File 9.

55. See Jim Babcock, "It Isn't Nice To Fool Mother Nature," *Dayton Journal Herald,* August 28, 1973.

56. "Newfields," unpublished manuscript, Wright State University Special Collections, Charles Simms Papers, Box 5, File 9.

57. See Thomas Grubisich, "New Towns Called Greatly Overrated," *Washington Post,* December 28, 1972; Brooks, *New Towns and Communal Values,* pp. 54–55, 143. See also Stuart MacCorkle, *Cities from Scratch: New Towns Planned for People* (San Antonio, TX: Naylor, 1974), p. 59, for a similar critique of Columbia and Reston.

58. Griscom Morgan, "Mental and Social Health and Population Density," unpublished manuscript, Antiochiana Collection, Olive Kettering Library, Antioch College, Community Service Inc., Box 27.

59. Letter from Don Huber to Montgomery County Commissioners, March 8, 1973, Wright State University Special Collections, Charles V. Sims Papers, Box 5, File 7; see also Frederick Steiner, *The Politics of New Town Planning: The Newfields Ohio Story* (Athens: Ohio University Press, 1981), esp. pp. 213–14.

60. U.S. Department of Housing and Urban Development, "New Communities: Problems and Potentials," unpublished manuscript, 1976, Library of Congress, p. 65.

61. Thomas Lippman, "Some Near Financial Collapse," *Washington Post,* November 15, 1974; "Federal Aid to 'New Towns' Is Reported Shutting Down," *New York Times,* January 11, 1975.

62. "New Town Blues," *Time,* October 16, 1978, p. 84.

63. Haar, quoted in Irving Lewis Allen, "New Towns and the Suburban Dream," in Irving Lewis Allen, ed., *New Towns and the Suburban Dream,* (Port Washington, NY: Kennikat Press, National University Publications, 1977), p. 4.

64. See "Thistles in the New Towns," *Time*, September 29, 1967.

65. Ken Ringle, "Reston At 7 Years: New Town Loses Its Innocence," *Washington Post*, July 16, 1972.

66. HUD, "New Communities: Problems and Potentials," pp. 8, 78–79.

67. "Brave New Towns that Aged Awkwardly," *Business Week*, January 9, 1971, pp. 22–24.

68. "Year of the Commune," *Newsweek*, August 18, 1969, p. 89; Hugh Gardner, *The Children of Prosperity* (New York: St. Martin's, 1978), p. 240; Timothy Miller, *The 60s Communes: Hippies and Beyond* (Syracuse: Syracuse University Press, 1999), p. 16; "A Strong Boost for 'New Towns,'" *Business Week*, May 31, 1969, p. 50. See also Rosabeth Moss Kanter, *Commitment and Community: Communes and Utopias in Sociological Perspective* (Cambridge, MA: Harvard University Press, 1972).

69. This migration had a small converse: some number of young people—artists, musicians, gays and lesbians—did move into places like the East Village in New York in search of social tolerance, like-minded community, and cheap rents. Thanks to Bryant Simon for pointing that out. It is also true that some activists from the 1960s rooted themselves in city neighborhoods and tried to create autonomous, almost utopian alternative communities. See Benjamin Looker, "Visions of Autonomy: The New Left and the Neighborhood Government Movement of the 1970s," *Journal of Urban History* 38 (2012): 577–98.

70. Sonya Rudikoff, "O Pioneers! Reflections on the Whole Earth People," *Commentary* 54 (1972): 64.

71. Charles Reich, *The Greening of America* (New York: Random House, 1970), p. 351.

72. *Antioch Review*, 30 (1970–71): 460; "The Greening of Black America," *Black Enterprise*, June 1979. Here, of course, "greening" has an entirely different connotation.

73. *Time*, February 2, 1970.

74. There are a number of histories of the environmental movement. See also Gregory Barton, "Sir Albert Howard and the Forestry Roots of the Organic Farming Movement," *Agricultural History* 75 (2001): 168–87.

75. Samuel P. Hays, "The Environmental Movement," *Journal of Forest History* 25 (1981):221. For a larger and more thematic examination of environmental politics in the second half of the 20th century, see Samuel P. Hays, *A History of Environmental Politics Since 1945* (Pittsburgh: University of Pittsburgh Press, 2000). In this book Hays takes what might be called an ecological approach to the question, emphasizing broad trends and contexts rather than tracing the chronology of specific events (see p. 3).

76. Stephen Diamond, *What the Trees Said: Life on a New Age Farm* (New York: Dell, 1971), p. 7; Tony Wagner, "Ecology of Revolution," *WIN*, August 1969, p. 6

77. Gardner, *Children of Prosperity*, pp. 249, 250. See also Robert Gottlieb, *Forcing the Spring: The Transformation of the American Environmental Movement* (Washington, DC: Island Press, 1993), p. 105, for more on the relationship between the counterculture and the environmental politics of everyday life.

78. Keith Melville, *Communes in the Counter Culture: Origins, Theories, Styles of Life* (New York: William Morrow, 1972), p. 11.

79. Melville, *Communes in the Counter Culture,* pp. 135, 144–45; letter to the editor, Igal Roodenko, *WIN,* September 1969, p. 33.

80. Observers have pointed out that plenty of communal living arrangements had sprung up in cities as well, but these tended more toward the rooming-house model, where communal living grew as an extension of real-estate convenience. As sociologist Benjamin Zablocki pointed out in his large field study of several rural communes, in the late 1960s "urban communes were still chiefly seen as way-stations to eventual rural settlement." Benjamin Zablocki, *Alienation and Charisma: A Study of Contemporary American Communes* (New York: Free Press, 1980), p. 51.

81. Melville, *Communes in the Counter Culture,* pp. 141–42.

82. Melville, *Communes in the Counter Culture,* pp. 63–64.

83. Diamond, *What the Trees Said,* p. 69.

84. Raymond Mungo, *Famous Long Ago* (Boston: Beacon Press, 1970), p. 165.

85. Albert H. Norman, "Take to the Hills," *Newsweek,* August 10, 1970, p. 76; Jack Newfield, *New York Times Book Review,* June 28, 1970, p. 29. The *Times* went on to name *Famous Long Ago* one of its notable books for 1970.

86. Norman, "Take to the Hills," p. 76; Melville, *Communes in the Counter Culture,* p. 67; *Times* quote from Raymond Mungo, *Total Loss Farm* (New York: E. P. Dutton, 1970), p. 45; "Radical's Suicide Puzzles Friends," *New York Times,* November 4, 1969.

87. As I can report from personal experience, even in the late-1990s the septic system at Montague Farm was notoriously fragile.

88. Bennett M. Berger, "American Pastoralism, Suburbia, and the Commune Movement," *Society* 16 (1979): 64.

89. Martin Jezer, *WIN,* August 1969, p. 5; Mungo, *Total Loss Farm,* p. 17; Diamond, *What the Trees Said,* p. 182.

90. Mungo, *Total Loss Farm,* p. 39.

91. Floyd McKissick, "The Free-Standing New Town: New Options?" in John C. DeBoer and Alexander Greendale, eds., *Are New Towns for Lower Income Americans Too?* (New York: Praeger, 1974), p. 20.

92. "Negroes To Build Their Own 'New Town'" *New York Times,* January 14, 1969.

93. Quoted in "The New Raid on Nader," *Christian Century* 87 (1970): 1176.

94. See "To Blacks, Ecology is Irrelevant," *Business Week,* November 14, 1970, p. 49; "The Rise of Anti-Ecology," *Time,* August 3, 1970, p. 42. In fairness, there were others who saw critical connections between the new issue of environmentalism and the older issues of the war, poverty, and race; who saw the issues of the city and the issues of the environment as linked in important ways. The *Christian Century* insisted that "there is no necessary contradiction between anti poverty and anti pollution strategies." Likewise, in Washington, D.C., one speaker told the crowd at a demonstration that the Vietnam War was "an ecological catastrophe" and warned

that "politicians and businessmen who are jumping on the environmental bandwagon don't have the slightest idea what they are getting into. They are talking about filters on smokestacks while we are challenging corporate irresponsibility." See "The New Raid on Nader," p. 1176; speaker quoted in Gottlieb, *Forcing the Spring*, p. 112. Andrew Hurley in his examination of the environmental justice has discovered that "in many instances, efforts to abate pollution and preserve existing landscapes coincided with the interests of workers and minorities, and at times, African American and blue-collar workers collaborated with environmentalists." He does acknowledge, however, that these coalitions "occurred infrequently." See Andrew Hurley, *Environmental Inequalities: Class, Race, and Industrial Pollution in Gary, Indiana, 1945-1980* (Chapel Hill: University of North Carolina Press, 1995), p. 11.

95. Zablocki, *Alienation and Charisma*, p. 89. In his later study of these communes, Timothy Miller offers a no more satisfying analysis. "The communes of the 1960s era were overwhelmingly white," he reiterates, and while "the communards considered themselves entirely open to accepting nonwhite members, [f]ew nonwhites...were interested." Miller, *The 60s Communes*, p. 170.

96. On a hot summer afternoon in 2008, I chatted with an elderly black man in North Philadelphia who described picking watermelons as a kid in South Carolina. He hated it so much he promised himself at the age of 12 that he would never do it again. He left the South and came to Philadelphia a few years later. We laughed at this because we were standing in the middle of his community garden where he was hoeing sweet potatoes.

97. Louie Robinson, "Life Inside a Hippie Commune," *Ebony* 26 (1970): 88, 91.

98. Paul Prensky, "End of the World Ecology of the World Beginning," *WIN*, August 1969, p. 21.

99. Quoted in Ron Roberts, *The New Communes* (Englewood Cliffs, NJ: Prentice-Hall, 1971), p. 142.

100. Reich, *Greening of America*, p. 350.

101. Wagner, "Ecology of Revolution," p. 6; booklet cited in Jim Bennett, "Ecological Planning," *WIN*, October 1969.

102. Melville, *Communes in the Counter Culture*, p. 80.

103. Mungo, *Famous Long Ago*, p. 187.

104. Personal conversation with Harvey Wasserman.

105. Gottlieb, *Forcing the Spring*, p. 113.

106. Richard Gale, "From Sit-In to Hike-In: A Comparison of the Civil Rights and Environmental Movements," in William R. Burch Jr., Neil H. Cheek Jr., and Lee Taylor, eds., *Social Behavior, Natural Resources, and the Environment* (New York: Harper & Row, 1972), pp. 280–305.

107. See "The Rise of Anti-Ecology," *Time*, August 3, 1970, p. 42.

108. See Gottlieb, *Forcing the Spring*, p. 97.

109. Thanks to Tom Sugrue and his blog "Rustbelt Intellectual" for bringing this to my attention.

110. See *Time*, February 2, 1970.

111. Jim Bennett, "Ecological Planning," *WIN*, October 1969, p. 21.

112. Paul Goodman, "Ungovernable Cities," *WIN*, August 1969, p. 37.

113. Muskie, quoted in Gottlieb, *Forcing the Spring*, p. 112.

114. Robert Park, "The City: Suggestions for the Investigation of Human Behavior in the City Environment," *American Journal of Sociology* 20 (1915): 608–609.

CHAPTER 9

1. Robert D. Putnam, *Bowling Alone: The Collapse and Revival of American Community* (New York: Simon & Schuster, 2000), p. 25.

2. From their website, communitariannetwork.org, accessed spring 2011. Others associated with communitarianism include Robert Bellah, Robert Putnam, Michael Sandel, and Michael Walzer.

3. Etzioni, quoted in Michael D'Antonio, "I or We?" *Mother Jones* 19 (May/June 1994): 20.

4. Amitai Etzioni, *The Spirit of Community* (New York: Touchstone, 1993), p. 134. For a particularly smart review see Robert Fogarty, "All Together Now," *Nation*, December 6, 1993, pp. 696–701.

5. Etzioni, *Spirit of Community*, p. 136.

6. D'Antonio, "I or We?" p. 20.

7. Amitai Etzioni, "Back to the Pillory," *American Scholar* 68 (Summer 1999): 43–50.

8. D'Antonio, "I or We?", p. 20.

9. Henry Tam, another communitarian, stressed the idea of "inclusive communities" in his book, and while Tam placed more emphasis on "market individualism" as a root of our current malaise than Etzioni did, he was similarly vague about how to negotiate the problem of inclusion and exclusion. Henry Tam, *Communitarianism: A New Agenda for Politics and Citizenship* (New York: New York University Press, 1998).

10. See Richard T. Ford's review essay "The Repressed Community: Locating the New Communitarianism," *Transition* 65 (1995): 96; Etzioni, *Spirit of Community*, p. 127.

11. Etzioni, "Back to the Pillory"; Etzioni, *Spirit of Community*, p. 121.

12. Putnam, *Bowling Alone*, p. 283.

13. Vincent Scully, "The Architecture of Community," and Todd Bressi, "Planning the American Dream," both in Peter Katz, ed., *The New Urbanism: Toward an Architecture of Community* (New York: McGraw-Hill, 1994), pp. 223–24, xxv.

14. Jay Tolson, "Putting the brakes on suburban sprawl," *U.S. News and World Report*, March 20, 2000, p. 64.

15. Andres Duany, Elizabeth Plater-Zyberk, and Jeff Speck, *Suburban Nation: The Rise of Sprawl and the Decline of the American Dream* (New York: North Point Press, 2000), p. xiii.

16. Duany, Plater-Zyberk and Speck, *Suburban Nation,* pp. x, xiii, 243.

17. Quoted in Duany, Plater-Zyberk, and Speck, *Suburban Nation,* p. 99; see Tim Padgett, "Saving Suburbia," *Time,* August 16, 1999, pp. 50–51.

18. Jay Tolson, "Putting the Brakes on Suburban Sprawl," *U.S. News and World Report,* March 20, 2000, p. 64; quoted in Padgett, "Saving Suburbia," p. 50.

19. See *Philadelphia Daily News,* March 31, 2009.

20. *New Urbanism: Comprehensive Report & Best Practices Guide* (Ithaca: New Urban Publications, 2001), pp. 2–5.

21. In 1997, Andrew Ross moved to Celebration, much as Herbert Gans had moved to Levittown a generation earlier, lived there for a year, and wrote a book about his experience. His goal was neither to bury nor to praise, and what he found was a population aware of the many contradictions about living in a Disney town, but prepared to live with them anyway. Andrew Ross, *The Celebration Chronicles* (New York: Ballantine, 1999), quote from p. 299.

22. Kathleen Howley, "Foreclosures Slam Utopian Disney Town," *Miami Herald,* December 18, 2010, quotes from this article.

23. Scully, "Architecture of Community," p. 266.

24. Alex Krieger, "Reinventing Public Space," *Architectural Record,* 183 (June 1995), pp. 76–77.

25. One of the first attempts to assess the effects of Reagan's policies—mostly budget-cutting—on American cities can be found in George E. Peterson and Carol W. Lewis, eds., *Reagan and the Cities* (Washington, DC: Urban Institute Press, 1986). Among the findings reported here is that cities suffered from the Reagan recession less than some had predicted. Given that cities found themselves dealing with thousands of newly homeless and with the tsunami of crack cocaine and its accompanying violence, some might beg to disagree with that sunny assessment. Assuming for a moment that the authors are right, it isn't clear whether this is attributable to Reagan's urban policies or to the inherent resilience of cities themselves.

26. See David Whitman, "Raising Hopes by Razing High-rises," *U. S. News & World Report,* February 21, 2000, p. 28; Sarah Downey and John McCormick, "Razing Vertical Ghettos," *Newsweek,* May 15, 2000, pp. 36–37.

27. I have taken this summary from John Ingram Gilderbloom, *Invisible City: Poverty, Housing and New Urbanism* (Austin: University of Texas Press, 2008), p. 115.

28. See *New Urbanism,* esp. sec. 3.

29. See Susan J. Popkin, Diane K. Levy, and Larry Buron, "Has HOPE VI Transformed Residents' Lives? New Evidence from the HOPE VI Panel Study," *Housing Studies* 24 (July 2009): 477–502; Margery Austin Turner, "Neighborhood Recovery, and the Health of Cities," in Henry Cisneros and Lora Engdahl, eds., *From Despair to Hope: HOPE VI and the New Promise of Public Housing in America's Cities* (Washington, DC: Brookings Institution Press, 2009), pp. 169–89.

30. Haya El Nasser, "Gated Communities More Popular, and Not Just for the Rich," *USA Today,* December 16, 2002.

31. See Edward J. Blakely and Mary Gail Snyder, *Fortress America: Gated Communities in the United States* (Washington, DC: Brookings Institution Press, 1997). Blakely and Snyder note that there are different kinds of gated communities and have created a typology of them. I have borrowed the phrase "governing by legal contract, not social contract" from them, p. 20.

32. From the website www.gatedcommunitiesusa.com, accessed February 2012.

33. Quoted in El Nasser, "Gated Communities More Popular." Setha Low has written about the relationship between these gated places and a larger discourse of fear. See Setha Low, *Behind the Gates: The New American Dream* (New York: Routledge, 2003).

34. Kevin Baker, "How The GOP Became The Anti-Urban Party," *New York Times*, October 6, 2012.

AFTERWORD

1. Frances Trollope, *Domestic Manners of the Americans*, (New York: Vintage Books, 1960).

2. Edward Glaeser, *The Triumph of the City* (New York: Penguin Press, 2011), p. 264.

3. See Jane Holtz Kay, *Asphalt Nation: How the Automobile Took Over America and How We Can Take It Back* (New York: Crown, 1997), p. 258. See also Douglas S. Kelbaugh, *Repairing the American Metropolis* (Seattle: University of Washington Press, 2002). Kelbaugh offers both a tally of what sprawl has cost us and a set of prescriptions for how to fix it.

4. Edmund Bacon, "The City Image," in Elizabeth Geen et al., eds., *Man and the Modern City*, (Pittsburgh: University of Pittsburgh Press, 1963), p. 26.

5. Quoted in Dolores Hayden, *Building Suburbia: Green Fields and Urban Growth, 1820–2000* (New York, Pantheon, 2003), p. 157.

6. See, for example, Glaeser, *Triumph of the City*,; Jane Jacobs, *Cities and the Wealth of Nations* (New York: Random House, 1984); and David Owen, "Green Manhattan," *The New Yorker*, October 18, 2004.

7. William Whyte, "Are Cities Un-American?" in William Whyte, *The Exploding Metropolis* (Garden City: Doubleday Anchor, 1958), p. 18.

8. Elijah Anderson, *Cosmopolitan Canopies: Race and Civility in Everyday Life* (New York: W. W. Norton & Company, 2011), p. 276.

9. Robert Wood, "The American Suburb: Boy's Town in a Man's World," in *Man and the Modern City*, p. 121. The real significance of Newt Gingrich was not that he was the first Speaker of the House from Georgia in the 20th century, but that he was the first Speaker from the suburbs. Kevin Kruse discusses this in the Epilogue to his *White Flight: Atlanta and the Making of Modern Conservatism* (Princeton: Princeton University Press, 2005).

10. Louis Wirth, "Urbanism as a Way of Life," *American Journal of Sociology* 44 (1938): 1–24.

11. Eric Hobsbawm, *The Age of Extremes: A History of the World, 1914-1991* (New York: Vintage, 1994), p. 428. See also John F. Friere, *Counterfeit Community: The Exploitation of Our Longing for Connectedness* (Lanham, MD: Rowman & Littlefield, 1998).

12. As long ago as 1970 the conservative commentator Irving Kristol believed that the real urban crisis was exactly this crisis of vision and value. "The challenge to our urban democracy," he wrote, "is to evolve a set of values and a conception of democracy that can function as the equivalent of the 'republican morality' of yesteryear." Irving Kristol, "Urban Civilization and its Discontents," *Commentary* 50 (July 1970): 35.

13. Richard Sennett has written a great deal about the relationship between cities and the public. See *The Fall of Public Man* (New York: Alfred A. Knopf, 1977). Like Whyte, Sennett believes in the civic importance of the impersonal interactions of the sort that happen regularly in the city. Richard Ford has also made these points about cities and communities in his essay "The Repressed Community: Locating the New Communitarianism," *Transition* 65 (1995): 96–117.

BIBLIOGRAPHY

Abbott, Carl. *The New Urban America: Growth and Politics in Sunbelt Cities*. Chapel Hill: University of North Carolina Press, 1981.

Adamic, Louis. *My America, 1928–1938*. New York: Harper & Brothers, 1938.

Adamic, Louis. "Tragic Towns of New England," *Harper's Monthly* 162 (1930–31): 748–60.

Adams, Henry. *The Education of Henry Adams*. Cambridge, MA: Riverside Press, 1918.

Addams, Jane. *The Spirit of Youth and the City Streets*. New York: Macmillan, 1909.

Addams, Jane. *Twenty Years at Hull House*. Boston: Bedford/St. Martin, 1999.

Allen, Irving Lewis, ed. *New Towns and the Suburban Dream*. Port Washington, NY: Kennikat Press, National University Publications, 1977.

Amsterdam, Daniel. *Building a Civic Welfare State: Businessmen's Forgotten Campaign to Remake Industrial America*. Philadelphia: University of Pennsylvania Press, forthcoming.

Anderson, Elijah. *Cosmopolitan Canopies: Race and Civility in Everyday Life*. New York: W. W. Norton, 2011.

Anderson, Larry. *Benton MacKaye: Conservationist, Planner, and Creator of the Appalachian Trail*. Baltimore: Johns Hopkins University Press, 2002.

Anderson, Martin. *The Federal Bulldozer*. New York: McGraw Hill, 1964.

Anderson, Martin. "The Sophistry that Made Urban Renewal Possible." *Law and Contemporary Problems* 30 (1965): 199–211.

Arnold, Joseph. *The New Deal in the Suburbs: A History of the Greenbelt Town Program, 1935-1954*. Columbus: Ohio State University Press, 1971.

Augur, Tracy. *Radburn: The Challenge of a New Town*. New York: City Housing Corporation, 1931.

Bacon, Mardges. *Le Corbusier in America: Travels in the Land of the Timid*. Cambridge, MA: MIT Press, 2001.

Bagaeen, Samer, and Ola Uduku, eds. *Gated Communities: Social Sustainability in Contemporary and Historical Gated Developments*. London: Earthscan, 2010.

Bailey, James. "A Case History of Failure." *Architectural Forum*, 23 (1965): 22–25.

Bailey, James, ed. *New Towns in America: The Design and Development Process*. New York: John Wiley, 1973.

Baker, Laura E. "Civic Ideals, Mass Culture, and the Public: Reconsidering the 1909 *Plan of Chicago.*" *Journal of Urban History* 36 (2010): 747–70.

Baltzell, E. Digby. *The Search for Community in Modern America.* New York: Harper & Row, 1968.

Barton, Gregory. "Sir Albert Howard and the Forestry Roots of the Organic Farming Movement." *Agricultural History* 75 (2001): 168–87.

Bauer, Catherine. "The Architects and Urban Renewal." *Journal of Architectural Education* 10 (1955): 37–38.

Bauer, Catherine. "The Swiss Family Borsodi." *Nation*, October 25, 1933, pp. 489–90.

Bauman, John. *Public Housing, Race, and Renewal: Urban Planning in Philadelphia.* Philadelphia: Temple University Press, 1987.

Bauman, John, Roger Biles, and Kristin Szylvian, eds. *From Tenements to the Taylor Homes: In Search of an Urban Housing Policy in Twentieth-Century America.* University Park: Pennsylvania State University Press, 2000.

Bayor, Ronald H. *Race and the Shaping of Twentieth Century Atlanta.* Chapel Hill: University of North Carolina Press, 1996.

Beauregard, Robert A. *When America Became Suburban.* Minneapolis: University of Minnesota Press, 2006.

Becker, Jane S. *Selling Tradition: Appalachia and the Construction of an American Folk, 1930-1940.* Chapel Hill: University of North Carolina Press, 1998.

Bender, Thomas. *Community and Social Change in America.* Baltimore: Johns Hopkins University Press, 1978.

Benedict, Ruth. *Patterns of Culture.* Boston: Houghton Mifflin, 1934.

Bennett, Charles A., "What Price Utopia?" *Harper's Monthly* 156 (1927-28): 782–84.

Bennett, James. *Frederick Jackson Turner.* Boston: Twayne, 1975.

Bennett, Larry. *Fragments of Cities: The New American Downtowns and Neighborhoods.* Columbus: Ohio State University Press, 1990.

Berger, Bennett M. "American Pastoralism, Suburbia, and the Commune Movement." *Society* 16 (1979): 64–69.

Bernard, Richard M., and Bradley R. Rice, eds. *Sunbelt Cities: Politics and Growth Since World War II.* Austin: University of Texas Press, 1983.

Biles, Roger. *A New Deal for the American People.* DeKalb: Northern Illinois University Press, 1991.

Blake, Casey Nelson. *Beloved Community: The Cultural Criticism of Randolph Bourne, Van Wyck Brooks, Waldo Frank and Lewis Mumford.* Chapel Hill: University of North Carolina Press, 1990.

Blakely, Edward, and Mary Gail Snyder. *Fortress America: Gated Communities in the United States.* Washington, DC: Brookings Institution Press, 1997.

Blevins, Brooks. "'In the Land of a Million Smiles': Twentieth-Century America Discovers the Arkansas Ozarks." *Arkansas Historical Quarterly* 61, no. 1 (Spring 2002): 1–35.

Bloom, Nicholas Dagen. *Merchant of Illusion: America's Salesman of the Businessman's Utopia*. Columbus: Ohio State University Press, 2004.

Bogue, Allan. *Frederick Jackson Turner: Strange Roads Going Down*. Norman, OK: University of Oklahoma Press, 1998.

Bone, Hugh. "Greenbelt Faces 1939." *American City* 54 (1939): 59–61.

Borsodi, Ralph. "Dayton, Ohio, Makes Social History." *Nation*, April 19, 1933, pp. 447–48.

Borsodi, Ralph. *Flight from the City: The Story of a New Way to Family Security*. New York: Harper Brothers, 1933.

Borsodi, Ralph. *This Ugly Civilization*. Philadelphia: Porcupine Press, 1975.

Bottles, Scott. *Los Angeles and the Automobile*. Berkeley: University of California Press, 1987.

Bouchard, Angeline. "Metropolis versus Province." *Free America* 2 (1938): 9–12.

Bourne, Randolph. "Trans-National America." *The Atlantic* 118 (July, 1916): 86–97.

Bowers, William. *The Country Life Movement in America, 1900-1920*. Port Washington, NY: Kennikat Press, 1974.

Breckenfeld, Gurney. *Columbia and the New Cities*. New York: Ives Washburn, 1971.

Bronner, Simon. *American Folklore Studies: An Intellectual History*. Lawrence: University of Kansas Press, 1986.

Brooks, Richard Oliver. *New Towns and Communal Values: A Case Study of Columbia, Maryland*. New York: Praeger, 1974.

Brooks, Van Wyck. *The Flowering of New England*. New York: E. P. Dutton, 1952.

Brown, Dona. *Back to the Land: The Enduring Dream of Self-Sufficiency in Modern America*. Madison: University of Wisconsin Press, 2011.

Brown, Philip S. "What Has Happened at Greenbelt?" *New Republic* 105 (1941): 183–85.

Brown, Victoria Bissell. *The Education of Jane Addams*. Philadelphia: University of Pennsylvania Press, 2004.

Brownell, Baker. "Doom of the City." *Free America* 1 (1937): 4–7.

Buckley, William F. Jr. *Did You Ever See a Dream Walking?: American Conservative Thought in the 20th Century*. Indianapolis: Bobbs-Merrill, 1970.

Burch, Jr., William R., Neil H. Cheek Jr., and Lee Taylor, eds. *Social Behavior, Natural Resources, and the Environment*. New York: Harper & Row, 1972.

Burgess, Ernest W. "Can Neighborhood Work Have a Scientific Basis?" *Proceedings of the National Conference of Social Work* 51 (1924): 406–11.

Burgess, Ernest W., ed. *The Urban Community: Selected Papers from the Proceedings of the American Sociological Society, 1925*. Chicago: University of Chicago Press, 1926.

Caldwell, William A., ed. *How to Save Urban America*. New York: New American Library for the Regional Planning Association, 1973.

Carlson, David. "Urban Renewal: Running Hard, Sitting Still." *Architectural Forum* 116 (April 1962): 99.

Carlton, Frank T. "Urban and Rural Life." *Popular Science Monthly* 68 (1906): 255–60.

Carriker, Robert M. *Urban Farming in the West: A New Deal Experiment in Subsistence Homesteads*. Tucson: University of Arizona Press, 2010.

Casillo, Robert. "Lewis Mumford and the Organicist Concept in Social Thought." *Journal of the History of Ideas* 53 (1992): 91–116.

Cayton, Andrew, and Susan Gray, eds. *The American Midwest: Essays in Regional History*. Bloomington: Indiana University Press, 2001.

Chapman, Edward M. *New England Village Life*. Cambridge, MA: Riverside Press, 1937.

Churchill, Henry. "America's Town Planning Begins." *New Republic* 87 (1936): 96–98.

Cisneros, Henry, and Lora Engdahl, eds. *From Despair to Hope: HOPE VI and the New Promise of Public Housing in America's Cities*. Washington, DC: Brookings Institution Press, 2009.

"The City and the Citizen." *Outlook* 74 (1903): 109–111.

Clark, Burton. *The Distinctive College*. New York: Aldine, 1970.

Clayton, Bruce. *Forgotten Prophet: The Life of Randolph Bourne*. Columbia, MO: University of Missouri Press, 1998.

Collier, John. *From Every Zenith: A Memoir*. New York: Sage Books, 1963.

"Columbus, Ohio Starts Big Physical Improvement Program." *American City* 72 (February, 1957): 112.

"The Columbus Riot," unpublished report. Columbus, OH: Planning and Research Bureau, 1969.

"The Commission on Country Life." *World's Work* 17 (1908): 10860–61.

"Community Life in Radburn," *Survey* 66 (1931): 99–100.

Comprehensive Plan—Houston Urban Area; 1c Population, Land Use, Growth. Houston: Houston City Planning Commission, 1959.

Conforti, John A. *Imagining New England: Explorations of Regional Identity from the Pilgrims to the Mid-Twentieth Century*. Chapel Hill: University of North Carolina Press, 2001.

Conkin, Paul. *A Requiem for the American Village*. New York: Rowman & Littlefield, 2000.

Conkin, Paul. *Tomorrow a New World: The New Deal Community Program*. Ithaca: Cornell University Press, 1959.

Conn, Steven, ed. *To Promote the General Welfare: The Case for Big Government*. New York: Oxford University Press, 2012.

Connery, Robert, and Richard Leach. "Southern Metropolis: Challenge to Government." *Journal of Politics* 26 (1964): 60–81.

Cooke, Morris Llewellyn. *Our Cities Awake: Notes on Municipal Activities and Administration*. Garden City, NY: Doubleday: 1918.

Cord, Steven. "Urban Renewal: Boon or Boondoggle?" *American Journal of Economics and Sociology* 33 (1974): 184–86.

Crepeau, Richard C. *Melbourne Village: The First Twenty-Five Years (1946-1971).* Orlando: University of Central Florida, 1988.

Danborn, David. "Romantic Agrarianism in Twentieth-Century America." *Agricultural History* 65 (1991): 1–12.

Daniels, Jonathan. *A Southerner Discovers New England.* New York: Macmillan, 1940.

D'Antonio, Michael. "I or We?" *Mother Jones* 19 (May/June 1994): 20.

Davidson, Donald. *The Attack on Leviathan: Regionalism and Nationalism in the United States.* Chapel Hill: University of North Carolina Press, 1938.

Davies, Richard. *Main Street Blues: The Decline of Small-Town America.* Columbus: Ohio State University Press, 1998.

Davis, F. James. "The Effects of a Freeway Displacement on Racial Housing Segregation in a Northern City." *Phylon* 26 (1965): 209–215.

Daynes, Bryan, William Pederson, Michael Riccards, eds. *The New Deal and Public Policy.* New York: St. Martin's, 1998.

DeBoer, John C., and Alexander Greendale, eds. *Are New Towns for Lower Income Americans Too?* New York: Praeger, 1974.

Deegan, Mary Jo. *Jane Addams and the Men of the Chicago School, 1892-1918.* New Brunswick, NJ: Transaction, 1988.

DeVoto, Bernard. "New England, There She Stands." *Harper's Monthly* 164 (1932): 405–15.

DeVoto, Bernard. "The Real Frontier." *Harper's Monthly* 163 (1931): 60–71.

Dewey, John. *The Public and Its Problems.* New York: Henry Holt, 1946.

Diamond, Stephen. *What the Trees Said: Life on a New Age Farm.* New York: Dell, 1971.

Diggs, Annie. "The Garden City Movement." *Arena* 28 (1902): 626–634.

Dilworth, Richardson. *The Urban Origins of Suburban Autonomy.* Cambridge, MA: Harvard University Press, 2005.

Dobriner, William M., ed. *The Suburban Community.* New York: G. P. Putnam, 1958.

"Does the Smaller City Have a Future?" *Changing Times* (June 1970): 25–28.

Donaldson, Scott. "City and Country: Marriage Proposals." *American Quarterly* 20 (1968): 547–66.

Dorman, Robert L. *Revolt of the Provinces: The Regionalist Movement in America, 1920-1945.* Chapel Hill: University of North Carolina Press, 1993.

Dorn, Jacob. "The Rural Ideal and Agrarian Realities: Arthur E. Holt and the Vision of a Decentralized America in the Interwar Years." *Church History* 52 (1983): 50–65.

Dorn, Jacob. "Subsistence Homesteading in Dayton, Ohio 1933-1935." *Ohio History* 78 (1969): 75–93.

"Downtown Area Plan," report prepared by the Planning Division, Department of Development, City of Columbus, 1970.

Doxiadis, C. A. *Urban Renewal and the Future of the American City.* Chicago: Public Administration Service for the National Association of Housing and Redevelopment Officials, 1966.

Drake, Richard B. *A History of Appalachia*. Lexington: University of Kentucky Press, 2001.

Dreiser, Theodore. "The Loneliness of the City." *Tom Watson's Magazine* 2 (1905): 474–75.

Duany, Andres, Elizabeth Plater-Zyberk and Jeff Speck, *Suburban Nation: The Rise of Sprawl and the Decline of the American Dream*. New York: North Point Press, 2000.

Dunn, Durwood. *Cades Cove: The Life and Death of a Southern Appalachian Community, 1818-1937*. Knoxville: University of Tennessee Press, 1988.

Dyckman, John. "The Changing Uses of the City" *Daedelus* 90 (1961): 111–31.

Eichler, Edward, and Marshall Kaplan, *The Community Builders*. Berkeley: University of California Press, 1967.

Ely, Richard. *The Coming City*. New York: Thomas Y. Crowell, 1902.

Etzioni, Amitai. *The Spirit of Community*. New York: Touchstone Books, 1993.

Etzioni, Amitai. "Back to the Pillory." *American Scholar* 68 (Summer 1999): 43–50.

Fairbanks, Richard B. "The Failure of Urban Renewal in the Southwest: From City Needs to Individual Rights." *Western Historical Quarterly* 37 (2006): 303–25.

Fairfield, John D. *The Public and its Possibilities: Triumphs and Tragedies in the American City*. Philadelphia: Temple University Press, 2010.

Faragher, John Mack. *Rereading Frederick Jackson Turner*. New York: Henry Holt, 1994.

"Farm and City and Factory." *Survey* 25 (1911): 896–97.

Feagin, Joe R. *Free Enterprise City: Houston in Political-Economic Perspective*. New Brunswick, NJ: Rutgers University Press, 1988.

Feuer, Lewis. "John Dewey and the Back to the People Movement in American Thought." *Journal of the History of Ideas* 20 (1959): 545–68.

Fishman, Robert. *Bourgeois Utopias: The Rise and Fall of Suburbia*. New York: Basic Books, 1987.

Fishman, Robert. "The Mumford-Jacobs Debate," *Planning History Studies* 10 (1996): 3–11.

Fishman, Robert. *Urban Utopias in the Twentieth Century: Ebenezer Howard, Frank Lloyd Wright, and Le Corbusier*. New York: Basic Books, 1977.

Flink, James. *The Automobile Age*. Cambridge, MA: MIT Press, 1988.

Flynn, John T. *Country Squire in the White House*. New York: Doubleday, Doran, 1940.

Flynn, John T. *The Road Ahead*. New York: Committee for Constitutional Government with Devin-Adair, 1949.

Fogarty, Robert. "All Together Now." *Nation*, December 6, 1993, pp. 696–701.

Fogarty, Robert. *All Things New: American Communes and Utopian Movements, 1860-1914*. Chicago: University of Chicago Press, 1990.

Ford, Richard T. "The Repressed Community: Locating the new communitarianism." *Transition* 65 (1995): 96–117.

Forsyth, Ann. *Reforming Suburbia: The Planned Communities of Irvine, Columbia, and the Woodlands*. Berkeley: University of California Press, 2005.

Freeman, Suzanne, and Morrow Wilson, eds. *Rural America*. New York: H. H. Wilson, 1976.

Frieden, Bernard. *The Future of Old Neighborhoods: Rebuilding for a Changing Population*. Cambridge, MA: MIT Press, 1964.

Frieden, Bernard J. and Robert Morris, eds. *Urban Planning and Social Policy*. New York: Basic Books, 1968.

Friedrich, Carl, ed. *Community*. New York: Liberal Arts Press, 1959.

Friere, John F. *Counterfeit Community: The Exploitation of Our Longings for Connectedness*. Lanham, MD: Rowan & Littlefield, 1998.

Fuermann, George. *Houston: Land of the Big Rich*. Garden City, NY: Country Life Press, 1951.

Gans, Herbert. "The Failure of Urban Renewal: A Critique and Some Proposals." *Commentary* 39, no. 4 (April 1965): 29–37.

Gardner, Hugh. *The Children of Prosperity*. New York: St. Martin's, 1978.

Geen, Elizabeth, Jeanne Low and Kenneth Walker, eds. *Man and the Modern City*. Pittsburgh: University of Pittsburgh Press, 1963.

Gelfand, Mark. *A Nation of Cities: The Federal Government and Urban America, 1933-1965*. New York: Oxford University Press, 1975.

Gershman, Carl. "Isolation of the New Left." *Nation* (1969): 666.

Gilbert, Richard L. Jr. "Phoenix Unreborn," *The Reporter* 29 (November 21, 1963): 48–49.

Gilderbloom, John Ingram. *Invisible City: Poverty, Housing and New Urbanism*. Austin: University of Texas Press, 2008.

Gillette, Howard. "Film as Artifact: The City." *American Studies* 2 (1977): 71–85.

Glaeser, Edward. *The Triumph of the City*. New York: Penguin Press, 2011.

Goist, Park Dixon, "City and 'Community': The Urban Theory of Robert Park." *American Quarterly* 23 (1971): 46–59.

Goist, Park Dixon. "Lewis Mumford and 'Anti-Urbanism.'" *Journal of the American Institute of Planners* 35 (1969): 340–47.

Goldwater, Barry. *The Conscience of a Conservative*. Shepardville, KY: Victor Publishing Co., 1960.

Gottlieb, Robert. *Forcing the Spring: The Transformation of the American Environmental Movement*. Washington, DC: Island Press, 1993.

"The Great Country Life Movement." *World's Work* 23 (1911–12): 616–19.

Greenbelt Towns. Washington, DC: Resettlement Administration, 1936.

Gura, Philip. *American Transcendentalism*. New York: Hill and Wang, 2007.

Gutfreund, Owen. *Twentieth-Century Sprawl: Highways and Reshaping of the American Landscape*. New York: Oxford University Press, 2004.

Gutkind, E. A. *The Twilight of Cities*. New York: Free Press of Glencoe, 1962.

Gutkind, E. A. *The Expanding Environment: The End of Cities—The Rise of Communities*. London: Freedom Press, 1953.

Habermas, Jurgen. *The Structural Transformation of the Public Sphere*. Cambridge, MA: MIT Press, 1989.

Hallenbeck, Wilbur. *American Urban Communities*. New York: Harper Brothers, 1951.

Handler, Richard. "Boasian Anthropology and the Critique of American Culture." *American Quarterly* 42 (1990): 252–73.

Handler, Richard. "Ruth Benedict, Margaret Mead, and the Growth of Anthropology." *Journal of American History* 71 (1984): 364–68.

Hartman, Chester. "Relocation: Illusory Promises and No Relief." *Virginia Law Review* 57 (1971): 745–817.

Hartt, Rollin Lynde. "A New England Small Town." *World's Work* 10 (1905): 6275–88.

Harvey, David. *The Condition of Post-Modernity: An Enquiry Into the Origins of Cultural Change*. London: Wiley, 1989.

Hayden, Dolores. *Building Suburbia: Green Fields and Urban Growth, 1820-2000*. New York: Pantheon, 2003.

Hayden, Dolores. *The Power of Place: Urban Landscapes as Public History*. Cambridge, MA: MIT Press, 1995.

Hays, Samuel P. *A History of Environmental Politics Since 1945*. Pittsburgh: University of Pittsburgh Press, 2000.

Hays, Samuel P. "The Environmental Movement," *Journal of Forest History* 25 (1981): 219–221.

Hayward, Stephen. "Legends of the Sprawl." *Policy Review* 91 (1998): 26–33.

Hewes, Thomas. *Decentralize for Liberty*. New York: E. P. Dutton, 1947.

Hicks, Granville. *Small Town*. New York: Macmillan, 1947.

Higham, John. *Writing American History: Essays on Modern Scholarship*. Bloomington: Indiana University Press, 1970.

Hillery, George A. Jr. "Definitions of Community: Areas of Agreement." *Rural Sociology* 20 (1955): 111–23.

Hines, Thomas S. *Burnham of Chicago: Architect and Planner*. New York: Oxford University Press, 1974.

Hirsch, Arnold. *Making the Second Ghetto: Race and Housing in Chicago, 1940-1960*. Chicago: University of Chicago Press, 1983.

Hirsch, Arnold, and Raymond Mohl, eds. *Urban Policy in Twentieth-Century America*. New Brunswick, NJ: Rutgers University Press, 1993.

Hiss, Tony. *The Experience of Place*. New York: Vintage, 1990.

Hobsbawm, Eric. *The Age of Extremes: A History of the World, 1914-1991*. New York: Vintage, 1994.

Hoffer, C. R. "The Development of Rural Sociology." *American Journal of Sociology* 32 (1926): 95–103.

Hollinger, David. *Postethnic America: Beyond Multiculturalism*. New York: Basic Books, 1995.

Holwerk, David. "Interstate 75: A Morality Play." *Nation* 215 (November 20, 1972): 492–95.

Horton, Paul David. *A Study of Administrative and Planning Deficiencies*, MA thesis, Ohio State University, 1964.

Howard, John. "An Urban Rehabilitation Program for Cleveland." *Journal of the American Institute of Planners* 10 (1944): 18–23.

Howe, Frederic. "In Defense of the American City." *Scribner's* 51 (1912): 484–85.

Howe, Frederic C. *The City: The Hope of Democracy*. New York: Charles Scribner's Sons, 1913.

Howe, Frederic C. *The British City: The Beginnings of Democracy*. New York: Charles Scribner's Sons, 1907.

Houston City Planning Commission. "Condition of Residential Structures Survey," 1959.

Hoyt, Homer. "Recent Distortions of the Classical Models of Urban Structure." *Land Economics* 40 (May, 1964): 199–212.

Hudson, Robert. *Radburn: A Plan for Living*. New York: American Association for Adult Education, 1934.

Hull House Maps and Papers. New York: Thomas Y. Crowell, 1895.

Hunt, D. Bradford. "What Went Wrong with Public Housing in Chicago?" *Journal of the Illinois State Historical Society* 94 (Spring 2001): 96–124.

Hunter, Robert. *The Tenement Conditions in Chicago*. Chicago: City Homes Association, 1901.

Hurley, Andrew. *Environmental Inequalities: Class, Race, and Industrial Pollution in Gary, Indiana, 1945-1980*. Chapel Hill: University of North Carolina Press, 1995.

Hynes, Emerson. "Fascists Please Copy." *Free America* 2, no. 8 (1938): 19–20.

"In the Path of Progress: Federal Highway Relocation Assurances." *Yale Law Journal* 82 (1972): 373–401.

Isenberg, Alison. *Downtown America: A History of the Place and the People Who Made It*. Chicago: University of Chicago Press, 2004.

Issel, William. "Ralph Borsodi and the Agrarian Response to Modern America." *Agricultural History* 41 (1967): 155–66.

Jackson, Kenneth T. *The Crabgrass Frontier: The Suburbanization of America*. New York: Oxford University Press, 1985.

Jacobs, Harvey. "The Small Town Comes Back." *Free America* 3 (1939): 15–16.

Jacobs, Jane. *Cities and the Wealth of Nations*. New York: Random House, 1984.

Jacobs, Jane. *The Death and Life of Great American Cities*. New York: Random House, 1961.

Jencks, Charles. *The Condition of Post-Modernity: An Enquiry Into the Origins of Cultural Change*. London: Wiley, 1989.

Jencks, Charles. *The Language of Post-Modern Architecture*. New York: Rizzoli, 1977.

Johnson, Donald Leslie. "Frank Lloyd Wright's Community Planning." *Journal of Planning History* 3 (February 2004): 3–28.

Johnson, Donald Leslie. "The Origin of the Neighborhood Unit," *Planning Perspectives* 17, no. 3 (2002): 227–46.

Jones, Louis C. *Three Eyes on the Past: Exploring New York Folk Life*. Syracuse: Syracuse University Press, 1982.

Kanter, Rosabeth Moss. *Commitment and Community: Communes and Utopias in Sociological Perspective*. Cambridge, MA: Harvard University Press, 1972.

Katz, Peter, ed. *The New Urbanism: Toward an Architecture of Community*. New York: McGraw-Hill, 1994.

Kaufman, Jason. *For the Common Good?: American Civic Life and the Golden Age of Fraternity*. New York: Oxford University Press, 2002.

Kay, Jane Holtz. "Architecture." *Nation*, September 24, 1973, pp. 284–86.

Kay, Jane Holtz. *Asphalt Nation: How the Automobile Took Over America and How We Can Take It Back*. New York: Crown, 1997.

Kelbaugh, Douglas S. *Repairing the American Metropolis*. Seattle: University of Washington Press, 2002.

Kelley, Ben. *The Pavers and the Paved*. New York: Donald W. Brown, 1971.

Kemmis, Daniel. *Community and the Politics of Place*. Norman: University of Oklahoma Press, 1990.

Kemp, Louis Ward. "Aesthetes and Engineers: The Occupational Ideology of Highway Design." *Technology and Culture* 27 (1986): 759–97.

Kilman, Ed, and Theon Wright. *Hugh Roy Cullen: A Story of American Opportunity*. New York: Prentice-Hall, 1954.

King, Paul Esmond. *The Spatial Aspects of Social Area Change: Columbus, Ohio 1950-1960*. MA thesis, Ohio State University, 1969.

Kirby, Jack Temple. *Rural Worlds Lost: The American South, 1920-1960*. Baton Rouge: Louisiana State University Press, 1987.

Kirchwey, Freda. "Sex in the South Seas." *Nation* (1928): 427.

Kirk, Russell, and James McClellan. *The Political Principles of Robert A. Taft*. New York: Fleet Press, 1967.

Klemek, Christopher. *The Transatlantic Collapse of Urban Renewal: Postwar Urbanism from New York to Berlin*. Chicago: University of Chicago Press, 2011.

Knepper, Cathy. *Greenbelt, Maryland: A Living Legacy of the New Deal*. Baltimore: Johns Hopkins University Press, 2001.

Kolson, Kenneth. *Big Plans: The Allure and Folly of Urban Design*. Baltimore: Johns Hopkins University Press, 2001.

Krieger, Alex. "Reinventing Public Space" *Architectural Record* 183 (June 1995): 76–77.

Kristol, Irving. "Urban Civilization and Its Discontents" *Commentary* 56 (July 1970): 29–35.

Kruse, Kevin. *White Flight: Atlanta and the Making of Modern Conservatism.* Princeton, NJ: Princeton University Press, 2005.

Kruse, Kevin M., and Thomas J. Sugrue, eds. *The New Suburban History.* Chicago: University of Chicago Press, 2006.

Kubly, Herbert. "Pittsburgh." *Holiday* 25 (March 1959): 152–56.

Kunitz, Stephen J. "The Social Philosophy of John Collier." *Ethnohistory* 18 (1971): 213–29.

Laidlaw, Walter. "The Church and the City Community." *American Journal of Sociology* 16 (1911): 794–800.

Langord, Letitia C., and Gwen Bell. "Federally Sponsored New Towns of the Seventies." *Growth and Change* 6, no. 4 (1975): 24–31.

Larner, Jeremy. *Nobody Knows: Reflections on the McCarthy Campaign of 1968.* New York: Macmillan, 1970.

Lassiter, Matthew. *The Silent Majority: Suburban Politics in the Sunbelt South.* Princeton, NJ: Princeton University Press, 2006.

Leach, Richard H. "The Federal Urban Renewal Program: A Ten-Year Critique." *Law and Contemporary Problems* 25 (1960): 777–92.

Lears, Jackson. *The Rebirth of a Nation: The Making of Modern America, 1877-1920.* New York: HarperCollins, 2009.

Lees, Andrew. *Cities Perceived: Urban Society in European and American Thought, 1820-1940.* New York: Columbia University Press, 1985.

Lehman, Edward W., ed. *Autonomy and Order: A Communitarian Anthology.* New York: Rowman & Littlefield, 2000.

Lerner, Max. *America as a Civilization: Life and Thought in the United States Today.* New York: Simon and Schuster, 1957.

Leverette, William, Jr., and David E. Shi, "Herbert Agar and 'Free America': A Jeffersonian Alternative to the New Deal." *Journal of American Studies* 16 (1982): 189–206.

Lewis, Tom. *Divided Highways: Building the Interstate Highways, Transforming American Life.* New York: Viking, 1997.

Lingeman, Richard. *Small Town America: A Narrative History, 1620-present.* New York: G. P. Putnam, 1980.

Looker, Benjamin. "Visions of Autonomy: The New Left and the Neighborhood Government Movement of the 1970s." *Journal of Urban History* 38 (2012): 577–98.

Lomax, John A., and Alan Lomax. *American Ballads and Folk Songs.* New York: Macmillan, 1934.

Low, Setha. *Behind the Gates: The New American Dream.* New York: Routledge, 2003.

Lubove, Roy. *Community Planning in the 1920s: The Contribution of the Regional Planning Association of America.* Pittsburgh: University of Pittsburgh Press, 1963.

Luccarelli, Mark. *Lewis Mumford and the Ecological Region: The Politics of Planning* New York: Guilford Press, 1995.

Luckingham, Bradford. *Phoenix: The History of a Southwestern Metropolis.* Tucson: University of Arizona Press, 1989.

MacCorkle, Stuart. *Cities from Scratch: New Towns Planned for People.* San Antonio: Naylor, 1974.

MacKaye, Benton. *The New Exploration: A Philosophy of Regional Planning.* New York: Harcourt, Brace, 1928.

MacManus, Susan A. *Federal Aid to Houston.* Washington: DC: Brookings Institution, 1983.

Madgwick, P. J. "The Politics of Urban Renewal." *Journal of American Studies* 5 (1971): 265–80.

Markey, Morris. *This Country of Yours.* Boston: Little, Brown, 1932.

Marlett, Jeffrey. "Harvesting an Overlooked Freedom: The Anti-Urban Vision of American Catholic Agrarianism, 1920-1950." *U.S. Catholic Historian* 16 (1998): 88–108.

Marsh, Benjamin Clarke. "City Planning in Justice to the Working Population." *Charities* 19 (1908): 1514.

Marsh, Benjamin Clarke. *An Introduction to City Planning: Democracy's Challenge to the American City.* New York: B. C. Marsh, 1909.

Mathews, Lois Kimball. *The Expansion of New England.* Boston: Houghton Mifflin, 1909.

Matthews, Fred H. *Quest for an American Sociology: Robert E. Park and the Chicago School.* Montreal: McGill-Queen's University Press, 1977.

McComb, David. *Houston: The Bayou City.* Austin: University of Texas Press, 1969.

McFarland, J. Horace. "The Growth of City Planning in the United States." *Charities* 19 (1908): 1523.

McGirr, Lisa. *Suburban Warriors: The Origins of the New American Right.* Princeton, NJ: Princeton University Press, 2001.

McGraw, B. T. "Urban Renewal in the Interest of All the People." *Phylon* 19 (1958): 45–55.

McWilliams, Cary. "Look What's Happening to California," *Harper's Magazine* (October 1949): 21–29.

Mead, Margaret. *Growing Up in New Guinea: A Comparative Study of Primitive Education.* New York: William Morrow, 1930.

Mead, Margaret. *And Keep Your Powder Dry.* New York: William Morrow, 1942.

Mead, Margaret. *Coming of Age in Samoa.* New York: William Morrow, 1928.

Mead, Margaret. "Growing up in the South Seas." *Forum* 87 (1932): 285–88.

Mead, Margaret. "Standardized America vs. Romantic South Seas." *Scribner's* 90 (1931): 486–91.

Melville, Keith. *Communes in the Counter Culture: Origins, Theories, Styles of Life.* New York: William Morrow, 1972.

Meyerson, Martin, ed. *The Conscience of the City.* New York: George Braziller, 1970.

Milgram, Stanley, and Paul Hollander. "The Murder They Heard." *Nation*, June 15, 1964, pp. 602–04.

Miller, Donald. *Lewis Mumford: A Life*. New York: Weidenfeld & Nicolson, 1989.

Miller, Randall M., and George E. Pozetta, eds. *Shades of the Sunbelt: Essays on Ethnicity, Race, and the Urban South*. Boca Raton: Florida Atlantic University Press, 1988.

Miller, Timothy. *The Quest for Utopia in Twentieth-Century America, 1900-1960*. Syracuse: Syracuse University Press, 1998.

Miller, Timothy. *The 60s Communes: Hippies and Beyond*. Syracuse: Syracuse University Press, 1999.

Miller, Zane. *Suburb: Neighborhood and Community in Forest Park, Ohio, 1935-1976*. Knoxville: University of Tennessee Press, 1980.

Miller, Zane, and Bruce Tucker. *Changing Plans for America's Inner Cities: Cincinnati's Over-the-Rhine and Twentieth-Century Urbanism*. Columbus: Ohio State University Press, 1998.

Mitchell, Jonathan. "Low-Cost Paradise." *New Republic* 84 (September 1935): 152–55.

Mitchell, Joseph Rocco, and David L. Stebenne. *A New City Upon a Hill: A History of Columbia, Maryland*. Charleston: History Press, 2007.

Modell, Judith Schachter. *Ruth Benedict: Patterns of a Life*. Philadelphia: University of Pennsylvania Press, 1983.

Mohl, Raymond. "Stop the Road: Freeway Revolts in American Cities." *Journal of Urban History* 30 (2004): 674–706.

Moore, Charles. *Daniel H. Burnham: Architect, Planner of Cities*. Boston: Houghton Mifflin, 1921.

Moore, Charles W. "You Have to Pay for Public Life" *Perspecta* 9-10 (1965): 57–106.

Morgan, Arthur. "Design for the Small Community." *Free America* 6 (1942): 3–6.

Morgan, Arthur. *Industries for Small Communities*. Yellow Springs, OH: Community Service, 1953.

Morgan, Arthur. *Nowhere Was Somewhere: How History Makes Utopias and How Utopias Make History*. Chapel Hill: University of North Carolina Press, 1946.

Morgan, Arthur. *The Small Community: Foundation of Democratic Life*. Yellow Springs, OH: Community Service, 1942.

Morgan, Arthur, ed. *Bottom-Up Democracy: The Affiliation of Small Democratic Units for Common Service*. Yellow Springs, OH: Community Service, 1954.

Morgan, George T. Jr., and John O. King. *The Woodlands: New Community Development, 1964-1983*. College Station: Texas A&M University Press, 1987.

Morris, Willie. "Houston's Superpatriots," *Harper's Magazine* (October 1961): 48–56.

Moskowitz, Ronald. "Education and Politics in Boomtown," *Saturday Review* (February 17, 1968): 52–54.

"Motor Traffic and Tomorrow's Cities." *Better Roads* 9 (1939): 19.

Moynihan, Daniel Patrick. "New Roads and Urban Chaos." *Reporter* 22 (April 14, 1960): 13–20.

Mumford, Lewis. *The City in History: Its Origins, Its Transformation, and Its Prospects.* New York: Harcourt, Brace, and World, 1961.

Mumford, Lewis. *The Culture of Cities.* New York: Harcourt, Brace and World, 1938.

Mumford, Lewis. "Mother Jacobs' Home Remedies," *The New Yorker* (December 1, 1962): 148ff.

Mumford, Lewis. "The Plan of New York." *New Republic* 71 (June 15 and 22, 1932): 121–26; 146–54.

Mumford, Lewis. "Regions—To Live In." *Survey* 54 (1925): 151–52.

Mumford, Lewis. "The Sky Line: Mr. Wright's City—Downtown Dignity," *The New Yorker*, April 27, 1935.

Mumford, Lewis. *Sticks and Stones.* New York: Boni and Liveright, 1924.

Mungo, Raymond. *Famous Long Ago.* Boston: Beacon Press, 1970.

Mungo, Raymond. *Total Loss Farm.* New York: E. P. Dutton, 1970.

"The Municipal Problem: The Ideal City." *Outlook* 93 (1909): 141–42.

Nachman, Larry David. "Obituary for SDS." *Nation* (1969): 558–61.

"The New Raid on Nader." *Christian Century* 87 (1970): 1176.

New Urbanism: Comprehensive Report & Best Practices Guide. Ithaca: New Urban Publications, 2001.

Norton, J. Pease. "Freeholders Wanted!" *Independent* 74 (1913): 1441–42.

Nusbaum, Roger. "16 Lanes Plus Mass Transit." *American City* 79 (1964): 14.

Nye, David, ed. *Technologies of Landscape.* Amherst: University of Massachusetts Press, 1999.

Ogden, Jean, and Jess Ogden. *Small Communities in Action.* New York: Harper Brothers, 1946.

Olsen, Joshua. *Better Places, Better Lives: A Biography of James Rouse.* Washington, DC: Urban Land Institute, 2003.

Orvell, Miles. *The Death and Life of Main Street: Small Towns in American Memory, Space, and Community.* Chapel Hill: University of North Carolina Press, 2012.

"The Overcrowded City." *Outlook* 97 (1911): 625–27.

Owen, David. "Green Manhattan." *The New Yorker*, October 18, 2004.

Page, Max. *The Creative Destruction of Manhattan, 1900-1940.* Chicago: University of Chicago Press, 2000.

Pangburn, Weaver. "The War and the Community Movement." *American Journal of Sociology*, 26 (1920): 82–95.

Papers in Honor of Josiah Royce on his Sixtieth Birthday. New York: Longmans, Green, 1916.

Park, Robert. "The City: Suggestions for the Investigation of Human Behavior in the City Environment." *American Journal of Sociology* 20 (1915): 577–612.

Park, Robert, Ernest Burgess & Roderick McKenzie. *The City.* Chicago: University of Chicago Press, 1925.

Park, Robert Ezra. *Human Communities: The City and Human Ecology*. Glencoe: Free Press, 1952.

Patterson, James. *Mr. Republican: A Biography of Robert A. Taft*. Boston: Houghton Mifflin, 1972.

Paxson, Frederic. "The Highway Movement, 1916-1935." *American Historical Review* 51 (1946): 236–53.

Pells, Richard. *Modernist America: Art, Music, Movies and the Globalization of American Culture*. New Haven, CT: Yale University Press, 2011.

Perloff, Harvey S., and Neil C. Sandberg, eds. *New Towns: Why—And for Whom?* New York: Praeger, 1973.

Perry, Clarence. "City Planning for Neighborhood Life." *Social Forces* 8 (1929): 98–100.

Perry, Clarence. *The Rebuilding of Blighted Areas: A Study of the Neighborhood Unit in Replanning and Plot Assemblage*. New York: Regional Planning Association, 1933.

Perry, David, and Alfred Watkins, eds. *The Rise of the Sunbelt Cities, Urban Affairs Annual Review* 14 (1977).

Peterson, Elmer. *Cities are Abnormal*. Norman: University of Oklahoma Press, 1946.

Peterson, George E. and Carol W. Lewis, eds. *Reagan and the Cities*. Washington, DC: Urban Institute Press, 1986.

Pfeiffer, Bruce Brooks, and Robert Wojtowicz, eds. *Frank Lloyd Wright & Lewis Mumford: Thirty Years of Correspondence*. New York: Princeton Architectural Press, 2001.

Pfretzschner, Paul A. "Panning the Planners," *Antioch Review* 22 (1962): 130–36.

Philp, Kenneth R. *John Collier's Crusade for Indian Reform, 1920-1954*. Tucson: University of Arizona Press, 1977.

Plan for New York City. New York: New York City Planning Commission, 1969.

Popkin, Susan J., Diane K. Levy, and Larry Buron, "Has HOPE VI Transformed Residents' Lives? New Evidence from the HOPE VI Panel Study." *Housing Studies* 24 (July 2009): 477–502.

Postel, Charles. *The Populist Vision*. New York: Oxford University Press, 2007.

Poston, Richard Waverly. *Small Town Renaissance: A Story of the Montana Study*. New York: Harper Brothers, 1950.

Pritchett, Wendell E. *Robert Clifton Weaver and the American City: The Life and Times of an Urban Reformer*. Chicago: University of Chicago Press, 2008.

Pritchett, Wendell. "The 'Public Menace' of Blight: Urban Renewal and the Private Uses of Eminent Domain." *Yale Law & Policy Review* 21 (2002): 1–52.

The Public Papers and Addresses of Franklin D. Roosevelt, compiled by Samuel Rosenman. New York: Harper Brothers, 1938–1950.

Putnam, Robert D. *Bowling Alone: The Collapse and Revival of American Community*. New York: Simon & Schuster, 2000.

Quandt, Jean B. *From the Small Town to the Great Community: The Social Thought of Progressive Intellectuals*. New Brunswick, NJ: Rutgers University Press, 1970.

Quinn, Patrick F. "Agrarianism and the Jeffersonian Philosophy." *Review of Politics* 2 (1940): 87–104.

Radford, Gail. *Modern Housing for America: Policy Struggles in the New Deal Era.* Chicago: University of Chicago Press, 1996.

Ralph, Julian. "Colorado and Its Capital." *Harper's New Monthly Magazine* 86 (1893): 935–48.

Raymond, George, Malcolm Rivkin and Herbert Gans. "Urban Renewal." *Commentary* 40, no. 1 (July 1965): 72–80.

Redfield, Robert. "Review of *Coming of Age in Samoa.*" *American Journal of Sociology* 34 (1929): 728–30.

Reich, Charles. *The Greening of America.* New York: Random House, 1970.

Report of the Commission on Country Life. New York: Sturgis & Walton, 1911.

Report of the National Advisory Commission on Civil Disorders. New York: E. P. Dutton, 1968.

"Report of the New York Congestion Commission." *Survey* 25 (1911): 977–79.

"Report on Cincinnati, Ohio and the Selection of a Site for Suburban Resettlement," Research Section Division of Suburban Resettlement, Resettlement Administration, 1936.

Rich, Louise Dickinson. *We Took to the Woods.* Philadelphia: J. B. Lippincott, 1942.

Ridgeway, James. "Missionaries in Darkest Ohio." *New Republic* 154 (February 5, 1966): 9–10.

Roberts, Ron. *The New Communes.* Englewood Cliffs, NJ: Prentice-Hall, 1971.

Rodgers, Daniel T. *Atlantic Crossings: Social Politics in a Progressive Age.* Cambridge, MA: Belknap, 1998.

Rodriguez, Joseph A. *City Against Suburb: The Culture Wars in an American Metropolis.* Westport: Praeger, 1999.

Roosevelt, Theodore. "Rural Life." *Outlook* 95 (1910): 919–22.

Rose, Mark. *Interstate: Express Highway Politics, 1939-1989.* Knoxville: University of Tennessee Press, 1990.

Ross, Andrew. *The Celebration Chronicles.* New York: Ballantine, 1999.

Royce, Josiah. *Race Questions, Provincialism and Other American Problems.* Freeport: Books for Libraries Press, 1967.

Royce, Josiah. *The Philosophy of Loyalty.* New York: Macmillan, 1924.

Royce, Josiah. "Provincialism." *Putnam's Magazine* 7 (1909): 232–40.

Royce, Josiah. *The Feud of Oakfield Creek: A Novel of California Life.* Boston: Houghton Mifflin, 1887.

Royce, Josiah. *The Hope of the Great Community.* New York: Macmillan, 1916.

Rudikoff, Sonya. "O Pioneers! Reflections on the Whole Earth People." *Commentary* 54 (1972): 62–74.

Russo, David J. *American Towns: An Interpretive History.* Chicago: Ivan R. Dee, 2001.

Rykwert, Joseph. *The Seduction of Place: The City in the Twenty-First Century.* New York: Pantheon Books, 2000.

Sanderson, Dwight. *The Rural Community: The Natural History of a Sociological Group*. New York: Ginn, 1932.

Sapir, Edward. "Culture, Genuine and Spurious." *American Journal of Sociology* 29 (1924): 401–29.

Satter, Beryl. *Family Properties: Race, Real Estate, and the Exploitation of Black Urban America*. New York: Henry Holt, 2009.

Schaffer, David. *Garden Cities for America: The Radburn Experience*. Philadelphia: Temple University Press, 1982.

Schoening, Niles Craig. *The Effects of Urban Renewal on the Pattern of Racial Segregation in Columbus, Ohio*. MA thesis, Ohio State University, 1969.

Schrag, Zachary. "The Freeway Fight in Washington, D.C.: The Three Sisters Bridge in Three Administrations." *Journal of Urban History* 30 (2004): 648–73.

Scott, Mel. *American City Planning Since 1890*. Berkeley: University of California Press, 1969.

Scully, Vincent. "The American City in 2025." *Brookings Review* 18 (Summer 2000): 4–5.

Sealander, Judith. *Private Wealth, Public Life: Foundation Philanthropy and the Reshaping of American Social Policy from the Progressive Era to the New Deal*. Baltimore: Johns Hopkins University Press, 1997.

Sears, Charles Hatch. *The Redemption of the City*. Philadelphia: Griffith & Rowland, 1911.

Sennett, Ricard, ed. *Classic Essays on the Culture of Cities*. New York: Meredith, 1969.

Sennett, Richard. *The Fall of Public Man*. New York: Knopf, 1977.

"Settlers in the City Wilderness." *Atlantic Monthly* 77 (1896): 118–23.

Sexton, Richard. *Parallel Utopias*. San Francisco: Chronicle Books, 1995.

Shapiro, Edward S. "Decentralist Intellectuals and the New Deal." *Journal of American History* 58 (1972): 938–57.

Shapiro, Henry D. *Appalachia on Our Mind: The Southern Mountains and Mountaineers in the American Consciousness, 1870-1920*. Chapel Hill: University of North Carolina Press, 1978.

Shelton, Beth Anne, Nestor Rodriguez, Joe Feagin, Robert Bullard, and Robert Thomas. *Houston: Growth and Decline in a Sunbelt Boomtown*. Philadelphia: Temple University Press, 1989.

Shermer, Elizabeth Tandy. *Sunbelt Capitalism: Phoenix and the Transformation of American Politics*. Philadelphia: University of Pennsylvania Press, 2013.

Shi, David E. *The Simple Life: Plain Living and High Thinking in American Culture*. New York: Oxford University Press, 1985.

Sims, Newell Leroy. *The Rural Community Ancient and Modern*. New York: Charles Scribner's Sons, 1920.

Slotboom, Erik. *Houston Freeways: A Historical and Visual Journey*. Cincinnati: C. J. Krehbiel, 2003.

Smalley, E. V. "The Isolation of Life on Prairie Farms." *Atlantic Monthly* 72 (1893): 378–82.

Smith, Carl. *The Plan of Chicago: Daniel Burnham and the Remaking of the American City*. Chicago: University of Chicago Press, 2006.

Smith, Geddes. "A Town for the Motor Age." *Survey* 59 (1927-28): 695–98.

Smith, Page. *As a City Upon a Hill: The Town in American History*. New York: Knopf, 1966.

Smith, Sherry L. *Reimagining Indians: Native Americans Through Anglo Eyes, 1880-1940*. New York: Oxford University Press, 2000.

Smith, T. V., and Leonard D. White, eds. *Chicago: An Experiment in Social Science Research*. Chicago: University of Chicago Press, 1929.

Spann, Edward K. *Designing Modern America: The Regional Planning Association of America and Its Members*. Columbus: Ohio State University Press, 1996.

Spears, Timothy B. *Chicago Dreaming: Midwesterners and the City, 1871–1919*. Chicago: University of Chicago Press, 2005.

Stein, Clarence. "Dinosaur Cities." *Survey* 54 (1925): 134–38.

Stein, Clarence. *Toward New Towns for America*. Liverpool: University of Liverpool Press, 1951.

Stein, Maurice. *The Eclipse of Community: An Interpretation of American Studies*, Princeton, NJ: Princeton University Press, 1960.

Steinberg, Alfred. "Pittsburgh, a New City." *National Municipal Review* 44 (March, 1955): 126–31.

Steiner, Frederick. *The Politics of New Town Planning: The Newfields, Ohio Story*. Athens: Ohio University Press, 1981.

Steiner, Jesse. "An Appraisal of the Community Movement." *Social Forces* 7 (1929): 333–42.

Sternsher, Bernard. *Rexford Tugwell and the New Deal*. New Brunswick, NJ: Rutgers University Press, 1964.

Strong, Josiah. *Our Country: Its Possible Future and Its Present Crisis*. New York: Baker & Taylor, 1885.

Strong, Josiah. *The Twentieth Century City*. New York: Baker & Taylor, 1898.

Sugrue, Thomas. *The Origins of the Urban Crisis: Race and Inequality in Postwar Detroit*. Princeton, NJ: Princeton University Press, 1996.

Sugrue, Thomas J. "Revisiting the Second Ghetto." *Journal of Urban History* 29 (2003): 281–290.

Swift, Earl. *The Big Roads: The Untold Story of the Engineers, Visionaries, and Trailblazers Who Created the American Superhighways*. Boston: Houghton Mifflin Harcourt, 2011.

Talbert, Roy Jr. *FDR's Utopian: Arthur Morgan of the TVA*. Jackson: University of Mississippi Press, 1987.

Tam, Henry. *Communitarianism: A New Agenda for Politics and Citizenship*. New York: New York University Press, 1998.

Tate, H. Clay. *Building a Better Home Town*. New York: Harpers Brothers, 1954.

Taylor, Carl. "The Field of Rural Sociology." *Journal of Social Forces* 1 (1923): 592–95.

Teaford, Jon. *The Rough Road to Renaissance: Urban Revitalization in America, 1940-1985*. Baltimore: Johns Hopkins University Press, 1990.

Teaford, Jon. *The Unheralded Triumph: City Government in America, 1870-1900*. Baltimore: Johns Hopkins University Press, 1984.

Thran, Sally. "No Room for the Poor." *Commonweal* 97 (1973): 292–93.

"A Town for Moderns." *Survey* 59 (1927-28): 621.

"'Town for the Motor Age' Finds Public Ready for Innovation," *Business Week*, July 9, 1930, p. 19.

Trollope, Frances. *Domestic Manners of the Americans*. New York: Vintage Books, 1960.

Tugwell, Rexford. *The Democratic Roosevelt*. Garden City, NY: Doubleday, 1957.

Tugwell, Rexford. *In Search of Roosevelt*. Cambridge, MA: Harvard University Press, 1972.

Tugwell, Rexford. "The Meaning of Greenbelt Towns." *New Republic* 90 (1937): 42–43.

Turner, Frederick Jackson. "The Significance of the Frontier in American History." Ann Arbor, MI: University Microfilms, 1966.

Twombly, Robert. "Undoing the City: Frank Lloyd Wright's Planned Communities." *American Quarterly* 24 (1972): 538–49.

Venkatesh, Sudhir. "Chicago's Pragmatic Planners: American Sociology and the Myth of Community." *Social Science History* 25 (2001): 275–317.

Ward, David. "Social Reform, Social Surveys, and the Discovery of the Modern City." *Annals of the Association of American Geographers* 80 (1990): 491–503.

Warren, Roland. *The Community in America*. Chicago: Rand McNally, 1963.

Warren, Roland. *Studying Your Community*. New York: Russell Sage Foundation, 1955.

"Way Out for the Farmer." *Survey* 25 (1911): 895–96.

Weaver, Robert C. *Dilemmas of Urban America*. Cambridge, MA: Harvard University Press, 1965.

Weber, Max. *The City*, ed. and trans. by Don Martindale. New York: The Free Press, London: Collier, 1968).

Webster, Clarence M. *Town Meeting Country*. New York: Duell, Sloan & Pearce, 1945.

Wedge, Bruce E. "The Concept 'Urban Renewal.'" *Phylon* 19 (1958): 55–60.

Weimer, Arthur M. "The Work of the Federal Housing Administration." *Journal of Political Economy* 45 (1937): 466–83.

Weller, George. "The City: America's First Decentralist Film." *Free America* 3, no. 8 (1939): 18–19.

Wellman, Walter. "Rise of the American City: The Wonderful Story of the Census of 1900." *McClure's* 17 (1901): 470–76.

"What Has Happened in an Unzoned City?" *American City* 68 (March 1953): 93.

Whisnant, David. *All That Is Native and Fine: The Politics of Culture in an American Region*. Chapel Hill: University of North Carolina Press, 1983.

Whitaker, Craig. *Architecture and the American Dream.* New York: Clarkson N. Potter, 1996.

White, Dana. *The Urbanists, 1865-1915.* New York: Greenwood, 1989.

White, Morton, and Lucia Morton. *The Intellectual Versus the City.* Cambridge, MA: Harvard University Press and MIT Press by arrangement with Mentor, 1962.

"Whither New England?" *New Republic* 57 (1928): 57–58.

Whiting, Edward E. *Changing New England.* New York: Century, 1929.

"Why Columbus?" *Saturday Review* April 30, 1977: 14.

Whyte, William, ed. *The Exploding Metropolis.* Garden City, NY: Doubleday Anchor, 1958.

Wiebe, Robert. *The Search for Order, 1877-1920.* New York: Hill and Wang, 1967.

Williams, C. Dickerman. "Decentralization Is Inevitable." *Free America* 1 (1937): 8–9.

Williams, Raymond. *The Country and the City.* New York: Oxford University Press, 1973.

Wills, Garry. *A Necessary Evil: A History of American Distrust of Government.* New York: Simon & Schuster, 1999.

Wilson, Charles Reagan, ed. *The New Regionalism.* Jackson: University of Mississippi Press, 1998.

Wilson, Harold Fisher. *The Hill Country of Northern New England.* Montpelier: Vermont Historical Society, 1947.

Wilson, R. Jackson. *In Quest of Community: Social Philosophy in the United States, 1860-1920.* New York: John Wiley, 1968.

Wilson, Warren H. *The Evolution of the Country Community: A Study in Religious Sociology.* Boston: Pilgrim Press, 1912.

Wilson, William H. *Coming of Age: Urban America, 1915-1945.* New York: John Wiley, 1974.

Winling, LaDale. "Students and the Second Ghetto: Federal Legislation, Urban Politics, and Campus Planning at the University of Chicago." *Journal of Planning History* 10 (2011): 59–86.

Wirth, Louis. "Urbanism as a Way of Life." *American Journal of Sociology* 44 (1938): 1–24.

Wood, Grant. *The Revolt Against the City.* Iowa City, IA: Clio Press, 1935.

Wood, Robert C. *Suburbia: Its People and their Politics.* Boston: Houghton Mifflin, 1958.

Woods, Ralph L. *America Reborn: A Plan for Decentralization of Industry.* London: Longmans, Green, 1939.

Woods, Robert. "The Neighborhood in Social Reconstruction." *American Journal of Sociology* 19 (1914): 577–91.

Woods, Robert. *The Neighborhood in Nation-Building.* Boston: Houghton Mifflin, 1923.

Woods, Robert A., ed. *The City Wilderness: A Settlement Study.* New York: Arno, 1970.

Woods, Robert A., and Albert J. Kennedy. *The Settlement Horizon: A National Estimate.* New York: Russell Sage Foundation, 1922.

Wright, Frank Lloyd. *The Disappearing City.* New York: William Farquhar Payson, 1932.

Wright, Frank Lloyd. *When Democracy Builds.* Chicago: University of Chicago Press, 1945.

Yin, Robert K. *The City in the Seventies.* Itasca, IL: F.E. Peacock, 1972.

Yoder, Don. *Discovering American Folklife: Studies in Ethnic, Religious and Regional Culture.* Ann Arbor: UMI Research Press, 1990.

Zablocki, Benjamin. *Alienation and Charisma: A Study of Contemporary American Communes.* New York: Free Press, 1980.

INDEX